Matthew Aernie and Don[...] thorough study of the Da[...] [...]ulogy. This comprehensive work studies the Day of the Lord in all the occurrences in Paul's writings and reflects the thoroughness of study from the Greek and Hebrew texts. There is no greater, more complete and thorough work on the Day of the Lord in Paul's writings than this study.

—**Paul Enns,** TH.D., Professor in Residence,
Idlewild Baptist Church

The Righteous and Merciful Judge is a careful overview of the Day of the Lord theme in Scripture ending with a detailed focus on Paul's letters. Judgment is not a popular theme today, but it runs through the whole of Scripture. This close look shows how important a part of theology the idea of accountability to the Creator God is. One can read this work with much profit to round out the understanding of how God holds us accountable to him in his world.

—**Darrell Bock,** Executive Director for Cultural Engagement,
Howard G. Hendricks Center for Christian Leadership and
Cultural Engagement and Senior Research Professor of
New Testament Studies, Dallas Theological Seminary

Aernie and Hartley have filled in a lacuna in Pauline scholarship with this work on the Day of the Lord. They consider carefully the OT background and Second Temple Jewish background and then set forth Paul's own understanding of the Day of the Lord. An important contribution which should be taken into account by those engaging in Pauline theology.

—**Thomas R. Schreiner,** James Buchanan Harrison Professor
of New Testament Interpretation and Professor of Biblical
Theology at The Southern Baptist Theological Seminary

The Righteous and Merciful Judge by Matthew Aernie and Donald Hartley makes an excellent addition to the Studies in Scripture and Biblical Theology series by Lexham Press. Aernie and Hartley have tackled a complicated and very important topic. Their study of Paul's theology through the lens of the Day of the Lord is fresh, exciting, and insightful. High recommended.

—**Craig A. Evans,** John Bisagno Distinguished Professor
of Christian Origins, Houston Baptist University

THE RIGHTEOUS & MERCIFUL JUDGE

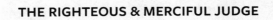

The *Righteous* & **Merciful Judge**

The Day of the Lord

in the Life and

Theology of Paul

MATTHEW AERNIE &
DONALD HARTLEY

STUDIES IN
**SCRIPTURE
& BIBLICAL**
THEOLOGY

LEXHAM PRESS

The Righteous and Merciful Judge
Studies in Scripture and Biblical Theology

Copyright 2018 Matthew D. Aernie, Donald E. Hartley

Lexham Press, 1313 Commercial St., Bellingham, WA 98225
LexhamPress.com

Print ISBN 9781683591023
Digital ISBN 9781683591030

Lexham Editorial Team: Derek R. Brown, Claire Brubaker, Sarah Awa, Danielle Thevenaz
Cover Design: Brittany Schrock
Typesetting: Scribe Inc.

Contents

Acknowledgments

Words cannot express how truly grateful I am for the privilege the Lord has afforded me to publish this monograph. It is my prayer that this work would bring him glory and encourage Christians to remember that the future impacts the present and therefore we must live in light of the day of the Lord.

No monograph is ever completed in isolation, and I am extremely grateful for the numerous conversations, criticisms, and insights from many individuals over the course of this work. Specifically, I would like to thank Dr. Brannon Ellis, who invited me to contribute this monograph to the Studies in Scripture and Biblical Theology series. Thanks also to Dr. Derek Brown, who served as an outstanding editor and offered numerous wise comments that have certainly enhanced this work. It has been a privilege to work with him. I also want to express my appreciation to Paul Roberts and Becky Owens, who were always diligent to locate all the interlibrary loans that I requested.

I want to also thank my colleague Dr. Donald Hartley for agreeing to join this project in its later stages. The demands of family, university responsibilities, and ministry made it seem that this work would never see completion. His contributions and expertise have not only made this project "see the light of day" much sooner but have tremendously enhanced the overall argument of the monograph. Don's scholarly abilities are unprecedented, and I am sincerely grateful not only for his contributions to this project but also for his friendship.

Finally, I want to express my deep appreciation and gratitude to my immediate family, who all sacrificed in numerous ways throughout the nearly four years of work on this project. My children, Andrew and Emma, are always a source of great joy, and I count it a tremendous privilege to be your dad. To my precious wife, Bonnie, for her constant encouragement and support: this book would not have been completed without her countless sacrifices. Her love and companionship have made me to better understand and appreciate Proverbs 18:22. I thank the Lord for blessing me with her.

Matthew D. Aernie

In addition to dittoing Matt's acknowledgments above, I would like to add my sincere appreciation to him as well as to Lexham Press for permitting me to be a part of this worthy monograph. Dr. Matthew Aernie and I served as colleagues at Southeastern Bible College for eight years, where we forged a deep and abiding friendship. Matt is not only a sound, careful, and humble scholar but also a sincere and kindly gentleman. Most of all, he is to me a true "soul brother."

For the first few years of this project, beginning in fall 2014, I merely observed Matt indefatigably yet not uninterruptedly labor in his office, which was situated adjacent mine. As his project progressed and grew, the teaching duties impinged all the more and family obligations multiplied to the point of making it nearly impossible for him to meet his objectives. So Matt subsequently (and hopefully not regrettably!) asked me to join him in completing the book in winter 2017. Over the past year, then, it has been my highest privilege and honor to engage in and contribute to this rewarding, refreshing, and rigorous research assignment on the day of the Lord in Paul and to bring it to within reach of its final stage of completion. For Matt's confidence and trust in doing so, I am sincerely grateful.

Thanks are also in order to my brother Doug for reading through some of my portion of the material and offering up helpful criticisms, critiques, and corrections. For the encouragement I daily receive from my son, Josh, observing him fighting the good fight of faith as a faithful soldier in God's day-of-the-Lord army within the battleground of ideas, I say to him, this bud is for you.

Finally and most of all, a huge thank you goes to my beautiful and understanding wife, Melissa, not only for tolerating the additional expenses (or excuses) of buying more books, scheduling superfluous lunches, and for the time I spent away from her preoccupied with the matters pertaining to the eschaton, but also for teaching me what it looks like to live each day as if the day of the Lord is indeed at hand. Your great faith as well as constant and consistent love and support mean more to me now than you will ever know. Thank you, my dear.

Donald E. Hartley

Abbreviations

ANCIENT SOURCES

1 Macc	1 Maccabees
2 Macc	2 Maccabees
3 Macc	3 Maccabees
1 En.	1 Enoch
2 En.	2 Enoch
LXX	Septuagint
MT	Masoretic Text
NT	New Testament
OT	Old Testament

MODERN SOURCES

AB	Anchor Bible Commentaries
ABD	*Anchor Bible Dictionary*. Edited by David Noel Freedman. New York: Doubleday, 1992.
AnBib	Analecta Biblica
AYBRL	Anchor Yale Bible Reference Library
BBMS	Baker Biblical Monograph Series
BBR	*Bulletin for Biblical Research*
BDAG	Bauer, Walter, Frederick William Danker, W. F. Arndt, and F. W. Gingrich. *A Greek-English Lexicon of the New Testament and Other Early Christian Literature*. 3rd ed. Chicago: University of Chicago Press, 2000.
BDB	Brown, Francis, Edward Robinson, S. R. Driver, Charles A. Briggs, and Wilhelm Gesenius. *A Hebrew and English Lexicon of the Old Testament: With an Appendix, Containing the Biblical Aramaic*. Oxford: Clarendon, 1979.

BDF	Blass, Friedrich, Albert Debrunner, and Robert W. Funk. *A Greek Grammar of the New Testament and Other Early Christian Literature*. Translated by Robert W. Funk. 4th ed. Chicago: University of Chicago Press, 1961.
BECNT	Baker Exegetical Commentary on the New Testament
Bib	*Biblica*
BibInt	Biblical Interpretation Series
BRS	Biblical Resource Series
BSac	*Bibliotheca Sacra*
BTB	*Biblical Theological Bulletin*
BZAW	Beihefte zur Zeitschrift für die alttestamentliche Wissenschaft
CBC	Cambridge Bible Commentary, New English Bible
CBQ	*Catholic Biblical Quarterly*
Colloq	*Colloquium*
ConBNT	Coniectanea Biblica: New Testament Series
COQG	Christian Origins and the Question of God
CTJ	*Calvin Theological Journal*
CTM	*Concordia Theological Monthly*
CTR	*Criswell Theological Review*
DJG	Green, Joel B., Jeannine K. Brown, and Nicholas Perrin, eds. *Dictionary of Jesus and the Gospels*. Downers Grove, IL: InterVarsity, 2013.
DNTB	*Dictionary of New Testament Background*
DOTP	Boda, Mark J., and J. G. McConville, eds. *Dictionary of the Old Testament: Prophets*. Downers Grove, IL: InterVarsity, 2012.
DPL	Hawthorne, Gerald F., Ralph P. Martin, and Daniel G. Reid, eds. *Dictionary of Paul and His Letters*. Downers Grove, IL: InterVarsity, 1993.
EDEJ	Collins, John J., and Daniel C. Harlow, eds. *Eerdmans Dictionary of Early Judaism*. Grand Rapids: Eerdmans, 2010.
ERT	*Evangelical Review of Theology*
EvQ	*Evangelical Quarterly*
ExpTim	*Expository Times*

FAT	Forschungen zum Alten Testament
FOTL	Forms of the Old Testament Literature
FRLANT	Forschungen zur Religion und Literatur des Alten und Neuen Testaments
HALOT	Köhler, Ludwig, Walter Baumgartner, and Johann Jakob Stamm, eds. *The Hebrew and Aramaic Lexicon of the Old Testament*. Rev. ed. 6 vols. Leiden: Brill, 1994–2001.
HTR	*Harvard Theological Review*
HTS	Harvard Theological Studies
HUCA	*Hebrew Union College Annual*
ICC	International Critical Commentary on the Holy Scriptures of the Old and New Testaments
Int	*Interpretation*
JBL	*Journal of Biblical Literature*
JBQ	*Jewish Biblical Quarterly*
JETS	*Journal of the Evangelical Theological Society*
JSJ	*Journal for the Study of Judaism in the Persian, Hellenistic, and Roman Periods*
JSOTSup	Journal for the Study of the Old Testament Supplement Series
JSNT	*Journal for the Study of the New Testament*
JSNTSup	Journal for the Study of the New Testament Supplement Series
JTS	*Journal of Theological Studies*
L&N	Louw, J. P., and Eugene A. Nida, eds. *Greek-English Lexicon of the New Testament Based on Semantic Domains*. 2 vols. New York: United Bible Societies, 1988.
LNTS	Library of New Testament Studies
LSJ	Liddell, Henry George, and Robert Scott. *A Greek-English Lexicon*. Rev. and aug. Henry Stuart Jones and Roderick McKenzie. 9th ed. Oxford: Clarendon, 1940. Rev. supplement, 1996.
MM	Moulton, J. H., and G. Milligan. *The Vocabulary of the Greek Testament: Illustrated from the Papyri and Other Non-Literary Sources*. London: Hodder & Stoughton, 1930.
MSJ	*Master's Seminary Journal*

NAC	New American Commentary
Neot	*Neotestamentica*
NIB	Seow, C. L., Leslie C. Allen, Ralph W. Klein, Irene Nowell, Sidnie Crawford White, and Lawrence M. Wills, eds. *New Interpreter's Bible.* Nashville: Abingdon, 1999.
NICNT	New International Commentary on the New Testament
NICOT	New International Commentary on the Old Testament
NIDNTTE	Silva, Moisés, ed. *New International Dictionary of New Testament Theology and Exegesis.* 2nd ed. 5 vols. Grand Rapids: Zondervan, 2014.
NIGTC	New International Greek Testament Commentary
NovT	*Novum Testamentum*
NovTSup	Supplements to Novum Testamentum
NSBT	New Studies in Biblical Theology
NTL	New Testament Library
NTS	*New Testament Studies*
OTL	Old Testament Library
OtSt	Oudtestamentische studiën
PBM	Paternoster Biblical Monographs
PNTC	Pillar New Testament Commentary
R&T	*Religion & Theology*
ResQ	*Restoration Quarterly*
RevExp	*Review & Expositor*
RTR	*Reformed Theological Review*
SBLDS	Society of Biblical Literature Dissertation Series
SBLSS	Society of Biblical Literature Symposium Series
SBT	Studies in Biblical Theology
SJT	*Scottish Journal of Theology*
SNTSMS	Society for New Testament Studies Monograph Series
SOTBT	Studies in Old Testament Biblical Theology
SP	Sacra Pagina
SUNT	Studien zur Umwelt des Neuen Testaments
SwJT	*Southwestern Journal of Theology*
TDNT	Kittel, Gerhard, and Gerhard Friedrich, eds. *Theological Dictionary of the New Testament.* 10 vols. Grand Rapids: Eerdmans, 1964–76.

TENTS	Texts and Editions for New Testament Study
Them	*Themelios*
TJ	*Trinity Journal*
TLNT	Spicq, Ceslas. *Theological Lexicon of the New Testament*. Edited and translated by James D. Ernst. 3 vols. Peabody, MA: Hendrickson, 1994.
TLOT	Jenni, Ernst, and Claus Westermann, eds. *Theological Lexicon of the Old Testament*. 3 vols. Peabody, MA: Hendrickson, 1997.
TOTC	Tyndale Old Testament Commentaries
TS	*Theological Studies*
TynBul	*Tyndale Bulletin*
VE	*Vox Evangelica*
VT	*Vetus Testamentum*
WBC	Word Biblical Commentary
WTJ	*Westminster Theological Journal*
WUNT	Wissenschaftliche Untersuchungen zum Neuen Testament
WW	*Word & World*
ZAW	*Zeitschrift für die alttestamentliche Wissenschaft*
ZECNT	Zondervan Exegetical Commentary Series on the New Testament
ZNW	*Zeitschrift für die neutestamentliche Wissenschaft und die Kunde der älteren Kirche*

Introduction

The subject of judgment often makes people uncomfortable. While this has certainly been the case since the fall of Adam and Eve, it seems even more prevalent in the modern era. Any type of behavior or speech that gives the impression of "judging others" is often considered offensive and intolerant. It seems that society applauds individuals and groups who bend over backward to avoid any appearance of judging others. Furthermore, it appears that this cultural mindset of being recalcitrant to any form of judgment has even infiltrated the church, at least in the West.

For many Christians, Matthew 7:1, "Do not judge so that you will not be judged," has arguably become more well known than John 3:16.[1] But what is even more alarming is the lack of conversation regarding *God's* judgment among believers. In many cases, the subject of divine judgment is rarely discussed among Christians, much less exposited from pulpits. Obviously people have no difficulty hearing or speaking about the richness of God's character, including his love, grace, mercy, forgiveness, and patience. But what about the fact that the Bible also teaches that God is angry and has indignation every day (Pss 7:11; 69:24)? Or that the wrath of God is coming on all who disbelieve (Rom 1:18–20; Rev 6:12–17)? Or that all will stand before the judgment seat of Christ (2 Cor 5:10)? However, it seems that the growing trend among many evangelicals, at least in the West, is that they would prefer to avoid the subject of God's divine judgment altogether.

---

1. In the context of Matthew 7:1–6 Jesus is *not* giving an absolute prohibition against judgment. Rather, he is teaching about *how* a person is to judge, namely with self-examination, humility, and love. See Grant R. Osborne, *Matthew*, ZECNT 1 (Grand Rapids: Zondervan, 2009), 258. Osborne offers this summary of Jesus' teaching in this passage, "Admonition has a humility that says, 'I love you enough to want to help you, and tomorrow you will need to correct me.' There is no sense of superiority, no desire to make yourself look good at the expense of another."

In addition to the subject of God's judgment being troublesome for people, another contributing factor for the neglect of this issue may stem from the tired cliché that says, "the God of the Old Testament is a God of justice, and the God of the New Testament is a God of grace." It is argued that the Old Testament depicts God as angry and vengeful, frequently administering divine retribution, whereas the New Testament focuses not on the anger and wrath of God but rather on his love, grace, and mercy. This kind of juxtaposition arguably destroys the unity of the Bible and leaves people with an extremely unbalanced and myopic view of God. Rather, the whole counsel of Scripture invariably demonstrates the consistency of God and his character in how he interacts with his creation throughout salvation history. And since one of the ways he relates is through divine judgment, any neglect of this motif is detrimental and inhibits a more erudite understanding of God. Peter Jensen writes, "The future of God's dealing with the whole world—and especially his judgment—may be regarded as essential to the framework of the gospel, without which it cannot be properly understood."[2] Therefore, because God's judgment is paramount to the overall message of Scripture, it is imperative for Christians to be acclimated with this important subject. In order for Christians to truly understand the whole counsel of God, a resurgence of preaching and teaching on this oft-neglected theme is arguably long overdue.

PRELIMINARY MATTERS REGARDING THE DAY OF THE LORD AND PAUL'S THEOLOGY

Studying Paul's theology is a complex task. One reason is that all of his letters are occasional, intending to address the specific needs of a particular audience. Thus, Paul's epistles were not meant to be a systematic treatment of his theology. Consequently, the situational nature of Paul's epistles has lead James Dunn to argue, "It is a wholly justified assumption that Paul himself had a much richer theology than he ever actually put on paper."[3]

2. Peter Jensen, *The Revelation of God*, Contours of Christian Theology (Downers Grove, IL: InterVarsity, 2002), 51.

3. James D. G. Dunn, *The Theology of Paul the Apostle* (Grand Rapids: Eerdmans, 1998), 14.

Many Pauline interpreters have attempted to determine whether there is an actual "center" or "core" of Paul's theology.[4] Suggestions as to what the "center" may be include justification by faith, reconciliation, the resurrection of Christ, participation in Christ, and God's apocalyptic triumph in Christ, and so on.[5] And while it may be helpful to identify the core of all of Paul's theology, the question must be asked, "Can any single theme explain every single letter and every single passage?"[6] This has persuaded some scholars to avoid using the term "center" or "core" because they contend it makes Paul too rigid and stifles the fluidity of his theology. For instance, Dunn comments, "The problem with the imagery of centre or core or principle, however, is that it is too fixed and inflexible. It encourages the impression from the start that Paul's theology was static and unchanging."[7] Thomas Schreiner also cautions regarding the use of the term "center" when he argues, "The image of a center could lead to a static conception of Pauline theology where one theme is given hegemony and other themes are slotted in accordingly. No vital connection is established between various themes, and the whole enterprise appears startlingly subjective."[8] Moreover, the discontent with the term "center" has prompted Johan Christiaan Beker to argue that the words "center" and "core" are imprecise and misleading, and thus he believes that Paul's theology is best described as a "coherent center."[9] Further complicating this

---

4. For discussion on this issue see ibid., 2–26; Don N. Howell, "The Center of Pauline Theology," *BSac* 151 (1998): 50–70; Joseph Plevnik, "The Center of Pauline Theology," *CBQ* 51 (1989): 461–78; Stanley E. Porter, "Is There a Center to Paul's Theology? An Introduction to the Study of Paul and His Theology," in *Paul and His Theology*, ed. Stanley E. Porter, vol. 3 of *Pauline Studies* (Leiden: Brill, 2006), 1–19; Thomas R. Schreiner, *Paul, Apostle of God's Glory in Christ: A Pauline Theology* (Downers Grove, IL: InterVarsity, 2001), 15–35; N. T. Wright, *Paul and the Faithfulness of God*, COQG 4 (Minneapolis: Fortress, 2013), 2:609–18.

5. For a survey of the various suggestions see David B. Capes et al., *Rediscovering Paul: An Introduction to His World, Letters, and Theology* (Downers Grove, IL: InterVarsity, 2007), 266–72; Frank Thielman, *Theology of the New Testament: A Canonical and Synthetic Approach* (Grand Rapids: Zondervan, 2005), 231.

6. Michael F. Bird, *Introducing Paul: The Man, His Mission and His Message* (Downers Grove, IL: InterVarsity, 2008), 22. See also Schreiner, *Paul, Apostle of God's Glory in Christ*, 17, where he argues, "The danger of imposing an alien center on Paul is a real one, and it may be the case that no single theme embraces the whole of Paul's thought."

7. Dunn, *Theology of Paul the Apostle*, 20.

8. Schreiner, *Paul, Apostle of God's Glory in Christ*, 17.

9. Johan Christiaan Beker, *The Triumph of God: The Essence of Paul's Thought*, trans. Loren T. Stuckenbruck (Minneapolis: Fortress, 1990), 13–19. For a critique of Beker see Paul J.

issue is the actual Pauline corpus used to determine a center. Some restrict their search by only examining the seven commonly accepted letters, while others make use of all thirteen. Yet regardless of the debate as to what actually constitutes the core of Paul's theology or which letters should be used, identifying a center can be valuable provided that certain components are envisaged. Scot McKnight offers a helpful summary of the apostle's fundamental theological convictions:

> Paul's theology is not systematics; instead, he is grasped best when at least the following seven principles are kept on the table as we proceed through his letters. *First*, the gospel is the grace of God in revealing Jesus as Messiah and Lord for everyone who believes; *second*, everyone stands behind one of the twin heads of humanity, Adam and Christ; *third*, Jesus Christ is the centre stage, and it is participation in him that transfers a person from the Adam line to the Christ line; *fourth*, the church is the body of Christ on earth; *fifth*, (salvation-) history does not begin with Moses but with Abraham and the promise God gave to him, and finds its crucial turning point in Jesus Christ—but will run its course until the consummation in the glorious Lordship of Christ over all; *sixth*, Christian behavior is determined by the Holy Spirit, not the Torah; *seventh*, Paul is an apostle and not a philosopher or systematic theologian. These principles spring into action when Paul meets his various threats (circumcision, wisdom, gifts, works of Torah, ethnocentrism, flesh rival leaders, and eschatological fights about the Parousia or general resurrection).[10]

While uniformity among scholars regarding the center of Paul's theology is elusive, it seems reasonable to conclude that any proposal should at the very least include all the above criteria to ensure that the whole of Paul's

---

Achtemeier, "Finding the Way to Paul's Theology: A Response to J. Christiaan Beker and J. Paul Sampley," in *Pauline Theology*, ed. Jouette M. Bassler, SBLSS 21 (Minneapolis: Fortress, 2002), 25–31.

10. Scot McKnight, *Jesus and His Death: Historiography, the Historical Jesus, and Atonement Theory* (Waco, TX: Baylor University Press, 2005), 374. See also Michael J. Gorman, *Apostle of the Crucified Lord: A Theological Introduction to Paul & His Letters* (Grand Rapids: Eerdmans, 2017), 131–44, where he offers "a dozen fundamental convictions" of Paul's theology; Plevnik, "Center of Pauline Theology," 477–78, who also provides specific criteria.

theology is correctly represented as presented by the apostle throughout his corpus.

Despite the variegated proposals regarding the center of Paul's theology, the intent of this work is *not* to rehash the various options that have been offered, *nor* is the intent here to propose a fresh hypothesis as to what the core may actually be. Rather, the purpose of this work is to examine how the day of the Lord should be understood as a major motif that influences all of Paul's theological paradigm. More specifically, the argument here is that the day of the Lord was so significant for Paul that every aspect of his theology was in some way affected by this concept. Even in contexts when he does not explicitly mention the day of the Lord, we will argue that the reality of this consummate day in some way shaped the totality of his theology. The argument here is not that the day of the Lord should be considered the center of Paul's theology but rather that the day of the Lord was a fundamental component influencing all of Pauline theology. Therefore, this work seeks to thematically examine the day of the Lord throughout Paul and to argue that his understanding of this theological concept has a much greater influence on the totality of his theology than has previously been understood.

METHODOLOGY AND OUTLINE

A few preliminary comments regarding the methodology and outline of this work are in order at the outset.

In chapter 1 the primary aim is to offer an overview of how contemporary scholarship has understood the day of the Lord. This survey will examine recent discussions so as to ascertain whether scholars have given full weight to the impact the day of the Lord has on Paul's theology or whether this concept has remained relatively obscure throughout Pauline studies.

In chapter 2 the primary aim will be to establish that the day of the Lord is based on the entire Old Testament. Knowing how the Old Testament defines, explicates, and is the basis for the day of the Lord motif will not only ensure a proper understanding of the concept in general, but it will also render greater perspicuity of how this motif influenced Paul's theology.

Chapter 3 will explore the day of the Lord in extracanonical literature and how the motif is understood throughout various texts from that era.

Chapter 4 will examine the importance of the Damascus road experience for Paul. The intent here will be to argue that Paul's conversion experience on the Damascus road was in a sense his personal *proleptic* day of the Lord experience. At Paul's conversion the Judge visibly appeared and gave him mercy instead of retribution. If it can be demonstrated that in some sense Paul viewed his Damascus road experience in this manner, then the case could be made that this had a tremendous influence for every facet of his theology. Paul's theological paradigm had been radically altered because he had experienced a *prefigured* day of the Lord.

Chapter 5 will provide a brief survey of the various terms and idioms that Paul uses when discussing the day of the Lord.

Chapter 6 follows with an examination of several Pauline texts intending to explore the various characteristics of the day of the Lord and the significance it had for Paul. Specific attention will be given to the realization that for Paul the day of the Lord in the Old Testament is fulfilled in Jesus. Consequently, an examination as to how the *day* relates to certain theological convictions of Paul will also be discussed, as well as how the day of the Lord impacts both the already and not yet. In other words, the day of the Lord is transformative and will irreducibly bring about communal effects.

Chapter 7 will offer a conclusion to the study and suggestions for future discussions on this subject.

1

The Day of the Lord in Recent Scholarship

The following is an examination of some of the major treatments pertaining to the day of the Lord in modern scholarship. Any perusal of the current literature on this subject quickly reveals that much of the discussion focuses on the *origin* of the concept. The purpose of this survey is to examine the various suggestions that have been put forth to determine what influenced the development of the day of the Lord motif evident in the Old Testament and how they affected the New Testament's interpretation of that concept. Examining a few of the prominent theories that have been proposed will help to elucidate a more precise understanding of the importance of the day of the Lord throughout the Old Testament and how this ultimately impacted Paul's theological framework.

R. H. CHARLES

In his monograph R. H. Charles proposes a thesis regarding the concept of the day of the Lord that has continued to influence scholars in the modern era.[1] He argues that the day of Yahweh was primarily understood to be a day of battle when Yahweh would come and destroy his enemies and bless his people. According to Charles, the day of Yahweh "means essentially the day on which [he] manifests Himself in victory over His foes, that is, the national foes of Israel."[2] The popular conception in Israel was that since they were solely Yahweh's chosen people and he was solely their God, he would eventually come to judge the nations and vindicate them. But as Charles rightly observes, this interpretation was reoriented by the preexilic prophets, such

---

1. R. H. Charles, *A Critical History of the Doctrine of a Future Life in Israel* (London: Adam & Charles Black, 1913).

2. Ibid., 86–87.

as Amos, Hosea, Isaiah, and Micah, who warned the Israelites that Yahweh's judgment would be "directed first and chiefly, against Israel."[3] Israel and Judah are urged *not* to look forward to the day of the Lord, for it would be a day of their doom. Charles also notes that the preexilic prophets did remind the nation that Yahweh had persevered a remnant and that the day of his coming would not only mean the "vindication of himself and his righteous purposes"[4] but also the reparation of those who truly belong to him. For Israel, Judah, and all the nations, the day of the Lord would culminate in Yahweh's absolute triumph over all those who oppose him as well as salvation for those who obey him. The military imagery that Charles assigns to the day of Yahweh continues to influence the discussion in recent times. Some have taken Charles's position of the military imagery and modified it further, while others have rejected his theory and argue for an alternative perspective.[5]

A further observation Charles offers is that from the beginning (that is, *before* the preexilic prophets), the day of the Lord was understood to be eschatological, describing the future hope of God's people.[6] However, scholars have challenged his theory.[7] For instance, K. J. Cathcart argues that Charles "may have been mistaken, since eschatology *proper* arose in the Exile at the earliest and since the eschatological aspect of the Day of Yahweh belongs to late prophecy."[8] But this critique may be somewhat overstated and in need of a qualification. Rather than insisting that eschatology proper *arose* in the exile at the earliest, it seems more reasonable to maintain that it *matured* during the exile. From the beginning, the Old Testament seems to indicate that God's covenant people had a

---

3. Ibid., 88.

4. Ibid., 89.

5. For those who have modified Charles's theory, see Gerhard von Rad, "Origin of the Concept of the Day of Yahweh," *Journal of Semitic Studies* 4 (1959): 97–108; Douglas K. Stuart, "The Sovererign's Day of Conquest," *Bulletin of the American Schools of Oriental Research* 221 (1976): 158–64. For those who have rejected Charles's view, see Sigmund Mowinckel, *He That Cometh: The Messiah Concept in the Old Testament and Later Judaism*, trans. G. W. Anderson, BRS (Grand Rapids: Eerdmans, 2005); Sigmund Mowinckel, *The Psalms in Israel's Worship*, trans. D. R. Ap-Thomas, BRS (Grand Rapids: Eerdmans, 2004); Meir Weiss, "The Origin of the 'Day of the Lord' Reconsidered," *HUCA* 37 (1966): 29–71.

6. Charles, *Critical History of the Doctrine of a Future Life in Israel*, 86.

7. Most notably, K. J. Cathcart, "Day of Yahweh," in *ABD*, 2:84; Mowinckel, *He That Cometh*; Mowinckel, *Psalms in Israel's Worship*.

8. Cathcart, "Day of Yahweh," 84, emphasis added.

future hope whereby they understood that he would one day ultimately restore righteousness. Yahweh's intervention in history, whether in blessing or cursing, served as a template pointing to the consummate day. This understanding certainly became more developed during the exilic and postexilic periods, but it is unlikely that the concept of a future hope did not originate until then.[9] Regardless of how Charles's thesis is interpreted, his study is helpful in that it illuminates and elaborates on the fact that the day of the Lord is both imminent and future and is simultaneously a day of retribution for Yahweh's enemies and a day of victory for those who belong to Yahweh.

JOHN M. P. SMITH

Similar to the view of Charles, John M. P. Smith also argues that the day of the Lord refers to a great battle where Yahweh fights against his enemies.[10] He also believes that during the preexilic era, prophets such as Amos modified the common understanding of the day of Yahweh as referring to a time of judgment and humiliation *against* Israel. Smith argues:

> In the hands of Amos this conception underwent a transformation. [Previously], it had been instrumental in stimulating the national spirit and life, so now, purified from its grosser elements, it is made to contribute to the development of the religious and moral life of the people. Instead of being the day of Israel's glorification at the expense of her enemies, it now became the day of her humiliation and chastisement at the hands of Yahweh. It was a complete reversal of all the hopes, which Israel had so long centered in this day. The first announcement of the new doctrine (Amos 5:8ff) must have fallen upon the people with startling suddenness; it was a rude awakening from a pleasant dream.[11]

Smith is correct in his assessment that Amos did warn Israel not to rejoice at the coming day of the Lord (5:18–20). The prophet warned the nation that their sin prevented them from looking forward to the day of

---

9. See chap. 2 for a discussion of how the day of the Lord is *thematically* evident throughout the OT.

10. John M. P. Smith, "The Day of Yahweh," *Ashland Theological Journal* 5 (1901): 505–33.

11. Ibid., 512–13.

Yahweh's coming. Rather, they should fear the Lord's arrival, for it would not be a day of celebration but of judgment. This leads Smith to conclude that such a perspective regarding the day of the Lord was a "new doctrine" for Israel. But such an inference is most likely untenable. Rather, it seems more evident that Amos was recapitulating the principle of Yahweh visiting his people in judgment as previously delineated throughout the Torah, specifically in contexts such as Deuteronomy 27–28, which outlines the curses the nation would face for their defiance of their covenant stipulations.[12] Amos' audience was certainly in need of a reminder that God would come to visit them in judgment if their sins persisted, but this was in all likelihood not a new doctrine that was being introduced to them for the first time.

HUGO GRESSMANN

Hugo Gressmann rejects the view of Charles and Smith that the day of the Lord refers to a day of battle and interprets the day of Yahweh as primarily an eschatological event having a cosmic impact.[13] He further argues, "Israelite eschatology was borrowed from an already developed foreign (Babylon) eschatology."[14] Understanding the day of the Lord with an eschatological framework is certainly viable. The Old Testament, particularly the prophetic literature, indicates that the consummate day of Yahweh is a future event that will have global ramifications impacting all the nations (Isa 13:9; Ezek 30:1–19; Amos 5:18–20). But in conjunction with the future orientation, there are passages that also indicate the day of Yahweh as a *past* event (Isa 22:1–14; Jer 46:2–20; Lam 1:2; Ezek 13:1–9). It seems, then, that the prophets understood there to be "days" of the Lord. They interpreted the various curses—such as plagues, famines, wars, and so on—to be an actual "day" of Yahweh. The catastrophes that the Israelites incurred (past and present) served as warnings to the nation, urging the people to repent and be restored back to Yahweh before the final day arrived. The Lord "visiting" his people with these various punishments served as a template pointing to the ultimate day of Yahweh. This eschatological framework of

---

12. See the discussion in chap. 2.

13. Hugo Gressmann, *Der Ursprung der israelitisch-jüdischen Eschatologie*, FRLANT 6 (Göttingen: Vandenhoeck & Ruprecht, 1905), 143–45.

14. Cathcart, "Day of Yahweh," 84.

the Lord having "visited" his people or coming to "visit" them with either judgment or blessing is arguably established as early as Genesis 3:8 and is ostensibly evident throughout the Torah.[15]

If this paradigm concerning the day of the Lord can be substantiated, then Gressmann's proposal that Israelite eschatology was dependent on Babylonian eschatology is doubtful. Ralph Klein even contends, "recent scholarship seems agreed that eschatology is a product of Israel's view of God and history, and it is not to be linked to a so-called pre-prophetic eschatology derived from Babylonia."[16] Consequently, if the evidence of the Old Testament testifies that the concept of the day of Lord was understood as early as the Torah, then a strong case could be made that Gressmann's view that Israelite eschatology had developed from Babylonian eschatology may actually be *mutatis mutandis*.

SIGMUND MOWINCKEL

Building on the thesis of Gressmann, Sigmund Mowinckel likewise argues that the day of the Lord was also evident in preexilic Israel and was influenced by Babylonian eschatology.[17] However, he differs from Gressmann's proposal by contending that the day of Yahweh was primarily connected to the autumn or new year's festivals, which he refers to as the "enthronement festival," which he believed symbolized God's triumph and enthronement as King. According to Mowinckel, the new year's festival occurred at the end of the year after the harvest had been completed and the land was barren. The desolation of the land symbolized that the earth was cursed and was on the verge of falling into utter chaos. Every day of the festival was a reminder to the nation that they should seek the Lord and he would bring another year of prosperity and protection.[18]

It was at this point that

> Yahweh came and revealed Himself, giving Himself to His own and making Himself known by His mighty acts. In and through the effectual rites of the cult, in which God's coming and conflict were

---

15. See the discussion in chap. 2.
16. Ralph W. Klein, "Day of the Lord," *CTM* 39 (1968): 523n22.
17. Mowinckel, *He That Cometh*; Mowinckel, *Psalms in Israel's Worship*.
18. See J. D. Barker, "Day of the Lord," in *DOTP*, 134.

displayed in dramatic symbolism, His appearance, His combat, and His victory really took place. He engaged with the powers of chaos, and defeated them as He did at the beginning, crushing or chaining them. He recreated the world; and behold, soon afterwards the autumn rains came, soaking the earth, watering its furrows, making it fertile and productive. The God of life had triumphed over the hostile powers of death and created the world anew.[19]

He believes that the Israelites borrowed this concept from both Canaanite and Babylonian practices, where after having triumphed over their enemies the gods sat enthroned over the kingdoms they had created. Mowinckel adduces that Israel transferred this same perspective and applied it to Yahweh, who comes to render judgment on his enemies and sits enthroned as the true King over all of creation. Mowinckel espouses that the primary reason that the nation of Israel observed these cultic festivals was to commemorate "Yahweh's cosmic conflict, victory, and enthronement."[20] And although the ultimate source for the day of the Lord, according to Mowinckel, was the new year festival, he strongly asserts that this was not an eschatological concept initially. Rather, the future orientation for the day of Yahweh was a later prophetic development.[21]

The controlling evidence for his proposal that the day of the Lord was founded on the cultic festivals is centered on five psalms (Pss 47; 93; 96; 98; 99)[22] and brief references in Isaiah and Amos. Mowinckel argues that there are certain characteristics found in the five psalms, which he refers to as enthronement psalms, that substantiate his thesis. He contends that specific expressions throughout these psalms depict the nation celebrating because Yahweh *has become* King, has taken his seat on the throne, and has sovereign rule. The notion that Yahweh *has become* King does not negate belief that he is eternally the true King; rather, the festival symbolizes that at his coming all the earth will witness his enthronement and will have no

---

19. Mowinckel, *He That Cometh*, 140.

20. Ibid.

21. Ibid., 132–33. See also Elizabeth Boase, *The Fulfilment of Doom? The Dialogic Interaction between the Book of Lamentations and the Pre-Exilic/Early Exilic Prophetic Literature*, Library of Hebrew Bible/Old Testament Series 437 (New York: T&T Clark, 2006), 107–8; Cathcart, "Day of Yahweh," 84.

22. Mowinckel, *Psalms in Israel's Worship*, 106–92.

choice but to recognize that Yahweh alone is the true King. Furthermore, Mowinckel contends that these psalms indicate that the enthronement festival was a graphic depiction of Yahweh's royal procession that included his victorious coronation and was accompanied by singing and dancing. The festival was intended to depict the personal presence of Yahweh ruling as King. Mowinckel writes:

> In the rites and psalms belonging to the festival of the enthrone-ment of Yahweh this idea was mirrored, or, rather, presented, expressed, and experienced. A main event was evidently the great festal procession, the victorious coronation entry of the Lord, to which reference is made in Ps. 47:6. It must have had a strongly dra-matic character, with playing, singing and dancing. The personal presence of Yahweh in the festive procession was most probably symbolized by his holy shrine (the ark). It is this appearance and enthronement day of Yahweh which originally was called "the day of the Lord," "the day of the feast of Yahweh."[23]

In addition to the enthronement psalms, Mowinckel contends that both Isaiah and Amos understood the annual festival day as depicting a royal day, namely the day of Yahweh's enthronement when he would return to restore his covenant people to himself, judge the nations, and demonstrate that he alone is the true King over the entire world. The nation of Israel longed for the day of the Lord, anticipating that it would be the day when Yahweh would vindicate them and punish their enemies. But, as Mowinckel cor-rectly observes, Isaiah and Amos reinterpret the day of Yahweh as a day when he would come to judge Israel (Isa 2:12–22; Amos 5:18–27). Amos in particular warns the people that the Lord actually denounces their festivals and that they should *not* look forward to the day of his coming. In spite of Amos' reinterpretation of the day of the Lord, the prophet understood that Yahweh has a remnant that he himself was preserving. The enthronement festival, according to Mowinckel, symbolized for the remnant a day "when Yahweh must remember his covenant, and appear as the mighty king and deliverer, bringing a 'day' upon His own and His people's enemies, (Isa 2:12ff), condemning them to destruction, and 'acquitting' and 'executing justice' for

---

23. Ibid., 115–16.

His own people."[24] However, Mowinckel claims that the annual enthrone-ment festival, intimated in the Psalms and early prophets, did not have any eschatological significance for those preexilic observers. The festival pri-marily demonstrated the nation's longing for Yahweh to come and restore favorable conditions for them.[25] It was the later prophets who implemented new meaning into the new year festival by envisaging a more future ori-entation to the day of the Lord.

The reaction to Mowinckel's enthronement theory is diverse, with both support and criticism. Scholars recognize that the later prophets perhaps had a more eschatological purview in their understanding of the day of Yahweh than their predecessors. But Mowinckel's conclusion that the day of the Lord found its origin in the so-called enthronement festivals, which he believes Israel adopted from Canaanite and Babylonian tradition, has been seriously challenged.[26]

LADISLAV CĚRNÝ

Ladislav Cěrný outright rejects Mowinckel's view that the day of the Lord refers to the reenthronement of Yahweh celebrated at the annual new year festival.[27] In Cěrný's estimation, any proper understanding of the day of the Lord would "abandon definitely any belief that the origin of the idea of the Day of Yahweh depended on the kingship of Yahweh and on his annual re-enthronement as king during the New Year Festival."[28] Instead, Cěrný proposes that originally the day of the Lord referred to a day in which Yahweh would act to "newly shape the fate of his nation."[29] Yahweh had cer-tainly acted on behalf of his nation throughout history, but those instances served as patterns pointing to the future day that had been decreed by God

---

24. Mowinckel, *He That Cometh*, 145.

25. Ibid., 132.

26. For advocates of Mowinckel's view, see the discussion in Derek Kidner, *Psalms 1–72: An Introduction and Commentary*, TOTC 15 (Downers Grove, IL: InterVarsity, 2008), 8–15. For those who disagree, see Roland de Vaux, *Ancient Israel: Its Life and Institutions*, trans. John McHugh, BRS (Grand Rapids: Eerdmans, 1997), 504–6; Gerhard von Rad, *Old Testament Theology: The Theology of Israel's Prophetic Traditions*, trans. D. M. G. Stalker (New York: Harper, 1962), 2:123n38.

27. Ladislav Černý, *The Day of* Yahweh *and Some Relevant Problems*, Práce z Vědeckých Ùstavù 53 (Praze: Nákl. Filosofické Fakulty University Karlovy, 1948).

28. Ibid., 74.

29. Ibid., 103.

when he would definitively shape the fate of his people. Černý argues that initially the day of the Lord referred to multiple days, but over the course of time it became much more future oriented, being focused on a single day. This change in perspective meant that the day of the Lord was understood to be the day that would establish a new and better order not only for Israel but also globally.[30] According to Černý, as the day of Yahweh developed, "the original narrow nationalistic scope was enlarged into something international, global, and universal, to become finally of cosmic significance."[31] This final day of the Lord will be catastrophic, described as a day of wrath, anger, and judgment. Even so, those who are faithful to Yahweh can take courage, knowing that he has ensured them a blissful future.

GERHARD VON RAD

One of the most influential theories regarding the origin of the day of the Lord has been offered by Gerhard von Rad.[32] His research led him to the following conclusions:

> First, The Day of Yahweh encompasses a pure event of war, the rise of Yahweh against his enemies, his battle and his victory. Secondly, the entire material for this imagery which surrounds the concept of the Day of Yahweh is of old-Israelitic origin. It derives from the tradition of the holy wars of Yahweh, in which Yahweh appeared personally, to annihilate his enemies. This does not, of course, dispute the possibility that one or the other individual idea can also be proved to have existed with neighboring peoples of the ancient Near East, but one thing has to be insisted upon, namely that the prophets have adopted the whole concept of the Day of Yahweh from the tradition of their own people and not from foreign sources.[33]

To substantiate his theory, von Rad focuses specifically on four texts that he believes delineate military imagery, therefore proving that the day of the Lord was derived from Israelite holy-war tradition and should be strictly

---

30. Ibid.
31. Ibid., 79.
32. Von Rad, "Origin of the Concept of the Day of Yahweh," 97–108.
33. Ibid., 103–4.

understood as an event of war.[34] His conclusions have been tremendously influential in the discussion regarding the origin of the day of Yahweh. Barker comments that von Rad's "hypothesis [has] probably garnered the most support in the discussion of the origins of the Day of the Lord and is the theory that provides the background for most of the subsequent discussion of the motif."[35]

However, von Rad's theory has also generated severe criticism. One substantial critique leveled against von Rad is that he limited analysis to only four texts. In doing so, he failed to include Amos 5:18–20 and Isaiah 2, which are arguably the two earliest texts that describe the day of the Lord.[36] His rationale for not including Amos 5:18–20 is that it "is not sufficiently unequivocal to be used as a suitable starting-point for an examination, it is advisable to begin with texts, which convey a more unequivocal, and at the same time a broader, conception of the Day of the Lord."[37] He defends his neglect of the Isaiah 2 passage by concluding that the day of the Lord "does not amount to more than an allusion."[38] But for von Rad to dismiss some of the earliest evidence not only is methodologically flawed but seemingly indicates a bias against any text that may disprove his theory. A further criticism offered is that von Rad believes that the day of the Lord derived from old Israelite holy-war tradition. However, critics have noted that what can actually be known about holy-war tradition in old Israel is scant. Cathcart argues that the conclusion that the day of the Lord originated from early Israelite war tradition is problematic because "the Deuteronomistic sources are scarcely sufficient for informing us about it. . . . Von Rad's claim that the Day of Yahweh is of old Israelite origin is not convincing."[39]

A final criticism directed against von Rad's theory is that military imagery does not seem to be the primary motif used to describe the day

---

34. The four texts he uses are Isa 13; 34; Ezek 7; and Joel 2.

35. Barker, "Day of the Lord," 134.

36. See Cathcart, "Day of Yahweh," 84–85; John A. Gray, "The Day of Yahweh in Cultic Experience and Eschatological Prospect," *Svensk exegetisk årsbok* 39 (1974): 5–37; Weiss, "Origin of the 'Day of the Lord' Reconsidered," 29–71.

37. Von Rad, "Origin of the Concept of the Day of Yahweh," 98.

38. Ibid., 105.

39. Cathcart, "Day of Yahweh," 84.

of the Lord. There are a variety of alliterations used throughout the Old Testament to depict the day of Yahweh, such as his judgment on his enemies, the establishment of his government, and various cosmic phenomena (e.g., earthquakes and darkness).[40] Critics agree with von Rad that there are texts that describe the day of the Lord by utilizing military imagery, but they argue such imagery is secondary and a more comprehensive origin is preferable. For instance, John Gray, who borrows from Mowinckel, contends that a more encompassing motif for the day of Yahweh is in all likelihood "the moment of his epiphany as King, which was the highlight of the autumn festival in Israel."[41] Although von Rad's methodology was arguably flawed, his work has had tremendous impact on the discussion regarding the day of the Lord and for many scholars his conclusions are considered to be authoritative and have generally gone unchallenged.[42]

FRANK M. CROSS

In his article, Frank Cross interacts with the views put forth by Mowinckel and von Rad.[43] He discusses the theories of each and concludes that their proposals for the origin of the day of the Lord do not oppose each other but rather complement each other. Cross does criticize von Rad for his failure to adequately consider the mythology from the Canaanite cult, which he believes influenced the day of Yahweh tradition in Israel. Cross contends that the weakness of von Rad's view is that he failed to recognize the many diverse elements that influenced Israel's understanding of the day of Yahweh. He argues that the development of the day of the Lord was more complex than von Rad had originally assumed, and his failure in ignoring these various elements does not afford a proper understanding for how the motif emerged. Cross concludes that a blending of Mowinckel and von Rad's views is the best solution for understanding the origin for the day of the Lord. For Cross, "It is the motifs from these

---

40. See Gray, "Day of Yahweh in Cultic Experience and Eschatological Prospect," 14.

41. Ibid., 16.

42. See Weiss, "Origin of the 'Day of the Lord' Reconsidered," 29n5.

43. Frank M. Cross, "The Divine Warrior in Israel's Early Cult," in *Biblical Motifs: Origins and Transformations*, ed. Alexander Altmann, Philip W. Lown Institute of Advanced Judaic Studies, Brandeis University Studies and Texts (Cambridge, MA: Harvard University Press, 1966), 11–30.

two traditions which provide the specific metaphors for eschatological passages in general, and for the day of Yahweh in particular."[44] According to Cross, the most precise interpretation regarding the origin of the day of the Lord is to understand that the day of Yahweh is both a day of victory in holy warfare and the day of Yahweh's festival where he comes in absolute victory demonstrating that he alone is the true King of the universe.[45]

FRANK C. FENSHAM

Frank Fensham contends that the hypotheses offered by Mowinckel and von Rad are unsatisfactory.[46] His criticism of Mowinckel's theory is that there is no direct proof that the Babylonian new year festival served as the starting point for Israel's understanding of the day of the Lord. Consequently, Fensham believes that Mowinckel's final analysis is untenable. However, he does acknowledge the contribution of Mowinckel's study, which he argues helped to demonstrate that "there were certain cultic peculiarities at certain periods in Israelite history."[47] His critique of von Rad's theory is that holy war imagery does not adequately explain all the day of the Lord passages. Furthermore, Fensham contends that von Rad did not sufficiently address the universal influence of the day of the Lord.[48] Fensham does agree with von Rad that the military motif is a veritable depiction of the day of Yahweh, but he says it is not all encompassing, as von Rod concludes. He also agrees with von Rad that the day of the Lord was not originally understood to be eschatological but rather was interpreted as the day when Yahweh would destroy his enemies.[49] However, Fensham ultimately concludes that von Rad's theory is unsatisfactory since it does not account for all the evidence.

---

44. Boase, *Fulfilment of Doom?*, 109.

45. Cross, "Divine Warrior in Israel's Early Cult," 30.

46. Frank C. Fensham, "A Possible Origin of the Concept of the Day of the Lord," in *Proceedings of the Ninth Meeting of Die Ou-Testamentiese Werkgemeenskap in Suid-Afrika Held at the University of Stellenbosch 26th–29th July 1966, and Proceedings of the Second Meeting of Die Nuwe-Testamentiese Werkgemeenskap van Suid-Afrika Held at the University of Stellenbosch 22nd–25th July 1966* (Potchefstroom: Bepeck, 1966), 90.

47. Ibid.

48. Ibid.

49. Ibid.

Fensham suggests that the concept of a treaty violation best explains the origin of the day of the Lord. According to Fensham, interpreting the day of the Lord in this manner was adapted from Near Eastern tradition, wherein violators of a treaty would be punished by their gods with various curses.[50] Fensham argues that the ancient Israelites applied this Near Eastern concept to the day of the Lord to explain that God would visit his people to enact various curses on them on account of their unfaithfulness to the covenant he had established with them. These curses would come in a variety of modes such as war, darkness, and other cosmological phenomena. Fensham writes: "The Day of the Lord is a day of judgment and punishment. The foreign enemies receive only punishment in the form of executed curses. The unfaithful Israel receives judgment as a result of the breach of covenant and the punishment in the form of executed curses. . . . The real background of the concept is a day of visitation and execution of curses."[51]

Fensham's theory is helpful because he seeks to explain the origin of the day of the Lord from a broader perspective rather than limiting it to strictly an event of holy war. However, in his final analysis Fensham seems to commit the same error for which he chastises von Rad, namely not interpreting the day of the Lord comprehensively. Certainly the Old Testament depicts the day of Yahweh as a day of judgment, but there are also several texts that describe it as a day of salvation and a day for those who are faithful to Yahweh to anticipate with great joy. Regarding Fensham's proposal, J. D. Barker observes that "the emphasis on punitive aspects of the Day of the Lord makes it difficult to account for its salvific [perspective], which various Day of the Lord passages explore in some detail."[52]

MEIR WEISS

Meir Weiss ardently opposes von Rad's thesis that the day of the Lord concept originated from the tradition of holy war.[53] Weiss rejects von Rad's assessment because he believes it was methodologically flawed. According

50. Ibid., 92–93, where he cites several examples.

51. Ibid., 95–96.

52. Barker, "Day of the Lord," 135.

53. Weiss, "Origin of the 'Day of the Lord' Reconsidered," 29–71.

to Weiss, von Rad considered fourteen texts to substantiate his thesis that the origin for the day of Yahweh was indeed the imagery of holy war. But as Weiss demonstrates, of those fourteen texts used by von Rad, five of them do not depict or even allude to an event of holy war.[54] Furthermore, Weiss observes that holy war imagery is absent from the earliest texts that describe the day of the Lord, namely Amos 5:18–20 and Isaiah 2:12–21. Weiss considers these two texts to be the earliest literary documents that address the day of the Lord, and he chastises von Rad for not including them along with the fourteen other texts relevant to the subject. Weiss observes, "From a methodological point of view it is most surprising for von Rad, in basing his conclusions on the Day of the Lord, to have disregarded the most ancient prophecies on the subject."[55] For these reasons Weiss argues that von Rad's thesis cannot be corroborated, and thus he rejects the notion that the origin of the day of the Lord was derived solely from the tradition of holy war.

According to Weiss, the origin for the day of Yahweh should not be interpreted as specifically as von Rad proposed. The concept encompasses a much wider range of meaning throughout Scripture than von Rad allowed. Weiss believes, "The variance in the working of the several expressions phrasing the concept of the [day of the Lord] indicates clearly that the [day of the Lord] was far from being a 'firm formula'—not to speak of a 'terminus technicus'—even in the words of the late prophets."[56] He contends that the day of Yahweh is "a 'neutral' concept, a formal one of a changing content which adapts itself to the nature of the individual [day of the Lord] implied by it. The [day of the Lord] *per se* signifies that action of the Lord, his might and power potential."[57] Weiss argues that the day of Yahweh concept is more "flexible" throughout the Old Testament, having a variety of different interpretations and applications depending on the context. However, he does propose that it is the self-manifestation of the Lord that embodies the meaning of this concept in every day of Yahweh prophecy.[58] Weiss concludes that the day of the Lord motif was *not* prepbrophetic

---

54. Ibid., 37. The five texts he lists are Isa 34:2–6; Joel 1:15; 3:4; Obad 15; Zeph 1:16.
55. Ibid.
56. Ibid., 45.
57. Ibid., 47.
58. Ibid.

but was coined by Amos, who did not derive his understanding of this day from holy war tradition but rather from the well-established tradition of theophany.[59]

The contribution of Weiss is helpful in that he demonstrates that the holy war tradition is not evident in every day of the Lord text. However, many day of the Lord texts do exhibit military imagery depicting Yahweh coming in battle as a warrior (Isa 13:1–22; Joel 2:1–11; Zech 9:14–17). Consequently, Weiss's indictment against von Rad's theory may be somewhat overstated. Ralph Klein observes, "Weiss certainly goes too far, but he is correct, perhaps, insofar as the passages will not all fit the schema of Israel's wars against her enemies. Nonetheless, Yahweh plays a central role as a warrior in many passages, and in this sense they are related to holy war."[60] Finally, Weiss's claim that the day of the Lord concept is not preprophetic seems tenuous. Although the explicit phraseology does not occur until the prophetic literature, the motif is arguably evident prior to the prophets, which the next chapter will seek to demonstrate.

RALPH KLEIN

Ralph Klein's essay provides a helpful survey of the various theories regarding the origin of the day of the Lord.[61] He discusses the various ways that the day of Yahweh is described throughout the Old Testament and suggests that these variegated descriptions are best understood as theophany. Klein contends that interpreting the day of the Lord as a theophany encapsulates the numerous titles and metaphors used throughout the Old Testament to describe that day. He agrees with von Rad that military imagery is used to describe the day, but this is only one aspect utilized to highlight the theophanic understanding. Other phenomena are used to describe the theophany of Yahweh on his day, such as darkness, gloom, a day of clouds, earthquakes, and so on.[62] In addition, Klein further contends that "imminence forms a persistent theme in discussions of the Day of Yahweh."[63] He supports this

---

59. Ibid., 60.
60. Klein, "Day of the Lord," 519n12.
61. Ibid., 517–25.
62. Ibid., 518–20.
63. Ibid., 521.

by examining eight texts, which he argues demonstrate that the Israelites interpreted that the day of the Lord was coming soon.[64]

Finally, Klein disagrees with earlier scholars such as von Rad and Fensham who argued that the day of the Lord was not originally an eschatological concept. He agrees that it is not strictly eschatological, since the day of Yahweh is referred to as a past event.[65] But this does not mean that the day of the Lord was completely devoid of any eschatological meaning. According to Klein, conclusions that suggest the absence of any eschatological nuance in the day of Yahweh are based on a much too narrow definition of eschatology. Klein contends: "If eschatology is more broadly defined as the study of ideas and beliefs concerning the end of the present world *order*, and the creation of a *new order*, thus emphasizing the intra-historical character of many of the happenings, then we can say that the pre-exilic prophets did have an eschatology of doom, and that, as we know from the rest of their message, they looked for a new day when God would intervene to reactivate His elections traditions."[66] Such a conclusion is seemingly helpful because it avoids placing unnecessary limitations on the concept of the day of Yahweh and allows for a more comprehensive understanding of this versatile motif.

DOUGLAS STUART

Douglas Stuart agrees with von Rad that the day of the Lord is "a day of decisive military action."[67] However, he disagrees with von Rad that the day of Yahweh was strictly an Israelite concept and that it is possible that the motif was borrowed from various Near Eastern traditions. Stuart contends that within ancient Near Eastern tradition there is ample evidence that non-Israelite people believed that there was a true king or sovereign who had universal authority and that through a single event of war this king would defeat all his enemies in one decisive day of battle. While most kings fought for weeks against their adversaries, the Near Eastern tradition believed that a true king could win the war in only one day.[68] Stuart argues

---

64. Isa 13:6; Ezek 30:3; Joel 1:15; 2:1; 3:14; Obad 15; Zeph 1:7, 14.

65. Klein, "Day of the Lord," 523.

66. Ibid.

67. Stuart, "Sovereign's Day of Conquest," 159.

68. See ibid., 161–62, where Stuart lists several non-Israelite sources in support of his argument.

that Israel was familiar with such a tradition and applied that to their understanding of the day of Yahweh. Since God alone is the true King, he has a day where he will come and destroy all those who oppose him. Although Stuart presents solid evidence that the day of Yahweh was understood as a decisive day of victory for God as he demonstrates his universal sovereignty, it seems that Stuart has also limited the overall biblical perspective of the day of the Lord. Certainly military imagery is frequently used to describe the day of Yahweh, but it is arguably not as exclusive as Stuart concludes.

YAIR HOFFMANN

Yair Hoffmann's article is a critique on the methodology of earlier scholars regarding the day of the Lord.[69] According to Hoffmann, only those texts that specifically use the phrase יוֹם יְהוָה (yôm yhwh), "day of the Lord," are eligible sources to be used to determine the meaning of the day of the Lord. He believes that scholars who deviate from this methodology and examine other texts that have variant expressions are unable to ascertain a proper understanding of the day of Yahweh. Hoffmann agrees that those variant expressions should not be overlooked, but they can only properly be understood after the principle locution yôm yhwh has been thoroughly investigated. Hoffmann writes, "Obviously, one must not ignore the related expressions. However, only after a careful philological examination of the proper phrase can one proceed to evaluate the significance of related phrases, for a comprehensive understanding of the concept."[70] After examining the various biblical texts that only use yôm yhwh, Hoffmann arrives at the following conclusions. First, the day of the Lord should be understood as a theophany, namely, God manifesting his presence to comfort his people and avenge his enemies.[71] Such manifestations are described as but not limited to an event of war or other cosmic phenomena. Second, divine judgment is a central focus within the theophany traditions. When Yahweh appears, he will bring judgment on the heathen and the unfaithful

---

69. Yair Hoffmann, "The Day of the Lord as a Concept and a Term in the Prophetic Literature," *ZAW* 93 (1981): 37–50.

70. Ibid., 38.

71. Ibid., 44.

Israelite.[72] Third, the phrase *yôm yhwh* was "never a non-eschatological term."[73] Hoffmann contends that *yôm yhwh* was a fixed term as early as the prophet Amos, since the Israelites understood the significance of the day of Yahweh and even looked forward to it. Fourth, the variant expressions related to *yôm yhwh* may or may not be eschatological depending on the context. Although Hoffmann has been severely criticized for focusing primarily on those texts that use the specific phrase *yôm yhwh*, his work is noteworthy in that he makes a strong case that ancient Israelites were familiar with the concept of the day of the Lord.

CONCLUSION

The above survey has demonstrated that scholarly consensus regarding the origin of the day of the Lord is elusive. The various theories examined throughout this chapter have demonstrated that the concept is fluid and has been approached from a variety of different angles. And while there is little agreement regarding the origin of the day, the majority of scholars surveyed do appreciate the diverse features used throughout the Old Testament to portray the day of Yahweh. These diverse features demonstrate that the motif is exceedingly broad and cannot be limited to only one specific nuance. To better appreciate the significance of the day of the Lord, the following chapter seeks to examine the concept throughout the entire Old Testament. The subsequent examination intends to only demonstrate how the day of Yahweh is *thematically* present throughout the whole Old Testament and the ramifications this has in the apostle Paul's theology.

---

72. Ibid., 45.
73. Ibid., 50.

2

The Day of the Lord in the Old Testament

A THEMATIC SURVEY

Both the Old and New Testaments unequivocally demonstrate that God's judgment of his enemies and vindication of his people is a central part of Scripture's overall message. As a result, the Scriptures incorporate a variety of terms and idioms to denote the concept of God's judgment. However, it is the phrase "the day of the Lord," along with its relevant derivatives, that finds pride of place throughout the canon. The intent of the present discussion is to thematically examine the concept of the day of the Lord—and several of the relevant terms and idioms—throughout the Old Testament.[1] The rationale for this is to demonstrate that the Old Testament serves as the foundation for the day of the Lord motif and thus served as the basis for Paul's understanding of this theme. Once it becomes evident that the concept of the day of the Lord is based solely on the Old Testament, this will enable a more appropriate understanding for how the Apostle Paul interpreted the phrase—along with its relevant terms—to be fulfilled in Jesus Christ.

The subject of judgment is extremely pervasive and is in some way evident throughout every portion of the Old Testament. This phenomenon has led Paul House to comment: "Even if one desires to analyse biblical statements about judgment, however, one faces a daunting task. Judgment appears in every segment of the canon and occurs in a variety of settings and as part of several theological emphases, which explains in part why the theme is treated in so many different ways and in such summary fashion in so many scholarly works."[2]

---

1. See chap. 5 for the discussion of these terms in Paul.

2. Paul R. House, "The Day of the Lord," in *Central Themes in Biblical Theology: Mapping Unity in Diversity*, ed. Scott J. Hafemann and Paul R. House (Grand Rapids: Baker, 2007), 181.

Since the subject of judgment is so comprehensive throughout the Old Testament, it is necessary to restrict the parameters of this survey. The following inquiry, then, seeks to only discuss the day of the Lord, "since it is one of the most important, if not the most important, of the biblical portrayals of divine judgment."[3] The intent here is to explore the day of the Lord *thematically* throughout the Old Testament while being textually responsible. The benefit of this discussion is that it will not only ensure a more firm understanding of this central theme as depicted throughout the Old Testament but will arguably enable a more accurate understanding of how this motif substantially affected Paul's theology.

THE DAY OF THE LORD IN THE TORAH?

The exact phrase "the day of the Lord" is not found in the Torah. The phrase does not occur—in relation to judgment—until the prophetic literature being referenced as early as Isaiah (13:9-6) and Amos (5:18). This has led Shimon Bakon to argue that there is not "any record of when there came to be a popular concept of such a day of judgment, in which the Lord would punish those who oppose Him and who oppressed His people Israel."[4] To some extent Bakon is correct in that there is no evidence as to when the actual phrase "the day of the Lord" became the moniker for judgment. However, his assertion that there is no record of when the *concept* of a day of judgment became popular is dubious. Rather, it is conceivable that the "day of the Lord" phrase used by the later Old Testament authors was ostensibly derived from their knowledge of the numerous theophanies or "parousias" of Yahweh depicted throughout the Torah. In other words, later authors may have viewed the many advents of Yahweh described in the Torah as a "day" when he would come and intervene to either bless or curse his people. The imagery of these "comings" of God found throughout the Torah is the likely catalyst that led later Old Testament authors to utilize the day of the Lord as an epithet that formalized the concept of

---

3. Ibid. House also comments that "every 'Day of the Lord' is an instance of judgment, although not every depiction of judgment is called a 'Day of the Lord.'" While this is certainly true, it should also be noted that there are also instances of the day of the Lord in contexts referring to salvation and deliverance.

4. Shimon Bakon, "The Day of the Lord," *JBQ* 38 (2010): 149.

God coming to judge or bless. A few examples will help to demonstrate this line of reasoning.

Genesis 3:8 may be the quintessential text illustrating the concept of the day of the Lord. In the immediate context, the Lord "comes" into the garden to judge Adam and Eve for their disobedience. In verse 8 the phrase "and they heard the voice of the Lord walking about" could arguably be a depiction of the Lord coming to judge Adam and Eve. The Hebrew term קוֹל (qôl), "voice," has an extensive field of meaning but is often translated as "voice" or "sound."[5] Scholars agree that in this context the term "voice" is not literally referring to God calling out to Adam and Eve, but rather the term refers to the sound of his coming.[6] This is further evident in other contexts, where the term qôl denotes the sound of coming footsteps (2 Sam 5:24; 1 Kgs 14:6; 2 Kgs 6:32). Other passages delineate that the qôl of Yahweh is similar to the sound of war, where God is described as a warrior charging into battle (Ps 18:13) or as loud thunder, symbolizing the terror that goes before him, causing people to tremble (Exod 19:16). Additional Old Testament contexts seem to support this interpretation that the qôl of Yahweh is oftentimes a theophany of judgment (Exod 19:16–18; Deut 4:9–12; Isa 30:31–33). The sound of Yahweh coming in the context of Genesis 3:8 is ostensibly more than just the cadence of footsteps but is arguably the distinctive sound of judgment. Meredith Kline contends, "What Adam and Eve heard was frighteningly loud. It was the shattering thunder of God's advent in judgment."[7] This interpretation is further substantiated with the participle מִתְהַלֵּךְ (mithallēk), which is typically translated as "walking." It should be noted that the subject of the participle is God, and thus the author likely wanted to stress that God himself was approaching. But to understand the term as "walking" in a general sense gives the misleading impression that Yahweh was merely strolling through the garden looking for Adam and Eve. Rather, mithallēk often denotes the idea of moving

---

5. See BDB 867; HALOT 3:1083.

6. See John Skinner, *A Critical and Exegetical Commentary on Genesis*, ICC 1 (Edinburgh: T&T Clark, 1969), 77; John Sailhamer, "Genesis," in *Expositor's Bible Commentary*, ed. Frank E. Gaebelein (Grand Rapids: Zondervan, 1990), 52; Gordon J. Wenham, *Genesis 1–15*, WBC 1 (Waco, TX: Word, 1987), 76.

7. Meredith G. Kline, "Primal Parousia," *WTJ* 40 (1978): 246.

with the intent to execute judgment.[8] In the context the term seems to express that the advent of Yahweh in the garden was not only thunderous but that his approaching is understood by Adam and Eve as a theophany of divine judgment, which is why they flee in terror. A further aspect in 3:8 that lends to understanding that this passage serves as nascent for the day of the Lord concept is the phrase לְרוּחַ הַיּוֹם (lĕrûaḥ hayyôm). This phrase is often translated by modern versions as "in the cool of the day."[9] Umberto Cassuto even offers an extensive defense for this rendering by arguing that the intent of this phrase was to stress the actual *time* when God approached Adam. He writes: "Scripture wished to emphasize that the word of the Lord God was wholly fulfilled, even in its literal meaning. The man was told that *in the day that he ate* from the tree of life he would surely die and lo! on that very day that he ate, in the afternoon of the self-same day the Lord God appeared and decreed that he should be banished from the garden of Eden."[10]

However, the phrase *lĕrûaḥ hayyôm* is a well-known *crux interpretum*, appearing only once throughout the Old Testament, making it difficult to translate and thus leading to interpretive conjecture. This is evident, for instance, in the LXX, which renders *lĕrûaḥ hayyôm* as δειλινός (*deilinos*), "evening," whereas the Vulgate construes *lĕrûaḥ hayyôm* as *ad auram post meridiem*, "in the cool afternoon," with most contemporary English versions following some sort of variation of this. The difficulty of translating this phrase has led Jeffrey Niehaus to conclude, "The translation 'in the cool/breeze of the day/afternoon' thus represents only a guess interpreters have made throughout the centuries about the meaning of the unusual Hebrew expression."[11] This peculiar phrase has led scholars to offer other alternatives for translating *lĕrûaḥ hayyôm*. For instance, Niehaus has

8. Ibid., 250.

9. E.g., NASB, NIV, NJB, NKJV, RSV.

10. Umberto Cassuto, *A Commentary on the Book of Genesis*, trans. Israel Abrahams, Publications of the Perry Foundation for Biblical Research in the Hebrew University of Jerusalem (Jerusalem: Magnes, 1961), 1:152–54. See also C. John Collins, *Genesis 1–4: A Linguistic, Literary, and Theological Commentary* (Phillipsburg, NJ: Presbyterian & Reformed, 2006), 151–52; Claus Westermann, *Genesis 1–11: A Commentary*, trans. John J. Scullion (London: Society for Promoting Christian Knowledge, 1984), 254.

11. Jeffrey Jay Niehaus, *God at Sinai: Covenant and Theophany in the Bible and Ancient Near East*, SOTBT (Grand Rapids: Zondervan, 1995), 156.

argued that the Akkadian term *ūmu*, "day," corresponds to the Hebrew word יוֹם (*yôm*), "day." He provides several examples demonstrating that the Akkadian term *ūmu* can also mean "storm" and is often used in certain contexts as an appellation for deity coming in anger and in judgment. He further demonstrates that the Akkadian *ūmu* also appears to be akin with a second Hebrew term for *yôm*, also meaning, "storm."[12] An example of this is found in Zephaniah 2:2, where the phrase כְּמֹץ עָבַר יוֹם (*kĕmōṣ ʿābar yôm*), commonly rendered as "the day passes on like chaff," might arguably be translated as "the storm that passes on like chaff." If this translation is accepted, it seems that Zephaniah is portraying the day of Yahweh's impending judgment as a "storm" that is fast approaching. This seemingly makes the most sense, since the overall context of Zephaniah 1–2 describes the Lord coming to judge.[13] Thus, Niehaus concludes that the phrase *lĕrûaḥ hayyôm* in Genesis 3:8 is a description of a judgment theophany where Yahweh is depicted as coming to Adam and Eve like a storm.

A further alternative for translating *lĕrûaḥ hayyôm* is offered by Meredith Kline, who contends that the phrase should be rendered "The Spirit of the Day." He argues that the traditional interpretation of this phrase in Genesis 3:8 is problematic because of the stress on temporality. In other words, what is the point for such a rare and ambiguous phrase as *lĕrûaḥ hayyôm* to mention that Yahweh came in the cool of the afternoon/ evening? Was the author implying that the Lord did not come until the late afternoon or early evening because he needed relief from the heat of the day? Certainly not, but the traditional rendering of "in the cool of the day" does implicitly give that impression. Kline believes that the conventional translation portrays "the momentous primeval judgment [as having] transpired just coincidentally to what began as an idyllic stroll."[14] The context is clearly narrating Yahweh's first act of judgment on humanity, and so it seems adverse to render *lĕrûaḥ hayyôm* as a reference to *when* the Lord came. Kline suggests that it is more reasonable to interpret *lĕrûaḥ hayyôm*

---

12. Ibid., 156–59. See also BDB 398; HALOT 2:401; William Lee Holladay and Ludwig Köhler, *A Concise Hebrew and Aramaic Lexicon of the Old Testament: Based upon the Lexical Work of Ludwig Köhler and Walter Baumgartner* (Grand Rapids: Eerdmans, 1971), 131.

13. See Johannes Vlaardingerbroek, *Zephaniah*, Historical Commentary on the Old Testament (Leuven: Peeters, 1999), 118–21; Ehud Ben Zvi, *A Historical-Critical Study of the Book of Zephaniah*, BZAW 198 (Berlin: de Gruyter, 1991), 295–98.

14. Meredith G. Kline, *Images of the Spirit*, BBMS (Grand Rapids: Baker, 1980), 103.

as designating the glory—theophany as the divine Spirit coming on a mission to execute judgment. He asserts that the judicial concept that exists between *ruaḥ*, "Spirit," and *yôm*, "day," is based on the creation account in Genesis 1. He argues that when the Spirit hovered in the darkness over the watery deep and created light, this served to demonstrate his sovereignty over the darkness, which was further confirmed by God calling the light "day." Kline understands "day" to be a "replication of the Glory—Spirit, which is itself, visually, light—the luminosity of the radiant Shekinah."[15] In other words, the Spirit's creation of the light is an archetype for later divine action.[16] The Spirit of God has overcome the darkness by creating "the day," and it is this paradigm of the "light of day" that Kline proposes serves as the foundation for the imagery of judgment, since the light reveals all things. Later Old Testament authors arguably drew on this motif as they often depicted the "day of judgment" as taking place at sunrise, revealing the light of God's glory.[17] The New Testament also corroborates this motif of the Sprit of God creating the light, which overcomes the darkness and thus exposes with the intent to judge.[18] Kline concludes that the conceptual bond with "the Sprit" and "day" evident in the creation of the primeval light of the first day stresses divine intervention. God will either act with benevolence or in judgment, and it is this paradigm that sets the stage for the forensic understanding of "the day of the Spirit" in Genesis 3:8 as an intervention of judgment.[19]

A final observation offered by Kline to support his thesis that *lĕrûaḥ hayyôm* should be rendered as "the Spirit of the day," as denoting a forensic day, is the phrase "and God saw that it was good." This phrase, which follows the completion of every "day" in the creation account, is more than just a casual observation, but rather, he argues, a divine judicial pronouncement where God is actually judging each day declaring it to be good. The seventh day or Sabbath was the consummate day, which God sanctified, making it "his day." This leads Kline to conclude, "In the Genesis prologue,

---

15. Ibid., 108.

16. Ibid., 108n38.

17. Ibid., 108n39 and the references listed.

18. See Kline, "Primal Parousia," 257n39.

19. See Kline, *Images of the Spirit*, 106–7, where he offers an extensive discussion to validate that *yôm* does have a judicial nuance in the Genesis prologue.

the day of the Spirit is a time when God takes action, and pronounces an assessment."[20] He believes this is predicated throughout the Old Testament, where the Spirit often functions in judicial roles, either rendering divine judgments or endowing individuals to function as agents of judgment on Yahweh's behalf.[21] Thus Kline asserts that the traditional rendering for the unusual Hebrew phrase *lĕrûaḥ hayyôm* is wanting. The author of Genesis in all probability did not intend *lĕrûaḥ hayyôm* to have a temporal nuance, referring to the time *when* Yahweh came to the first couple, but rather *how* he came to the first couple, namely as a roaring sound of a judgment theophany, a precursor for the day of the Lord.

The above discussion of Genesis 3:8 was necessary since this passage arguably functions as the quintessential text for the concept of the day of the Lord throughout Scripture. The traditional interpretation of the verse is somewhat misleading, since it gives the impression that in the cool of the afternoon/evening Yahweh was taking a chimerical stroll through the garden, calling out to Adam. But this seems to be contrary to the evidence. Rather, it seems more plausible that Genesis 3:8 describes the thunderous sound of Yahweh coming in a judgment theophany to render his divine retribution on the first couple for their disobedience. Kline offers a helpful summary of Genesis 3:8:

> They heard the sound of Yahweh God traversing in the garden as the Spirit of the day. The frightening noise of the approaching Glory theophany told them that God was coming to enter into judgment with them. The sound of judgment day preceded the awesome sight of the parousia of their Judge. It was evidently heard from afar before the searching, exposing beams of the theophanic light pierced through the trees in the midst of the garden. Momentarily, then, it seemed to them possible to hide from the eyes of Glory among the shadows of the foliage. Thus, inadvertently, they positioned themselves at the place of judgment in the garden, at the site of the tree of judicial discernment between good and evil.[22]

20. Ibid., 109.
21. Ibid., 104.
22. Ibid., 106.

A second plausible example of the Torah depicting the concept of the day of the Lord is the golden calf incident in Exodus 32–34. The absence of Moses for forty days on Sinai caused the nation to doubt whether or not their leader would return. Consequently, the people implore Aaron to make "gods who will lead us."[23] Succumbing to the pressure, Aaron fashions a golden calf, declares it to be their god who led them out of Egypt, and presents offerings to the image, all of which are clear transgressions of their covenant with Yahweh. God informs Moses that the people have acted corruptly and that his anger burns against them to such an extent that he desires to destroy them and make a new nation with Moses as the progenitor. Moses, however, intercedes on behalf of the people, asking God to spare them because of the promises he made to their ancestors. Yahweh relents from wiping out the nation completely, but by no means will he allow them to go unpunished. On his descent from the mountain, Moses witnesses firsthand the debauchery of the people, resulting in his destruction of the two tablets, which serves as a sign that Israel violated the covenant.[24] He then proceeds to burn the calf and grind it into a powder, which he mixes in their water, forcing the people to drink it. Furthermore, at the command of Yahweh, Moses carries out divine justice by assembling the Levites, who go throughout the camp killing three thousand of the idolaters. The massacre, however, is not carried out arbitrarily, but rather the Levites are instructed to "go back and forth from entrance to entrance," indicating that they are "to carefully and systematically approach everyone and find out whether or not they intended to return to Yahweh, abandoning their idolatry. Those found to be committed to idolatry must be killed.

---

23. Several scholars agree that אֱלֹהִים ('ĕlōhîm) should be translated as plural, since the verb יֵלְכוּ (yēlĕkû) in the following relative clause is plural and the context seems to indicate that the people were dissatisfied with one god. See John I. Durham, *Exodus*, WBC 3 (Waco, TX: Word Books, 1987), 419; John N. Oswalt, "The Golden Calves and the Egyptian Concept of Deity," *EvQ* 45 (1973): 13–20; Douglas K. Stuart, *Exodus*, NAC 2 (Nashville: Broadman & Holman, 2006), 663n12. For those who argue that 'ĕlōhîm should be translated as singular, see Victor P. Hamilton, *Exodus: An Exegetical Commentary* (Grand Rapids: Baker, 2011), 530–32; Rolf A. Jacobson, "Moses, the Golden Calf, and the False Images of the True God," *WW* 33 (2013): 130–39.

24. See T. Desmond Alexander, *From Paradise to the Promised Land: An Introduction to the Pentateuch* (Grand Rapids: Baker, 2012), 219–20; John H. Sailhamer, *The Pentateuch as Narrative: A Biblical-Theological Commentary*, Library of Biblical Interpretation (Grand Rapids: Zondervan, 1992), 313; Nahum M. Waldman, "The Breaking of the Tablets," *Judaism* 27 (1978): 442–47.

Those sorry for being caught up in it but now actively repenting must be spared."[25] Although Yahweh relents from obliterating the nation, he does warn them that there will come a time when he will punish them for this sin. Following a plague the Lord sends on the nation, he instructs Moses to continue leading the people to the place he has designated for them.

What is notable throughout the narrative of the golden calf incident in Exodus 32–34 is that while Yahweh does demonstrate his mercy and relents from annihilating the nation, he certainly does not acquit them. Rather, he informs Moses that the day will come when he will "visit" the people to punish them for this sin (32:34). The verb פָּקַד (pāqad), "visit," often connotes the idea of visiting with the intent to avenge or punish (Ps 59:6 [MT]; Isa 26:14; Jer 6:15; 49:8).[26] Thus it seems that in 32:34 Yahweh relates to Moses that he has reserved a future day of visitation when he will mete out retribution on the people for this sin. But what about the plague mentioned in verse 35? Is that plague an immediate fulfillment of the Lord's day of visitation expressed in verse 34? Or is the plague a more immediate punishment, which serves to auspicate a future day when Yahweh will "visit" to enact vengeance on the nation? It seems that a future visitation is likely in view here for at least two reasons. First, in the overall context of Exodus 32–34 the author describes both the rupture and the renewal of the covenant relationship between Yahweh and his people. The focus of the narrative is arguably on the character of Yahweh, namely that he is "merciful and gracious, slow to anger, and abounding in steadfast love and faithfulness," but he is also just and will not exonerate the guilty (34:6–7). There will come a time when he will enact divine retribution on the people for their violation of the covenant by committing this *particular* sin. In other words, it could be that while Israel certainly transgressed the covenant by constructing the golden calf, it was not a "comprehensive" violation like what is described later in Deuteronomy 28–32. The full-scale curses that brought an end to the covenant privileges for Israel would not come until much later, during the Babylonian exile.[27] Therefore, in 32:35 it

---

25. Stuart, *Exodus*, 681.

26. BDB 823; HALOT 3:955; W. Schottroff, "פקד," in *TLOT*, 2:1018–31.

27. Stuart, *Exodus*, 689. See also Brevard S. Childs, *The Book of Exodus: A Critical, Theological Commentary*, OTL 2 (Philadelphia: Westminster, 1974), 571–72; Martin Noth, *Exodus: A Commentary*, trans. J. S. Bowden, OTL (Philadelphia: Westminster, 1962), 251–52.

seems that the author intentionally accentuates that the plague is specifically for the golden calf that Aaron made. In other words, the punishment
was for this particular incident, but it was not *the* day of visitation that
would bring about the full-scale curses.[28] Despite Israel's unfaithfulness,
Yahweh remains faithful to his covenant promises by allowing the nation
to live and commands Moses to continue leading the people to the land he
promised their ancestors. It is plausible, then, that the immediate punishment of the plague in 32:35 serves as "small-scale warning, a sample of
God's wrath, but by no means the actual full punishment for abandoning
the covenant."[29]

Second, the prophets regularly echo the context of Exodus 32–34, particularly 34:6–7, when discussing that Yahweh is slow to anger but that the
day is coming when he will visit with divine punishment (Hos 9:7; Joel 2:2,
12–13; Amos 3:14; Jonah 3:8–10; 4:2; Mic 7:18–20).[30] For example, in Amos 3:14
the prophet declares the coming judgment of God on his people. His
announcement that the Lord will destroy Bethel's altars is a reference to
the golden calves that Jeroboam I constructed for the people to worship at
both Bethel and Dan (1 Kgs 12:25–33). But it also seems reasonable to surmise that the prophet may have also been alluding to Exodus 32:34, since
he markedly repeats the wording found there.[31] Furthermore, just as the
punishment issued at Sinai was in all likelihood for that particular incident coupled with a warning of a future day of judgment, so also in Amos
the temporal particle כִּי (*kî*), "when," indicates that the time for the day of
Yahweh to punish his people is still to come. Shalom Paul rightly comments

---

28. See David E. Fass, "The Molten Calf: Judgment, Motive, and Meaning," *Judaism* 39
(1990): 171, who understands the plague to be a separate act. Contra Walter C. Kaiser, *Exodus*,
Expositor's Bible Commentary 2 (Grand Rapids: Zondervan, 1990), 481, where he suggests
that the plague in v. 35 is a reference back to the killing of those mentioned earlier in v. 28.
He notes that "the order of events is probably not in strict chronological sequence; hence the
plague may well be the slaughter of the three thousand mentioned in v. 28. The plague came
on the people because they caused the calf to be made or asked for it."

If Kaiser's assessment is correct, then v. 35 functions as a recapitulation transitioning to
the subsequent events in chaps. 33–34.

29. Stuart, *Exodus*, 689. See also the discussion in Herbert Chanan Brichto, "The Worship
of the Golden Calf: A Literary Analysis of a Fable on Idolatry," *HUCA* 54 (1983): 1–44.

30. See also Jan P. Bosman, "The Paradoxical Presence of Exodus 34:6–7 in the Book of
the Twelve," *Scriptura* 87 (2004): 233–43.

31. See Willis Beecher, "The Day of the Lord before Joel's Time," *Homiletical Review* 18
(1889): 449–51; Shalom M. Paul, *Amos*, Hermeneia (Minneapolis: Fortress, 1991), 124–25.

about these parallel motifs when he notes, "The sins of the past which abide in the present, will . . . be extirpated."[32] Borrowing from Exodus 32–34, Amos warns the people that though the Lord is slow to anger and may not execute final vengeance against sins immediately, the day of his reckoning will certainly come.

Third, the New Testament borrows from Exodus 32–34 in contexts that issue warnings about both the delay and the incurring of God's judgment (Acts 7:38–41; 1 Cor 10:7; 2 Pet 3:8–10).[33] For instance, in 2 Peter 3:8–10 the author has denounced the heretics who have infected the church by falsely teaching that there will be no future judgment, since time continues to move forward status quo without any apparent divine intervention (3:3–7). Peter corrects this misunderstanding by citing Psalm 90:4 to illustrate that humanity's calculation of time is not applicable to God because for him one day is as a thousand years. The psalmist encourages his readers to consider the brevity of human life and the reality that God's judgment is imminent (Ps 90:3, 5–11). In light of the fact that the divine and human perceptions of time differ, Peter reminds his audience that the delay of God's final judgment is a direct result of his mercy as he patiently affords people time to come to repentance. But the motif regarding the delay of Yahweh's judgment here in 2 Peter 3 and Psalm 90 is arguably derived from the template of Exodus 34:6–7, which serves as one of the nascent texts exhibiting the Lord's patience with his people by postponing his judgment on them.[34] Although Yahweh is slow to anger and abounding in loving-kindness, he has prescribed the day of

---

32. Paul, *Amos*, 125.

33. The most salient reference is 2 Cor 3:7–4:6, where Paul recounts Exod 34:29–35, where the glory that shone from Moses' face had to be veiled because the Israelites could not look at him. Since this does not directly relate to the theme of the day of the Lord, it is not included in the list of references. The literature here is extensive, but see Linda L. Belleville, "Tradition or Creation? Paul's Use of the Exodus 34 tradition in 2 Corinthians 3.7–18," in *Paul and the Scriptures of Israel*, ed. Craig A. Evans and James A. Sanders (Sheffield: JSOT, 1993), 169–86; Scott J. Hafemann, "The Glory and Veil of Moses in 2 Cor 3:7–14: An Example of Paul's Contextual Exegesis of the OT—A Proposal," *HBT* 14 (1992): 31–49; Richard B. Hays, *Echoes of Scripture in the Letters of Paul* (New Haven: Yale University Press, 1989), 122–53; Carol Kern Stockhausen, *Moses' Veil and the Glory of the New Covenant: The Exegetical Substructure of II Cor. 3,1–4,6*, AnBib 116 (Rome: Editrice Pontificio Istituto Biblico, 1989), 87–152; N. T. Wright, *The Climax of the Covenant: Christ and the Law in Pauline Theology* (Minneapolis: Fortress, 1992), 175–92.

34. See House, "Day of the Lord," 186; Gene L. Green, *Jude and 2 Peter*, BECNT (Grand Rapids: Baker, 2008), 324–31.

final judgment where he will carry out divine retribution on the guilty. Thus it seems reasonable to conclude that Exodus 34:6–7 served as the foundational paradigm for both 2 Peter 3 and Psalm 40 in their understanding of God's patience and eschatological judgment.[35]

A final example where the Torah is arguably divulging the concept of the day of the Lord is found in Deuteronomy 27–28. These chapters relate the blessings that Yahweh would bestow on his people for their covenantal obedience as well as the curses they would experience for their covenantal disobedience. After a description of the benefits the nation would receive in 28:1–14 for their fidelity to the covenant stipulations, the author provides a lengthy and graphic account of the curses the nation would suffer for their failure to uphold the covenant sanctions (28:15–68). The author stresses the severity of covenant violation by detailing the horrific consequences that would come on the nation. Similar to Exodus 34:6–7, it is again the character of Yahweh that is of primary importance. In the context of Deuteronomy 27–28, God demonstrates that he is slow to anger in that he sends multiple warnings to the nation urging them to repent or judgment will eventually come. As Paul House comments, "These passages indicate clearly that the Lord will send persons and circumstances to warn Israel to change their ways prior to punishing them. The purpose of these warnings was to ward off judgment."[36] The point is that Yahweh is patient and offers ample time for the nation to change. However, failure to repent will ensure future judgment.

The blessings and curses found in Deuteronomy 27–28 arguably allude to the concept of the day of the Lord in a twofold manner. First, failure to heed the warnings found in Deuteronomy 27–28 will ultimately bring divine retribution, both imminent and final. These warnings are intended to demonstrate not only the forbearance of Yahweh but also that he will ultimately make things right by one day conclusively punishing the guilty. This theme is further echoed by the Prophets, who frequently exhort their readers that judgment will come because of their failure to observe Yahweh's admonitions, which culminates in their return to exile

---

35. See Richard J. Bauckham, *Jude, 2 Peter*, WBC 50 (Waco, TX: Word, 1983), 311–12.

36. House, "Day of the Lord," 186. See also J. G. McConville, *Deuteronomy*, Apollos Old Testament Commentary 5 (Downers Grove, IL: InterVarsity, 2002), 410.

(Isa 27:13; Jer 11:8, 39, 52; Hos 8:13; 9:3; Amos 4:6–13).[37] The prophets seemingly understand divine punishments in Deuteronomy 27–28 as *patterns* depicting what the final day of the Lord will be like. Second, the consequences forewarned in Deuteronomy 27–28 are more imminent and indicate that the final judgment will come at an undisclosed time in the future. Again, the gracious character of Yahweh is evident as "the consequences accrue after a long period of time. They are not quick responses on God's part."[38] However, as the Prophets later warn, the people should not be foolish in thinking that the interval of time before the day of the Lord indicates any passiveness from Yahweh, but rather this demonstrates his patience and mercy, allowing the nation ample time to repent. As Duane Christensen observes, "The curses reverse the blessings of God and constitute a final and awesome warning for future generations."[39]

Although the phrase "the day of the Lord" does not explicitly appear in the Torah, the preceding discussion has argued that *conceptually* the day of the Lord is evident throughout. The passages discussed above demonstrate that Yahweh does "visit" his people with both blessing and judgment, and they anticipate the final day when the Lord will ultimately reward the righteous and judge the wicked. The conclusion here is that the Torah serves as the origin for the *concept* of the day of the Lord, which is further developed by later Old Testament authors, especially the Prophets.

THE DAY OF THE LORD IN THE OLD TESTAMENT PROPHETS

The day of the Lord is a prominent theme throughout the Old Testament prophetic literature, particularly in the Book of the Twelve, and is portrayed as both historical and eschatological in nature.[40] Exactly when

---

37. See Peter M. Head, "The Curse of the Covenant Reversal: Deuteronomy 28:58–68 and Israel's Exile," *Churchman* 111 (1997): 218–26.

38. House, "Day of the Lord," 186.

39. Duane L. Christensen, *Deuteronomy 21:10–34:12*, WBC 6B (Nashville: Thomas Nelson, 2002), 701.

40. Several scholars have argued that the day of the Lord is the major unifying feature of the Minor Prophets. See further Paul R. House, "Endings and New Beginnings: Returning to the Lord, the Day of the Lord, and Renewal in the Book of the Twelve," in *Thematic Threads in the Book of the Twelve*, ed. Paul L. Redditt and Aaron Schart, BZAW 325 (Berlin: de Gruyter, 2003), 313–39; Richard H. Hiers, "Day of the Lord," in *ABD*, 2:82; James D. Nogalski, "The Day(s) of YHWH in the Book of the Twelve," in Redditt and Schart, *Thematic Threads in the Book of the*

the day of the Lord became the Prophets' standard phrase for judgment remains elusive. However, if the conclusion from the previous discussion is correct and the Torah serves as the progenitor for the concept of the day when Yahweh will come and "visit" his people with either judgment or blessing, then it seems reasonable to surmise that the prophets would have been familiar with this motif, further elaborating and developing it into the *terminus technicus* for the final day of judgment.

The exact phrase *yôm yhwh*, "day of the Lord," occurs fifteen times throughout the prophetic literature, specifically in contexts referring to final judgment (Isa 13:6, 9; Ezek 13:5; Joel 1:15; 2:1, 11; 3:4; 4:14; Amos 5:18, 20; Obad 15; Zeph 1:7, 14 [*bis*]; Mal 2:22). In addition, this expression also occurs in several variant forms. For example, there are instances where the preposition ב (*b*) precedes *yôm*, which stresses the temporal nuance of *at* or *when* the day will occur (Obad 8; Zeph 1:18; 2:3). In other instances the preposition *l* comes before the term *yhwh*, likely denoting possession, and would then convey the meaning "the day *belonging* to Yahweh" (Isa 2:12; 12:4; Zech 14:1). What is noteworthy is that all fifteen occurrences of *yôm yhwh* are found in forensic contexts where the prophets announce that the Lord has an indictment against his people and that the day of Yahweh's judgment is inevitable. Furthermore, in these texts the prophets refer to the day of the Lord from different vantage points: (1) The day is described in retrospect by referring to past events where the Lord has previously rendered punishment (e.g., exile). The prophets want their audience to interpret those past incidences as a warning to later generations regarding the future judgment. (2) Judgment may be more imminent in that the Lord will send foreign nations as his agents to carry out retribution on his people. (3) Judgment may be specifically eschatological in nature, looking forward to the consummate day when Yahweh renders the final verdict on all the nations of either divine judgment or divine blessing.[41] The point is that the prophets understood that *yôm yhwh* referred to a specific day when the Lord would intervene to bring about divine justice or divine blessing.

Twelve, 192–213; Rolf Rendtorff, "How to Read the Book of the Twelve as a Theological Unity," in *Reading and Hearing the Book of the Twelve*, ed. James Nogalski and Marvin A. Sweeney, SBLSS 15 (Atlanta: Society of Biblical Literature, 2000), 76–87.

41. A. Joseph Everson, "Days of Yahweh," *JBL* 93 (1974): 328–37.

The prophets, however, typically do not use the specific locution *yôm yhwh* when referring to the motif of the day of the Lord and the events associated with that time.[42] In most instances the phrase has been replaced by a variety of different idiomatic expressions that are conceptually parallel to *yôm yhwh*, such as הַיּוֹם (*hayyôm*), "the day," בַּיָּמִים (*bayyāmîm*), "in those days," בַּיּוֹם (*bayyôm*), and so on.[43] Moreover, James Nogalski has observed: "In addition to the[se] formulas, references to the day of YHWH's intervention using idiomatic expressions appear in over 100 texts. These expressions include terms for YHWH's destructive activity (e.g., wrath, vengeance), the effect of that activity (your overthrow), or the name of the recipient (e.g., Egypt, Midian). The majority of these terms refer to contexts of judgment and punishment, but both the idiomatic expressions and the[se] formulas also appear in contexts which speak of salvation or deliverance."[44]

The significance of these various idioms is that (1) they overwhelmingly refer to a day when Yahweh would intervene to either judge or bless. Depending on the context, the intervention can be either imminent or eschatological; and (2) the comprehensive use of these various collocations demonstrates that the prophets and their audiences more than likely interpreted them to be synonymous with *yôm yhwh*.[45] Furthermore, the extensive use of these idioms throughout the prophetic literature demonstrates that this was colloquial language for the prophets and their audiences, and communicating about the day of the Lord and the events pertaining to it was accomplished in multifaceted ways. But regardless of the locution used, the prophets all agree that there was a day when the King would come to visit his subjects, and his arrival meant disaster for some and blessing for others.

---

42. See Hoffmann, "Day of the Lord as a Concept and a Term in the Prophetic Literature," 37–50, who argues that any examination of the day of the Lord that does not begin with those passages that use the exact phrase *yôm yhwh* is methodologically flawed and produces unreliable conclusions. This assessment, however, has been seriously criticized by Daniella Ishai-Rosenboim, "Is יום ה (Day of the Lord) a Term in Biblical Language?," *Bib* 87 (2006): 395–401.

43. For a comprehensive list of the various expressions see Weiss, "Origin of the 'Day of the Lord' Reconsidered," 29–60, particularly table B after p. 60.

44. Nogalski, "Day(s) of YHWH in the Book of the Twelve," 195.

45. Ibid., 194. Nogalski mentions that the phrase "in those days" occurs thirty-nine times in the Hebrew Bible, and the expression "on that day" occurs 206 times, with 170 of these instances found throughout the prophetic literature. His point is to demonstrate that these idioms were clearly understood to be interchangeable with the day of the Lord.

Since the day of the Lord motif is so pervasive throughout the prophetic literature, a brief survey of a few texts will help to elucidate the general consensus of the Prophets' understanding and portrayal of *yôm yhwh*. For example, the concept of the day of Yahweh is a prominent theme throughout the book of Isaiah. Although the exact phrase *yôm yhwh* occurs only twice in the book (13:6, 9) the prophet utilizes several of the typical locutions mentioned earlier to describe the final day (1:24–25; 2:2, 12, 20; 3:19). While Isaiah has much to say regarding the day of the Lord, there are two features that are most notable for this current study. First, the oracles in Isaiah that pertain to the day of the Lord seemingly demonstrate that the prophet understands that there are actually *days* of Yahweh.[46] Throughout the book, Isaiah repeatedly warns that the Lord will come to punish all who oppose him and that such "visits" are intended to serve as both a warning and a pattern. Isaiah warns not only God's people but all the nations, urging them to repent of their sins and be restored to him (14:1–2, 28–32; 15:1–16:14; 17:1–11). These *days* or judgments are likely intended to serve as typological patterns that are indicative of the consummate day of the Lord. Isaiah describes how Yahweh will punish those who defy him by means of military invasion, agricultural ruin, depopulation of cities and nations, and cosmic disorder as Yahweh's day approaches (13:1–22). But these crises likely serve as a prescience to describe how destructive and terrible the ultimate judgment will be.[47] Thus John Goldingay aptly comments, "A pattern characteristic of prophecy appears here. It speaks as if the end of the world is imminent; what fulfills such prophecies is not the actual end, but a particular historical expression of God's ultimate purpose receiving a fulfillment in time."[48] Furthermore, these judgments are also a demonstration of Yahweh's mercy, and those who correctly interpret these divine warnings and respond with genuine repentance will experience the Lord's redemption. It also seems that for Isaiah these *days* are reminiscent of Exodus 34:6–7 and stress the character of Yahweh, who is slow

---

46. See John Goldingay, *The Theology of the Book of Isaiah* (Downers Grove, IL: InterVarsity, 2014), 39–41; Herbert M. Wolf, *Interpreting Isaiah: The Suffering and Glory of the Messiah* (Grand Rapids: Academie Books, 1985), 293–94.

47. See House, "Day of the Lord," 188; and the discussion in Donald C. Polaski, *Authorizing an End: The Isaiah Apocalypse and Intertextuality*, BibInt 50 (Leiden: Brill, 2001), 104–17.

48. Goldingay, *Theology of the Book of Isaiah*, 39–40.

to anger and abounding in steadfast love but will by no means leave the guilty unpunished. In keeping with the pattern established in the Torah, Isaiah understands that the final day of the Lord is on the horizon. In the interim Yahweh demonstrates his compassion by "visiting" both Israel and the nations, admonishing them to repent before the final day arrives. Those who fail to heed God's warnings will face his condemnation, while those who respond appropriately will celebrate Yahweh's universal rule on that day.[49]

A second feature regarding the day of the Lord is Isaiah's mention of the coming Messiah, who will reign on David's throne forever (9:1–7; 11:1–16). This king will lead Yahweh's army into battle and will destroy all of God's enemies. Isaiah understands that it is the prerogative of this final Davidic king to render divine judgments on all those opposing Yahweh. But for those who are faithful to the Lord, the advent of this king is a message of hope, for his sovereign reign will be characterized by peace, justice, and righteousness (11:5; 32:1–2, 16–18). For the remnant, the promise of the coming Davidic heir is a message of hope and cause for great rejoicing, since his arrival will mean their vindication and the establishment of his universal sovereignty. It seems, then, that Isaiah's vision of this coming Davidic king is intended to reveal the "glory of his person and the perfection of his reign and the worldwide spread of his dominion."[50] This understanding of Isaiah's message concerning the coming Davidic heir is prevalent throughout many of the Old Testament Prophets. For instance, prophets such as Jeremiah (23:5–6), Ezekiel (34:23–24), Hosea (3:4–5), Amos (9:11–12), and Micah (5:1–4) all relate how the people will return to God and the Davidic king.[51] They anticipate the future day of Yahweh, when he will come and eradicate all sin, ultimately restore his people to himself, and permanently rule in Zion. This understanding from the Old Testament

---

49. Marvin A. Sweeney, *Isaiah 1–39: With an Introduction to Prophetic Literature*, FOTL 16 (Grand Rapids: Eerdmans, 1996), 41–48.

50. J. Alec Motyer, *The Prophecy of Isaiah: An Introduction and Commentary* (Downers Grove, IL: InterVarsity, 1993), 37. This interpretation also seems substantiated when considering the various epithets that are used to describe him. See also Brevard S. Childs, *Isaiah*, OTL (Louisville, KY: Westminster John Knox, 2001), 80–81.

51. Michael Rydelnik, *The Messianic Hope: Is the Hebrew Bible Really Messianic?*, NAC Studies in Bible & Theology 9 (Nashville: Broadman & Holman, 2010), 75. See also the discussion in Young S. Chae, *Jesus as the Eschatological Davidic Shepherd: Studies in the Old Testament, Second Temple Judaism, and in the Gospel of Matthew*, WUNT 216 (Tübingen: Mohr Siebeck, 2006), 25–31.

is also in continuity with the New Testament authors, who interpret the true Davidic king and ultimate restoration of God's people as finding fulfillment in the person of Jesus Christ.[52] For the New Testament writers, the restoration and eternal reign inaugurated by Christ at his first advent will be consummated at his parousia, when he returns to bring judgment and salvation. Thus from the vantage point of the New Testament the day of the Lord is ultimately fulfilled at the return of Jesus, who is both Lord and Christ and sits on the throne wielding absolute authority to render the final verdict on all the nations (Acts 2:36; 2 Cor 5:10; 2 Thess 1:6–10).[53] Isaiah's prophecy regarding the coming Davidic king is a message of hope for those who are faithful to Yahweh (i.e., the remnant) because justice and righteousness will characterize his universal reign. But for those who rage against Yahweh, the day of the king's arrival will result in their condemnation.

A second example to consider is found in the prophet Joel, where the day of the Lord is arguably the controlling theme of the book. Numerous idiomatic expressions relating to "the day" permeate the three chapters that comprise the book. Nogalski has observed that there are eleven *yôm* texts that explicitly refer to and delineate the austerity of this day. Some of these locutions include: יוֹם חֹשֶׁךְ וַאֲפֵלָה (*yôm ḥošek wa'ăpēlâ*), "day of darkness and gloom" (2:2); יוֹם עָנָן וַעֲרָפֶל (*yôm 'ānān wa'ărāpel*), "day of clouds and darkness" (2:2); and יוֹם יְהוָה, "The day of Yahweh" (1:15; 2:1, 11; 3:4).[54] The prophet begins his message by announcing a "locust plague" so catastrophic that even future generations will know about it (1:3).[55] This use of the locust imagery is not unique to the prophet Joel, since it occurs

52. See Childs, *Isaiah*, 81; Walter C. Kaiser, *The Messiah in the Old Testament*, SOTBT (Grand Rapids: Zondervan, 1995), 155–85; Richard L. Schultz, "The King in the Book of Isaiah," in *The Lord's Anointed: Interpretation of Old Testament Messianic Texts*, ed. P. E. Satterthwaite, Richard S. Hess, and Gordon J. Wenham, Tyndale House Studies (Grand Rapids: Baker, 1995), 141–65.

53. Mark D. Vander Hart, "The Transition of the Old Testament Day of the Lord into the New Testament Day of the Lord Jesus Christ," *Mid-America Journal of Theology* 9 (1993): 3–25.

54. Nogalski, "Day(s) of YHWH in the Book of the Twelve," 200, where he also mentions that there are eleven specific references to the day of the Lord in Joel.

55. The identity of the locusts is contested among scholars. Whether Joel was referring to a literal locust plague or intended the plague to be a metaphor for an army invasion does not impact the point of this brief overview regarding the prophet's understanding and portrayal of the day of the Lord. For relevant discussions on this issue see Pablo R. Andiñach, "The Locusts in the Message of Joel," *VT* 42 (1992): 433–41; Duane A. Garrett, "Joel, Book of," in *DOTP*, 452–54; Douglas K. Stuart, *Hosea-Jonah*, WBC 31 (Waco, TX: Word Books, 1987), 232–34.

in several places throughout the prophetic writings (Amos 4:9; Nah 3:16–17; Mal 3:10). For Joel use of such imagery may function as an allusion to certain texts from the Torah where Yahweh either sends or threatens to send a locust plague as a manifestation of his judgment. For instance, in Exodus 10:1–19 the Lord sends a locust plague on the Egyptians because of Pharaoh's refusal to emancipate the people of Israel. Several scholars have observed that Joel probably had Exodus 10 in the foreground of his mind when he penned his work.[56] Joel's dependence on the Exodus narrative is evident by the numerous lexical parallels that exist between the two texts.[57] These intertextual similarities have led John Strazicich to conclude, "Joel was indeed *influenced* by the Exodus tradition of the locust plague, together with the darkness and earthquake themes as theophanic motifs for the Day of Yahweh."[58] Furthermore, Joel also seems to draw on the covenantal curses from Leviticus 26 and Deuteronomy 28, where Yahweh informs his people that their unfaithfulness will result in divine judgment. The nation is even warned that Yahweh will manifest his judgment on them by means of a locust plague that will ravage their harvest (Deut 28:38). Therefore, it seems that from the outset Joel may have intentionally alluded to the locust plagues mentioned in the Torah as a reminder to the inhabitants of Jerusalem that Yahweh visits not only the nations in judgment but his covenant people also.

Joel continues to describe the day of the Lord by comparing it to an army invasion (2:1–11). Similar to the locust plague, Joel proclaims that Yahweh will initiate an unprecedented military attack on Judah that will bring great destruction. While the coming locust plague will obliterate the agriculture, the coming military invasion emphasizes that the attack is specifically aimed at the people of the land, for no one will be able to

---

56. Leslie C. Allen and R. K. Harrison, *The Books of Joel, Obadiah, Jonah, and Micah*, NICOT (Grand Rapids: Eerdmans, 1976), 68–69; Duane A. Garrett, *Hosea, Joel*, NAC 19A (Nashville: Broadman & Holman, 1997), 314–15; John Strazicich, *Joel's Use of Scripture and Scripture's Use of Joel: Appropriation and Resignification in Second Temple Judaism and Early Christianity*, BibInt 82 (Leiden: Brill, 2007), 62–66; Marvin A. Sweeney, *The Twelve Prophets*, Berit Olam (Collegeville, MN: Liturgical, 2000), 1:154; Hans Walter Wolff, *Joel and Amos*, trans. Waldemar Janzen, S. Dean McBride Jr., and Charles A. Muenchow, Hermeneia 14 (Minneapolis: Fortress, 1977), 44.

57. See Strazicich, *Joel's Use of Scripture and Scripture's Use of Joel*, 63–66, where he observes and comments on fourteen lexical parallels evident in Joel and Exod 10.

58. Ibid., 63, emphasis original.

escape the destruction this army will bring (2:10–11).[59] Joel arguably wants his audience to realize that this invasion is of divine origin: "Indeed, this is God's army and God's Day (2:11)."[60] Understanding the nearness of this day should serve as a warning to the people to return to the Lord and not face his divine judgment. The people of Judah are called on to come before the Lord with fasting, weeping, and mourning, for he is merciful and slow to anger (2:13). The nation assembles as they appeal to Yahweh's mercy and await his response, confident that he will treat them favorably.[61] The book concludes indicating that if the people sincerely humble themselves and repent, they can rejoice, for Yahweh will deliver them from his judgment on the day of the Lord. If the nation heeds Joel's warnings, the day of the Lord will no longer be something for them to fear but rather a reason for them to celebrate.

For the prophet Joel, the day of the Lord is both imminent and future.[62] He calls on his listeners from every stratus of society to heed Yahweh's warning of the coming judgment. The warnings of the locust plague and coming military invasion are used as an exhortation to the inhabitants of Judah that they should return to the Lord before he visits them on that day. Drawing on the motif of Yahweh come to visit his people in judgment, Joel arguably interprets the locust plague and army invasion as *a* day of the Lord intended to serve as typological warnings urging God's people to repent before *the* day of the Lord arrives. There is a sense of urgency in Joel's message, for the day of Yahweh is on the horizon, and all who fail to identify with the Lord on that day will suffer his divine wrath, while those who belong to him will dwell in his presence, enjoying him forever (3:16–21).

A final example demonstrating the prominence of the day of the Lord motif throughout the prophets is found in the book of Zephaniah. The prophet incorporates a variety of different idioms throughout this book, such as *bəyôm*, "on that day"; *bəyômʿebrat yhwh*, "the day of Yahweh's wrath"; and *yôm*, "the day," as synonyms of *yôm yhwh* to depict

---

59. Nogalski, "Day(s) of YHWH in the Book of the Twelve," 200.

60. House, "Day of the Lord," 192.

61. See Marvin A. Sweeney, *Form and Intertextuality in Prophetic and Apocalyptic Literature*, FAT 45 (Tübingen: Mohr Siebeck, 2005), 195–97, and his discussion relating to the purpose of the nation's assembly.

62. David Fleer, "Exegesis of Joel 2:1–11," *ResQ* 26 (1983): 153.

what that day will be like (1:9–18).[63] The oracles the prophet delivers regarding the day of Yahweh are some of the most extremely detailed accounts regarding the severity of the judgment to be rendered on *this day* within the prophetic literature. Willem VanGemeren has noted:

> Zephaniah most extensively and dramatically developed the prophetic concept of the Day of the Lord. . . . It is compared to the judgment of the Flood in Noah's day, but it is more extensive. Nothing will escape the purifying judgment of the Lord as it affects human beings, animals, the birds of the sky, and the fish of the sea. But it is unlike the Flood since it will be as by fire: "The whole world will be consumed by the fire of my jealous anger" (see 3:8; and 2 Peter 3:10). The wrath and jealousy of the Lord will come to expression against everything, and thus he established his everlasting kingdom.[64]

Zephaniah underscores for his audience that the divine retribution on this day is both comprehensive and universal. For instance, in 1:1–3 the prophet borrows from both the creation account in Genesis 1 and the flood narrative in Genesis 6–8 to stress the gravity of the destruction Yahweh will unleash. The allusion to the creation narrative in this context seems to be at the forefront of Zephaniah's message. Scholars have observed that the prophet's echo of the creation narrative is evident in (1) that he reverses the order of creation in verse 3 by beginning with humanity, whereas in Genesis 1 humanity is created last; (2) the assonance that is evident in the terms ברא (*brʾ*), "create," and כרת (*krt*), "cut off," as well as עשׂה (*ʿśh*), "to make," and אסף (*ʾsp*), "come to an end"; and (3) the wordplay between הָאָדָם (*hāʾādām*), "the man," and הָאֲדָמָה (*hāʾădāmâ*), "the earth."[65] The colloca-

---

63. See Adele Berlin, *Zephaniah*, AB 25A (New York: Doubleday, 1994), 92–93; Greg A. King, "The Day of the Lord in Zephaniah," *BSac* 152 (1995): 17; Victor Harold Matthews, *The Hebrew Prophets and Their Social World: An Introduction* (Grand Rapids: Baker, 2012), 130–34; Ralph L. Smith, *Micah-Malachi*, WBC 32 (Waco, TX: Word Books, 1984), 130–33. The exact phrase *yôm yhwh* appears only three times in the entire book (1:7, 14 [2x]).

64. Willem VanGemeren, *Interpreting the Prophetic Word: An Introduction to the Prophetic Literature of the Old Testament* (Grand Rapids: Zondervan, 1996), 174–75.

65. For instance, Michael De Roche, "Zephaniah 1:2–3: The 'Sweeping' of Creation," *VT* 30 (1980): 107; Kenneth L. Barker and D. Waylon Bailey, *Micah, Nahum, Habakkuk, Zephaniah*, NAC 20 (Nashville: Broadman & Holman, 1999), 411–15; Richard Duane Patterson, *Nahum, Habakkuk, Zephaniah*, Wycliffe Exegetical Commentary (Chicago: Moody, 1991), 300–303; Marvin A. Sweeney, *Zephaniah: A Commentary*, Hermeneia (Philadelphia: Fortress, 2003), 62–64.

tion of these items in Zephaniah's message arguably stresses that sinful humanity is the primary recipient of Yahweh's judgment on *his day*. This is further accentuated in that humanity is mentioned twice in verse 3 and that the remainder of the book stresses that the Lord's judgment will come on specific groups of people while simultaneously those who fear Yahweh and remain faithful to him will be able to rejoice on that day (1:4; 2:4–9, 12–13; 3:15–20).[66] The point that Zephaniah reiterates with his allusion to the creation account is that the Lord's judgment is universal in scope and not only impacts humanity but also all animate life. As Greg King observes, "the judgment on the day of the Lord will be the most complete ever experienced."[67] Consequently, Zephaniah is reminding his audience that since the day of the Lord is absolutely ubiquitous, then Judah and the inhabitants of Jerusalem should not be under the delusion that they will be exempt from Yahweh's verdict on that day.

The allusion to the flood in 1:2–3 is evident in the phrase מֵעַל פְּנֵי הָאֲדָמָה (mē'al pǝnēy hā'ǎdāmâ), "from the face of the earth," which is used in the flood narrative to describe Yahweh's judgment on humanity (Gen 6:7; 7:4). Ivan Ball has noted that "this exact phrase is found thirteen times in the MT, all but one involving punishment."[68] It seems that Zephaniah intended to stress that the judgment to occur at the day of the Lord will be much more comprehensive than the flood. In addition, the prophet may have utilized the flood narrative to also qualify the stipulations of the Noachian covenant. Yahweh promised to never destroy the earth *by means of a flood*, but that does not prohibit another type of universal destruction. Thus Zephaniah warns his audience that the day of the Lord is coming, and no one is exempt from standing before the Judge on the final day. But like all

---

66. King, "Day of the Lord in Zephaniah," 23.

67. Ibid. See also De Roche, who observes, "Yahweh's destruction will be just as bleak as his creating was abundant" ("Zephaniah 1:2–3," 107). He further argues that the reference to the creation narrative in Zephaniah is actually a "reversal of creation," meaning that humanity will "experience a loss of dominion over the earth" (ibid., 106). This has been criticized by Patterson, *Nahum, Habakkuk, Zephaniah*, 301–2, who argues that it is unlikely that humanity's loss over creation is the point. Patterson contends that "Indeed, the order of creation with man at its head is fixed by God and guaranteed in perpetuity (cf. Ps 8:5–9 [HB 8:6–10]), a reality ultimately realized in Christ (Col. 1:15–20; Heb. 2:5–9). Rather the creation account is employed by Zephaniah to remind his hearers of the continued importance of mankind."

68. Ivan Jay Ball, "A Rhetorical Study of Zephaniah" (PhD diss., Graduate Theological Union, 1972), 46.

the prophets, Zephaniah also reminds those who are faithful to the Lord that this final day will be a day of celebration, where Yahweh himself will rejoice over his people (3:17). The duality of the day of the Lord is again evident in Zephaniah, for he has stressed that even though Yahweh has threatened to utterly destroy all living creatures from the earth, he has preserved a remnant of those who have persevered and remained faithful to him. For the covenant people, the day of the Lord "signifies the day of vindication, glorification, and full redemption . . . (3:14–20). Theirs is the kingdom and theirs is the enjoyment of God's presence in kingship."[69]

The day of the Lord is a pervasive theme throughout the prophetic writings of the Old Testament. It is also a flexible concept in that the final day brings either cursing or blessing. It seems apparent, however, that this was not an original concept with the prophets, but rather they derived their understanding of this theme from the Torah, where God "visits" his people, bringing either judgment or blessing. The prophets seemingly expound on these divine theophanies evident in the Torah and interpret them with both an imminent and an eschatological flavor. Imminently, there are *days* of Yahweh, whereby through a variety of agents and events he urges his people to repent and be restored to him. These *days*, however, likely serve as typological patterns pointing to the consummate day of the Lord, where he will render the final verdict on all the nations. Barker offers a helpful summary of the day of Yahweh throughout the prophetic literature:

> The Day of the Lord [motif] admirably highlights the creativity and rhetorical power of the OT prophets as they invoke images relating to warfare, creation and chaos, and theophany in an attempt to capture the power inherent in this day. . . . For the prophets, human affairs do not proceed unnoticed by Yahweh; indeed the Day of the Lord provides a powerful reminder of Yahweh's presence and ability to shape events according to the divine purpose. This purpose does not cease at the conclusion of the OT, but continues to speak into the NT and contemporary contexts.[70]

---

69. VanGemeren, *Interpreting the Prophetic Word*, 176.
70. Barker, "Day of the Lord," 142.

THE DAY OF THE LORD IN THE WRITINGS

The day of the Lord is not as prevalent in the Writings of the Old Testament as it is throughout the prophetic literature. Nevertheless, the books of Lamentations and Daniel seemingly demonstrate noticeable reliance on both the Torah and the Prophets regarding their understanding of this theological motif.

Most scholars conclude that the historical setting for the book of Lamentations is the fall of Jerusalem in 586/7 BC.[71] The author relates the agony and despair the Israelites endured as they suffered the divine consequences they incurred for disobeying the covenant stipulations that Yahweh commanded. Through the means of the prophets, God repeatedly warned the people of Judah to repent of their sins and be restored to him. However, the nation's continued defiance brought the covenant curses on them that Yahweh had promised centuries earlier (Deut 28:47–57). Even those living in Jerusalem understood that the divine sanction and the horrific repercussions (2:1–9) that followed were simply the righteous acts of Yahweh (1:5, 8, 18).[72] But the author of Lamentations also speaks of hope of renewal and assures his readers that Yahweh will not completely abandon his covenant people (3:19–24, 33).

Following the theme of the Old Testament, Lamentations likewise interprets Yahweh's judgment on Judah as a day of the Lord. House has argued that Lamentations "is nothing less than a report on the Day of the Lord from those who have experienced it in space and time."[73] The author demonstrates familiarity with this biblical theme in at least two ways. First, the book utilizes the typical idioms identifiable throughout the Old Testament that describe the day of the Lord. The author incorporates several of these collocations throughout the book, describing the punishment Yahweh inflicts on his people in the day of his visitation.[74] For instance, Lamentations 2

---

71. See the discussions in Duane A. Garrett and Paul R. House, *Song of Songs/Lamentations*, WBC 23B (Nashville: Thomas Nelson, 2004), 283–85; Robert B. Salters, *A Critical and Exegetical Commentary on Lamentations*, ICC (London: T&T Clark, 2010), 7–9; Claus Westermann, *Lamentations: Issues and Interpretation*, trans. Charles A. Muenchow (Minneapolis: Fortress, 1994), 54–55.

72. House, "Day of the Lord," 203.

73. Ibid.

74. 1:12: בְּיוֹם חֲרוֹן אַפּוֹ (bayôm hărôn 'apô), "in his day of fierce anger"; 1:21: הֵבֵאתָ יוֹם קָרָאתָ (hēbē'tā yôm-qārā'tā), "bring on the day you announced;" 2:1, 21: בְּיוֹם אַפּוֹ (běyôm 'apô), "in his day of anger;" 2:22: בְּיוֹם אַף יְהוָה (běyôm 'ap-yhwh), "on the day of the Lord's anger."

offers vivid imagery describing that this is the day of Yahweh's anger and he is ultimately responsible for the punishment the nation has encountered because of its sin. The author depicts Yahweh as a warrior who fights *against* Jerusalem and its inhabitants, bringing destruction and misery on the city and the nation (2:4, 5, 21; 3:43). Yahweh is likened to an enemy who refused to aid the city when it was under siege (2:5, 8–9). In addition to destroying the city, Yahweh is also responsible for abrogating both the religious and political arenas (2:6–10). The inhabitants lament because Yahweh has destroyed the temple, made the people forget the Sabbath and the festivals, rejected the sanctuary, scorned the altar, and left the nation without leadership.[75] With such dire consequences, it is no wonder the people are in mourning. But what the author of Lamentations repeatedly accentuates, not only in this chapter but also throughout the book, is that Yahweh is the one responsible for the calamity that has befallen the nation of Judah. And although God visiting his people to punish them is a common motif, particularly throughout the prophetic literature, the unique perspective of Lamentations is that the day of the Lord has *already happened*. Yahweh has visited his people, made evident by the destruction of Jerusalem and the temple.[76] As the preexilic prophets such as Amos and Isaiah warned the people to repent because the day of the Lord was imminent, the author of Lamentations recounts the divine devastation that Judah had already incurred for their failure to heed Yahweh's message. But even though the writer of Lamentations focuses on the day of the Lord as a *past event*, this does not mean that the writer understood this day to be the culmination of history. Norman Gottwald has observed that "It should be abundantly clear that [the] Day of Yahweh . . . at least for the poet of Lamentations, could scarcely have been regarded as the culmination of history, i.e., the point at which history ends in one great act of God. If it had been so regarded, it would have been impossible to equate the fall of the city, however calamitous, with that Day, for it was obvious that history was still in process."[77] Furthermore, Lamentations offers a word of hope, reminding its hearers

---

75. See Adele Berlin, *Lamentations: A Commentary*, OTL (Louisville, KY: Westminster John Knox, 2002), 69–72.

76. Boase, *Fulfilment of Doom?*, 134–35; Norman K. Gottwald, *Studies in the Book of Lamentations*, SBT 14 (Eugene, OR: Wipf & Stock, 2009), 84–85.

77. Gottwald, *Studies in the Book of Lamentations*, 84.

that the Lord does not completely abandon his own, for "when the 'day' is over the remnant still exists. Yahweh still maintains a covenantal relationship with his people."[78]

Second, while the backdrop for Lamentations' understanding of the day of the Lord is primarily from the preexilic prophets, the author also seemingly interprets the punishment Judah suffered from the perspective of the covenant curses outlined in the Torah. There are several instances where Lamentations specifically echoes the theological tradition found in Deuteronomy 28 to delineate what the day of the Lord would entail (Lam 1:3, 5, 9; 2:20; 3:45; 4:10, 16; 5:12).[79] For instance, enemies triumph over the nation, people are eating their children, Judah will be an object of reproach to the nations, and ultimately the inhabitants experience exile. Yahweh warned his people that their continual disobedience would not only result in these curses but that Yahweh himself would be responsible for meting them out. From the perspective of Lamentations, the day of the Lord has occurred, for the curses of Deuteronomy 28 have become the reality for the inhabitants of Judah. But the author also understands that there is hope for the people, and Lamentations concludes with an allusion to Deuteronomy 30, reminding the people of the faithfulness of Yahweh, who promises to restore them if they truly repent. Such a motif is reminiscent of the Lord's character delineated in Exodus 34:6–7.

The book of Lamentations describes the day of the Lord as a past event where Yahweh has intervened in history to bring judgment on Judah and her inhabitants. The author interprets the catastrophic events that have happened against Judah as a day of Yahweh. The nation had continuously repudiated Yahweh's warnings that he established in Deuteronomy, which were later reiterated by the preexilic prophets, urging the people to repent and be restored or they would face terrible judgments. The nation's failure to heed the Lord's warnings has led to his visitation, in which he has faithfully upheld his covenant stipulations by enacting on Judah the Deuteronomic curses he had previously prescribed. But even in the midst of great tragedy, Lamentations offers a word of hope to the remnant. As

---

78. House, "Day of the Lord," 204.

79. See the discussion in Barry G. Webb, *Five Festal Garments: Christian Reflections on the Song of Songs, Ruth, Lamentations, Ecclesiastes, Esther*, NSBT 10 (Downers Grove, IL: InterVarsity, 2000), 76–77.

Elizabeth Boase observes, "The events may have had epochal significance in that they marked the end of life as it was known, but life continued after the event and *hope* existed for future decisive action by Yahweh."[80]

A final example from the Writings to briefly consider is found in the book of Daniel. Although the actual phrase "the day of the Lord" or any of the typical idioms denoting that day are not found in the book, the concept of the day of the Lord is seemingly evident in the vision Daniel receives in chapter 7.[81] The vision describes four beasts that symbolically represent four different kings/kingdoms and their dominion over the earth. These four kingdoms are juxtaposed to the ultimate kingdom of the Ancient of Days, that is, God. The four kingdoms are earthly and temporal, while the kingdom of Yahweh is heavenly and eternal. Having permitted the four earthly kings to rule for a time, Yahweh has removed their authority and is ready to administer judgment on them. The Ancient of Days takes his seat on the throne, accompanied by thousands of his attendants, and presides over the final courtroom as the supreme judge. As the vision continues, Daniel sees the Ancient of Days give the kingdom to *kĕbar ʾĕnāš*, "one like a son of man."[82] House comments, "Yahweh may give the kingdom to whomever he wills, for all the kingdoms of the earth are his."[83] The "one like a son of man" is distinct from the Ancient of Days, for he is both human and divine, but he is similar in that he is also worshiped and served by the nations. The "son of man" serves as the judicial agent of the Ancient of Days, executing final justice on all the nations, for his reign is eternal and the epitome of righteousness (vv. 13–14). The eternal rule of the son of man offers tremendous hope to the remnant living in exile, for he will share

---

80. Boase, *Fulfilment of Doom?*, 136, emphasis mine.

81. House, "Day of the Lord," 205.

82. The identity of "one like a son of man" in Dan 7 is rigorously debated among scholars. It is not the intent of the current discussion to rehearse the various interpretations. For thorough discussions regarding this issue see Matthias Albani, "'The One Like a Son of Man' and the Royal Ideology," in *Enoch and Qumran Origins: New Light on a Forgotten Connection*, ed. Gabriele Boccaccini (Grand Rapids: Eerdmans, 2005), 47–53; Stefan Beyerle, "'One Like a Son of Man': Innuendoes of a Heavenly Individual," in Boccaccini, *Enoch and Qumran Origins*, 54–58; Darrell L. Bock, "Son of Man," in *DJG*, 894–900; Chrys C. Caragounis, *The Son of Man: Vision and Interpretation*, WUNT 38 (Tübingen: Mohr Siebeck, 1986), 61–81; Maurice Casey, *The Solution to the "Son of Man" Problem*, LNTS (London: T&T Clark, 2009), 56–115; James M. Hamilton, *With the Clouds of Heaven: The Book of Daniel in Biblical Theology*, NSBT 32 (Downers Grove, IL: InterVarsity, 2014), 135–54; George W. E. Nickelsburg, "Son of Man," in *ABD*, 6:137–50.

83. House, "Day of the Lord," 205.

his kingdom with them.[84] Sigurd Grindheim offers a helpful summary regarding the son of man described in Daniel 7:13–14: "The Son of Man is a heavenly being appearing as a human, he is the eschatological judge (cf. the Similitudes of 1 Enoch), he is the representative of the people of God and will experience vindication subsequent to his suffering."[85]

The coming eternal rule of the son of man offered great encouragement to Daniel and the remnant living in exile, for it reminded them of their eventual restoration to Yahweh and their participation in his kingdom. For the faithful who were suffering in exile, the vision reminded them that Yahweh is triumphant, for his kingdom will eventually abolish all earthly rule and authority. The remnant can be encouraged knowing that in spite of their suffering they will "triumph only because [God] comes to sit in judgment (7:26–27)."[86] The coming of the Ancient of Days to judge and ultimately reign in many respects parallels concepts related to the day of the Lord motif found throughout the Old Testament, which reminds God's people that the day is coming when he will abolish all who oppose him and establish his sovereign rule once and for all.

CONCLUSION

The preceding survey has demonstrated that the day of the Lord is *thematically* evident throughout the entire Old Testament. The concept, while certainly embryonic, is evident throughout the Torah, where in several contexts Yahweh either comes or will come to visit his people with blessings or curses depending on their faithfulness to the covenant stipulations he prescribed.

The day of Yahweh's visitation may be a day that his people should fear, or it may be a day they can joyfully anticipate. It seems that this

---

84. There is much discussion surrounding the identity of "the holy ones of the Most High" (7:18, 22, 25, 27). Scholars primarily argue that the holy ones are angelic or refer to the saints. For those who advocate an angelic interpretation, see Luc Dequeker, "'The Saints of the Most High' in Qumran and Daniel," in *Syntax and Meaning: Studies in Hebrew Syntax and Biblical Exegesis*, ed. C. J. Labuschagne, OtSt 18 (Leiden: Brill, 1973), 108–87; Martin Noth, *The Laws in the Pentateuch, and Other Studies*, trans. D. R. Ap-Thomas (Philadelphia: Fortress, 1967), 215–28. For those who identify them as saints, see Louis Francis Hartman and Alexander A. Di Lella, *The Book of Daniel*, AB 23 (Garden City, NY: Doubleday, 1978), 207; Vern S. Poythress, "Holy Ones of the Most High in Daniel 7," *VT* 26 (1976): 208–13.

85. Sigurd Grindheim, *God's Equal: What Can We Know about Jesus' Self-Understanding?*, LNTS 446 (London: T&T Clark, 2011), 203.

86. House, "Day of the Lord," 206.

phenomenon of the Lord coming to visit his people likely served as the foundation for the origin of the "day of the Lord" phrase that was later annotated by the Prophets.

Building on the foundation established in the Torah, the Prophets interpreted the day of the Lord as a *terminus technicus* for the final day of judgment. But the Prophets also revealed that they understood there to be "days" of the Lord.[87] The circumstances that affected God's people (famine, sickness, war, exile, etc.) were seemingly understood as typological patterns pointing to the consummate day of the Lord. The hardships that the covenant people faced were to be interpreted as warnings to repent of their sins and return to Yahweh before the ultimate day arrived and all the nations would appear before him at the final assize. For the Prophets, the day of the Lord describes imminent judgment, while in other passages the locution clearly refers to the final eschatological judgment when God will ultimately make all things right.[88]

Finally, a brief exposition of the Writings demonstrated that the people understood the consequence of exile as a day of the Lord in which they were currently living. The authors of Lamentations and Daniel interpreted life in exile as an actual day of the Lord but were encouraged by God that the final day had not arrived and that Yahweh would restore his people and share his kingdom with them. The benefit of this survey not only ensures a firmer understanding of the day of the Lord as a central theme depicted throughout the Old Testament, but it also sets the stage for properly understanding Paul's theology of this major motif, which he interprets as finding fulfillment at the second coming of Jesus.

---

87. William J. Dumbrell, *The Search for Order: Biblical Eschatology in Focus* (Grand Rapids: Baker, 1994), 109, observes that "the concept of the day of the Lord, as considered by the prophets, is not singular in meaning; the connotation can be determined only by examining each context in which the phrase appears."

88. See George Eldon Ladd, *A Theology of the New Testament* (Grand Rapids: Eerdmans, 1993), 198–99.

3

The Day of the Lord in Extracanonical Literature

The following chapter seeks to briefly explore the day of the Lord motif as found throughout the extracanonical literature. The intent here is not to rehearse every occurrence where the concept is evident but rather to provide a sampling of the various texts that demonstrate that the authors of these ancient writings were familiar with this theme. Although the exact phrase "day of the Lord" occurs infrequently throughout this literature, the concept is certainly demonstrable. The authors of the extracanonical literature were arguably familiar with the concept because of their knowledge of the Old Testament, where (as the previous chapter demonstrated) the day of the Lord is a prominent theme.

THE DAY OF THE LORD IN THE OLD TESTAMENT APOCRYPHA

The Old Testament Apocrypha is a collection of Jewish literature composed during the Second Temple period.[1] While Protestants and Jews do not consider these books to be canonical or inspired, the Greek Orthodox, Russian Orthodox, Roman Catholic, and Coptic Churches do accept most of them.[2] The value of these books cannot be overestimated, as they provide valuable insights into what life was like for Jews living in the Second Temple

---

1. For helpful introductions on the Apocrypha see David Arthur deSilva, *Introducing the Apocrypha: Message, Context, and Significance* (Grand Rapids: Baker, 2002); Daniel J. Harrington, *Invitation to the Apocrypha: Message, Context, and Significance* (Grand Rapids: Eerdmans, 1999); Bruce M. Metzger, *An Introduction to the Apocrypha* (New York: Oxford University Press, 1957); W. O. E. Oesterley, *An Introduction to the Books of the Apocrypha* (London: SPCK, 1958).

2. There are some books, however, that are not regarded to be canonical by these churches. For instance, the Roman Catholic Church does not accept 1 and 2 Esdras, whereas the Russian Orthodox Church does. A helpful chart indicating which books these various churches accept is found in Craig A. Evans, *Ancient Texts for New Testament Studies: A Guide to the Background Literature* (Peabody, MA: Hendrickson, 2005), 341.

period. From a historical perspective, the Apocrypha provide information about how the Jews lived after the exile under the regime of empires
that attempted to force the Israelites into conformity with the prevailing
Hellenistic culture. In addition to the historical insights, the Apocrypha
also have much to say regarding the theology of those Jews living in their
Hellenistic milieu. The theology evident throughout the Apocrypha is vast
and covers a wide range of doctrines.[3] In a general sense, "these books bear
witness to what it meant to remain faithful to the God of Israel during
a tumultuous period of history."[4] Thus exploring the theology of the
Apocrypha provides "a deeper understanding into the world of Judaism
at the turn of the century and into the matrix of early Christianity."[5]
Understanding the theology of the Apocrypha can be a source of encouragement to all Christians, as these books testify about those who remained
faithful to Yahweh in the midst of persecution, trusting that he would
ultimately accomplish their deliverance and vindication, both imminent
and eschatological.

Although the Apocrypha cover a vast range of theological topics, one
that appears in some sense throughout all the books is the issue of suffering. Regarding the theology of suffering found in the Apocrypha, Daniel
Harrington writes, "This theological focus touches upon a universal human
experience, and it naturally raises broader questions about God, the human
condition, the meaning of human life and history, ethics, and so forth."[6]
While there are certainly many other theological issues raised throughout the Apocrypha, the theology of suffering is closely related to the day
of the Lord motif in that those who suffer for righteousness's sake can be
assured that Yahweh will ultimately deliver them. The intent of the following discussion is to demonstrate that the apocryphal writers were familiar
with the concept of the day of the Lord as delineated throughout the Old
Testament. The authors of the Apocrypha were likely familiar with the
Old Testament's teaching on this subject and utilized this theme to remind
their readers that God would eventually vindicate his covenant people and

---

3. For a sampling of the theological doctrines evident throughout the Apocrypha see
Oesterley, *Introduction to the Books of the Apocrypha*, 74–120.

4. DeSilva, *Introducing the Apocrypha*, 16.

5. Ibid., 40.

6. Harrington, *Invitation to the Apocrypha*, 8.

bring retribution on his enemies. Thus the Apocrypha have consanguinity with the Old Testament in that they also envision the day of the Lord as a day of salvation and a day of judgment.

Like the Old Testament, there are numerous epithets used to describe the day of the Lord throughout the Apocrypha.[7] For instance, the book of 2 Esdras provides numerous examples describing the day of the Lord. Second Esdras was likely composed initially in Aramaic or Hebrew and later translated into Greek.[8] The book is customarily divided into three sections: chapters 1–2 (5 Ezra), chapters 3–14 (4 Ezra), and chapters 15–16 (6 Ezra). The day of the Lord motif is primarily evident in chapters 3–14, which are considered to be a Jewish apocalypse that was likely written thirty years after the destruction of the temple in AD 70 (3:1).[9] Chapters 3–14 open with Ezra complaining to God about the current hardships Israel is experiencing. He is utterly perplexed as to why God would allow the righteous to suffer while the wicked prosper. In response, God gives Ezra seven different visions reassuring him that Yahweh is in fact just and that he will ultimately bring vindication for his chosen people on that final day. The most relevant of these chapters as pertains to the day of the Lord is the third vision, found in 6:35–9:25. In this vision Ezra is given a complete picture regarding the final day of judgment (7:26–44). Ezra is informed that at the end of the messianic age all humanity will die, which will then be followed by the resurrection and judgment. After the resurrection, God will be revealed sitting on his judgment seat to render the final verdicts. Nothing is hidden from God, and he rewards both the righteous and unrighteous impartially. The detailed descriptions shown to Ezra concerning this eschatological day are relevant to the purposes here because of the conceptual parallels drawn from the Old Testament. For instance, the cosmic phenomena mentioned in 7:39–40 are likely direct allusions to Genesis 8:22; Psalm 73:16–17 (LXX); Amos 5:18–20; and Zechariah 14:6. In recounting this vision given to Ezra, the author seemingly demonstrates great familiarity

---

7. For example, "day of judgment," "day of his anger," "day of wrath," "the day."

8. See R. J. Coggins and Michael A. Knibb, *The First and Second Books of Esdras*, CBC (Cambridge: Cambridge University Press, 1979), 76.

9. The book also mentions in 10:20–24 that Jerusalem had been destroyed. For a helpful discussion regarding the date of 2 Esdras, see Michael E. Stone, *Features of the Eschatology of IV Ezra*, Harvard Semitic Studies 35 (Atlanta: Scholars Press, 1989), 1–11.

with the Old Testament's teaching regarding the day of the Lord in that he does not assume it necessary to expound on it. The interpretation Ezra is given concerning the vision of the day of the Lord is not *what* the day is but *why* so few will experience God's mercy. The dilemma for Ezra is not that there *is* a day of the Lord, but rather that he is overwhelmed with grief as he discovers that the majority of humanity will experience God's wrath rather than his salvation on that final day (7:47-48).[10] Additional passages could also be mentioned that describe the day of the Lord (7:102, 104, 113; 12:34). However, the point here is to establish that the day of the Lord was likely a conventional motif for the author of 2 Esdras because of his familiarity with the Old Testament's teaching regarding this theme.

Another example of the day of the Lord motif evident in the Apocrypha is found in the book of Judith. Likely written around 150 BC by an unknown author, the book of Judith is considered to be a rescue story recounting the exploits of the pious heroine Judith, who saves her village from being destroyed by the Assyrian general Holofernes.[11] The book is divided into two sections: chapters 1-7 and 8-16. The first seven chapters detail the numerous victories of the Assyrian army. These opening chapters "serve to demonstrate the might of the Assyrians and thus underline the depth of faith required to counteract such might. In so doing, they set the stage for the appearance of Judith in chap. 8."[12] Chapters 8-16 introduce Judith, a devout follower of Yahweh and highly respected within her village. She prays that God would use her to destroy the Assyrians, who have desecrated the temple (9:9). The Lord answers Judith's prayers as she is granted access into the Assyrian camp and allowed to speak with Holofernes. Judith tricks the Assyrian general by convincing him that invading her village is unnecessary because God will hand it over to him on account of the people's disobedience, and Holofernes' throne will be established in Jerusalem (11:18-19). Holofernes permits Judith to go out every evening to pray to God

---

10. Jacob Martin Myers, *I and II Esdras: Introduction, Translation and Commentary*, AB 42 (Garden City, NY: Doubleday, 1974), 253-54; Tom W. Willett, *Eschatology in the Theodicies of 2 Baruch and 4 Ezra*, Journal for the Study of the Pseudepigrapha Supplement Series 4 (Sheffield, UK: JSOT, 1989), 60-61.

11. See Benedikt Otzen, *Tobit and Judith*, Guides to Apocrypha and Pseudepigrapha (London: Sheffield Academic Press, 2002), 68-69.

12. John F. Craghan, *Esther, Judith, Tobit, Jonah, Ruth*, Old Testament Message 16 (Wilmington, DE: Glazier, 1982), 67.

in order to discern when his victory will take place. On the fourth evening the Assyrian general holds a banquet for his attendants and invites Judith to attend so that he can seduce her. When the banquet is finished and the guests have left, Judith is alone with an inebriated Holofernes lying on his bed. She then cuts off his head, puts it in a bag, leaves the camp, and returns to her town, where she recounts to the residents how the Lord gave them victory over their enemies. The next day the Israelites defeat the Assyrians and pillage their camp.

In the final chapter of the book, Judith sings a hymn of praise to God for the deliverance he has accomplished for his people (16:1–17). This hymn has many parallels with the one sung by Moses in Exodus 15:1–18, where he praises God for delivering his people from the pursuing Egyptians at the Red Sea.[13] Like the Song of the Sea in Exodus 15, the hymn of Judith 16 recognizes that God is directly involved in bringing deliverance for his people. Yahweh comes as the Divine Warrior fighting for his people and triumphing over his enemies. This concept of the Lord coming to take vengeance on his enemies is clearly delineated in 16:17, where the author seemingly indicates a familiarity with the day of the Lord motif. Verse 17 mentions that any nation that rises up against God's people will experience his vengeance on the day of judgment. The imagery of this "day of judgment" is likely dependent on the Old Testament, where the theme of Yahweh enacting retribution on his enemies is prominent. But as the previous chapter demonstrated, the Old Testament can describe the day of the Lord as being imminent or future depending on the context. The issue, then, is to discern whether the phrase "day of judgment" in verse 17 should be interpreted as imminent or future.

Benedikt Otzen argues that the "day of judgment" in verse 17 is strictly referring to the defeat of Holofernes and his army as described in chapter 15.[14] Certainly Judith and the residents in her town had in essence experienced a "day" of the Lord with the recent triumph over the Assyrians. But Otzen appears too myopic in his interpretation, as the language of verse 17 seemingly suggests a more eschatological interpretation.

---

13. Carey A. Moore, *Judith: A New Translation with Introduction and Commentary*, AB 40 (Garden City, NY: Doubleday, 1985), 256. See also deSilva, *Introducing the Apocrypha*, 96, who contends that Judith 16 is also dependent on the song of Deborah in Judg 5.

14. Otzen, *Tobit and Judith*, 99.

The future indicative ἐκδικήσει (*ekdikēsei*), "he will take vengeance," in verse 17 arguably looks forward to a future time, from the perspective of the speaker, when Yahweh will punish the nations.[15] This seems substantiated since the reference point of this future vengeance is the prepositional phrase ἐν ἡμέρᾳ κρίσεως (*en hēmera kriseōs*), "in the day of judgment." This phrase likely indicates the time when this vengeance will occur. Furthermore, the other two occurrences of *en hēmera kriseōs* in the LXX also indicate a future day when retribution will come (Prov 6:34; Pss. Sol. 15:12).[16] Finally, Judith mentions that these nations will weep in pain forever, which also seems to support the eschatological nature of the day of judgment. The killing of Holofernes and the defeat of his army described in chapters 13–15 arguably illustrate the day of the Lord in a more immediate sense. But the language of verse 17 also has eschatological overtones, which point to the consummate day when those who oppose Yahweh will suffer for eternity.[17] It seems reasonable, then, to surmise that because of the familiarity with the Old Testament's teaching regarding the day of Yahweh, the writer of Judith interpreted the most recent defeat of Holofernes' army as a paradigmatic "day" of the Lord where the recent judgment on the Assyrians and the deliverance of the Israelites were pointing to the ultimate day of the Lord, when he would enact both final vengeance on his enemies and salvation for his people.

A final example to briefly consider is found in the Additions to Esther. The Greek version of Esther includes six passages that are absent from the

---

15. There is debate among grammarians regarding the aspectual nature of the future, namely, is the future aspectual or aspectually neutral? Nevertheless, in reference to time, it is widely held that the future tense always refers to a future occurrence from the speaker's point of view. See Constantine R. Campbell, *Verbal Aspect, the Indicative Mood, and Narrative: Soundings in the Greek of the New Testament*, Studies in Biblical Greek Series 13 (New York: Lang, 2012), 127–60; Buist M. Fanning, *Verbal Aspect in New Testament Greek*, ed. Barton, R. C. Morgan, B. R. White, J. MacQuarrie, K. Ware, and R. D. Williams, Oxford Theological Monographs (Oxford: Clarendon, 1990), 120–25; Stanley E. Porter, *Verbal Aspect in the Greek of the New Testament, with Reference to Tense and Mood*, Studies in Biblical Greek 1 (New York: Lang, 1989), 403–39; Daniel B. Wallace, *Greek Grammar beyond the Basics: An Exegetical Syntax of the New Testament* (Grand Rapids: Zondervan, 1996), 566–67.

16. This prepositional phrase also occurs five times in the NT, all referring to the eschatological day of judgment (Matt 10:15; 11:22, 24; 12:36; 1 John 4:17).

17. Harrington, *Invitation to the Apocrypha*, 40. See also Toni Craven, *Artistry and Faith in the Book of Judith*, SBLDS 70 (Chico, CA: Scholars Press, 1983), 110. She notes that many scholars understand v. 17 as a witness to developing ideas of eschatology. Craven, however, is not entirely convinced of this.

Masoretic Text. These additions, which are typically referred to as A–F, are believed to have been included for the "purpose of introducing God and religion into a book which originally did not once mention the name of God."[18] Additions A and F are pertinent for the present study because the author indicates a familiarity with the day of the Lord concept. Addition A (11:2–12:6) recounts a dream of Mordecai. Carey Moore notes that the dream consists of three parts: the setting of the dream (vv. 1–3); the dream itself, which contains several elements of apocalyptic imagery (e.g., dragons fighting, darkness, chaos on the earth), which initially puzzles Mordecai (vv. 4–10); and Mordecai's discovery of the plot against the king (vv. 11–17).[19]

The interpretation of the dream is found in Addition F (10:4–11:1), where the symbolism of the dream is expounded for Mordecai (10:4–7). The interpretation reveals that God heard the cry of his people and that he alone was responsible for delivering them from gentile oppression. However, the dream not only was about the ethnic oppression and religious antagonism between Jews and gentiles in Mordecai's day, but warrants a more eschatological understanding. Sidnie Crawford observes that the dream reflects the eternal, cosmic struggles between God's people and the rest of the world, in which God is on the side of his people.[20] The eschatological nature of the interpretation is evident in how the author describes Yahweh ultimately vindicating his people at the final assize. In 10:10–11 [F 7–8] the author mentions that God has divided humanity into two "lots." In this particular context the term "lots" is likely used in its figurative sense to mean "portion" or "destiny."[21] This meaning is evident in both the Old

---

18. Evans, *Ancient Texts for New Testament Studies*, 14. See also the helpful discussions in W. J. Fuerst, "The Rest of the Chapters of the Book of Esther," in *The Shorter Books of the Apocrypha: Tobit, Judith, Rest of Esther, Baruch, Letter of Jeremiah, Additions to Daniel and Prayer of Manasseh* (Cambridge: Cambridge University Press, 1972), 132–38; Michael V. Fox, *Characters and Ideology in the Book of Esther* (Columbia: University of South Carolina Press, 1991), 265–73; George W. E. Nickelsburg, "The Bible Rewritten and Expanded," in *Jewish Writings of the Second Temple Period: Apocrypha, Pseudepigrapha, Qumran Sectarian Writings, Philo, Joseph*, ed. Michael E. Stone, Literature of the Jewish People in the Period of the Second Temple and the Talmud 2 (Philadelphia: Fortress, 1984), 135–38.

19. Carey A. Moore, "The Origins of the LXX Additions to the Book of Esther," *JBL* 92 (1973): 386.

20. Sidnie White Crawford, "The Additions to Esther: Introduction, Commentary, and Reflections," in *NIB*, 3:969.

21. Ibid. See also David J. A. Clines, *The Esther Scroll: The Story of the Story*, JSOTSup 30 (Sheffield, UK: JSOT, 1984), 172; Carey A. Moore, *Daniel, Esther, and Jeremiah: The Additions*, AB 44 (Garden City, NY: Doubleday, 1977), 247.

Testament and Qumran literature, where it is found in contexts emphasizing the different outcomes or "destinies" that await humanity when all appear before God on that final day (Isa 17:14; Jer 13:25; Dan 12:13; 1QS 1.10, 2.17, 4.26; 4Q495, et al.). Further, the author specifically mentions the time will come when the two "lots" (God's people and the nations) will stand before him εἰς ἡμέραν κρίσεως (eis hēmeran kriseōs) "on the day of judgment." Considering the context, it seems reasonable to surmise that the author understood this phrase as an epithet for the consummate day of the Lord. God had delivered his people from the evil schemes of Haman, and this act of deliverance points to a greater reality, namely that God will ultimately deliver his people from the nations at the final judgment. The struggle of God's people is not solely with Haman but the entire world, and just as Yahweh had demonstrated his faithfulness in delivering his people from the genocide Haman plotted, so likewise he will accomplish their eschatological vindication at the final day.

Additional examples could be explored regarding the day of the Lord motif throughout the Apocrypha.[22] However, the previous discussion has demonstrated that the authors were not unfamiliar with the day of the Lord concept, which was made evident by the various epithets used to describe that final day. Taking its cue from the Old Testament, the Apocrypha understands that while there are "days" of the Lord where he has intervened in the past or in the present to bring deliverance for his people and judgment on his enemies, these visits served as reminders pointing to the final day of the Lord, when judgment and vindication will be rendered once and for all.

THE DAY OF THE LORD IN THE OLD TESTAMENT PSEUDEPIGRAPHA

The Old Testament Pseudepigrapha is a collection of writings dating from 200 BC–AD 200. The term "pseudepigrapha" means "falsely ascribed" and is similar to what contemporary readers may refer to as writing under a pen name.[23] For many scholars, the label "Old Testament Pseudepigrapha" is misleading and in some cases incorrect.[24] While attempts have been made

---

22. E.g., 2 Esdras 7:102, 104, 113; 12:34; Sirach 5:7; 18:24.

23. Evans, *Ancient Texts for New Testament Studies*, 27.

24. For a discussion on why the label "Old Testament Pseudepigrapha" is considered inaccurate see James H. Charlesworth, "Pseudepigrapha, OT," in *ABD*, 5:537–40; James R. Davila,

to offer a more precise label for these diverse writings, no suggestion has achieved consensus. However, James Charlesworth seems to capture the nature of what constitutes "Pseudepigrapha" when he writes:

> The present description of the Pseudepigrapha is as follows: Those writings 1) that, with the exception of *Ahiqar*, are Jewish or Christian; 2) that are often attributed to ideal figures in Israel's past; 3) that customarily claim to contain God's word or message; 4) that frequently build upon ideas and narratives present in the OT; 5) and that almost always were composed either during the period 200 B.C. to A.D. 200 or, though late, apparently preserve, albeit in an edited form, Jewish traditions that date from that period.[25]

From this perspective it cannot be overestimated how valuable the Old Testament Pseudepigrapha are for understanding the background of early Judaism and Christianity. Furthermore, careful investigation of the Pseudepigrapha arguably enables a more precise interpretation of how various doctrines were understood by those living in the Second Temple period, particularly in those writings that predate AD 70.

One prominent doctrine evident throughout the Pseudepigrapha is the final judgment. There are numerous instances where these documents exhibit a familiarity with the Old Testament's teaching that on the final day the Lord will execute justice by exacting retribution on his enemies and vindicating his own. The authors of the Pseudepigrapha seemingly borrow many of the idioms used throughout the Old Testament to describe this final day, such as "the day of judgment," "the day of distress," and "the day." Although numerous examples of this theological motif abound, a brief survey of some relevant texts will establish that the day of the Lord was a familiar theme for many of the authors of these works.[26]

"Pseudepigrapha, Old Testament," in *EDEJ*, 1110–14; Leonhard Rost and Robert Morris Johnston, *Judaism outside the Hebrew Canon: An Introduction to the Documents [Review]*, trans. David E. Green, Andrews University Seminary Studies 18 (Berrien Springs, MI: Andrews University Press, 1980), 30–31; Loren T. Stuckenbruck, "Apocrypha and Pseudepigrapha," in *Early Judaism: A Comprehensive Overview*, ed. John J. Collins and Daniel C. Harlow (Grand Rapids: Eerdmans, 2012), 191–92.

25. James H. Charlesworth, ed., *The Old Testament Pseudepigrapha*, AYBRL (New York: Doubleday, 1985), xxv.

26. Some examples include 1 En. 10:12; 22:11–13; 27:3–4; 2 En. 65:5–11; 2 Baruch 83:1–7; Testament of Levi 1.1; Apocalypse of Abraham 29.14–21; Life of Adam and Eve 12.1; 26.4.

No other book in the Pseudepigrapha discusses the day of the Lord more distinctly than 1 Enoch. First Enoch is typically divided into five sections, with each section varying in date of composition.[27] The book is often categorized as apocalyptic literature because a primary theme evident throughout the work is the coming final judgment.[28] From the author's perspective the eschatological judgment is universal, affecting not only humanity but also fallen angels and demons (10:6; 41:1–2).[29] The writer repeatedly declares that at the final assize God will punish the wicked for breaking his laws and oppressing his children. In contrast, those who were faithful to God will be rewarded with eternal life. Because the concept of the day of the Lord is so prevalent throughout 1 Enoch, a few brief comments on the salient sections of the book will establish that the day of the Lord was a standard theological viewpoint for the author.

The initial section of 1 Enoch is commonly known as the Book of Watchers (chaps. 1–36). In the opening chapters Enoch receives a heavenly vision that describes in vivid detail God coming to bring final judgment (1–5).[30] For example, the theophany evident in 1:1–9 is arguably dependent on numerous Old Testament texts that portray God as a divine warrior who will ultimately come as the final Judge to punish his enemies and bring redemption for his people.[31] The author utilizes similar language

---

27. The five sections include (1) the Book of Watchers (chaps. 1–36); (2) the Book of Similitudes/Parables (chaps. 37–71); (3) the Book of Luminaries (chaps. 72–82); (4) the Book of Dream Visions (chaps. 83–90); (5) the Epistle of Enoch (chaps. 91–107). Chapter 108 serves as an excursus reassuring the readers of the punishment the wicked will receive and the blessings the righteous will receive.

28. For discussions regarding what constitutes apocalyptic literature and the various emphases therein, see David E. Aune et al., "Apocalypticism," in *DNTB*, 45–58; John J. Collins, "Apocalyptic Literature," in *DNTB*, 40–45; Larry R. Helyer, *Exploring Jewish Literature of the Second Temple Period: A Guide for New Testament Students* (Downers Grove, IL: InterVarsity, 2002), 112–47; Michael E. Stone, "Apocalyptic Literature," in *Jewish Writings of the Second Temple Period: Apocrypha, Pseudepigrapha, Qumran Sectarian Writings, Philo, Josephus*, ed. Michael E. Stone, Compendia Rerum Iudaicarum ad Novum Testamentum 2 (Philadelphia: Fortress, 1984), 383–441; James C. VanderKam, *From Revelation to Canon: Studies in the Hebrew Bible and Second Temple Literature*, Supplements to the Journal for the Study of Judaism 62 (Leiden: Brill, 2000), 241–54.

29. George W. E. Nickelsburg, "Deliverance, Judgment, and Vindication," in *Faith and Piety in Early Judaism: Texts and Documents*, ed. George W. E. Nickelsburg and Michael E. Stone (Philadelphia: Fortress, 1983), 122–26.

30. For a fuller discussion of 1 En. 1–5 see Lars Hartman, *Asking for a Meaning: A Study of 1 Enoch 1–5*, ConBNT 12 (Lund: LiberLaromedel/Gleerup, 1979).

31. See the discussion in chap. 2.

and themes reminiscent from the Old Testament's description of the day of the Lord. For instance, the author mentions that this final day will be a ἡμέραν ἀνάγκης (*hēmeran anankēs*), "a day of distress" (v. 1); it will be a day when God ἐξελεύσεται ... ἐκ τῆς κατοικήσεως (*exeleusetai ek tēs katoikēseōs autou*), "will come forth from his dwelling place" (v. 3); a day when God ἐπὶ γῆν πατήσει (*epi gēn patēsei*), "will march/trample upon the earth" (v. 4); and a day when κρίσις ἔσται κατὰ πάντων (*krisis estai kata pantōn*), "judgment will be upon all" (v. 7). This eschatological day is also described in terms of cosmic phenomena such as σεισθήσονται καὶ πεσοῦνται καὶ διαλυθήσονται ὄρη (*seisthēsontai kai pesountai kai dialythēsontai orē*), "mountains will be shaken and will fall" (v. 6); they will also τακήσονται ὡς κηρὸς ἀπὸ προσώπου πυρὸς ἐν φλογί (*takēsontai hōs kēros apo prosōpou pyros en phlogi*), "melt as wax before fire" (v. 6); the earth διασχισθήσεται ἡ γῆ σχίσμα (*diaschisthēsetai hē gē schisma*), "will be torn asunder" (v. 7); and all that is on the earth will be *apoleitai*, "destroyed," on this final day (v. 7). The vision also stresses the universal nature of the final judgment, resulting in the absolute destruction of all the wicked (humanity, angels, and demons), while in contrast all the elect will experience eternal peace, mercy, and blessing (vv. 8–9). Thus the initial chapters of 1 Enoch demonstrate a familiarity with the day of the Lord motif as portrayed throughout the Hebrew Scriptures. As VanderKam concludes, there is "remarkable dependence of the author . . . upon the Old Testament both for theophanic motifs and even for vocabulary."[32] First Enoch looks forward to the future with great anticipation to the day of the Lord because on that day God's enemies will ultimately be removed, and the righteous will be saved.

Further evidence of the day of the Lord motif in 1 Enoch is found in chapters 6–11. These chapters are an elaboration of Genesis 6:1–8, describing in further detail the rebellion of the Watchers (angels), who take human women as their wives, producing giant offspring, whose need for food is so voracious that they proceed to eat humans (7:1–5). In addition to their sexual immorality with human women and producing cannibalistic offspring, the Watchers plunge humanity further into depravity by teaching them magic and incantations (7:1; 8:3). This crisis leads the people to cry out to heaven for help. Their petitions are heard by four heavenly

---

32. James C. VanderKam, "Theophany of Enoch 1:3b–7, 9," VT 23 (1973): 150.

beings—Michael, Sariel, Raphael, and Gabriel—who present them to God (9:1–3). The Lord instructs the four heavenly beings to destroy the wicked from the earth, which will be accomplished by means of the flood (10:2). However, the fate of the Watchers is that they will be imprisoned for seventy generations τῆς γῆς μέχρι ἡμέρας κρίσεως (*tēs gēs mechri hēmeras kriseōs*), "until the day of judgment" (10:12). Enoch is commissioned to inform the Watchers of their imminent punishment (12:4–6). After hearing of their fate, the Watchers implore Enoch to petition God on their behalf for forgiveness (13:4). Enoch is given a vision affirming that God will not show the Watchers mercy but will bring destruction on them (14:5–7). Once the Watchers are released from prison they, along with all the wicked, will be sentenced to eternal torment (10:13). Once the purging of the wicked is complete, God will bring restoration on the earth, and all nations will come and worship him (10:21–22).

This narrative seems to demonstrate, at least *conceptually*, an affinity with the Old Testament's teaching regarding the day of the Lord for at least two reasons. First, the people's sin provoked God to "visit" them in judgment by means of the deluge, which arguably serves as a pattern pointing to the consummate day of the Lord. Second, the fates of both the unrighteous and the righteous at the final judgment are outlined; the former receive eternal damnation, and the latter receive eternal absolution. George Nickelsburg contends, "[This] tradition interprets the events of Genesis as a prototype of eschatological violence, judgment, and restoration in which evil that originated in demonic rebellion would find its cure in divine intervention."[33]

A further example relating to the day of the Lord motif in 1 Enoch is found in the Book of Parables (chaps. 37–71).[34] The title of the book is predicated on the fact that it is essentially comprised of three "parables" or "similitudes" (chaps. 38–44; 45–57; 58–69).[35] These parables describe Enoch's journeys into heaven, where he is shown various visions. In general, these

33. George W. E. Nickelsburg, "Enoch, First Book of," in *ABD*, 2:510; George W. E. Nickelsburg, *1 Enoch 1: A Commentary on the Book of 1 Enoch Chapters 1–36*, Hermeneia (Minneapolis: Fortress, 2001), 224–25.

34. For a fuller discussion regarding these chapters see George W. E. Nickelsburg, *Jewish Literature between the Bible and the Mishnah: A Historical and Literary Introduction* (Minneapolis: Fortress, 2005), 248–56.

35. Ibid., 248; VanderKam, *From Revelation to Canon*, 294.

visions consist of cosmological phenomena that are interpreted as being anticipatory to the final judgment (43:1–44:1); the "Elect One," who is victorious over the wicked, brings restoration to the earth, and presides over the final judgment (46:1–5; 55:4); the final judgment (chaps. 61–63); and the eternal blessing the righteous receive after the final judgment (62:13–16). Nickelsburg observes, "The major and unique component in these chapters . . . is a series of heavenly tableaux that portray the judgment and the events leading up to it."[36] These chapters relate how the coming final judgment will be carried out primarily by one referred to as "the Elect One," "the Chosen One," and the "Son of Man." What is most notable is that this individual serves as God's agent who comes to pronounce the final verdicts on the righteous and unrighteous (62:1–16).[37] To further elaborate on the final judgment, the author recounts the story of Noah and the judgment that took place in his day (chaps. 65–68). The inclusion of the Noachian tradition arguably reveals that the author viewed the judgment during the time of Noah as typological, pointing to the final judgment. Michael Knibb contends, "The story of Noah functions in 1 Enoch as a paradigm of the judgment that will occur at the end of the age, and this is probably why the material concerning Noah was included."[38] The author of 1 Enoch seems to have appropriated the Old Testament's teaching concerning the day of the Lord to remind his readers that just as God "visited" the earth in judgment in the days of Noah, so he will come again to render the ultimate judgment on the righteous and the unrighteous.

A final example to consider regarding the day of the Lord motif in 1 Enoch is the section referred to as the Epistle of Enoch (chaps. 91–107). The opening chapters of this epistle, specifically 91:11–17 and 93:1–10, are known as the Apocalypse of Weeks. VanderKam notes that these chapters comprise a "short apocalypse which divides the sacred past, present, and future

---

36. Nickelsburg, 1 Enoch 1, 7.

37. It should be noted that the Book of Parables has been the catalyst for much discussion regarding the identity of the Son of Man as described in these chapters and the connection with Jesus identifying himself as the Son of Man in the Gospels. Helpful discussions of this issue can be found in Gabriele Boccaccini, ed., Enoch and the Messiah Son of Man: Revisiting the Book of Parables (Grand Rapids: Eerdmans, 2007); George W. E. Nickelsburg, Resurrection, Immortality, and Eternal Life in Intertestamental Judaism and Early Christianity, HTS 56 (Cambridge, MA: Harvard University Press, 2006), 281–314.

38. Michael A. Knibb, "Enoch, Similitudes of (1 Enoch 37–71)," in EDEJ, 586.

into periods called *weeks*."[39] In a series of ten weeks Enoch recounts his birth (week 1); events throughout biblical history (weeks 2–6); the present wicked generation and the rising of the "righteous ones" to carry out judgment (week 7); leading up to the final judgment (weeks 8–10). Beginning in week eight, the "righteous ones" are given a sword and commanded to execute judgment on the wicked. VanderKam contends, "The battle against the wicked in *week* eight is rather to be interpreted as an eschatological conflict against the nations, not as a historical war."[40] The purging of the wicked carried out with the sword wielded by the "righteous ones" ushers in the great day of divine intervention when God, through means of his angels, will bring about the eternal judgment (91:15). After the final judgment of the tenth week, the first heaven passes away, and a new heaven appears, whose number of weeks is without end (91:16–17). What is described in this brief apocalypse embedded in the Epistle of Enoch arguably reveals a conceptual familiarity with the day of the Lord.

The day of the Lord motif is further evident throughout the epistle as the author utilizes various Old Testament collocations to encourage his audience that their vindication was certain. Enoch reminds his children to avoid the company of the wicked and those who commit oppression, for the eschatological day is coming, and it is "a day of darkness and of great judgment" (94:1–9). He exhorts the "righteous ones" to persevere and be confident, knowing that the final day of destruction will soon come on "the sinners" at the "day of destruction" (96:8). He reminds the wicked that all their sinful deeds are written down day after day so that on *the day* they will face God's judgment (98:7). Enoch offers encouragement to the righteous, reminding them that they need not fear the final day, but rather they can be assured that on that day they will experience the joy and honor God has prepared for them (103:1–3).

The previous survey has shown that the book of 1 Enoch manifestly demonstrates an affinity with the Old Testament's teaching regarding the final day. The author utilizes the numerous idioms found throughout the Hebrew Scriptures to communicate to his readers that Yahweh does

---

39. James C. VanderKam, "Studies in the Apocalypse of Weeks (1 Enoch 93:1–10, 91:11–17)," *CBQ* 46 (1984): 511.

40. Ibid., 522.

in fact have a final day when he will come and ultimately render the righteous verdicts, sentencing the wicked to eternal condemnation and the righteous to eternal paradise.

Another pseudepigraphal text exhibiting the concept of the day of the Lord is the Psalms of Solomon. The work consists of eighteen psalms that were likely written by multiple authors around mid- to late first century BC.[41] Kenneth Atkinson contends, "A close examination of all the historical allusions in the Psalms of Solomon suggests that the entire collection was composed in Jerusalem between 62–30 BCE."[42] The psalms reflect the struggles that many Jews faced as they attempted to make sense of the nation's recent defeat by a foreign enemy.[43] Nevertheless, the author(s) understands that it was Israel's sin that brought about their defeat and subsequent persecution at the hand of foreigners (2:11–13; 8:9–14; 17:5–8). The psalms, however, assert that Israel's defeat was an act of God's discipline on them and that eventually Yahweh will restore his people, whom he has mercy on forever (7:3–10; 9:8–11). But the psalms not only exhibit confidence that God will spare the righteous; they also describe the final day when God will "visit" and bring eternal judgment on the wicked. There are several passages throughout the psalms where the author(s) incorporates the typical idioms associated with the day of the Lord concept that arguably demonstrate a familiarity with the Old Testament's teaching of this doctrine.[44]

---

41. The most well known are psalms 17–18. These texts are arguably some of the earliest texts to use the title "Son of David." Many scholars believe that these chapters are pre-Christian and provide valuable insight for understanding the Jewish concept of the Messiah and his role. These chapters describe the Son of David as the Lord's Messiah who will come to destroy the "sinner," restore the city of Jerusalem, and reign as king forever. For helpful discussions of psalms 17–18 see Michael Lattke, "Psalms of Solomon," in DNTB, 853–57; Johannes Tromp, "The Sinners and the Lawless in Psalm of Solomon 17," NovT 35 (1993): 344–61; H. Daniel Zacharias, "The Son of David in Psalms of Solomon 17," in "Non-Canonical" Religious Texts in Early Judaism and Early Christianity, ed. Lee Martin McDonald and James H. Charlesworth, Jewish and Christian Texts in Contexts and Related Studies Series (London: T&T Clark, 2012), 73–87.

42. Kenneth Atkinson, "Theodicy in the Psalms of Solomon," in Theodicy in the World of the Bible, ed. Antti Laato and Johannes C. de Moor (Leiden: Brill, 2003), 553. See also Mikael Winninge, Sinners and the Righteous: A Comparative Study of the Psalms of Solomon and Paul's Letters, ConBNT 26 (Stockholm: Almqvist & Wiksell International, 1995), 12–16.

43. The foreign enemy is believed to be the Roman general Pompey and his conquest of Jerusalem. See David Arthur deSilva, The Jewish Teachers of Jesus, James, and Jude: What the First Family of Christianity Learned from the Apocrypha and Pseudepigrapha (New York: Oxford University Press, 2012), 144–48; Richard A. Horsley, Revolt of the Scribes: Resistance and Apocalyptic Origins (Minneapolis: Fortress, 2010), 143–57.

44. E.g., 3:3–12; 13:1–12; 14:1–10; 15:1–13.

For example, in psalm 15 the author has experienced persecution at the hand of "sinners" but nevertheless offers praise to God for delivering him from such oppression. The psalmist can rejoice in the midst of calamity, knowing that God has "marked" him for salvation and thus has full assurance that the unrighteous will not be able to touch him (15:1–6). In contrast, the psalmist describes the fate of the unrighteous as those who are "marked" for destruction, which is described as both imminent and future (15:9–12). For the "sinners," famine, sword, and death are both proximate and inescapable. Their inheritance, however, is described in typical day of the Lord fashion. The author understands that the unrighteous will inherit ἀπώλεια καὶ σκότος (apōleia kai skotos), "destruction and darkness" (v. 10); they will ἀπολοῦνται . . . ἐν ἡμέρα κρίσεως κυρίου εἰς τὸν αἰῶνα (apolountai hēmera kriseōs kyriou eis ton aiōna), "perish forever on the day of the Lord's judgment" (v. 12). And this will transpire ὅταν ἐπισκέπτηται ὁ θεὸς τὴν γῆν ἐν κρίματι αὐτοῦ (hotan episkeptētai ho theos tēn gēn en krimati autou), "when God visits the earth at his judgment" (v. 12). From the author's perspective it seems not only that judgment was near for the unrighteous because of their lawless deeds but that the imminent punishment they experience arguably serves as a pattern pointing to the eschatological judgment that God will render at his return on the final day. At the final day the righteous will live by God's mercy, and the unrighteous will perish forever (15:13). Nickelsburg writes, "Since the psalmist describes the sinners' destruction as terminal, he may be referring to an eschatological day of judgment, when the sinners' destruction is sealed and the righteous dead are raised to life."[45] Thus the context of psalm 15 approximates with the Old Testament's teaching regarding the day of the Lord, for the day is both near (or has already happened) and future, as well as a day of both judgment and salvation.

A final example from the Pseudepigrapha regarding the doctrine of the day of the Lord is found in the apocalyptic work 2 Baruch. The author, probably a Jew writing under the pseudonym Baruch, likely wrote the book sometime after the fall of Jerusalem in 70 AD.[46] The setting for 2 Baruch is

---

45. Nickelsburg, *Resurrection, Immortality, and Eternal Life in Intertestamental Judaism and Early Christianity*, 166.

46. The date of 2 Baruch is unknown. However, the consensus seems to be that the work was composed sometime between AD 70 and 135. A helpful discussion relevant to the date

the events surrounding the destruction of Jerusalem in 586 BC. However, it is typically understood that the author's description of the destruction of the temple in 586 BC is a "literary device used to allude to the destruction of Jerusalem and the Second Temple in 70 CE."[47] The opening chapters (1–5) describe a dialogue between Baruch and God where Baruch is told about the coming destruction of Jerusalem. He is greatly concerned about this, because if enemies conquer Jerusalem that would not only profane God's name, but also it would be disastrous for his chosen people (5:1). The Lord informs Baruch that he is ultimately responsible for destroying Jerusalem and that this by no means infringes on his promises. Rather, the destruction is temporary and serves only as a chastisement, for God will preserve the true Jerusalem, which comes from heaven (4:1–6). Baruch questions God's fairness and wrestles with the difficulty of Babylon flourishing and Israel suffering. But God reveals to Baruch that the time is coming when he will ultimately bring judgment on his enemies and salvation for the righteous (24:1–2). Baruch pleads with God that the "end of days" would come soon.

The eschatological judgment that God will bring about at the consummation of time is arguably understood to be the day of the Lord. The author incorporates typical Old Testament language to describe this final day. For instance, in chapter 48 Baruch offers a prayer to God in which he specifically focuses on the "end times." Baruch prays for God to continually be merciful to his people as they persevere in obeying his commands (48:18–24). In the second half of the prayer God responds to Baruch, describing the judgment that will come upon the wicked. In verse 47 God informs Baruch that this judgment will happen on "your day." This phrase is arguably synonymous with the Old Testament idiom הַיּוֹם (hayyôm), "the day," and in this particular context emphasizes the consummate day when God will come to render the final verdicts.[48] This interpretation is further

---

of 2 Baruch is found in Gwendolyn B. Sayler, *Have the Promises Failed? A Literary Analysis of 2 Baruch*, SBLDS 72 (Chico, CA: Scholars Press, 1984), 103–18.

47. Rivkah Nir, *The Destruction of Jerusalem and the Idea of Redemption in the Syriac Apocalypse of Baruch*, Early Judaism and Its Literature 20 (Atlanta: Society of Biblical Literature, 2003), 1.

48. See the discussions in Lars Hartman, *Prophecy Interpreted. The Formation of Some Jewish Apocalyptic Texts and of the Eschatological Discourse Mark 13 Par*, ConBNT 1 (Lund: Gleerup, 1966), 23–49; Nir, *Destruction of Jerusalem and the Idea of Redemption in the Syriac Apocalypse of Baruch*, 121–64; Sayler, *Have the Promises Failed?*, 63–67; Willett, *Eschatology in the Theodicies of 2 Baruch and 4 Ezra*, 77–125.

validated in the overall context, as the author not only repeats the phrase "your day" in 49:2 but also describes how after "this day" (51:1) the righteous will be changed and inherit eternal glory, while the wicked will inherit eternal torment (51:1–12).

There are other texts in the Pseudepigrapha that could be explored for their familiarity with the day of the Lord motif.[49] Nevertheless, the above discussion has shown that this diverse collection of writings utilizes much of the same language and collocations found throughout the Old Testament regarding the day of the Lord theme. Like the Old Testament, the authors of the Pseudepigrapha understood that the "day" has both an imminent and future orientation and encompasses both judgment and salvation.

THE DAY OF THE LORD IN THE
DEAD SEA SCROLLS

The Dead Sea Scrolls are a collection of writings from a Jewish sect commonly identified as the Essenes who lived in the region of Qumran.[50] Since their discovery in 1947, the number of scrolls, many of which are fragmentary, totals approximately 875.[51] In general, the scrolls consist of both biblical and nonbiblical material. The biblical material comprises about 220 scrolls and includes every Old Testament book with the exception of Esther. The importance of these biblical scrolls cannot be overestimated. They have tremendously enhanced the areas of Old Testament studies such as textual criticism and linguistics. Regarding the benefit the scrolls have on Old Testament studies, Michael Wise comments: "Their . . . importance is obvious when one considers that prior to their discovery the oldest complete manuscript of the Hebrew Bible dated from the tenth century A.D.

---

49. E.g., Jubilees 23:16–32; Testament of Levi 1.1; 3.2–3; Life of Adam and Eve 12.1; 26.4; Apocalypse of Abraham 29.14–21; 2 En. 65:5–11.

50. Literature pertaining to the Dead Sea Scrolls is extensive. For some helpful introductions see Joseph A. Fitzmyer, *The Impact of the Dead Sea Scrolls* (New York: Paulist, 2009); Eibert Tigchelaar, "The Dead Sea Scrolls," in *EDEJ*, 163–80; Michael O. Wise et al., eds., *The Dead Sea Scrolls: A New Translation* (San Francisco: HarperSanFrancisco, 1996), 3–43; Michael O. Wise, "The Dead Sea Scrolls: General Introduction," in *DNTB*, 252–66.

51. See Stephen A. Reed, *The Dead Sea Scrolls Catalogue: Documents, Photographs, and Museum Inventory Numbers*, Resources for Biblical Study 32 (Atlanta: Scholars Press, 1994).

The DSS lifted the curtain to a period over a millennium earlier in the formation of the text."[52]

They have also helped to advance knowledge of the intertestamental period as well as New Testament background. The vast majority of the scrolls consist of the nonbiblical writings, encompassing a wide range of diverse material such as rules for community life, various hymns and prayers, apocryphal texts, and apocalyptic and eschatological texts.[53] Regarding the value of the Scrolls, Craig Evans comments, "The Dead Sea Scrolls probably constitute the single most important biblically related discovery of the twentieth century."[54]

The Qumran community had much to say about eschatology and the events that would take place in the future. With respect to the day of the Lord, the Scrolls rely heavily on the Old Testament's portrayal of the consummate day when God will visit to render either punishment or salvation. This is evident in several texts that incorporate the typical Old Testament idioms when speaking about the final day.[55] For example, one common phrase found throughout the scrolls is אחרית הימים (ʾḥryt hymym) "end of days," which occurs more than thirty times.[56] Although there is some debate regarding the precise meaning of this phrase, a general interpretation is that, first, it indicates the Qumran community understood that they were living in the last days, which are characterized by many trials and tribulations. The difficulties of these final days require the community members to be steadfast in their perseverance, as they remain firm in their commitment to God and persistent in righteous living. Second, the Qumran community believed that there was a definitive end coming in the future. They understood that there was a fixed day when God would come to bring both judgment and salvation (1QpHab 7.6–13, 16). John Collins aptly notes, "The belief that God would ultimately intervene to put an end

52. Wise, "Dead Sea Scrolls," 253.

53. For a listing and annotation of the various topics covered in the nonbiblical Scrolls, see Evans, *Ancient Texts for New Testament Studies*, 89–154.

54. Ibid., 80.

55. Such as "the day of vengeance," "the day of judgment," and "the day of visitation."

56. See John J. Collins, "The Expectation of the End in the Dead Sea Scrolls," in *Eschatology, Messianism, and the Dead Sea Scrolls*, ed. Martin Abegg Jr. and Peter W. Flint, Studies in the Dead Sea Scrolls and Related Literature (Grand Rapids: Eerdmans, 1997), 74–90; Annette Steudel, "'CHRYT HYMYM in the Texts from Qumran," *Revue de Qumran* 16 (1993): 225–46.

to wickedness was no doubt essential to the worldview of the community, as it was the source of their hope."[57]

Any cursory reading of the Scrolls reveals that the Qumran sect was an eschatologically oriented community. The members genuinely believed they were living in the "end of days" but that this time was limited since God had already determined a day when he would come and destroy all wickedness (1QS 4.18–19). Despite the fact that the timing of this final day was a mystery,[58] the Qumran sect did not lose hope, for they believed that God had chosen them and would ensure that they would receive their eternal possession (1QS 11.7–9). Thus, much like the Old Testament prophets, the Qumran community was ardently concerned about godly living in the present as they joyfully anticipated the future blessings that God had reserved for them, which would ultimately be realized on the final day.

This "end of days" mentality evident throughout many of the Scrolls arguably demonstrates that the day of the Lord was a prominent theme for the Qumran community.[59] The most notable text that provides evidence for the day of the Lord is arguably the War Scroll (1QM). The author of this text describes an eschatological battle where the Sons of Light wage war against the Sons of Darkness, who are led by Belial. The scroll provides detailed information regarding military formations, tactics, the equipment used, and the prominent role of the priests in these battles.[60] The war takes place over a forty-year period, culminating in a final battle. At this final battle the author declares it to be the day that God has appointed to come and in which he will definitively "lift up his hand against Belial and against all the forces of his dominion for an eternal slaughter" (1QM 18.1). During the final battle the author describes seven different "lots" (i.e., confrontations)[61] between the Sons of Light and the Sons of Darkness. After the

---

57. Collins, "Expectation of the End in the Dead Sea Scrolls," 90.

58. See Florentino García Martínez, "Apocalypticism in the Dead Sea Scrolls," in *The Continuum History of Apocalypticism*, ed. Bernard McGinn, John J. Collins, and Stephen J. Stein (New York: Continuum, 2003), 100–101. He notes that though the community attempted to calculate when the "end of days" would conclude, "the precise limits of the end of days are nowhere clearly stated, but it is said that this period of time will be closed by God's 'visitation.'"

59. A few examples include: 1QpZeph; 1QS 4.18–19, 26; 10.19–20; 1QM 7.5; 13.14; 4Q174; 4Q202.

60. See Martin Abegg, "War Scroll (1QM) and Related Texts," in *DNTB*, 1260–63; Fitzmyer, *Impact of the Dead Sea Scrolls*, 73.

61. See Hans Heinrich Schmid, "גורל," in *TLOT*, 1:311.

first six confrontations, the two sides are "deadlocked in a 3–3 tie."[62] At the seventh and final confrontation the hand of God comes to utterly destroy all the Sons of Darkness forever (1QM 1.14–15). Similar to the teachings of the Old Testament prophets, the author of the War Scroll understood that on that eschatological day the Lord would not only defeat all the pagan nations that rebelled against him but that he would completely obliterate all evildoers, including rebellious Israelites.[63] Following the victory, a celebration ensues for the chosen ones, who rejoice because they have experienced their ultimate vindication on the final day that God had appointed.

Another example of the day of the Lord motif can be found in the Rule of the Community scroll (1QS). This manuscript outlines the beliefs and rules that were expected of the members of the Qumran community. Such ordinances included how community life was to be carried out, the organization of leadership within the community, the separation from outsiders, and the acceptance of new members.[64] Nickelsburg concludes that the scroll "lays out the rules and regulations that governed the lifestyle and religious practices of the community, together with their theological rationale."[65] The Qumran sect believed that they were living in the last days, which were dominated by Belial. These last days are described as the time of struggle between the "two spirits," that is, the spirit of truth and the spirit of falsehood (1QS 3.13–4.26). Those who are of the spirit of truth are ruled by the Prince of Light, who governs all the righteous, in stark contrast to those of the spirit of falsehood, who are ruled by the Angel of Darkness (1QS 3.19–21). The scroll reminds the members of Qumran that though they were living in the last days, which were characterized by injustice, they could maintain hope, for the day of God's visitation would eventually come (1QS 4.18–19). That final day is described as both a day of vengeance when the Lord returns to render judgment and a day of ultimate renewal (1QS 4.18–26). Thus, in light of the coming day of the Lord, the scroll exhorts the Qumran members to faithfully

---

62. Wise et al., *Dead Sea Scrolls*, 151.

63. Martínez, "Apocalypticism in the Dead Sea Scrolls," 106.

64. See James H. Charlesworth, "Community Organization in the Rule of the Community," in *Encyclopedia of the Dead Sea Scrolls*, ed. Lawrence H. Schiffman and James C. VanderKam (New York: Oxford University Press, 2000), 2:133–36; Sarianna Metso, "Rule of the Community/ Manual of Discipline (1QS)," in *DNTB*, 1018–24.

65. Nickelsburg, *Jewish Literature between the Bible and the Mishnah*, 137.

observe the commands of God and the community rules until the consummate day when Yahweh will put an end to all injustice (1QS 4.19; 10.19–20).[66]

A final example from the Dead Sea Scrolls portraying familiarity with the day of the Lord is the Pesher on Habakkuk. The discovery of this commentary is significant because it is one of the most complete of all the pesharim, likely preserved in its entirety.[67] The text primarily deals with two events. First, it deals with the description of the Teacher of Righteousness and his conflict with the Man of the Lie and the Wicked Priest. The Teacher of Righteousness speaks on behalf of Yahweh, explaining everything that will come on his people. Those who oppose the Teacher demonstrate their rejection of God and his covenant and their allegiance to the Wicked Priest, who will eventually face final judgment (2.1–5; 8.3–11.17). The second event is a description of the Roman army and the extreme cruelty they unleash as they march throughout the land pillaging the cities (2.10–6.17).[68] Much like the canonical book of Habakkuk, the author of 1QpHab wrestles with the question of God's presence in the midst of the injustices the community faced at the hand of a foreign power. However, the community can be assured that God is still present and the time is coming when he will eventually defeat their enemies on the final day. The author encourages his readers that even though the last days will be longer than the prophets had foretold, the final day has been ordained by God and will come at the appointed time (7.13). On the final day, God will execute retribution on his enemies, while those who were loyal to him and faithfully observed his law will experience eternal blessings.

---

66. See Daniel C. Timmer, "Variegated Nomism Indeed: Multiphase Eschatology and Soteriology in the Qumranite Community Rule (1QS) and the New Perspective on Paul," *JETS* 52 (2009): 341–56.

67. Moshe J. Bernstein, "Pesher Habakkuk," in Schiffman and VanderKam, *Encyclopedia of the Dead Sea Scrolls*, 2:647–50; Evans, *Ancient Texts for New Testament Studies*, 147; Peter W. Flint, "Habakkuk Commentary (1QpHab)," in *DNTB*, 437–38; Helyer, *Exploring Jewish Literature*, 228; Shani Berrin Tzoref, "Pesher on Habakkuk," in *EDEJ*, 1054.

68. The pesher refers to the foreign power as the "Kittim," which most scholars believe to be Rome. See Wise et al., *Dead Sea Scrolls*, 114–15.

CONCLUSION

The above discussion has demonstrated that the extracanonical literature was familiar with the day of the Lord. In keeping with the Old Testament's teaching, these ancient texts are replete with numerous idioms that depict the final day when God will render perfect justice. The authors of these writings understood that God had decreed that the consummate day would come at the appointed time. Until then, the readers are encouraged to remain steadfast in their obedience to God and his commands as they suffer persecution at the hands of his enemies. Those who are loyal to Yahweh can have a firm hope, knowing that on this final day God will come to put all things right. These extracanonical texts echo the Old Testament's teaching that the day of the Lord is a day of judgment and salvation, a day to be feared or celebrated, a day of doom or rejoicing, but whatever the outcome may be, it is clear that this is the consummate day toward which all history is heading.

4

The Day of the Lord and Paul's Damascus Road Encounter

It has been established that the day(s) of the Lord concept is not only founded on the Old Testament but is also a prominent motif throughout extracanonical literature. The familiarity that the authors of the Hebrew Scriptures and other ancient Jewish writings demonstrate regarding the day of the Lord, and the frequency of this motif, has led to the conclusion that this was a significant part of their theological matrix. For them the day(s) of the Lord characterize how God deals with both his covenant people and his enemies in the past, present, and future. The day(s) of the Lord theme intimated throughout the Old Testament was a concrete expression that had great impact on the lives of its hearers. Furthermore, the significance of the day(s) of the Lord motif for the Old Testament was carried over into the extracanonical literature of the Second Temple period. The authors of these texts demonstrate their awareness of the Old Testament's teaching regarding the day of the Lord, evident in how pervasive it is thematically throughout the literature.

Understanding how both the Hebrew Scriptures and the Second Temple literature depict the day of the Lord affords a more complete picture of how the Apostle Paul interpreted the day of the Lord. While Paul's theology was first and foremost grounded in the Old Testament, he would have likely been familiar with some of the extracanonical texts and their teaching regarding the day of the Lord.[1] In addition to the Old Testament, there were likely other components that contributed to Paul's understanding of the day of the Lord. One of the primary components that arguably made a tremendous impact

---

1. Several texts in the Pseudepigrapha are obviously too late and would have not influenced Paul. However, some works, such as Jubilees and 1 Enoch, are likely early enough to have been relevant for the apostle. For a discussion on Paul's use of the Pseudepigrapha see Tom Holland, *Contours of Pauline Theology: A Radical New Survey of the Influences on Paul's Biblical Writings* (Fearn, UK: Mentor, 2004), 55–68.

on Paul's view of the day of the Lord was his Damascus road experience. Therefore, the following chapter will explore what impact Paul's Damascus road experience had on his understanding of the day of the Lord. The contention here is that the apostle understood the day of the Lord as more than just an eschatological event and, like the Old Testament prophets, recognized that the day of the Lord also affects the lives of Christians *in the present*. And although the day of the Lord is primarily discussed throughout the Pauline corpus in contexts with a future orientation, it must be remembered that the "already/not-yet" reality was always at the forefront of his mind. In Paul's estimation the certainty of the future radically impacted the present. Thus the following discussion seeks to demonstrate two points: (1) that the Damascus road completely reoriented Paul's understanding about the day of the Lord and (2) that the day of the Lord, with all its various nuances, profoundly influenced Paul's entire theological paradigm.

To substantiate these two claims, the following chapter will address three specific areas. First, there is a brief analysis regarding the significance of the Damascus road encounter based on Paul's own testimony. Second, there is an overview of the three accounts in the book of Acts that outline the Damascus road event. Third, there is an examination of some important elements, based on the *composite* portrayal from Paul's writings and Acts, as to how the Damascus road event framed the apostle's understanding regarding the day of the Lord. The conclusions reached from this discussion will arguably ensure a more complete interpretation for how the day of the Lord seemingly influences every facet of Paul's theology.

THE DAMASCUS ROAD EVENT
ACCORDING TO PAUL

What actually happened to Paul on the Damascus road? The traditional view understands Paul's encounter with the risen Christ as a *conversion* experience.[2] Peter O'Brien explains, "In the Damascus encounter Paul underwent a significant 'paradigm shift' in his life and thought; his own self-consciousness was that of having undergone a conversion. At the same time, he viewed his commitment to Jesus as being in line with God's ancient

---

2. See, e.g., Bruce Corley, "Interpreting Paul's Conversion—Then and Now," in *The Road from Damascus: The Impact of Paul's Conversion on His Life, Thought, and Ministry*, McMaster New Testament Studies (Grand Rapids: Eerdmans, 1997), 1–17; Seyoon Kim, *The Origin of Paul's Gospel* (Tübingen: Mohr Siebeck, 1981).

promises, and knew that he belonged to the 'remnant' or 'elect of Israel.' In this sense, he had not rejected his ancestral faith."[3] Others, however, have challenged the traditional view, contending that Paul's encounter with the risen Christ on the Damascus road was primarily concerned with his *calling* to be the apostle to the gentiles.[4] According to Krister Stendahl, Paul's encounter with the risen Jesus meant that he had been given a new assignment. Stendahl argues, "The emphasis in the [New Testament] accounts is always on this assignment, not on the conversion. Rather than being 'converted,' Paul was called to the specific task—made clear to him by his experience of the risen Lord—of apostleship to the Gentiles, one hand-picked through Jesus Christ on behalf of the one God of Jews and Gentiles."[5] The result of this divine calling for Paul was the realization that he had been working *against* God's Messiah, but now he would be commissioned as an agent working *for* the Messiah, and the remainder of his life would be dedicated to fulfilling this divine commission by taking the gospel to the gentiles. But while the debate continues as to whether the Damascus road experience was Paul's conversion or call, it would seem that they are not mutually exclusive. The accounts of Paul's encounter with the risen Lord recorded in the New Testament suggest that his *calling* was subsumed in the overall event of his *conversion*. In other words, it is arguably a false dichotomy to separate Paul's conversion and his calling. Rather, it seems reasonable that Paul's calling is one of the effects of his conversion. As D. A. Carson and Douglas Moo contend, "For Paul . . . conversion and call are bound up together."[6] Thus it seems appropriate to refer to the Damascus

---

3. Peter T. O'Brien, "Was Paul Converted?," in *Justification and Variegated Nomism: A Fresh Appraisal of Paul and Second Temple Judaism*, ed. D. A. Carson and Peter T. O'Brien (Grand Rapids: Baker, 2004), 2:390. See also D. A. Carson and Douglas J. Moo, *An Introduction to the New Testament* (Grand Rapids: Zondervan, 2005), 359, who rightly argue, "But whatever the continuity between Judaism and Christianity, the New Testament makes clear that the two are distinct, that only within Christianity is salvation found."

4. See, e.g., James D. G. Dunn, "Paul's Conversion—A Light to Twentieth Century Disputes," in *Evangelium, Schriftauslegung, Kirche: Festschrift für Peter Stuhlmacher zum 65. Geburtstag*, ed. Jostein Ådna, Scott J. Hafemann, and Otfried Hofius (Göttingen: Vandenhoeck & Ruprecht, 1997), 77–93; Dunn, "Paul and Justification by Faith," in Longenecker, *Road to Damascus*, 85–101; Calvin J. Roetzel, *Paul, a Jew on the Margins* (Louisville, KY: Westminster John Knox, 2003), 10–12; Krister Stendahl, *Paul among Jews and Gentiles, and Other Essays* (Philadelphia: Fortress, 1976); N. T. Wright, *Paul and the Faithfulness of God*, COQG 4 (Minneapolis: Fortress, 2013), 2:1427–26.

5. Stendahl, *Paul among Jews and Gentiles, and Other Essays*, 7.

6. Carson and Moo, *Introduction to the New Testament*, 359.

road experience as Paul's conversion, for he was radically transformed by the revelation of the risen Christ. Paul's thinking had undergone a complete metamorphosis about the person of Jesus, whom he now understood to be the Son of God who alone saves his people from their sins. As the apostle himself put it, he had been made a new creature in Christ (2 Cor 5:17). But it is also evident, as Stendahl argues, that inseparably linked with Paul's conversion was his "new assignment," or his calling to proclaim the good news about Jesus Christ to the gentiles. The conclusion here and one that seems most reasonable is that Paul experienced both a *conversion* (Acts 9:1-18; Phil 3:4-11) and a *calling* (Acts 22:6-21; Gal 1:11-23) on the Damascus road.[7]

The revelation that Paul received on the Damascus road that Jesus is both God and Messiah radically affected every facet of his life. His encounter with the risen Lord enabled him to understand that Jesus of Nazareth was the anointed one spoken of in the Law and the Prophets as the one who would fulfill all of God's covenant promises. This divine revelation transformed Paul in such a way that this former persecutor had now pledged total allegiance to Christ, becoming his ambassador.

The result of Paul's conversion was a reorientation of his theological paradigm. Every facet of his theology would now be viewed in light of the revelation he received that Jesus is both God and Christ. For Paul, the Damascus road event meant that his entire theological framework would now be understood through his faith in Jesus Christ. His knowledge of the Torah, justification, sanctification, the people of God, the kingdom, redemption, atonement, eschatology, and so on were now interpreted through Christ and what he had accomplished through his life, death, and resurrection. What follows is a brief examination of how this divine encounter with the risen Lord Jesus affected Paul's understanding regarding the day of the Lord. Exploring Paul's references about his Damascus road experience and its subsequent effects on him will provide a more precise understanding of how he interpreted the day of the Lord. Following the brief discussion of Paul's writings, a short examination of the Damascus road narratives recorded in the book of Acts will also serve to illustrate

---

7. See Craig S. Keener, *Acts: An Exegetical Commentary*, vol. 3., *Acts 15:1–23:35* (Grand Rapids: Baker, 2014), 1615.

how his encounter with the risen Son of God illumined his understanding about the day of the Lord.

There are several instances in Paul's epistles where he specifically mentions his Damascus road experience and the consequences from it (1 Cor 15:8–10; Gal 1:13–16; Phil 3:4–11; 1 Tim 1:12–16).[8] Moreover, he also makes some veiled allusions to the Damascus road experience throughout his writings (1 Cor 9:1; Eph 3:1–13; Col 1:23–29).[9] Interestingly, in none of these passages does the apostle give any *explicit* details surrounding the events of the Damascus road incident. Michael Bird notes, "Paul never recounts the exact circumstances of his encounter with Christ, but does offer snippets along the way as to what happened."[10] But why would the apostle choose not to relate the specific details surrounding his divine encounter? After all, this was *the* life-changing event that radically transformed his entire existence, so why not enumerate for his readers what exactly transpired on the Damascus road? The most plausible solution is that Paul had likely informed his readers about the divine encounter during his initial visit with them. Consequently, since they were already familiar with what had happened to him on the Damascus road, it was unnecessary to rehearse it again.[11] Furthermore, it must be kept in mind that all of Paul's letters were *situational*. His epistles were written, in many instances, as a means of offering the recipients further instruction or clarification regarding specific challenges or concerns they were experiencing. These unique issues afforded Paul an opportunity to briefly reference his Damascus road experience as a way to provide the necessary information his audience needed to remedy their particular issue. For example, in Galatians 1:11–17 Paul stresses that he did not receive the gospel by means of any human instruction, but rather he received it directly through a revelation from the risen Lord. He contrasts

---

8. Some would also include here 2 Cor 4:4–6, arguing that Paul may have had his conversion in mind when writing these verses. See the discussions in John B. Polhill, *Paul and His Letters* (Nashville: Broadman & Holman, 1999), 53; Seyoon Kim, *Paul and the New Perspective: Second Thoughts on the Origin of Paul's Gospel*, WUNT 140 (Tübingen: Mohr Siebeck, 2002), 165–213; N. T. Wright, *The Resurrection of the Son of God*, COQG 3 (Minneapolis: Fortress, 2003), 384–86.

9. See J. M. Everts, "Conversion and Call of Paul," in *DPL*, 156–63; Timothy J. Ralston, "The Theological Significance of Paul's Conversion," *BSac* 147 (1990): 198–215.

10. Michael F. Bird, *Introducing Paul: The Man, His Mission and His Message* (Downers Grove, IL: InterVarsity, 2008), 34.

11. See Kim, *Origin of Paul's Gospel*, 29.

his former manner of life and how he progressed within the traditions of Judaism more than any of his contemporaries with the sovereign grace of God, who revealed his Son to Paul, enabling him to carry out his divine call of preaching the gospel to the gentiles. Paul likely included this brief autobiographical excerpt to combat certain opponents who were attempting to convince the Galatian believers that they needed to be physically circumcised if they were to be considered legitimate children of God (1:7; 3:1; 5:10, 12; 6:12–13).[12] In his initial preaching of the gospel in Galatia, Paul had said nothing about the need for physical circumcision, and thus the Galatians began to wonder about the legitimacy of his gospel. The desire of the Galatians to adhere to the opponents' teaching demonstrated that they were on the verge of following after a false gospel. But Paul uses his testimony to accentuate that the source of his gospel was Christ himself and that the divine origin of his gospel was something none of his opponents could claim. The apostle, then, alludes to his Damascus road experience to remind the Galatians that he was a legitimate apostle, equal with those in Jerusalem, and that what he had received from the risen Lord he faithfully passed on to them.

Likewise, in 1 Corinthians 15:8–10 Paul briefly alludes to his encounter with the risen Lord on the Damascus road because many in the Corinthian church were questioning the validity of the resurrection. In verses 1–4 he reminds the church of the tradition that had been passed down to them regarding the certainty of Christ's resurrection. He then proceeds in verses 5–7 by recounting those who were eyewitnesses of Christ's postresurrection appearances, such as Peter, the Twelve, more than five hundred at a time, the rest of the apostles, and James. He concludes his eyewitness accounts by reminding them that Christ had also appeared to him. His mention of the Damascus road Christophany is further proof intended to reiterate for the Corinthians the certainty of the resurrection. Therefore, since Christ has been raised, he himself being the firstfruits, then those who

---

12. For helpful discussions regarding the identity of these "opponents" see A. E. Harvey, "Opposition to Paul," in *The Galatians Debate: Contemporary Issues in Rhetorical and Historical Interpretation*, ed. Mark D. Nanos (Peabody, MA: Hendrickson, 2002), 321–33; Richard N. Longenecker, *Galatians*, WBC 41 (Dallas: Word Books, 1990), lxxxviii–c; Douglas J. Moo, *Galatians*, BECNT (Grand Rapids: Baker, 2013), 19–31; Thomas R. Schreiner, *Galatians*, Exegetical Commentary on the New Testament (Grand Rapids: Zondervan, 2010), 39–52. Cf. Martinus C. de Boer, *Galatians: A Commentary*, NTL (Louisville, KY: Westminster John Knox, 2011), 50–61, who argues that these "opponents" are actually "new preachers" whose version of the gospel was different from Paul's.

belong to him will also be raised in like manner (vv. 20–57). Consonant with the first apostles, Paul also saw the risen Christ and this revelation, along with the evidence already mentioned, as more than enough to substantiate the truth of the resurrection.[13]

Other examples from Paul's letters could be explored (1 Cor 9:1; Phil 3:4–11; 1 Tim 1:12–16), but the point here is to reiterate that every instance where the apostle alludes to his Damascus road encounter is found in contexts that address his readers' specific circumstances. The recipients of Paul's epistles were in all likelihood already familiar with the events that had transpired on the Damascus road, making it unnecessary to recapitulate the specific details. This, however, should by no means lead to the assumption that the Damascus road experience was peripheral in Paul's estimation. Rather, the Damascus road encounter was one of the major components in the overall process that formulated his doctrinal framework. To fully appreciate "Paul's theological method of developing new theological insights and conceptions [there must be regard for] the Damascus revelation, the Jesus tradition, the Scriptures, and the early church kerygma for mutual interpretation and confirmation."[14] With respect to Paul's understanding of the day of the Lord as seen throughout his corpus, it seems that his divine encounter on the Damascus road served as a primary catalyst in reorienting and developing his understanding of this theological criterion. How exactly Paul interpreted the day of the Lord in light of the Damascus road experience will be discussed below. However, a brief survey of the Damascus road encounter as portrayed in the book of Acts is in order.

---

13. For helpful discussions on the overall context of 1 Cor 15:1–11 see Roy E. Ciampa and Brian S. Rosner, *The First Letter to the Corinthians*, PNTC (Grand Rapids: Eerdmans, 2010), 742–53; Wayne Coppins, "Doing Justice to the Two Perspectives of 1 Corinthians 15:1–11," *Neot* 44 (2010): 282–91; Gordon D. Fee, *The First Epistle to the Corinthians*, NICNT (Grand Rapids: Eerdmans, 2014), 796–818; Michael Licona, *The Resurrection of Jesus: A New Historiographical Approach* (Downers Grove, IL: InterVarsity, 2010), 223–35; Anthony C. Thiselton, *The First Epistle to the Corinthians: A Commentary on the Greek Text*, NIGTC (Grand Rapids: Eerdmans, 2000), 1182–1213; Wright, *Resurrection of the Son of God*, 312–31.

14. Kim, *Paul and the New Perspective*, 296. See also Udo Schnelle, *Apostle Paul: His Life and Theology*, trans. M. Eugene Boring (Grand Rapids: Baker, 2005), 98–102.

THE DAMASCUS ROAD EVENT
ACCORDING TO ACTS

There are three instances in the book of Acts where Luke recounts Paul's Damascus road experience (Acts 9:1–22; 22:1–16; 26:1–18). In these accounts Luke provides more information about the occasion in that he relates specific details that Paul himself never mentions in his own letters. In addition, Acts portrays the Damascus road encounter with a deliberate focus on Paul's *conversion*, whereas in the apostle's own writings he tends to focus on his *calling*. However, John Polhill rightly comments, "His conversion seems to lie behind many of Paul's references in his letters to his apostleship and ministry."[15]

Each instance of the Damascus road experience recounted in Acts is unique in its retelling of the events that transpired on that occasion. Much like Paul's references to this event, found in specific contexts addressing the particular issues of his audiences, so Luke also strategically places his descriptions of the Damascus road event at specific places in Acts to augment his overall purpose for writing the book.[16] For example, in Acts 9:1–19 Luke narrates the events surrounding Paul's conversion/call, narrated at this point in the book for a specific purpose. In 1:1–6:7, Luke relates how the gospel was spreading to those in Jerusalem and how the Lord was adding to their number those who were being saved (2:47). Moreover, in spite of opposition from outsiders (3:1–4:31; 5:12–42), a troubling circumstance within the church (4:32–5:11), and an administrative dilemma regarding the distribution of food among the members (6:1–6), the gospel continued to progress, the number of disciples in Jerusalem increased rapidly, and the church continued to expand (6:7). Subsequent to the increase in the number of disciples in Jerusalem, Luke relates how the gospel would spread into Judea and Samaria (6:8–9:31). Stephen's bold testimony before the Sanhedrin results in both his martyrdom and great persecution against the disciples in Jerusalem, forcing many of the Christians to flee to

---

15. Polhill, *Paul and His Letters*, 44.

16. It is generally recognized that Acts 1:8 functions as the summary outline for the book. See F. F. Bruce, *The Acts of the Apostles: The Greek Text with Introduction and Commentary* (Grand Rapids: Eerdmans, 1990), 103; Craig S. Keener, *Acts: An Exegetical Commentary*, vol. 1, *Introduction and 1:1–2:47* (Grand Rapids: Baker, 2012), 697; I. Howard Marshall, *The Acts of the Apostles*, New Testament Guides (Sheffield: Sheffield Academic Press, 1997), 29; J. C. O'Neill, *The Theology of Acts in Its Historical Setting* (London: SPCK, 1970), 54–70.

Judea and Samaria (6:8–8:1). Those who fled Jerusalem carried the gospel message with them to these regions, and ironically the persecution that was intended to squelch the Christian movement actually caused it to flourish. In chapter 9, Luke sets the stage for the advancement of the gospel to "the ends of the earth" by recounting Paul's conversion. The Damascus event is strategically placed here in this context because it prepares the reader for the rest of the events that transpired in the book. Eckhard Schnabel observes that from a literary standpoint, Paul's conversion/call as related in Acts 9:1–19 "points forward to the later extensive description of his missionary work in the synagogues and among the Gentiles outside of Judea. Even though Peter's role in the conversion of Cornelius, the first pagan to come to faith in Jesus, is a major factor in the move of the gospel from Jerusalem toward the ends of the earth, the mission of Philip and the conversion of Saul are important developments as the gospel moves into new regions."[17] One major assertion that Luke stresses regarding Paul's conversion and commission is that the Lord utilized it as the means for the gospel to spread rapidly throughout the Mediterranean world, eventually making its way to Rome.[18]

The final two accounts of the Damascus road event are located in contexts where Paul offers a bold defense of the gospel. In Acts 21:26–31 a group of Jews falsely accuses Paul of teaching contrary to the law of Moses and profaning the inner temple courts by bringing gentiles into it. Consequently, an angry mob seizes Paul and, seeking to kill him, they throw him out of the temple courts and proceed to beat him. The uproar grabs the attention of the Roman soldiers, who then descend on the situation to break up the chaos, arrest Paul, and secure him with chains in order to determine what he had done (21:33). The anger of the mob, however, hinders the soldiers' investigation, forcing them to bring Paul into the barracks. Before entering the barracks Paul is allowed to address the angry mob, which affords him an opportunity to describe how God used the Damascus road event to convince Paul that Jesus is the risen Lord who had commissioned Paul to bring the gospel to the gentiles (22:6–21). Hearing that the gospel is for the gentiles enrages the mob, and they demand that Paul be executed. The

---

17. Eckhard J. Schnabel, *Acts*, ed. Clinton E. Arnold, ZECNT 5 (Grand Rapids: Zondervan, 2012), 433–34.

18. The theological significance of Paul's Damascus experience is discussed below.

volatile situation forces the soldiers to escort Paul into the barracks, where he is interrogated by means of scourging (22:22–24).

The final account in 26:1–6 is located in a judicial context where Paul is brought before the civil authorities to stand trial before King Agrippa, where he is granted permission to offer his defense. The apostle relates certain events regarding his Damascus road encounter once again, testifying that Jesus is Lord and that he appointed Paul to take the gospel to the gentiles so that they would repent and turn to God (26:13–18). Agrippa determines that Paul has done nothing deserving of death and could have been released had he not appealed to Caesar (26:30–32). Despite Paul's innocence, he will be sent to Rome, as this was God's sovereign plan to advance the gospel to the ends of the earth.

Luke records all three accounts of Paul's Damascus road experience in strategic contexts throughout Acts. Even though in each instance some details are excluded while others are emphasized, it seems that he records each account as a means to carry forward the purpose of the book as delineated in 1:8.[19] In general, the first account sets the stage for the gospel to progress beyond Jerusalem, the second emphasizes Jewish rejection and Paul's gentile commission, and the final account describes the gospel making it to Rome. Acts concludes by recognizing that despite the many attempts to stop the progress of the gospel, God ensured that the message not only reached the ends of the earth but that it continued to advance unhindered (28:31).

THE DAMASCUS ROAD EVENT AND THE DAY OF THE LORD: COMPOSITE CONCLUSIONS

In spite of the differences in how the Damascus event is portrayed in the book of Acts and Paul's epistles, when looking at them collectively "they complement one another, giving a multifaceted view of this pivotal event in Paul's life as a Christian."[20] It is clear that this event serves as one of the foundational moments in Paul's life that radically affected and reoriented

---

19. See Charles W. Hedrick, "Paul's Conversion/Call: A Comparative Analysis of the Three Reports in Acts," *JBL* 100 (1981): 415–32; David M. Stanley, "Paul's Conversion in Acts: Why the Three Reports?," *CBQ* 15 (1953): 315–38; Ralston, "Theological Significance of Paul's Conversion," 200; Ronald D. Witherup, "Functional Redundancy in the Acts of the Apostles: A Case Study," *JSNT* 48 (1992): 67–86.

20. Polhill, *Paul and His Letters*, 44.

his theology. God had graciously enabled Paul to understand that Jesus was both Lord and Messiah, who had fulfilled all of God's covenant promises and inaugurated the new era. This had enormous repercussions for how the apostle thought about God and the progression of redemptive history. Paul's entire theological purview would now be shaped and interpreted by the divine revelation he had received from the risen Lord. And while every aspect of Paul's theology was in some way affected by his Damascus road experience, the following discussion seeks to only explore how this divine encounter affected his understanding regarding the day of the Lord.

A *composite* examination of Paul's writings and Acts arguably reveals some important elements as to how the Damascus road event framed the apostle's understanding regarding the day of the Lord. First, on the Damascus road Paul experienced a *Christophany*. The risen Lord physically *appeared* to Paul, as he had earlier to several others (1 Cor 15:5–8; Acts 9:17; 26:16). Furthermore, Paul also alludes to this *Christophany* when he reminds the Corinthians and the Galatians that he had *seen* the Lord (1 Cor 9:1) and that God was pleased to *reveal* his Son to him (Gal 1:16). The book of Acts also describes this *Christophany* as Paul seeing a *light from heaven* (Acts 9:3; 22:6; 26:13). The descriptions of this divine manifestation help in formulating how the apostle interpreted the day of the Lord. It seems that an important caveat that both Acts and Paul stress regarding the Damascus road experience is how this *Christophany* was in many respects analogous to the *theophanies* found in the Old Testament.[21] Throughout the Old Testament Yahweh manifests himself or "comes down" in various forms to confront his people regarding judgment (i.e., warning them of it or unleashing it on them) and salvation (Exod 3:2–4; 19:16; 24:15–20; Ps 18:14; Hab 3:12–13; etc.). In the many instances where Yahweh *appears* or *reveals* himself to people, these visitations are often associated with either judgment or salvation. As was argued earlier, these visits from Yahweh, particularly in the prophetic literature, are understood to be a day of the Lord.[22] An important element of the *theophanies* throughout the Old Testament is that they serve as a type or pattern pointing to the consummate day of the Lord.

---

21. See G. K. Beale, *A New Testament Biblical Theology: The Unfolding of the Old Testament in the New* (Grand Rapids: Baker, 2011), 244–47.

22. See the discussion in chap. 3.

Such parallels lend themselves to suggest that Paul likely understood his *Christophany* to be analogous with the Old Testament *theophanies*.[23] On the Damascus road, the apostle experienced firsthand the *theophany* tradition recounted in the Old Testament. Just as Yahweh had made himself visible in some form to individuals in past generations, so also Jesus, in his glorified state, made himself visible to Paul (1 Cor 9:1; 15:8; Gal 1:12, 16). Therefore, it also seems reasonable to conclude that because the *Christophany* Paul experienced in many ways correlated to the Old Testament *theophanies*, the Damascus road encounter for Paul was in essence a *proleptic* day of the Lord. Paul had once believed that it was his duty before God to extinguish this new movement that proclaimed a crucified and risen Messiah. But the pursuer was actually being pursued. And when the risen Christ appeared he pronounced a severe indictment against Paul, namely that he was guilty of fighting against God (Acts 9:4–5; 26:14). This accusation forced Paul to realize that he actually stood before the Lord, the Judge of all the earth, guilty, having no defense and utterly condemned. However, on this day when the final Judge appeared to Paul, he was given mercy rather than judgment. Thus the outcome from this *Christophany* radically altered Paul's entire theological framework. In some manner this *proleptic* day of the Lord influenced not only every aspect of Paul's theology but also how he would carry out his commission as the apostle to the gentiles.

A second element to consider regarding Paul's Damascus road experience and the day of the Lord are the many similarities of his commission to be the apostle to the gentiles to that of the Old Testament prophets. It is, however, beyond the scope of this study to exhaustively address the numerous parallels evident between Paul's divine calling with respect to the calling of the Old Testament prophets.[24] Nevertheless, in the matter of Paul's understanding of the day of the Lord, a few brief comments are in order.

---

23. See Larry R. Helyer, *The Witness of Jesus, Paul, and John: An Exploration in Biblical Theology* (Downers Grove, IL: InterVarsity, 2008), 290–94.

24. Comprehensive discussions regarding Paul's relationship to the Old Testament prophets are found in Jeffrey W. Aernie, *Is Paul Also among the Prophets? An Examination of the Relationship between Paul and the Old Testament Prophetic Tradition in 2 Corinthians*, LNTS 467 (London: T&T Clark, 2012); Tony Costa, "Is Saul of Tarsus Also among the Prophets? Paul's Calling as Prophetic Divine Commissioning," in *Christian Origins and Hellenistic Judaism: Social and Literary Contexts for the New Testament*, ed. Stanley E. Porter and Andrew W. Pitts, TENTS 10 (Leiden: Brill, 2013), 203–35; Scott J. Hafemann, *Paul, Moses, and the History of Israel: The Letter/Spirit Contrast and the Argument from Scripture in 2 Corinthians 3*, WUNT 81 (Tübingen:

Although Paul never explicitly calls himself a prophet, scholars have long recognized numerous parallels between his divine appointment and the calling of the Old Testament prophets. The book of Acts and Paul's epistles describe the apostle's new covenant ministry by drawing on similar vocabulary and themes related to the Old Testament prophetic tradition. Indeed, Paul's commission and vocation that he received on the Damascus road exhibit many similarities with such figures as Moses, Isaiah, Jeremiah, and Ezekiel. Some of the more commonly observed parallels include seeing a *theophany* (Exod 3–4; Isa 6:1; Ezek 1:26–28; compare Acts 9:3; 22:6; 26:13; 1 Cor 9:1; Gal 1:16a), the prophet declaring his unworthiness/inadequacies (Exod 4:10; Isa 6:5; Jer 1:6; Ezek 1:28; compare 1 Cor 15:9; 2 Cor 2:16; 3:5), the Lord overcoming the prophet's inadequacies and enabling him to carry out the ministry (Isa 6:6–7; Jer 1:7–8; compare 2 Cor 12:10), the prophet being given the divine message from the Lord (Exod 4:12; Jer 1:9–10; Ezek 2:4; compare 1 Cor 15:1–3; Gal 1:11–12), and the Lord granting the prophet authority to carry out the ministry (Exod 4:1–17; Isa 6:8–9; Jer 1:10; Ezek 2:3; compare 2 Cor 10:8, 17; 3:10).[25]

Paul ostensibly indicates in his writings that he interpreted his divine appointment to be pursuant with the calling of the Old Testament prophets. For instance, in Galatians 1:15–16 Paul uses language reminiscent of the prophetic callings, particularly of Isaiah and Jeremiah, when reminding the Galatians that God had also set him apart, called him by his grace, and appointed him as the apostle to the gentiles (Isa 49:1–6; Jer 1:5). He also mentioned to them in verse 16a that "God had revealed his Son to me." This may arguably serve as a reference to his Damascus road *Christophany*, which in many respects resembles the *theophanies* experienced by the Old Testament prophets.[26] Regarding Paul's echo of the prophetic tradition in verses 15–16, Tony Costa has concluded, "The linguistic parallels that Paul draws between

---

Mohr Siebeck, 1995); Karl Olav Sandnes, *Paul, One of the Prophets? A Contribution to the Apostle's Self-Understanding*, WUNT 43 (Tübingen: Mohr Siebeck, 1991).

25. These elements were adopted from Hafemann, *Paul, Moses, and the History of Israel*, 50–59; Polhill, *Paul and His Letters*, 50–51. See also Craig A. Evans, "Prophet, Paul as," in *DPL*, 762–65. See also 2 Cor 4:1–6; Eph 2:19–3:7, etc.

26. Sandnes, *Paul, One of the Prophets?*, 60, rightly points out there are both continuity and discontinuity with Paul's *Christophany* and the *theophanies* in the Old Testament. He notes that the primary difference is *christological*, meaning that Paul's revelation "concentrated on the Son of God and Paul's commission was to preach him. . . . The Old Testament prophets were normally commissioned to preach a message."

himself and the commissioning of the Old Testament prophets are evident in Gal 1:15–16."[27] A further example of the correlation with Paul's ministry with respect to the Old Testament prophets is those texts, particularly in 2 Corinthians, where Paul recognizes his insufficiencies and understands that only by God's grace can he carry out his new covenant ministry. Just as Moses (Exod 4:10), Isaiah (Isa 6:5), and Jeremiah (Jer 1:6) all recognized their inadequacies, Paul also affirms his insufficiency and thus acknowledges his need to be constantly dependent on God's grace and power (2 Cor 3:5; 4:7–18; 12:10). A primary assertion for Paul in 2 Corinthians is that "he declares that *from* himself he is not sufficient to reckon anything as *of* himself; he rejects even the capacity to discern that anything could emanate from him. But, he affirms, our sufficiency is from God."[28] Like the Old Testament prophets before him, Paul understood that his sufficiency derived only from God, which is why he can say, "for when I am weak then I am strong."

Although additional examples could be mentioned, the intent here is to merely demonstrate that Paul's calling on the Damascus road exhibits several parallels in relation to the divine calling found in the Old Testament prophetic tradition. The many corollaries evident throughout Paul's epistles and the book of Acts reasonably substantiate the conclusion that "Just as the prophets of old were confronted by Yahweh and sent to preach, Paul was confronted by the risen Jesus and commissioned to evangelize the nations."[29] But how is the correlation between Paul's calling and the calling of the Old Testament prophets relevant to the apostle's understanding of the day of the Lord? Do Paul's divine commission on the Damascus road and subsequent ministry affect his theological perspective about the day of the Lord?

Earlier we argued that in one sense the Damascus road experience for Paul functioned as a *proleptic* day of the Lord. Paul was guilty of fighting against the Son of God, the ultimate Judge, and deserved condemnation.

---

27. Costa, "Is Saul of Tarsus Also among the Prophets?," 213. See also the discussion in Sandnes, *Paul, One of the Prophets?*, 59–65.

28. Paul Barnett, *The Second Epistle to the Corinthians*, NICNT (Grand Rapids: Eerdmans, 1997), 173. See also Aernie, *Is Paul Also among the Prophets?*, 118–19; Timothy B. Savage, *Power through Weakness: Paul's Understanding of the Christian Ministry in 2 Corinthians*, ed. Margaret E. Thrall, SNTSMS 86 (Cambridge: Cambridge University Press, 1996).

29. Carey C. Newman, "Christophany as a Sign of 'The End,'" in *Israel's God and Rebecca's Children: Christology and Community in Early Judaism and Christianity: Essays in Honor of Larry W. Hurtado and Alan F. Segal*, ed. David B. Capes (Waco, TX: Baylor University Press, 2007), 156.

However, instead of retribution the Judge gave Paul mercy, making him a new creature and commissioning him as the apostle to the gentiles. Like the Old Testament prophets, the apostle carried out his divine vocation by faithfully proclaiming the message he had received. However, Paul's message was distinct from the older prophets in that he specifically preached repentance and faith in Jesus Christ. Understanding Jesus to be the Son of God meant that Paul also realized that Jesus was the climax and fulfillment of redemptive history.[30] Yet throughout his letters Paul certainly understands the reality of the already/not yet. In other words, as Thomas Schreiner observes, "The eschatological promises of the OT are now fulfilled in Christ. . . . God's promises have been realized in Jesus Christ, and yet have not reached their consummation. God's saving promises have been inaugurated but not yet consummated."[31] This realization would have certainly affected Paul's entire theological paradigm. But more specifically, how did such knowledge affect his understanding regarding the day of the Lord? It seems feasible to argue that when it was revealed to Paul that Jesus was the culmination of the Old Testament promises, the one who inaugurated the end of the age, the apostle would have also understood that the day of the Lord was fulfilled in Jesus. In other words, on the Damascus road Paul personally identified with the message that the Old Testament prophets had announced concerning the day of the Lord, namely that Paul himself experienced a "day" of the Lord and that day pointed toward the final eschatological day. The first coming of Christ (also a day of the Lord), his death, burial, and resurrection, meant that his second coming, namely the consummate day of the Lord, could emerge at any moment. Indeed, Paul realized that what the Old Testament prophets declared about the final day of the Lord was now far more imminent than ever because of Jesus Christ. The *proleptic* day of the Lord that Paul experienced on the Damascus road meant that he was markedly aware "that the time was short. . . . For the present shape of the world is passing away" (1 Cor 7:29–31).[32]

---

30. See G. K. Beale, *Handbook on the New Testament Use of the Old Testament: Exegesis and Interpretation* (Grand Rapids: Baker, 2012), 95–102; Christopher J. H. Wright, *Knowing Jesus through the Old Testament* (Downers Grove, IL: InterVarsity, 1995); N. T. Wright, *What Saint Paul Really Said: Was Paul of Tarsus the Real Founder of Christianity?* (Grand Rapids: Eerdmans, 1997), 176.

31. Thomas R. Schreiner, *The King in His Beauty: A Biblical Theology of the Old and New Testaments* (Grand Rapids: Baker, 2013), 543.

32. See also Thiselton, *First Epistle to the Corinthians*, 578–86; Bruce W. Winter, "'The Seasons' of this Life and Eschatology in 1 Corinthians 7:29–31," in *"The Reader Must Understand":*

Therefore, one of the primary aspects of Paul's divine commission to the apostolate in relation to the Old Testament prophetic tradition was that it was *missional*. Just as the Old Testament prophets urged repentance and faith in God and warned the people about the coming day(s) of the Lord, in the same manner Paul also exhorts people to repent and believe in Jesus, who is coming again as the eschatological Judge. The Old Testament prophets warned people of the coming day of the Lord, when Yahweh would come and render his perfect verdicts. Similarly, Paul proclaimed the imminence of the day of the Lord but realized that this final day was fulfilled in the Son of God, who functions as the Father's judicial agent to whom all must give an account. Thus, when Paul writes that "now is the day of salvation" (2 Cor 6:2), he means in a general sense that God is presently at work redeeming his people through his Son.[33] But when the Father completes his work of reconciliation, then the day of the Lord will commence as Christ comes to render judgments at the final assize.[34] Similar with the Old Testament prophets before him, Paul also proclaimed that for those who identify with Christ by faith, the day of the Lord will be a day of vindication, while those who reject Christ will find it to be a day of condemnation.

A final element as a result of the Damascus road episode is that Paul likely understood the day of the Lord *forensically*. The final Judge appeared, casting an indictment against Paul, who was vehemently opposing the living God. In essence, on the Damascus road, Paul was brought before the bench of the final Judge guilty, with no defense. However, the Judge granted Paul mercy, transformed his life, and appointed him with

---

Studies in Eschatology in Bible and Theology, ed. K. E. Brower and M. Elliot (Leicester, UK: Apollos, 1997), 323–34; Ben Witherington III, "Transcending Imminence: The Gordian Knot of Pauline Eschatology," in *Eschatology in Bible & Theology: Evangelical Essays at the Dawn of a New Millennium*, ed. K. E. Brower and M. Elliott (Downers Grove, IL: InterVarsity, 1997), 171–86.

33. For helpful discussions on 2 Cor 6:2, see Aernie, *Is Paul Also among the Prophets?*, 150–52; Peter Balla, "2 Corinthians 6:2," in *Commentary on the New Testament Use of the Old Testament*, ed. G. K. Beale and D. A. Carson (Grand Rapids: Baker, 2007), 766–68; G. K. Beale, "The Old Testament Background of Reconciliation in 2 Corinthians 5–7 and Its Bearing on the Literary Problem of 2 Corinthians 6:14–7:1," in *The Right Doctrine from the Wrong Texts? Essays on the Use of the Old Testament in the New*, ed. G. K. Beale (Grand Rapids: Baker, 1994), 217–47; Mark S. Gignilliat, "2 Corinthians 6:2: Paul's Eschatological 'Now' and Hermeneutical Invitation," *WTJ* 67 (2005): 147–61; Jan Lambrecht, "The Favorable Time: A Study of 2 Cor 6,2a in Its Context," in *Vom Urchristentum zu Jesus: für Joachim Gnilka*, ed. Hubert Frankemölle and Karl Kertelge (Freiburg: Herder, 1989), 377–91.

34. This is discussed more fully in the following chapter.

a new vocation. Paul's forensic interpretation of the day of the Lord is seemingly evident throughout his letters as he utilizes judicial language and idioms to describe the eschatological day. Much like the Old Testament prophets, Paul repeatedly exhorts his readers that the final assize is coming and that everyone has been subpoenaed to stand before the Lord Jesus Christ, who as the Father's judicial agent has full authority to pronounce the final verdict.[35]

The preceding discussion has argued that Paul's encounter with the risen Christ on the Damascus road was in essence a *proleptic* day of the Lord. The final Judge appeared to Paul and instead of administering retribution granted him mercy. Paul was not only transformed into a Christ follower but was also divinely appointed to a new vocation that was parallel with the Old Testament prophetic tradition in many respects. Paul was made aware of the true identity of Jesus, who was the culmination of all the Old Testament promises and the one who inaugurated the end of the age. This "day" on the Damascus road verified for the apostle that the final day was closer than ever. Consequently, the day of the Lord arguably became one of the primary components of Paul's theological matrix, made evident by the numerous references and allusions to the eschatological day throughout his writings. In other words, for Paul the day of the Lord was exceedingly more than just an afterthought in his theological arsenal. Rather, the day of the Lord, and the many implications associated with it, are notably pervasive throughout his letters. Paul repeatedly mentions or alludes to the fact that Jesus' coming again on that last Day to bring final judgment and salvation veritably affects every facet of his theology. In other words, it seems that there is no part of Paul's theological schema that is not in some way influenced by the day of the Lord. Thus the following chapter seeks to substantiate these claims by thematically exploring how Paul both describes and understands the day of the Lord by examining several salient texts in his corpus.

---

35. The subsequent chapter discusses this claim more fully.

5

The Day of the Lord in Paul's Theology

PAULINE TERMINOLOGY

The preceding analysis has argued that the doctrine of the day of the Lord is a familiar concept found throughout the Old Testament, particularly the prophetic literature. We also put forth that the day of the Lord is also notably evident in the Second Temple literature, which drew heavily on the Old Testament for its interpretation of this motif. These ancient authors and their readers understood that the day(s) of the Lord was both near and far. Throughout the course of history people had experienced instances where Yahweh would visit, bringing either judgment or salvation. These days served as a typological pattern pointing to the final eschatological day of the Lord, when God would return and ultimately set things right once and for all. Consequently, the day of the Lord will either be a day of celebration that God's people should joyfully anticipate or will be a day of great fear and trepidation, when God will enact final vengeance on those who oppose him.

As a devout Jew, Paul would have been familiar with such teachings concerning the day of the Lord. Indeed, it would seem reasonable to conclude that because of his familiarity with and commitment to the Old Testament Scriptures that the doctrine of the day of the Lord was by no means unfamiliar territory for him. However, Paul's understanding about the day of the Lord was completely reoriented because of his encounter with the risen Son of God on the Damascus road. The pinnacle of redemptive history was found in the person of Jesus Christ, whose life, death, burial, and resurrection fulfilled all of God's Old Testament promises and inaugurated the end of the age. Seeing the risen Lord made Paul understand that the consummation of all things was more imminent than ever before. In other words, Paul's Damascus road experience brought him to the realization that Jesus was the eschatological

Judge who fulfills the day of the Lord. The consummation of "the end of the ages" would take place when the risen Lord Jesus returned on that ultimate day. In essence, Paul's Damascus road experience was a *proleptic* day of the Lord, as he stood before the final Judge guilty but was granted mercy, which resulted in his conversion and new vocation. Knowing that this eschatological day was on the horizon, the apostle spent the rest of his life urging people to be reconciled to God through Christ, who would preside as Judge on the final day of the Lord.

The contention here is that the doctrine of the day of the Lord is a major component that affects all of Paul's theology. The apostle's personal *proleptic* day of the Lord experience significantly affected him and reoriented his entire theological framework. In other words, the day of the Lord motif should not be something merely reserved for discussions about eschatology, but rather this concept to some degree affects the entirety of Paul's theology. In order to substantiate these claims, the following discussion seeks to analyze how Paul perceived the day of the Lord throughout his writings. This will be accomplished by the following: (1) offering a brief overview of the various terms and idioms found throughout Paul's epistles that are synonymous with the day of the Lord motif and (2) exploring several texts throughout Paul's writings relevant to the day of the Lord. The intention here is not to provide a detailed exegesis of either the various terms or passages, but rather the goal is to offer a *thematic* analysis of how Paul understood the day of the Lord throughout his epistles.

There are a variety of words and expressions that Paul uses to describe the day of the Lord throughout his letters. All of these terms that the apostle employed to communicate his doctrine of the day of the Lord are used in connection with Jesus Christ. This is significant because it demonstrates that Paul understood that Jesus has assumed the prerogatives that Yahweh was to perform on that day. Paul understood that when the Old Testament spoke about the day of the Lord, it was most certainly referring to Yahweh as the one who will bring about final judgment and salvation on that day. It was revealed to Paul on the Damascus road that Jesus is Lord and that the Father was pleased to have all his fullness dwell in him (Col 1:19). Paul concludes that since Jesus is fully God he naturally possesses all of the divine attributes and therefore has sovereign authority to preside as final Judge on the day of the Lord. Joseph Kreitzer rightly concludes, "For

Paul, the Day of the Lord Yahweh has become the Day of the Lord Jesus
Christ."[1] The various words and phrases Paul incorporates throughout
his writings arguably demonstrate that the apostle believed that the Son
was coming again as the Father's judicial agent, having been granted full
authority to subject all things under his feet, after which he himself will
be subjected to the Father so that God will be all in all (1 Cor 15:27-28). What
follows is a brief overview of some of the terms and phrases used by Paul
to describe his perception of the day of the Lord. The intent of this survey
is to obtain a more complete understanding surrounding the terminology
Paul utilized to describe the day of the Lord.

ἡμέρα κυρίου (hēmera kyriou)

The most frequent expression Paul uses to discuss the final return of Christ
is ἡμέρα κυρίου (hēmera kyriou), "the day of the Lord."[2] The use of this phrase
and its various locutions throughout the Old Testament and Second Temple
literature have been discussed extensively in the previous chapters. Thus
the following survey focuses on the use of the expression strictly in the
Pauline corpus.

Paul uses the expression hēmera kyriou only twice throughout his
epistles (1 Thess 5:2; 2 Thess 2:2). His tendency, however, is to use a variety of different variations of this idiom, as is evident from the numerous
examples throughout his corpus. Some of these include: ἡμέρα τοῦ κυρίου
Ἰησοῦ Χριστοῦ (hēmera tou kyriou Iēsou Christou), "day of the Lord Jesus
Christ" (1 Cor 1:8); τῇ ἡμέρᾳ τοῦ κυρίου ἡμῶν Ἰησοῦ (te hēmera tou kyriou
hēmōn Iēsou), "day of our Lord Jesus" (2 Cor 1:14); ἡμέρας Χριστοῦ Ἰησοῦ

---

1. L. Joseph Kreitzer, *Jesus and God in Paul's Eschatology*, JSNTSup 19 (Sheffield, UK: JSOT,
1987), 129. See also Larry R. Helyer, *The Witness of Jesus, Paul, and John: An Exploration in Biblical
Theology* (Downers Grove, IL: InterVarsity, 2008), 289-90; Paul R. House, "The Day of the
Lord," in *Central Themes in Biblical Theology: Mapping Unity in Diversity*, ed. Scott J. Hafemann
and Paul R. House (Grand Rapids: Baker, 2007), 214; Ben Witherington III, *Jesus, Paul, and
the End of the World: A Comparative Study in New Testament Eschatology* (Downers Grove, IL:
InterVarsity, 1992), 152-69.

2. This is an instance of Apollonius's corollary, which states that when one anarthrous
noun governs another anarthrous noun they both have the same semantic force. The Genitive
construction *hēmera kyriou* is understood here as definite and thus renders the translation
"the Day of the Lord." For a discussion of this rule see C. F. D. Moule, *An Idiom Book of New
Testament Greek* (Cambridge: Cambridge University Press, 1959), 114-17; Daniel B. Wallace,
Greek Grammar beyond the Basics: An Exegetical Syntax of the New Testament (Grand Rapids:
Zondervan, 1996), 250-52.

(*hēmeras Christou Iēsou*), "day of Christ Jesus" (Phil 1:6); ἡμέραν Χριστοῦ (*hēmeran Christou*), "day of Christ" (Phil 1:10); ἡ ἡμέρα (*hē hēmera*), "the day" (1 Cor 3:13; 1 Thess 5:4); and ἐκείνην τὴν ἡμέραν (*ekeinēn tēn hēmeran*), "that day" (1 Tim 1:12, 18; 4:8). The significance of these numerous expressions is that they all demonstrate at least two important aspects of Paul's understanding of this final day. First, these renderings demonstrate that Paul undoubtedly understood that the day of the Lord was in fact the day of the Lord Jesus Christ. Second, as will be discussed below, these idioms suggest a forensic nuance. The manner in which the apostle utilizes these various expressions reveals that he was heavily influenced by the Old Testament's teaching regarding the eschatological day of the Lord as both a day of judgment and vindication. The uniqueness of these various locutions is that they reveal that Paul undoubtedly realizes that Jesus fulfills the role as consummate Judge to whom all must give an account at the final assize. The day of the Lord Jesus is the final court day when all will appear before his judgment bench, where he will render the final verdicts (2 Cor 5:10).

παρουσία (parousia)

The term παρουσία (parousia) typically means the "coming" or "arrival" of an individual or group in a general sense.[3] However, in specific contexts throughout the Old and New Testaments as well as extracanonical literature, the word involves a more eschatological nuance and is at times found in contexts referring to such events as the arrival of the day of redemption, the coming of God as king, and the coming of the day of the Lord.[4] Although the MT does not have an equivalent noun for parousia, it does utilize certain verb forms in contexts that are related to the coming of the Lord.[5] The word is found four times in the LXX, none of which refer to the day of the Lord (Judith 10:18; 2 Macc 8:12; 15:21; 3 Macc 3:17). Nevertheless, the concept is certainly evident in passages such as Daniel 7:13, where one like a son of man comes to the Ancient of Days and is given royal authority over all the nations. The importance of this concept is evident in that "Son

---

3. BDAG 780; LSJ 1343; Albrecht Oepke, "παρουσία, πάρειμι," in *TDNT*, 5:858–71; Moisés Silva, "παρουσία," in *NIDNTTE*, 3:647–57.

4. See Oepke, "παρουσία, πάρειμι," 861–62, who provides numerous references.

5. E.g., אתה ('*th*); בוא (*bôʾ*). See also *HALOT* 102, 113; BDB 97.

of Man" was Jesus' favorite self-designation. By referring to himself as the Son of Man, Jesus "ultimately tied that association to the picture of Daniel 7, where a human with transcendent capability comes on the clouds to the Ancient of Days to share in judgment, rule and vindication."[6] In addition, the Pseudepigrapha incorporate parousia twelve times, five of which are in contexts referring to the day of Lord (Apoc. Sedr. 1.0; Testament of Judith 22.2; Apocalypse of Abraham 13.4; 13.6; Liv. Pro. 2.12).[7] The Hebrew verb בּוֹא (bô') is also used in the Dead Sea Scrolls in connection with the final coming of the Lord (1QpZeph; 4Q88 9.4–7; 4Q171).

Paul uses the term parousia fourteen times throughout his writings, always followed by a qualifying word or phrase.[8] Seven of these occurrences are found in contexts related to the final day of the Lord (1 Cor 15:23; 1 Thess 2:19; 3:13; 4:15; 5:23; 2 Thess 2:1; 2:8).[9] Based on the Old Testament's teaching regarding the return of Yahweh, it seems that the apostle employed the term parousia as a locution referring to the final return of the Lord Jesus. In particular, the apostle may have based his understanding of parousia on the Old Testament *theophany* passages.[10] Texts such as Exodus 19:10–18 and Deuteronomy 32:2 illustrate the Lord "coming" down to meet with his people and the events associated with that glorious occasion. Paul may have been drawing on the background of these Old Testament *theophanies* and then "reformulated these traditional images in a creative fashion in order

---

6. Darrell L. Bock, "Son of Man," in *DJG*, 900. See also the discussion in N. T. Wright, *The New Testament and the People of God*, COQG 1 (Minneapolis: Fortress, 1992), 291–300.

7. Apoc. Sedr. was likely written between the second and fifth centuries, and Liv. Pro. sometime in the first century. These documents may have had Christian origins and were perhaps influenced by the New Testament's use of the term. See Craig A. Evans, *Ancient Texts for New Testament Studies: A Guide to the Background Literature* (Peabody, MA: Hendrickson, 2005), 36, 50.

8. Osvaldo D. Vena, *The Parousia and Its Rereadings: The Development of the Eschatological Consciousness in the Writings of the New Testament*, Studies in Biblical Literature 27 (New York: Lang, 2001), 107.

9. Some would dispute Pauline authorship of Ephesians, Colossians, 2 Thessalonians, 1–2 Timothy, and Titus. Nevertheless, the evidence seems to overwhelmingly substantiate the authenticity of these epistles. Consequently, this work assumes these letters to be genuinely Pauline. For helpful discussions on the disputed letters, see the relevant chapters in Luke Timothy Johnson, *The Writings of the New Testament: An Interpretation* (Minneapolis: Fortress, 2010), 255–57; Stanley E. Porter, *The Apostle Paul: His Life, Thought, and Letters* (Grand Rapids: Eerdmans, 2016).

10. See Jacques Dupont, *ΣΥΝ ΧΡΙΣΤΩΙ: L'union avec le Christ Suivant Saint Paul* (Leuven: Desclée de Brouwer, 1952), 73.

to incorporate the features specific to Christ's coming and to Christian hope centered on that coming."[11] Although there are a number of parallels between the *theophany* passages and Paul's writings concerning the day of the Lord, these narratives may not have served as the *only* background for his portrayal of the final coming of Christ.[12] For instance, the pervasiveness of the day(s) of the Lord motif and its various depictions found throughout the entire Old Testament tradition likely influenced Paul's use of parousia in connection with Christ's final return. Additionally, Paul may have also been familiar with the meaning of parousia from Classical Greek, where the word is used as a technical term referring to the arrival or coming of the emperor, a king, or dignitary.[13] The arrival of the emperor or royal official was highly celebrated and characterized by much pomp and circumstance. The coming of the emperor was such a momentous event that coins were often minted commemorating the occasion.[14] When Paul proclaimed that Jesus is Lord and that he was coming again, such a proclamation would have been interpreted as a threat to the emperor. Such threats were viewed as sedition and often led to persecution for the apostle and those associated with him (Acts 17:1–9). But despite the persecutions they experienced, Christians boldly proclaimed the parousia of Christ because they understood that at his final coming the entire world will recognize that Jesus is Lord.

Every believer greatly anticipates the parousia of Christ, for that is their day of vindication. Paul arguably derives his understanding of parousia from the backgrounds of the Old Testament Jewish literature as well as its technical use in Hellenistic Greek as a term delineating the eschatological

---

11. Joseph Plevnik, *Paul and the Parousia: An Exegetical and Theological Investigation* (Peabody, MA: Hendrickson, 1997), 10. See also Vena, *Parousia and Its Rereadings*, 156, who also argues that "the manifestation of the glorified Christ resonated with some of the OT theophanies."

12. See the discussion in Plevnik, *Paul and the Parousia*, 10.

13. See LSJ 1343; W. Harold Mare, "A Study of the New Testament Concept of the Parousia," in *Current Issues in Biblical and Patristic Interpretation: Studies in Honor of Merrill C. Tenney Presented by His Former Students*, ed. Gerald F. Hawthorne (Grand Rapids: Eerdmans, 1975), 336; G. H. R. Horsley and S. R. Llewelyn, *New Documents Illustrating Early Christianity: Greek and Other Inscriptions and Papyri Published 1988–1992* (Grand Rapids: Eerdmans, 1981–2012), 4:168; NIDNTTE 3:647.

14. See Adolf Deissmann, *Light from the Ancient East: The New Testament Illustrated by Recently Discovered Texts of Graeco-Roman World*, trans. Lionel R. M. Strachan (New York: Dorian, 1927), 368–73.

arrival of Christ. In other words, Paul understands parousia as a synonym for the day of the Lord.

ἀποκάλυψις (apokalypsis)

The term ἀποκάλυψις (apokalypsis) usually means "revelation" in the sense of making something known.[15] The noun form, apokalypsis, occurs only three times in the LXX (1 Sam 20:30; Sirach 11:27; 22:22), while the verb form, ἀποκαλύπτω (apokalyptō), is found seventy-nine times. The various meanings of apokalypsis include the act of uncovering something (Gen 18:13), the indecent exposure of individuals (Lev 18:6–19); the receiving of a divine word from the Lord (1 Sam 3:21), and the revealing of something that was previously unknown (Ps 98:2).[16] In addition, both the noun and verb forms are found several times throughout the apocalyptic literature of the Pseudepigrapha in contexts referring to the eschatological judgment and redemption that God will reveal (3 Baruch 4:1–16; 1 En. 38:2–3; 4 Ezra 7:23). The Hebrew equivalent, גָּלָה (gālâ), occurs in the Dead Sea Scrolls also, with the primary meaning of God revealing something that was previously hidden (CD 3.13–14; 1QHᵃ 26.15; 4Q266).

Paul uses apokalypsis throughout his writings with the standard meaning of "to reveal or disclose something previously hidden" (Rom 16:25; Eph 3:5; Phil 3:15). He also uses the term to describe his encounter with the risen Lord on the Damascus road (Gal 1:16) and how he received the gospel directly through the revelation of Jesus Christ (Gal 1:12). However, in specific contexts Paul does incorporate the expression as a reference to the final revelation of Christ and his appearing at the day of the Lord. The noun apokalypsis is found seven times throughout his writings; four occurrences are in contexts related to the second coming of Christ and the eschatological judgment (Rom 2:5; 8:19; 1 Cor 1:7; 2 Thess 1:7). The verb apokalyptō is found thirteen times, three in passages relating to the day of the Lord (Rom 1:18; 8:18; 1 Cor 3:13).[17] Paul's affinity for the Old

---

15. BDAG 112; LSJ 201.

16. See also Plevnik, *Paul and the Parousia*, 41n111; *TLNT* 2:244–50.

17. The term is also found three times in 2 Thess 2:1–8 but is related to the revealing of the "man of lawlessness." However, the overall context of the passage is clearly focused on the events surrounding Jesus' final return, when he will ultimately destroy the man of lawlessness on the day of the Lord.

Testament's portrayal of Yahweh coming to reveal himself to pronounce either judgment or blessing offers insight as to how the apostle used *apokalypsis* in connection with the day of the Lord. In specific contexts Paul describes the final advent of Christ as the day when he will reveal himself in full glory and power. On this day it will be revealed to all that Jesus is Lord and thus has all authority to judge. This final revelation will be a day of calamity for those who rejected Jesus' Lordship, as they are sentenced to eternal punishment, whereas this final day also encompasses a celebration, as those who confessed his Lordship are ushered into eternal paradise.

ἐπιφάνεια (epiphaneia)

Another term related to the day of the Lord is ἐπιφάνεια (*epiphaneia*). This word is a synonym of *apokalypsis* denoting "coming" or "appearing."[18] It occurs twelve times in the LXX, predominantly in contexts describing a manifestation of God (2 Sam 7:23; Amos 5:22; 2 Macc 2:21; 3:24; 5:5; 12:22; 14:15; 15:27; 3 Macc 2:9; 5:8, 51). There are twenty instances of the verb form, ἐπιφαίνω (*epiphainō*), which has the meaning of either "provide illumination" or "make one's presence known."[19] In almost every occurrence the term is used in reference to God favorably making his presence known either to an individual or to a group (Gen 35:7; Num 6:25; Deut 33:2; Ps 118:135 [LXX]; 2 Macc 3:30). There are, however, a few instances where *epiphainō* along with the adjective ἐπιφανής (*epiphanēs*) is used in reference to the day of the Lord, when he appears to judge his people as well as all the nations, who in turn bow down and worship him (Joel 2:11; 3:4 [LXX]; Zeph 2:11; Mal 3:22 [LXX]).[20] The predominant Hebrew rendering of *epiphainō* is the verb אוֹר (*'ôr*), meaning "shine" or "illuminate."[21] Although the semantic domain of this term is extensive, it is frequently used in specific contexts where "light" is a reference to God and salvation, in contrast to "darkness" or impending judgment. This nuance is particularly evident in the prophetic literature, where "imminent judgment

---

18. BDAG 385; LSJ 669; Moisés Silva, "ἐπιφάνεια," in *NIDOTTE*, 4:585–90.

19. BDAG 358.

20. See Plevnik, *Paul and the Parousia*, 43.

21. BDB 21; *HALOT* 24; M. Sæbø, "אוֹר," in *TLOT*, 1:63–66.

transforms the light of salvation into the darkness of approaching catastrophe on the Day of Yahweh (Isa 5:30, 13:10; Amos 5:18, 20, 8:9) . . . [while] on the other hand, the prophetic salvation-eschatology transforms the darkness of distress into the light of dawning salvation (Isa 10:17, 42:16; Mic 7:8–20)."[22]

The term in its various forms occurs sixteen times throughout the Pseudepigrapha. There is only one instance where it is found in a context of final judgment, but this reference is late (Greek Apocalypse of Ezra 3:3).[23] The Hebrew equivalent, 'ôr, is found numerous times throughout the Dead Sea Scrolls. Most of the occurrences use the general meaning of "give light" or "illuminate." The term does not appear to be used directly in reference to the day of the Lord. There are, however, several places throughout 1QM where the word refers to the Sons of Light, who fight against the Sons of Darkness at the final eschatological battle prior to the day of the Lord. But in this context the term is merely used to distinguish those who fight for Yahweh as opposed to those who fight against him (1QM 1.8–10, 14–15).

Paul employs the noun *epiphaneia* six times in his writings, all of which refer to the day of the Lord (2 Thess 2:8; 1 Tim 6:14; 2 Tim 1:10; 4:1, 8; Titus 2:13). He uses the verb *epiphainō* twice, and neither instance refers to the final day. What seems fairly certain is that Paul's familiarity with the LXX likely influenced his use of *epiphaneia*; there the term often describes God manifesting himself in either judgment or salvation. The apostle borrows this meaning from the Old Testament and incorporates *epiphaneia* as a reference to the final coming of Christ. Harold Mare rightly concludes, "There can be no doubt, then, that [Paul] uses the word *epiphaneia* and its cognates for the glorious, visible, physical appearance of Jesus, both at the time of his incarnation and of his Second Advent at the end of the age."[24]

---

22. Sæbø, "אוֹר," 66.

23. For a helpful survey of this issue see Michael E. Stone, "Greek Apocalypse of Ezra," in *The Old Testament Pseudepigrapha*, ed. James H. Charlesworth, AYBRL (New York: Doubleday, 1983), 1:561–70.

24. Mare, "Study of the New Testament Concept of the Parousia," 339. See also Helyer, *Witness of Jesus, Paul, and John*, 42–43.

ADDITIONAL TERMS RELATED TO
THE DAY OF THE LORD IN PAUL

Paul also used various other terms and expressions when communicating about the day of the Lord. Although these terms are not primarily used as a reference to the second advent of Christ, the apostle does incorporate them in certain contexts when discussing the final eschatological day. A few examples include: ἔρχομαι (erchomai), "come" or "arrive" (1 Cor 4:5; 11:26; 2 Thess 2:10); φανερόω (phaneroō), "reveal" or "manifest" (Col 3:4); and τέλος (telos), "end" or "goal" (1 Cor 1:8; 15:24).[25] For Paul these terms connote a future orientation in their specific contexts, and he therefore considers them valid expressions for describing the day of the Lord.

---

25. The term μαράνα θά (marana tha) or μαρὰν ἀθά (maran atha) or μαραναθα (maranatha) could also be included. The term is a Greek transliteration of the Aramaic מָרַן אֲתָא (māran ʾātāʾ). This expression can be rendered either as "our Lord come" or "our Lord has come." The term occurs only once in the Pauline corpus in a context that is not overtly eschatological in nature (1 Cor 16:22). However, see Kreitzer, Jesus and God in Paul's Eschatology, 260, who argues, "Maranatha is a prayer, uttered with a liturgical context, that may call for the future parousia of the Lord. The parallel in Rev 22:20 would support such a conclusion."

6

The Day of the Lord

A THEMATIC SURVEY OF VARIOUS PAULINE TEXTS

As the previous survey demonstrates, Paul had a sizable arsenal of terms and expressions at his disposal related to the concept of the day of the Lord. The nuances of these various expressions not only seem to be conventional for the apostle and his understanding of Christ's final advent but also were familiar to the recipients of his letters, who were likewise well acquainted with the day of the Lord motif and the expressions associated with it. Such a common understanding is due to the fact that Paul primarily borrowed from the language of both the Old Testament and Second Temple literature, where the final coming of God is a prominent theme.

What follows is a *thematic* survey of several Pauline texts relevant to the day of the Lord. The purpose of this discussion is strictly to analyze Paul's perception of the day of the Lord and to explore how this was a major theological motif for the apostle and not merely reserved only for eschatological contexts. In other words, the intent here is to investigate how the concept of the day of the Lord, to some degree, influenced Paul's entire theological purview.

This survey will follow the *chronological* rather than canonical order of Paul's epistles. One reason for such an approach is that "It can be claimed with confidence that the coming again of Christ was a firm part of Paul's theology, *maintained consistently from first to last in our written sources.* Paul's convictions that the parousia was imminent and becoming ever closer also seems to have remained remarkably untroubled by the progress of events and passing of time."[1] In other words, the apostle certainly understood that the day of the Lord *could* happen at any moment, but he does not teach that it *would* happen in

---

1. James D. G. Dunn, *The Theology of Paul the Apostle* (Grand Rapids: Eerdmans, 1998), 313.

his lifetime.[2] Moreover, tracing the theme of the day of the Lord from Paul's earliest to final writings arguably substantiates that his understanding of this doctrine was fully formed because of his conversion on the Damascus road, the teachings of Jesus, and his familiarity with the Old Testament.

THE THESSALONIAN CORRESPONDENCE

First and Second Thessalonians[3] are probably two of the apostle's earliest epistles, written during his second missionary journey, around AD 49–50.[4] According to Acts 17, Paul and Silas arrived in Thessalonica and began to preach the gospel in the local synagogue for at least three Sabbaths. This resulted in many converting to Christianity and the formation of a local church. The residents of Thessalonica, however, took issue with Paul's message that there was "another king named Jesus" and formed a mob to bring charges of sedition against the apostle and those who welcomed him (v. 7).[5] Paul and Silas were then forced to leave Thessalonica because of the ensuing hostility from its citizens. Following their departure, the residents of Thessalonica continued their attempts to discredit the missionaries' character, accusing them of being motivated by greed and personal gain (1 Thess 2:1–12).[6] The city also

---

2. See Johan Christiaan Beker, *Paul's Apocalyptic Gospel: The Coming Triumph of God* (Philadelphia: Fortress, 1982), 51–53; Herman Ridderbos, *Paul: An Outline of His Theology*, trans. John Richard De Witt (Grand Rapids: Eerdmans, 1975), 487–92; Ben Witherington III, *Jesus, Paul, and the End of the World: A Comparative Study in New Testament Eschatology* (Downers Grove, IL: InterVarsity, 1992), 34–35.

3. It is beyond the sphere of this work to discuss the issues surrounding the authorship of 2 Thessalonians. Historically, the consensus has been in favor of the Pauline authorship for the letter. It was primarily during the twentieth century that many began to question the authenticity of the epistle. Nevertheless, the arguments against Pauline authorship have been largely refuted, and therefore the authenticity of 2 Thessalonians is assumed here. For full discussions of this issue see Paul Foster, "Who Wrote 2 Thessalonians? A Fresh Look at an Old Problem," *JSNT* 35 (2012): 150–75; Abraham J. Malherbe, *The Letters to the Thessalonians: A New Translation with Introduction and Commentary*, AB 32B (New York: Doubleday, 2000), 364–74; Jeffrey A. D. Weima, *1–2 Thessalonians*, BECNT (Grand Rapids: Baker, 2014), 46–54.

4. See, for instance, the discussions in Gordon D. Fee, *The First and Second Letters to the Thessalonians*, NICNT (Grand Rapids: Eerdmans, 2009), 3–5, 237–41; Gary Steven Shogren, *1 and 2 Thessalonians*, ZECNT (Grand Rapids: Zondervan, 2012), 29–30.

5. For a discussion on the severity of this accusation see Matthew D. Aernie, *Forensic Language and the Day of the Lord Motif in 2 Thessalonians 1 and the Effects on the Meaning of the Text*, West Theological Monographs Series (Eugene, OR: Wipf & Stock, 2011), 56–66; Edwin A. Judge, "The Decrees of Caesar at Thessalonica," *RTR* 30 (1971): 1–7.

6. See Todd D. Still, *Conflict at Thessalonica: A Pauline Church and Its Neighbours*, JSNTSup 183 (Sheffield: Sheffield Academic Press, 1999), 137–49.

concentrated its anger toward the Christians, severely persecuting the newly formed congregation (1 Thess 1:6; 2:14; 3:3; 2 Thess 1:4, 6–7).

The combination of these circumstances—Paul's forced departure, the defamation of his character, and the intense persecution the Thessalonian believers were suffering—seemingly led to the occasion for the writing of these epistles. As the Thessalonians faithfully lived out the gospel in the midst of great affliction, some concerns surrounding the parousia inevitably arose amid the congregation that the apostle needed to address. Consequently, the Thessalonian letters offer some of the most detailed accounts of the day of the Lord motif found in the Pauline corpus. Todd Still has observed, "One should note that eschatology is nowhere far from the fore of Paul's mind in these—and (most) all of his other—epistles."[7] For instance, in 1 Thessalonians the church was troubled because they wondered whether fellow Christians who had died would miss the parousia. Why the congregation struggled with this issue is speculative, since it appears they were well acquainted with that doctrine (1 Thess 5:2). Nevertheless, "Paul's immediate desire [was] to allay his converts' fear that the dead in Christ will miss out on or be disadvantaged at the parousia."[8] The apostle exhorts the Thessalonian church not to grieve and reminds them that just as Christ rose from the dead so also the Christians who had died will rise again and accompany the Lord at his parousia (1 Thess 4:14). Likewise, in 2 Thessalonians the church had somehow become deceived by a false claim that the day of the Lord had come. Paul offers both correction and encouragement by reminding the Thessalonians not to be shaken from their composure, for the day of the Lord had not yet arrived, for certain events had to occur before the eschatological day could arrive, and therefore they must remain steadfast in their faith despite their circumstances (2 Thess 2:3).[9] With Paul's reminder that the

---

7. Todd D. Still, "Eschatology in the Thessalonian Letters," *RevExp* 96 (1999): 195.

8. Ibid., 197. See also Richard S. Ascough, "A Question of Death: Paul's Community Building Language in 1 Thessalonians 4:13–18," *JBL* 123 (2004): 520–23; Raymond F. Collins, "Παρουσία to Ἐπιφάνεια: The Transformation of a Pauline Motif," in *Unity and Diversity in the Gospels and Paul: Essays in Honor of Frank J. Matera*, ed. Christopher W. Skinner and Kelly R. Iverson (Atlanta: Society of Biblical Literature, 2012), 273–99.

9. For helpful discussions regarding the nature of the false claim and why it was so alarming for the Thessalonians, see John M. G. Barclay, "Conflict at Thessalonica," *CBQ* 55 (1993): 527–29; F. F. Bruce, *1 & 2 Thessalonians*, WBC 45 (Waco, TX: Word Books, 1982), 163, 75; Charles A. Wanamaker, *The Epistles to the Thessalonians: A Commentary on the Greek Text*, NIGTC (Grand Rapids: Eerdmans, 1990), 237–41.

day of the Lord had not yet occurred, the Thessalonians were encouraged to continue advancing the gospel, fully assured that their ultimate justification was still to come when Christ would return to sentence the persecutors to condemnation and to exonerate the church.

The following discussion seeks to survey a few texts within the Thessalonian correspondence to further delineate the significance of the day of the Lord theme in Paul's entire theological framework.

FIRST THESSALONIANS 1:9–10

First Thessalonians 1:2–10 functions as the opening thanksgiving to the letter. The contents of the thanksgiving set the stage for what Paul will address throughout the remainder of the epistle. In general, scholars consider verses 2–10 as comprising the following outline.[10] First, Paul and Silas offer thanksgiving specifically to God (v. 2a). Second is the manner in which their thanksgiving is offered, namely through their constant prayers of thanks to God for the church (v. 2b). Third, their ultimate cause for thanksgiving was God's love and choosing the Thessalonians, which was made evident in the church's proper reception of the gospel, their welcoming of the apostles, and their godly example to other congregations (vv. 3–8). Finally, Paul and Silas offer thanksgiving to God because the Thessalonians eagerly awaited the return of the Lord. Throughout this entire section, Paul and Silas direct all of their thanksgiving to God, for he alone has accomplished these realities for the Thessalonians.

Paul concludes in verses 9–10 by offering additional thanks to God for the Thessalonians' conversion. Moreover, it seems feasible to argue that the subject matter of these two verses is driving the remainder of the letter and the apostle's discussion regarding the day of the Lord. Indeed, the topics found in 1:9–10, such as "conversion, dualism between idols and God, waiting, resurrection, deliverance and *orgē* contribute to a characteristic eschatological discourse in the letter (Paul returns to many of these motifs). . . . This discourse [arguably] plays a fundamental role in his purposes for writing."[11]

---

10. What follows is primarily adopted from Weima, *1–2 Thessalonians*, 80. But see also Gene L. Green, *The Letters to the Thessalonians*, PNTC (Grand Rapids: Eerdmans, 2002), 86–87; Shogren, *1 and 2 Thessalonians*, 54; Wanamaker, *Epistles to the Thessalonians*, 73.

11. David Luckensmeyer, *The Eschatology of First Thessalonians*, Novum Testamentum et Orbis Antiquus, Studien zur Umwelt des Neuen Testaments 71 (Göttingen: Vandenhoeck & Ruprecht, 2009), 75.

Consequently, it could be inferred that 1:9–10 serves as the outline for the entire letter.[12]

Paul delineates two additional reasons in verses 9–10 that have prompted his thanksgiving.[13] First, the believers in Macedonia and Achaia were reporting concerning *us* the kind of "entrance" *we* had among you. Initially, this may appear strange, since the apostle's focus in the preceding verses has been on the Thessalonians, whereas at the beginning of verse 9 he abruptly shifts his focus to himself and Silas but then returns his focus back to the Thessalonians in verses 9b–10.[14] Further compounding the alleged difficulty of verse 9a is the translation of the term εἴσοδον (*eisodon*) as "reception."[15] Several English translations give the impression that in verse 9a Paul is referring to the kind of reception the *Thessalonians* gave himself and his coworkers. However, the term *eisodon* does not here refer to reception but rather "entrance" or "visit."[16] Consequently, the intent in verse 9a then seems to be for Paul to defend his motivation for visiting the Thessalonians and his conduct among them. Although the citizens of Thessalonica ardently slandered Paul and Silas, the apostle thanks God that the Thessalonian believers repudiated the attacks leveled on the missionaries' character and welcomed them and their message.

Second, Paul thanks God for the Thessalonians' conversion, evident by the fact that they "turned to God from idols."[17] He then further expounds on the goal or result of their conversion with two infinitival clauses.[18] The first clause, δουλεύειν θεῷ ζῶντι καὶ ἀληθινῷ (*douleuein theō zōnti kai alēthinō*), "to serve the living and true God," focuses on the ethics of their salvation, namely that the Thessalonians are "to serve the living and true God" (v. 9b).

---

12. Ibid., 77. See also Earl Richard, *First and Second Thessalonians*, SP 11 (Collegeville, MN: Liturgical, 1995), 75.

13. The explanatory γάρ (*gar*) at the beginning of v. 9 indicates that Paul's intention was to expound on his comments from v. 8.

14. Some manuscripts attempt to alleviate this alleged awkwardness by replacing the pronoun ἡμῶν (*hēmōn*), "our," with ὑμῶν (*hymōn*), "you."

15. See, for example, ESV, NIV, HCSB, NASB.

16. BDAG 294; *NIDNTTE* 3:451–60; Wilhelm Michaelis, "εἴσοδος, ἔξοδος, διέξοδος," in *TDNT*, 103–9.

17. The verb ἐπιστρέφω (*epistrephō*), "turned," is used thirty-six times in the NT, and nearly half of these occurrences refer to spiritual conversion. Similar usage of the term is found throughout the LXX as well the MT, where the Hebrew rendering is typically שׁוּב (*šûb*). *NIDNTTE* 4:386 observes that שׁוּב is used in over one hundred instances as a reference to spiritual conversion.

18. See Luckensmeyer, *Eschatology of First Thessalonians*, 89n88.

The result of their conversion was a complete shift of not only *how* they lived but also *whom* they lived for. The second infinitival clause, ἀναμένειν τὸν υἱὸν αὐτοῦ ἐκ τῶν οὐρανῶν (*anamenein ton huion autou ek tōn ouranōn*), "to wait for his Son from the heavens," emphasizes that a further result of their conversion is that the Thessalonians now have a future hope.[19] This hope, Paul explains, is found only in Jesus, the one whom God raised from the dead and who is our deliverer from the coming wrath. This is the first explicit mention of the day of the Lord motif in the epistle and lays the foundation for the remainder of the apostle's instructions and exhortations, particularly in 4:13–18 and 5:1–11. However, Paul's intent in verses 9–10 seems to be that "the coming [wrath] makes *imperative* a certain holiness/ sanctification in the present, so that one remains blameless at the parousia of Jesus."[20] In other words, Paul understands that the day of the Lord has tremendous ethical implications. The Thessalonians' conversion afforded them the assurance that despite living in a hostile environment they could be encouraged to live worthily of the gospel as they awaited their vindication at the final day. There is a real sense in this context and the letters as a whole that from Paul's perspective the future day of the Lord impacts the present and thus guides the church's orientation for living.[21]

FIRST THESSALONIANS 4:13–5:11

In 4:1–12 Paul praises the Thessalonians because they are genuinely living holy lives even to the extent that the church's godly behavior has influenced other congregations throughout the province of Macedonia (4:10). The apostle mentions a litany of Christian behaviors that he encourages the Thessalonians to continue practicing all the more, such as abstaining from sexual immorality, demonstrating love for fellow believers, and living respectable lives so as not to offend outsiders. After admonishing them to continue in these holy pursuits, Paul begins to address some concerns the Thessalonians had regarding the day of the Lord.

In general, Paul deals with two issues in 4:13–5:11 regarding the day of the Lord. First, in 4:13–18 Paul addresses the grief that the Thessalonian

---

19. See also Weima, *1–2 Thessalonians*, 111–12, who offers helpful comments on this clause.

20. Luckensmeyer, *Eschatology of First Thessalonians*, 105n90, emphasis original.

21. See Frank J. Matera, *New Testament Theology: Exploring Diversity and Unity* (Louisville, KY: Westminster John Knox, 2007), 109–10.

congregation has regarding fellow believers who had died before the day of the Lord had come.[22] The Thessalonian church was likely concerned that their fellow Christians who had died before the parousia were at some sort of disadvantage in comparison with those living at the day of the Lord. Paul reassures the Thessalonians that their departed loved ones have only "fallen asleep"[23] and that just as God raised Jesus from the dead he will likewise raise them. Not only will deceased Christians participate in the day of the Lord, but they will actually be raised *before* those who are alive at Christ's final coming. Paul goes on to describe the parousia in verses 14–16 with imagery borrowed from the Old Testament, intertestamental literature, and Jesus' teaching associated with the day of the Lord in order to further encourage the grieving Thessalonian congregation. For example, Paul's reference to Jesus as Lord[24] in verse 16 demonstrates that he understood Jesus to be equal with God. This is further substantiated by Paul's mention in verse 14 of how God "will bring with him those who have fallen asleep," and then immediately in verse 16 he attributes that role to the Lord Jesus and his second coming. In other words, "It is not surprising to find the title [Lord] in close association with traditions of resurrection, exaltation, and parousia. . . . Thus, if by Jesus' resurrection he is considered *Kyrios* then exaltation is confirmation of that lordship. Further, Jesus as *Kyrios* at his parousia emphasizes his role as eschatological agent, exercising God's authority."[25] Additionally, the imagery of the command is likely drawing on multiple influences, such as the Old Testament theophanies as well as the first-century political arena. In the theophany traditions, God's command demonstrates his sovereign authority over the universe, nature, spirits, his enemies, and all humanity.[26] In the political realm the command imagery often referred to an imperial edict or decree coming from the emperor, and thus it may be that Paul purposefully used this imagery because it communicated to the Roman world

---

22. Why the church grieved over this issue is difficult to determine, since Paul seems to have provided instruction about the Lord's return while he was among them (1 Thess 5:2). For helpful surveys of the numerous theories related to this issue see, for example, Luckensmeyer, *Eschatology of First Thessalonians*, 194–211; Wanamaker, *Epistles to the Thessalonians*, 165–66; Weima, *1–2 Thessalonians*, 310–13.

23. Paul always uses the verb κοιμάω (koimaō), "sleep," as a euphemism for death.

24. The intensive pronoun αὐτός (autos), "himself," stresses that the Lord is Jesus.

25. Luckensmeyer, *Eschatology of First Thessalonians*, 238.

26. Plevnik, *Paul and the Parousia*, 84.

that only the Lord Jesus was vested with full authority to pronounce the final edict, which all will be forced to obey.[27] The remaining imagery in verse 16 of the archangel, the trumpet of God, and the rising of the dead is also likely influenced from the day of the Lord tradition evident throughout the Old Testament, extracanonical literature, and the teachings of Jesus.[28] Paul's intent in 4:13–18 is to remind the church not to grieve over the loss of their loved ones for those who have "fallen asleep" actually have an advantage over those who remain because the Lord Jesus will raise them first. The Thessalonian congregation can be encouraged knowing that deceased believers "would see the light of immortality first."[29]

The second issue Paul addresses is the timing of the Lord's return (5:1–11). For whatever reason, the Thessalonian congregation was concerned about the timing of the day of the Lord. Essentially the Thessalonians wanted to know when the day of the Lord would come. Paul deals briefly with this concern because they have already received adequate instruction regarding this topic (vv. 1–3). He employs a variety of allusions from the Old Testament and Jesus' teaching to remind the church that the day of the Lord could arrive at any moment (vv. 1–3). For instance, the description that the day of the Lord will come "as a thief in the night" is an echo from the teaching of Jesus where he emphasizes the unpredictability of the final eschatological day and the need for believers to be prepared for its arrival (Matt 24:42–44; Luke 12:39).[30] The reference in verse 3a of people declaring "peace and security" is likely derived from the Old Testament prophetic literature where the false prophets were deceiving the people declaring that there were "peace and security" in the land when in reality judgment was imminent (Jer 6:13–14; Ezek 13:1–16). The imagery of "labor pains" in verse 3b is also a motif found in the Old Testament and the teachings of Jesus, used to describe suffering and calamity associated with judgment on this final day (Jer 4:31; Hos 13:13; Mark 13:8). However, Paul's intention in

27. See Luckensmeyer, *Eschatology of First Thessalonians*, 239–40.

28. See, for example, Seyoon Kim, "The Jesus Tradition in 1 Thess 4:13–5:11," *NTS* 48 (2002): 225–42; J. Julius Scott, "Paul and Late-Jewish Eschatology: A Case Study of 1 Thess 4:13–18 and 2 Thess 2:1–12," *JETS* 15 (1972): 133–40; Murray J. Smith, "The Thessalonian Correspondence," in *All Things to All Cultures: Paul among Jews, Greeks, and Romans*, ed. Mark Harding and Alanna Nobbs (Grand Rapids: Eerdmans, 2013), 289–98; C. Henry Waterman, "The Sources of Paul's Teaching on the 2nd Coming of Christ in 1 and 2 Thessalonians," *JETS* 18 (1975): 105–13.

29. Vena, *Parousia and Its Rereadings*, 119.

30. This metaphor is also used by other NT authors (2 Pet 3:10; Rev 3:3; 16:15).

verses 1–3 is not to inform the Thessalonians as to *when* the day of the Lord will occur but rather to remind them that the day will come unexpectedly and will utterly shock those who are unprepared.[31]

Having reminded the Thessalonians about the suddenness of the day of the Lord, Paul focuses his attention on the ethical implications this has for these persecuted believers. In his typical pastoral fashion, the apostle exhorts the Thessalonian congregation to continue living in a state of preparedness (vv. 4–10). He employs several metaphors to encourage this church to remain steadfast in righteous living as they anticipate the day of the Lord. As David Luckensmeyer has observed, Paul utilizes several sets of rhetorical pairs intended to exhort the Thessalonians to remain steadfast. These pairs include day/night, light/darkness, awake/sleep, sober/drunk, and salvation/wrath.[32] These metaphors remind these believers of the distinction between themselves and their persecutors. God had chosen the Thessalonians, and this is evident in their perseverance and moral living as they await their vindication at the day of the Lord. In contrast, those who are outside Christ are unaware of the coming judgment and are destined only for wrath. Paul's description of unbelievers as "of the darkness, sleeping, and getting drunk" is used to highlight their manner of life, depicting not only their hostility toward Christ but that they are oblivious to their impending judgment. Furthermore, Paul borrows from Isaiah 59:17 with his allusion to the armor that the Thessalonians have put on (v. 8). This reminder serves to further encourage the congregation to continue faithful and righteous living for the sake of the gospel, knowing that the battle has already been won. Having been endowed with this divine armor, the Thessalonians can be encouraged to persevere until the day of the Lord.[33] Thus Paul's point in verses 4–11 is to offer a moral exhortation to the Thessalonians that the church must continue to spur one another on to moral living as they anticipate the day of the Lord. Garland Young offers a helpful summary of 5:1–11 when he writes, "For Paul, eschatology and ethics were partners which required and implied each other. . . . The imminence of Christ's return required upright, moral living. Yet those

---

31. Still, "Eschatology in the Thessalonian Letters," 199.

32. Luckensmeyer, *Eschatology of First Thessalonians*, 295.

33. R. Garland Young, "The Times and the Seasons: 1 Thessalonians 4:13–5:11," *RevExp* 96 (1999): 272.

who do live uprightly . . . are to live their lives totally under the influence of the parousia of Christ."[34]

SECOND THESSALONIANS

The second letter to the Thessalonians further displays Paul's pastoral concern for this persecuted church and their concerns surrounding the day of the Lord. In 1 Thessalonians Paul wanted to relieve the angst the congregation had regarding deceased Christians and their participation at the day of the Lord. He reminds the church that those who are "asleep" actually have an advantage at Christ's parousia, for they will be resurrected first. Furthermore, Paul reminds the church about the timing of the day of the Lord. The Thessalonians are encouraged to continue living moral and upright lives in preparation for the day of the Lord.

In 2 Thessalonians the apostle continues to address further concerns the congregation had regarding the day of the Lord. In typical pastoral fashion, Paul arguably composes this letter as a means to encourage this persecuted church to persevere amid difficult circumstances until the day of the Lord arrives. In general, Paul provides encouragement for the Thessalonians in two ways. First, he reminds them that the day of the Lord is their day of ultimate vindication. When the Lord Jesus returns on this final day, he will render his righteous verdicts on those who have both obeyed and disobeyed him (1:3–12). Paul utilizes several forensic terms and allusions throughout chapter 1 to emphasize that the day of the Lord is a judicial day.[35] More specifically, the day of the Lord is the day when all will stand before God's eschatological tribunal and receive their just recompense. Paul's understanding of the judicial nature of the final day is likely based on numerous intertextual parallels originating primarily from the Old Testament and extrabiblical literature, where the day of the Lord motif is often described as a forensic concept.[36] "Much like the prophets in the Old Testament who referred to the Day of Yahweh in a judicial sense, Paul seemingly understood the parousia of Jesus to be a direct parallel. . . . The

---

34. Ibid., 273.

35. For a thorough discussion of the forensic language in 2 Thess 1 see Aernie, *Forensic Language*, 69–115, who examines twelve judicial terms and idioms evident throughout the context of 2 Thess 1.

36. See the discussions in chaps. 2 and 3.

judicial language in 2 Thess 1 served to emphasize that Christ's return will be the eschatological Day of the Lord where, as the righteous Judge, he will render the final verdict."[37] The Thessalonians can be encouraged, for their vindication will come on the day of the Lord, when God vindicates them in the presence of their enemies. The believers can take heart knowing that justice will come and they will be found not guilty at the final assize.

Second, Paul encourages the Thessalonians by reminding them that the day of the Lord has not yet occurred. Some of the members have apparently been deceived into thinking that they have missed the day of the Lord (2:1–17). The apostle is uncertain as to how this false claim infiltrated the church (2:2), but he recognizes that such a claim has caused the church to become σαλεύω (saleuō), "frightened," and θροέω (throeō), "disturbed." These two verbs are often used in contexts describing tremendous fear and terror.[38] Paul's concern, therefore, is not that the Thessalonians are overzealous about the day of the Lord but rather that this false claim is causing tremendous angst for this suffering church. Being under the duress of constant persecution combined with the false claim that the day of the Lord has already occurred has seemingly left many in the congregation terrified as they wonder whether they have actually missed their vindication. In other words, "the idea that the Day of the Lord had come, literally understood, would naturally have been received by 'the Thessalonians' as bad news, undermining the essence of their Christian hope for judgment, both reward and vengeance."[39] Paul needed to quiet the fears of the congregation and reassure them that the day of the Lord had not yet happened. He does this by explicating the judicial nature of the day, reminding the Thessalonian believers that at God's final court they will be vindicated and their enemies will be punished, as well as reminding them that certain events must first take place before the day of the Lord will commence. When the final day does arrive, Christ will destroy those who oppose him and will set all things right.

---

37. Aernie, *Forensic Language*, 180.

38. For an excellent semantic analysis of these terms see Colin R. Nicholl, *From Hope to Despair in Thessalonica: Situating 1 and 2 Thessalonians*, SNTSMS 126 (Cambridge: Cambridge University Press, 2004), 126–32.

39. Ibid., 131. See also Glenn Stanfield Holland, "The Tradition That You Received from Us: 2 Thessalonians in the Pauline Tradition" (PhD diss., University of Chicago Divinity School, 1988), 68–69; Maarten J. J. Menken, *2 Thessalonians*, New Testament Readings (London: Routledge, 1994), 96–101.

Paul concludes the epistle admonishing the church about the ethical implications that coalesce with the reality that the day of the Lord is still to come. Being under the duress of persecution and believing that they have missed the day of the Lord have apparently led some in the congregation to become lackadaisical and to begin to live undisciplined lives (3:7–8). Many have stopped working and grown idle "because they believed that if the Day of the Lord had already occurred then their daily responsibilities would be futile."[40] However, Paul exhorts the Thessalonians to follow the example of him and his companions, who worked diligently while they were with them. Therefore, since the final day is yet to occur, the Thessalonians are urged to continue living in a manner worthy of the gospel in the midst of a hostile environment, being fully assured that their ultimate vindication is still to come on the day of the Lord, when all will appear before God's eschatological tribunal.

In general, then, it seems that the overall purpose for the Thessalonian correspondence was to encourage the persecuted congregation to remain steadfast in their faith as they waited for the return of the Lord, for on that consummate day, both those who have fallen asleep as well as those who remain will gain their ultimate vindication.

The day of the Lord is the overarching theme throughout the Thessalonian epistles. This is evident by the fact that Paul refers to this topic numerous times throughout both letters (1 Thess 1:10; 2:19; 3:13; 4:6, 13–18; 5:1–11, 23; 2 Thess 1:6–10; 2:1–12, 14). Such frequency lends itself to the conclusion that the day of the Lord is the hermeneutical key to these epistles.[41] The Thessalonian correspondence demonstrates how the day of the Lord motif greatly affects Paul's theological framework. The apostle reminds the Thessalonian congregation that Christian living must be carried out in view of the day of the Lord. The letters reveal how the

---

40. Aernie, *Forensic Language*, 170–71. See also Ronald Russell, "The Idle in 2 Thess 3:6–12: An Eschatological or a Social Problem?," *NTS* 34 (1988): 105–19; B. N. Kaye, "Eschatology and Ethics in 1 and 2 Thessalonians," *NovT* 17 (1975): 47–57; Judy Skeen, "Not as Enemies, but Kin: Discipline in the Family of God; 2 Thessalonians 3:6–12," *RevExp* 96 (1999): 287–94. Bruce W. Winter, "'If a Man Does Not Wish to Work . . .' A Cultural and Historical Setting for 2 Thessalonians 3:6–16," *TynBul* 40 (1989): 303–15, offers helpful discussions as to why some in the Thessalonian church were living undisciplined and idle lives.

41. See Luckensmeyer, *Eschatology of First Thessalonians*, who offers exhaustive support for this claim. Although his study focuses only on 1 Thessalonians, it seems more than reasonable to understand 2 Thessalonians in the same manner, particularly because of the overwhelming eschatological nature of the epistle.

imminent arrival of the Lord calls the church to holy and disciplined living, encouraging one another as they await their vindication on that final day. Paul also focuses on the judicial aspect of the day of the Lord in order to encourage the Thessalonians. The congregation can be assured that they have not missed the day of the Lord and that justice will ultimately be served. The Thessalonians can therefore rejoice, for at God's final court they will receive their ultimate justification while their enemies are sentenced to eternal destruction (2 Thess 1:9). It seems reasonable, then, to conclude that within the Thessalonian epistles Paul intentionally "highlights the centrality of the Day of the Lord in both and the importance of ethical living in the light of this coming day. Thus, ethics, the wrath of God and the future all received vital treatment, just as they do in the Old Testament and Gospel passages."[42]

THE CORINTHIAN CORRESPONDENCE

A cursory reading of these letters quickly reveals that the church in Corinth struggled with a litany of problems. In 1 Corinthians the primary issue seems to be that dissensions and quarrels were prevalent within the church (1:10–17). Paul was informed "by Chloe's household"[43] about such factions and composed 1 Corinthians to address those issues. The intent of 2 Corinthians is much more debated. Traditionally, scholars have believed that the epistle focuses on Paul's defense of his apostolic ministry. It is argued that certain opponents within the church were maligning Paul's ministry, which therefore necessitated a response from the apostle, who in turn offers a defense for the legitimacy of his new covenant ministry.[44]

---

42. House, "Day of the Lord," 215. House offers a helpful summary of the significance of the day of the Lord motif in the Thessalonian epistles (ibid., 218–19).

43. The phrase ὑπὸ τῶν Χλόης (hypo tōn Chloēs), lit. "by those of Chloe," could refer to those in her household or to business associates whom she employed. Although certainty is elusive, Gerd Theissen, The Social Setting of Pauline Christianity: Essays on Corinth (Philadelphia: Fortress, 1982), 57, observes that "members of a family would have used their father's name, even if he were deceased." Thus it seems most reasonable that the phrase is a reference to either slaves or employees of Chloe who traveled between Ephesus and Corinth on her behalf and were likely members of the church in Ephesus. See also Roy E. Ciampa and Brian S. Rosner, The First Letter to the Corinthians, PNTC (Grand Rapids: Eerdmans, 2010), 77; Gordon D. Fee, The First Epistle to the Corinthians, NICNT (Grand Rapids: Eerdmans, 2014), 55; David E. Garland, 1 Corinthians, BECNT (Grand Rapids: Baker, 2003), 43–44; Anthony C. Thiselton, The First Epistle to the Corinthians: A Commentary on the Greek Text, NIGTC (Grand Rapids: Eerdmans, 2000), 121.

44. See, for example, Paul Barnett, The Second Epistle to the Corinthians, NICNT (Grand Rapids: Eerdmans, 1997), 33–40; George H. Guthrie, 2 Corinthians, BECNT (Grand Rapids: Baker,

Recent studies, however, contend that Paul's defense was grounded in his "apostolic self-understanding and not simply in response to the historical situation at Corinth."[45] Despite these differing perspectives, it is clear that the continual struggles within the Corinthian church demanded Paul's attention.

As Paul dealt with the various circumstances within the Corinthian church, he oftentimes approached their issues from an eschatological perspective. Regarding 1 Corinthians Gordon Fee writes, "As much as in any of his writings, the essentially eschatological framework of Paul's theological thinking stands out in bold relief in this letter."[46] There are several instances throughout the Corinthian correspondence demonstrating that the day of the Lord motif served as a prominent theological framework for the apostle as he admonished this church. A brief sampling of a few texts will continue to demonstrate how the day of the Lord ties in directly with all of Paul's theology.

FIRST CORINTHIANS 1:4–9

Paul begins the epistle with a thanksgiving prayer to God for what he has and will continue to accomplish among the Corinthians. Although it is typical for Paul to open his letters with a prayer, it seems that one reason he does so here is to prepare them for his austere comments that are to follow. The prayer reminds the Corinthians that Paul *does* consider them to be fellow believers and that he cares for them deeply despite the fact that he must offer some stern comments regarding the troubles the congregation is experiencing.

The apostle offers thanks to God for the grace he has bestowed on the Corinthians and how he has enriched them with every spiritual gift as they

---

2015), 41–50; Murray J. Harris, *The Second Epistle to the Corinthians: A Commentary on the Greek Text*, NIGTC (Grand Rapids: Eerdmans, 2004), 67–87; Mark A. Seifrid, *The Second Letter to the Corinthians*, PNTC (Grand Rapids: Eerdmans, 2014), xxviii–xxix.

45. Jeffrey W. Aernie, *Is Paul Also among the Prophets? An Examination of the Relationship between Paul and the Old Testament Prophetic Tradition in 2 Corinthians*, LNTS 467 (London: T&T Clark, 2012), 114. For further discussion see Timothy B. Savage, *Power through Weakness: Paul's Understanding of the Christian Ministry in 2 Corinthians*, ed. Margaret E. Thrall, SNTSMS 86 (Cambridge: Cambridge University Press, 1996), 3–12.

46. Fee, *First Epistle to the Corinthians*, 17. This same sentiment could arguably be applied to 2 Corinthians also; see, for example, Stephan Joubert, "Paul's Apocalyptic Eschatology in 2 Corinthians," in *Eschatology of the New Testament and Some Related Documents*, ed. Jan G. van der Watt, WUNT (Tübingen: Mohr Siebeck, 2011), 225–38.

eagerly wait for the revelation of our Lord Jesus Christ. Paul's purpose for connecting the Corinthians' reception of every spiritual gift with the fact that they are eagerly waiting for the return of Christ is likely to empha- size that they have not yet arrived, for the consummate day is still to come. Since the Corinthians are still waiting for the day of the Lord, they should not abuse their spiritual gifts but should ardently behave in a manner that edifies others and promotes unity, for at the parousia the gifts will cease. In verse 8 Paul continues this theme of Christian character as he reminds the Corinthians that God is the one who sustains them until the end, ensuring that the Corinthians will be blameless as they stand before the Lord Jesus on that final day. Being blameless on the day of the Lord Jesus is a legal metaphor that reminds the Corinthians that they will be found innocent when they appear at the eschatological court. For Paul, the term ἀνέγκλητος (anenklētos), "blameless," often has a judicial flavor, emphasizing that "no accusation can be brought against them"[47] when they stand before the final Judge. Furthermore, the phrase ἐν τῇ ἡμέρᾳ οὗ κυρίου ἡμῶν Ἰησοῦ Χριστοῦ (en tē hēmera ou kyriou hēmōn Iēsou Christou), "in the day of our Lord Jesus Christ," is one of Paul's favorite idiomatic expressions, derived from the Old Testament and referring to the great assize, which is both a day of judgment and a day of redemption.

Not only does Paul's opening prayer in 1 Corinthians 1:4–9 consist of great theological truths about God and what he has done in and among the Corinthian church, but the content of this prayer serves as the launch pad for what the apostle will address throughout the remainder of the letter. Furthermore, this brief prayer continues to showcase how the day of the Lord motif greatly affected Paul's theology in at least two ways. First, the apostle emphasizes that the day of the Lord greatly affects how Christians ought to live. More specifically, it is evident that Paul is not just primar- ily focused on how the eschatological day affects Christian ethics in gen- eral, but rather he seems to stress that the day of the Lord is *relational*. In other words, it seems that one of the characteristic traits of the day of the Lord that Paul repeatedly stresses throughout the letter is that being in Christ radically impacts all the relationships within the new-covenant

---

47. Walter Grundmann, "ἀνέγκλητος," in *TDNT*, 1:357. See also BDAG 76; L&N 2:438; *NIDNTTE* 1:293.

community.[48] This communal nature of the day of the Lord is evident in how Paul corrects and instructs the Corinthian congregation. He is concerned how the Corinthian church is living in community within itself and how their behavior is impacting the culture. Second, Paul understands that the day of the Lord is a judicial day. The forensic nature of the day of the Lord is made evident in the fact that God has justified the Corinthians in Christ and that because of their right standing with him they will be found blameless on that final court day.[49] Even though many in the Corinthian church are struggling with numerous issues, Paul reminds them in his opening prayer that at the day of the Lord they will be found not guilty.

FIRST CORINTHIANS 5:1-13

A further example of how the day of the Lord motif functions as one of the primary components for Paul's theological framework is 1 Corinthians 5:1-13. In this passage the apostle chastises the congregation for allowing one of its members to be engaged in an incestuous relationship with his stepmother.[50] While such behavior is even deplorable among pagans (v. 1), the overarching problem for Paul is that the church did not mourn over this situation but actually took pride in it (v. 2).[51] Consequently, Paul admonishes *the congregation* to carry out appropriate discipline against this man by literally "turning such a one over to Satan for the destruction of the flesh, in order that the spirit may be saved in the Day of the Lord"

48. See, for example, David Emory Lanier, "The Day of the Lord in the New Testament: A Historical and Exegetical Analysis of Its Background and Usage" (PhD diss., Southwestern Baptist Theological Seminary, 1988), 224n3, who observes, "One finds many times in the New Testament that mention of the Day of the Lord, or the last judgment, often serves as a platform from which to launch an ethical exhortation to moral purity in holiness, even though the actual mention of the judgment may not be elaborate."

49. See also Ciampa and Rosner, *First Letter to the Corinthians*, 66-67; Richard Oster, *1 Corinthians*, College Press NIV Commentary (Joplin, MO: College Press, 1995), 48.

50. The phrase γυναῖκά τινα τοῦ πατρὸς ἔχειν (*gynaika tina tou patros echein*), "has his father's wife," is a euphemism referring to an ongoing sexually immoral relationship between the two individuals. This phrase is borrowed from Lev 18:7-8, where a clear distinction is made between a son's biological mother (v. 7) and "his father's wife" (v. 8). The phrase "his father's wife" emphasizes that a son is prohibited from fornicating with any woman connected with his father by marriage. See Craig Steven De Vos, "Stepmothers, Concubines, and the Case of Πορνεία in 1 Corinthians 5," *NTS* 44 (1998): 104-14.

51. See Bruce W. Winter, *After Paul Left Corinth: The Influence of Secular Ethics and Social Change* (Grand Rapids: Eerdmans, 2001), 44-57, who argues that the reason the congregation was prideful was possibly due to the son's elite social status.

(v. 5).[52] Turning the man over to Satan in all likelihood means casting him out into the *realm* of Satan. In other words, Paul wants the Corinthians to remove this man from the church, which represents a sphere of holiness, and place him outside in the world, which represents the realm of Satan. The purpose of this excommunication is for the "destruction of the flesh." The term "destruction" in all probability does *not* refer to the man's physical death, since Paul clearly states that his desire is for the individual to be saved. The term "destruction" is likely metaphorical and is similar to Paul's teaching that believers are not to live according to the flesh but rather are to put to death the deeds of the body (Gal 5:24; Rom 8:13; Col 3:5). Therefore, the destruction of the flesh is intended to be *remedial*, with the ultimate goal of the incestuous man's salvation in the day of the Lord.

Paul's mention of the day of the Lord in verse 5 reminds the Corinthians of two important realities. First, that the incestuous man's situation is not hopeless, but it is critical. The apostle reminds the Corinthians that anyone who persists in sexual sin will not inherit the kingdom of God (6:9–11). Thus the purpose of expelling this individual is for his own benefit; it is to spur him on to repentance. Paul likely derived his understanding of expelling someone from the community from various Old Testament texts such as Deuteronomy 19:16–20 and 22:22–23:1, where the judgment rendered on covenant violators is carried out corporately; as well as Jesus' instruction in Matthew 18, where the community is responsible for expelling a fellow Christian who refuses to repent of sin.[53] Drawing from his knowledge of the Old Testament and Jesus' teaching, Paul urges the Corinthians to swiftly expel the incestuous man for his benefit. In other words, the church must also recognize that removing the man from the community functions as a temporal judgment that is intended to spare him from eternal judgment.[54] The Corinthians must carry out this judgment on the incestuous man in

---

52. For helpful discussions regarding the various interpretations of v. 5 see, for example, Fee, *First Epistle to the Corinthians*, 228–35; Mario Phillip, "Delivery into the Hands of Satan—A Church in Apostasy and Not Knowing It: An Exegetical Analysis of 1 Corinthians 5:5," *ERT* 39 (2015): 45–60; Thiselton, *First Epistle to the Corinthians*, 392–400; Guy Waters, "Curse Redux? 1 Corinthians 5:13, Deuteronomy, and Identity in Corinth," *WTJ* 77 (2015): 237–50.

53. See, for example, Richard B. Hays, *The Conversion of the Imagination: Paul as Interpreter of Israel's Scripture* (Grand Rapids: Eerdmans, 2005), 21–24; Brian S. Rosner, *Paul, Scripture and Ethics: A Study of 1 Corinthians 5–7*, Biblical Studies Library 22 (Grand Rapids: Baker, 1999), 81–93.

54. Lanier, "Day of the Lord in the New Testament," 231–32.

hopes that he will come to his senses while there is still time to repent, before he stands before the final Judge on the day of the Lord. Guy Waters comments, "The position of the offender is not a hopeless one. His expulsion from the community is not designed to be an act of final, eschatological judgment. That judgment awaits the Day of the Lord. And it may be that the offender, upon repentance, will find himself among those who are saved on that day."[55]

Second, Paul understands that the day of the Lord is also irreducibly communal. While it is certainly evident that Paul is concerned for the incestuous man, his primary concern is arguably for the *congregation*.[56] Earlier in 3:16–17 the apostle reminds the Corinthians, "You [plural] are God's temple and that God's Spirit dwells in you [plural]. . . . Anyone who destroys God's temple, God will destroy him. For God's temple is holy, which is what you [plural] are."[57] This temple imagery would have probably still been fresh on their minds as Paul chastises them in chapter 5 for allowing unholy behavior to pollute God's temple. As God's chosen community, they are holy, and they must adamantly maintain their holiness. The apostle provides additional imagery borrowed from the Passover to further stress the sanctity of the church by reminding them that they are a new batch of dough without leaven and that by allowing the incestuous man to continue in their midst they are all being contaminated (vv. 6–13). Just as leaven penetrates the entire batch of dough, so also this sin negatively affects the entire congregation.[58] Paul admonishes the Corinthians to live as what they

---

55. Waters, "Curse Redux?," 249.

56. Verse 5 presents an interesting *crux interpretum*. The standard translation is "Turn this man over to Satan for the destruction of the flesh, so that *his* spirit may be saved in the Day of the Lord" (e.g., NET, NIV, ESV, HCSB). The focus of this translation is on the incestuous man and the purging of his sinful behavior so that he will be saved on the day of the Lord. The Greek text, however, does not include the pronoun αὐτοῦ (*autou*), "his," and may indicate that Paul's primary focus in v. 5 was not the man but rather the church. This has led some scholars to contend that the apostle was urging the church to turn the incestuous man over to Satan for the destruction of *their* flesh so that the community would continue to live in fellowship with the Spirit, who ensures they will be saved in the day of the Lord. For helpful discussions related to this particular interpretation see, for example, Barth Lynn Campbell, "Flesh and Spirit in 1 Cor 5:5: An Exercise in Rhetorical Criticism of the NT," *JETS* 36 (1993): 331–42; Adela Yarbro Collins, "The Function of 'Excommunication' in Paul," *HTR* 73 (1980): 251–63; Karl P. Donfried, "Justification and Last Judgment in Paul," *Int* 39 (1976): 150–52.

57. See 1 Cor 6:19, where the temple metaphor is also used regarding how the Spirit indwells individual believers.

58. See James K. Howard, "Christ Our Passover: A Study of the Passover-Exodus Theme in 1 Corinthians," *EvQ* 41 (1969): 97–108; Charles L. Mitton, "New Wine in Old Wine Skins: IV," *ExpTim* 84 (1973): 339–43.

are, namely unleavened, and they must do so in light of the coming final day. More specifically, in the overall context of chapter 5 it seems that these ethical exhortations are framed in the reality that the day of the Lord significantly affects ecclesiastical life, and this should actually motivate the congregation to grow in holiness. As "one batch," the Corinthian church must collectively act to eradicate the offender, not only for their continued sanctification but also so they can effectively maintain their witness as God's people in the city of Corinth, all of which is accomplished with an eschatological orientation since the day of the Lord is drawing near.

FIRST CORINTHIANS 15

Another example regarding how the day of the Lord motif influences Paul's theology is evident in his understanding of the resurrection. First Corinthians 15 is the apostle's most comprehensive discussion on the resurrection. The chapter was likely prompted by the report from Chloe's house that some within the congregation were denying the future bodily resurrection of the dead (v. 12). Why some in the church had come to this conclusion is not stated, but since the resurrection is the bedrock of Christianity, Paul's objective in chapter 15 is seemingly to reestablish the absolute certainty of Christ's bodily resurrection and how his resurrection guarantees the bodily resurrection of all believers (vv. 20–28).[59]

It is generally recognized that chapter 15 divides into two parts: verses 1–34 and verses 35–57.[60] In the first section the apostle begins by reminding the Corinthians about their mutually held belief that Christ was in fact raised bodily from the dead (vv. 1–11). What Paul is strongly emphasizing at the beginning of this chapter is that "the resurrection of Jesus was a real event . . . and it underlay the future real event of the resurrection of all God's people."[61] Not only did the Corinthians hear and receive this

---

59. For a helpful discussion on the various theories as to why some in the church were denying the resurrection see, for example, Joost Holleman, *Resurrection and Parousia: A Traditio-Historical Study of Paul's Eschatology in I Corinthians 15*, NovTSup 84 (Leiden: Brill, 1996), 35–40.

60. Martinus C. de Boer, *The Defeat of Death: Apocalyptic Eschatology in 1 Corinthians 15 and Romans 5*, JSNTSup 22 (Sheffield, UK: JSOT, 1988), 93–95; Holleman, *Resurrection and Parousia*, 40–48. More detailed outlines of chap. 15 can be found in Ciampa and Rosner, *First Letter to the Corinthians*, 741–42; Fee, *First Epistle to the Corinthians*, 793–96; Wright, *Resurrection of the Son of God*, 312–61.

61. Wright, *Resurrection of the Son of God*, 317–18.

message from Paul, but it had become their personal commitment. Having reestablished that they all believed in Christ's bodily resurrection, Paul moves on to refute those who are denying this foundational truth. He does this by arguing that if those who deny the resurrection are right, then the logical outcome of their position would be catastrophic, for it would mean that Christ was not raised and believers are still dead in their sins and without hope (vv. 12–19). Essentially Paul's point is that "if [this] position prevails, they have neither a past nor a future."[62]

But the apostle adamantly rejects such a notion and stresses that Christ has indeed been raised from the dead, and he presses forward reminding the Corinthians that Christ's resurrection guarantees their bodily resurrection. Paul substantiates this premise by asserting that Christ is the ἀπαρχὴ (aparchē), "firstfruits," specifically for τῶν κεκοιμημένων (tōn kekoimēmenōn), "those who have fallen asleep."[63] The term aparchē is prevalent throughout the Old Testament in cultic contexts, where the first or best portion of a crop or an animal from the flock was offered to God in thanksgiving for his provision. Moreover, the term is also used metaphorically and "signifies the pledge of the remainder and, concomitantly, the assurance of a full harvest which in effect is attributed to God's providential care. Used figuratively . . . 'first fruits' symbolizes the first installment and that part which includes, as by synecdoche, the whole."[64] To further illustrate how Christ's resurrection leads to the final resurrection of believers, Paul uses an Adam-Christ analogy. The purpose of the analogy is to emphasize that death came through one man (Adam), and consequently all humanity, being identified with Adam, will die. But the defeat of death came through a man (Christ), by means of his resurrection. Therefore, all who are in Christ will be made alive. "The inevitable process of death begun in Adam will be reversed by the equally inevitable process of 'bringing to life' that was begun in Christ."[65] Paul's intent here is to stress that Christ's resurrection is the down payment that guarantees the future bodily resurrection of all believers. As

---

62. Fee, First Epistle to the Corinthians, 819.

63. The verb κοιμάω (koimaō), "sleep," in vv. 18, 20 is used euphemistically as a reference to believers. In this particular context Paul is not concerned with the general resurrection of humanity. Rather, he is focused on the resurrection of those who have fallen asleep ἐν Χριστῷ (en Christō), "in Christ." See the helpful discussion in ibid., 830–31n163.

64. De Boer, Defeat of Death, 109.

65. Fee, First Epistle to the Corinthians, 833.

Katherine Grieb notes, "The whole point of Paul's argument . . . is that in the destiny of Jesus Christ, the one 'raised from the dead, the firstfruits of those who have fallen asleep' (1 Cor 15:20), is our destiny."[66] It is therefore absurd for some in the Corinthian congregation to deny the future resurrection. Paul's use of the firstfruits metaphor underscores the reality that Christ's bodily resurrection guarantees that there will be an eschatological harvest (i.e., resurrection), which occurs at the parousia (v. 23).[67]

Having reminded the Corinthians that their future bodily resurrection is completely anchored in Christ's resurrection, Paul concludes chapter 15 with a note of triumph (vv. 50-57). At the day of the Lord, believers will be transformed as their bodies are changed from "their present state to the one required for God's future."[68] Now that they are assured of their eschatological resurrection and ultimate glorification, Paul once again reminds the Corinthians that these truths must presently affect their ethics. The guarantee of their future resurrection should spur them on to be steadfast in their work of the Lord (v. 58). Knowing that death has been defeated and they have victory through Christ, the Corinthians should be all the more diligent in their service to God as they look forward to their resurrection, awaiting them at the parousia. The Corinthians can be assured knowing that they will be resurrected on the day of the Lord.

Certainly, the main thrust of chapter 15 is to defend the doctrine of the resurrection. Paul reestablishes for the Corinthians that since Christ has been raised, this then necessitates their future resurrection. But this understanding is also seemingly connected to Paul's theology of the day of the Lord. In other words, implicit in the apostle's discussion throughout chapter 15 is that the resurrection of Christ both inaugurates the parousia and anticipates its consummation. As G. R. Beasley-Murray observes, "The resurrection is the anticipation of the parousia, the parousia is the

---

66. A. Katherine Grieb, "Last Things First: Karl Barth's Theological Exegesis of 1 Corinthians in the Resurrection of the Dead," *SJT* 56 (2003): 55.

67. There has been much discussion surrounding the fact that Paul mentions other "events" that take place as part of the parousia (vv. 24-28). In general, the debate focuses on the interpretation of the adverb ἔπειτα (*epeita*), "then," and the timing of these "events." This discussion is beyond the purview of the present work's primary focus on the day of the Lord motif. For helpful discussions on this particular issue see Ciampa and Rosner, *First Letter to the Corinthians*, 765-67; Holleman, *Resurrection and Parousia*, 51-54; Plevnik, *Paul and the Parousia*, 125-29.

68. Wright, *Resurrection of the Son of God*, 357.

fulfillment of the promise for humanity and the cosmos implied in the resurrection. . . . The Easter resurrection made plain the eschatological reality of the process, the parousia completes it."[69] Believers can look forward
to the day of the Lord with great joy and eagerness only because Christ's
resurrection guarantees that they too will be raised immortal.

Finally, the day of the Lord also affects the theology in 2 Corinthians. The
letter opens in typical Pauline fashion with a greeting followed by a thanksgiving prayer offered to God (1:1–7). The opening prayer sets the tone of the
letter, as the apostle offers thanks to God, who provides comfort in the midst
of suffering for the cause of Christ. The apostle had suffered much in the
province of Asia (1:7–11; Acts 19) but also experienced tremendous despair
due to his tenuous relationship with the Corinthians. But despite his afflictions and apparent weakness, Paul offers a defense for the legitimacy of his
ministry by reminding the Corinthians that the nature of his sufferings
reveals the authenticity of his apostolic ministry, for it is strictly by God's
power that he is able to serve as a minister of the new covenant (2 Cor 3:5–6).[70]

For Paul the concept of the day of the Lord is both a present and future
reality, and it seems to have impacted his self-understanding regarding the
ministry he had been given. For example, in 1:12–16 Paul offers a defense of
his motivation for not coming to visit the Corinthians as he had planned.
It seems that some within the congregation accused Paul of being fickle
and insincere because he revised his early travel plans. However, the apostle reminds them that he has always carried out his ministry with pure
motives and integrity. Paul expresses genuine concern for the Corinthians
because they have only partially understood his ministry, and he implores
them to give him a fair hearing in order to bring further reconciliation
in their strained relationship. Timothy Savage comments, "Clearly Paul
had a reason for joy (7:7, 9, 13, 16). Yet on a deeper level he remains troubled. His converts have yet to grasp the full significance of his ministry. . . .
They understand it only in part."[71] Although the congregation has partially

---

69. G. R. Beasley-Murray, "Resurrection and Parousia of the Son of Man," *TynBul* 42
(1991): 309. See also G. K. Beale, *A New Testament Biblical Theology: The Unfolding of the Old
Testament in the New* (Grand Rapids: Baker, 2011), 249–316; Gordon D. Fee, "Toward a Theology
of 1 Corinthians," in *Pauline Theology*, ed. David M. Hay (Minneapolis: Fortress, 2002), 55–58;
Vena, *Parousia and Its Rereadings*, 133–34.

70. See also Aernie, *Is Paul Also among the Prophets?*, 114.

71. Savage, *Power through Weakness*, 68.

understood, Paul reminds them that they all have a common boast, namely what God has accomplished in their relationship through the gospel. The Corinthians can take pride in Paul, knowing that he has always carried out his ministry among them with the utmost sincerity. Moreover, the Corinthians will be a source of pride for Paul at the day of the Lord. The apostle's hope is that the Corinthians will *presently* accept what he is saying about his motives for ministry, but if not his motives will ultimately be revealed in the future at the day of the Lord.[72] Once more this passage demonstrates that a characteristic of the day of the Lord motif is that it is relational. In other words, the day of the Lord affects the communal relationship of believers in the present and the future. Both Paul and the Corinthians can presently boast because of their relationship despite the strain that exists between some of the members of the congregation toward the apostle. But their relationship also has a future orientation and should be understood within the context of the day of the Lord.[73] As Donald Guthrie notes, "Part of the hope for Paul is that he and the Corinthians will be able to make a mutual boast on that day, that they will be able to take pride in Paul and he will be able to take pride in them."[74] In essence, the day of the Lord motif significantly affects Paul's relationship with the Corinthians. The apostle notably values his relationship with this congregation and in turn exhorts them to have a high regard for him and his new covenant ministry *in the present*, knowing that their mutual boasting will ultimately be fulfilled at the day of the Lord.[75]

Last, the day of the Lord motif is also conceptually evident throughout the apostle's discussion in 4:7–5:10. In this passage Paul reminds the Corinthians that the incessant suffering he has encountered throughout his new covenant ministry is based on the paradigm of Jesus' own suffering and death.[76] But like Jesus before him, the apostle understands that his current suffering is linked to future victory. As previously argued, the day of the Lord has both present and future aspects, and the sufferings

---

72. Ralph P. Martin, *2 Corinthians*, WBC (Waco, TX: Word, 1986), 19.

73. See Guthrie, *2 Corinthians*, 98; Harris, *Second Epistle to the Corinthians*, 187–89.

74. Guthrie, *2 Corinthians*, 99.

75. Seifrid, *Second Letter to the Corinthians*, 53–54. Cf. Barnett, *The Second Epistle to the Corinthians*, 97–98; Victor Paul Furnish, *II Corinthians*, AB 32A (Garden City, NY: Doubleday, 1984), 131–32.

76. Aernie, *Is Paul Also among the Prophets?*, 191.

that Paul experiences are a means of sanctification as his inner man is being renewed daily despite his physical body being destroyed (vv. 16–18). However, the apostle recognizes the temporal nature of his current sufferings and that the consummate day of the Lord is still to come, when all believers will stand before the judgment seat of Christ.[77] The purpose for appearing before Christ's tribunal is that each one "may receive recompense" for what has been done, whether good or bad.[78] When believers come before the final Judge on the day of the Lord, it is not their status with God that is on trial, since they have been justified by faith; but it is an appraisal of their actions and character.[79] Therefore, Paul makes it his ambition to do all things to please Christ, to whom he will give an account at the final assize. Thus it seems that Paul's point in this passage is that "the present is full of suffering, especially for the apostle; but he sees it as organically connected to the future in which there is resurrection (4:14), glory (4:17), a new body (5:1), and judgment (5:10)."[80] Paul can take great comfort in his present afflictions because at the day of the Lord he will be raised, given a new body, comforted, and vindicated in the sight of his persecutors.

Paul's discourse throughout the Corinthian correspondence demonstrates the various characteristics that the day of the Lord had on his theological framework. The numerous issues addressed throughout both epistles reveal that the day of the Lord serves as a major component for Paul, as it influenced his understanding on such areas as ethics, communal

---

77. Scholarship is divided on the issue of whether Paul had in mind a general judgment of all humanity or strictly believers in this passage. Certainly the apostle understands that Christ is the ultimate Judge of all humanity (Rom 2:6–16; 2 Tim 4:1). In this particular context, however, the consensus is that Paul is strictly referring to believers. See Guthrie, 2 Corinthians, 288–89; Harris, Second Epistle to the Corinthians, 406–7; Jan Lambrecht, "The Paul Who Wants to Die: A Close Reading of 2 Cor 4:16–5:10," in Theologizing in the Corinthian Conflict: Studies in the Exegesis and Theology of 2 Corinthians, ed. R. Bieringer, Ma. Marilou S. Ibita, Dominika Kurek-Chomycz, and Thomas A. Vollmer, Biblical Tools and Studies 16 (Leuven: Peeters, 2013), 158–59.

78. The verb κομίζω (komizō), "receive back," may connote the idea of recompense and focuses more on evaluation and commendation. See Guthrie, 2 Corinthians, 289; Harris, Second Epistle to the Corinthians, 408–9; Fredrick J. Long, 2 Corinthians: A Handbook on the Greek Text, Baylor Handbook on the Greek New Testament (Waco, TX: Baylor University Press, 2015), 100. Contra Fredrik Lindgård, Paul's Line of Thought in 2 Corinthians 4:16–5:10, WUNT 189 (Tübingen: Mohr Siebeck, 2005), 217–19, who contends that scholars have taken this meaning for granted and argues that the term is better understood as "reaping one's deeds."

79. Harris, Second Epistle to the Corinthians, 409. See also Martin, 2 Corinthians, 115–16.

80. Wright, Resurrection of the Son of God, 361.

relationships, resurrection, glorification, and his own perception of his apostolic ministry. The apostle recognizes that the eschatological day is both already and not yet. Consequently, the day of the Lord means that every facet of the Christian life must be lived out in the present in light of the future, since all believers' actions and character will ultimately be assessed at the great assize.

ROMANS

Paul's book of Romans refers to the day of the Lord as "the Day of wrath and the revelation of the righteous judgment of God" (2:5), "the Day" when "God will judge the secrets of men's hearts" (2:16), and a day that is prophetically "near" (13:12). These judgments are in accordance with truth (2:2), involve the conviction of the guilty (2:3), and will be carried out as a just condemnation (3:8). They are on the one hand precipitated by inbreakings into the present era, evidenced by the increase of immorality (1:18–23), and on the other hand foreshadowed through the creaturely jurisprudence of God-ordained government (13:2). In Romans Paul's interest in the day of the Lord focuses almost entirely on the wrath associated with that day. Much of the theological portions of the book are designed to provide a forensic, formal, or functional means of escaping this wrath (3:21–5:21; 9:22–23; 10:13; 12:19–20; 13:1–14).[81] The proleptic guilty verdict on the day of the Lord (3:9–20) forms the immediate background for Paul's subsequent soteriological sections (3:21–5:21; 6–8; 9–11). How does one escape the judgment of the day of the Lord? In the later paraenetic section of Romans (12–16), the imminence of that day provides motivation for fulfilling one's religious, civic, and moral duties to God and humanity (13:8–14). In addition, the promise of ultimate and just recompense to one's enemies benefits in ameliorating feelings of injustice as well as motivates one to exercise patience in the face of such unjust treatments (12:19–20). Short of insisting that the day of the Lord is the center on which Romans orbits, it certainly functions as an essential component in understanding its theological emphases and structure.

---

81. On Rom 10:13 see Joel D. Estes, "Calling on the Name of the Lord: The Meaning and Significance of ἐπικαλέω in Romans 10:13," *Them* 41 (2016): 20–36. Estes refers to Rom 10:13 (which quotes Joel 3:5) as "the theological heart and rhetorical hinge of 9:30–10:21" and to Rom 10:13 in particular as a "prayer for deliverance" (ibid., 23, 26). He also notes that "the solution in 10:13 matches the problem in chapter 1, and both concern the issue of worship" (ibid., 33).

ROMANS 1:18–3:20

No sooner than Paul introduces the gospel (1:16–17) does he interject the necessity of divine wrath. This wrath is in some ways deemed to be *revelatory* both in terms of its inauguration into the present time and with respect to the nature of its specific operations (1:18–32). The "wrath of God" being "revealed" in Romans 1:18 introduces the inbreaking of the eschatological day of the Lord rather than merely forecasting the inevitability of the final judgment.[82] "It is not only an eschatological event but also a present reality."[83] This inbreaking is *revelatory* in the sense that the retaliatory recompense in some way commences in the present time, continues until its culmination, but also closely corresponds to the nature and intensity of the judgments that will occur in the last day and beyond. Given his background as a Pharisee and in light of his conversion/call experience on the Damascus road, Paul most likely reached his views about God's present wrath by contemplating what he knew of the day of the Lord and applying features of it not only typologically to his experience in particular but also hermeneutically and paradigmatically to other aspects of his theology as well.[84] In recognizing

---

82. Other texts in Paul (Rom 2:6–10; 9:22–23; 2 Thess 1:6–10; Eph 5:6–7) are used "um das zukünftige Zorngericht Gottes zu beschreiben" (Hans-Joachim Eckstein, "'Denn Gottes Zorn wird vom Himmel her offenbar werden': Exegetische Erwägungen zu Röm 1:18," ZNW 78 [1987]: 74). Eckstein notes that the earliest attempt to limit this wrath in Rom 1:18 to the future was Irenaeus (*Against Heresies* 4.27.4); but he provides an impressive list of early fathers to support this *only future wrath* interpretation as well as other scholars who argue it is present as a promise of the coming wrath. The nuance of the present tense of ἀποκαλύπτaι is most likely *customary* or *gnomic* rather than *futuristic* (Stanley E. Porter, *Idioms of the Greek New Testament*, Biblical Languages 2 [Sheffield: Sheffield Academic Press, 1994], 39). Besides many German scholars, other English commentators parallel the present eschatological event of the revelation of the gospel (1:16–17) to this concurrent eschatological wrath. See Thomas R. Schreiner, *Romans*, BECNT (Grand Rapids: Baker, 1998), 84–85; Grant R. Osborne, *Romans*, IVP New Testament Commentary Series (Downers Grove, IL: InterVarsity, 2004), 46; Kevin W. McFadden, *Judgment according to Works in Romans: The Meaning and Function of Divine Judgment in Paul's Most Important Letter* (Minneapolis: Fortress, 2013), 21–25; Michael J. Gorman, *Apostle of the Crucified Lord: A Theological Introduction to Paul & His Letters* (Grand Rapids: Eerdmans, 2017), 413. Gorman concludes, "The wrath of God is experienced now proleptically, before the actual coming day of judgment and wrath" (ibid., 414).

83. Charles M. Horne, "Toward a Biblical Apologetic," *Bulletin of the Evangelical Theological Society* 4 (1961): 89. See John William Drane, *Introducing the New Testament* (Minneapolis: Fortress, 2011), 72–75.

84. See David Arthur deSilva, *An Introduction to the New Testament: Contexts, Methods, and Ministry Formation* (Downers Grove, IL: InterVarsity, 2004), 479. Geerhardus Vos did hold that in the New Testament "it was eschatology which shaped soteriology . . . and not the other way around" (Anthony A. Hoekema, *The Bible and the Future* [Grand Rapids: Eerdmans, 1979], 299). On the general tenor of Christian theology as eschatological see Jürgen Moltmann, *Theology of Hope: On the Ground and the Implications of a Christian Eschatology* (New York: Harper & Row, 1967), 16; Scott M. Lewis, *What Are They Saying about New Testament Apocalyptic?* (New York: Paulist, 2004), 7–21.

these eschatological features of the day of the Lord, Paul doubtlessly inferred the intersection or overlapping of the present and future ages, especially considering them in light of Jesus' resurrection as "an apocalyptic event."[85] As a consequence of his radical reorientation derived from his conversion and calling, Paul may then have utilized an eschatological perspective to reinterpret and better understand how God's justice is meted out in the *now* in light of the *then*. Because of the overlapping of ages, one may infer an already/not-yet or eschatological aspect to practically every tenet of Pauline theology. Therefore the day of the Lord as part of an inaugurated eschatology would appear to be no exception.[86] One should then expect an already/not-yet perspective connected with the day of the Lord including a major component of that day—the wrath of God.

Among Paul's epistles, the term for "wrath" (ὀργή [*orgē*]) occurs mostly in Romans (1:18; 2:5 [2x], 8; 3:5; 4:15; 5:9; 9:22 [2x]; 12:19; 13:4–5).[87] Although the term signifies more of a juridical component of justice, its combination with another term for "anger" (θυμός [*thymos*]) argues for an "unceasing, consciously felt retribution" suggesting an element of just temperamental acrimony from God (Rom 2:5).[88] Kevin McFadden writes, "The two words

---

85. Lewis, *What Are They Saying about New Testament Apocalyptic?*, 27. Paul saw the resurrected Jesus, according to his own testimony (1 Cor 9:1; 15:1–11; see also Acts 22:7–10; 26:14–18). "Paul differs from traditional apocalyptic, however, in his faith that the end time has begun with the resurrection of Christ" (Vincent P. Branick, "Apocalyptic Paul?," *CBQ* 47 [1985]: 666). See also W. D. Davies, *Paul and Rabbinic Judaism: Some Rabbinic Elements in Pauline Theology* (Philadelphia: Fortress, 1980), 293–323; Ulrich Luz, *Das Geschichtsverständnis des Paulus* (München: Kaiser, 1968), 393; Drane, *Introducing the New Testament*, 405–6.

86. Hoekema sets forth seven eschatological themes from the OT that the NT believer would expect to become realities: the coming redeemer, the kingdom of God, the new covenant, the restoration of Israel, the outpouring of the Spirit, the day of the Lord, and the new heaven and the new earth. See Hoekema, *Bible and the Future*, 3–12. Each one of these aspects has multiple fulfillments leading up to a par-excellent scenario.

87. The term occurs thirty-six times in the NT, twenty-one in Pauline epistles, and twelve in Romans alone, more than any other Pauline epistle (Matt 3:7; Mark 3:5; Luke 3:7; 21:23; John 3:36; Rom 1:18; 2:5 [2x], 8; 3:5; 4:15; 5:9; 9:22 [2x]; 12:19; 13:4–5; Eph 2:3; 4:31; 5:6; Col 3:6, 8; 1 Thess 1:10; 2:16; 5:9; 1 Tim 2:8; Heb 3:11; 4:3; Jas 1:19–20; Rev 6:16–17; 11:18; 14:10; 16:19; 19:15). See Mary Schmitt, "Peace and Wrath in Paul's Epistle to the Romans," *Conrad Grebel Review* 32 (2014): 67.

88. James E. Rosscup, "Paul's Concept of Eternal Punishment," *MSJ* 9 (1998): 170. See the excellent treatment of God's wrath/anger in Michael C. McCarthy, "Divine Wrath and Human Anger: Embarrassment Ancient and New," *TS* 70 (2009): 845–74. McCarthy argues that there is a history of rejecting the notion that God has wrath/anger mostly due to projection of evil feelings to God or the inability to "distinguish between human and divine predicates" (ibid., 861). The underlying assumption is that all human wrath/anger is evil, and therefore divine wrath is problematic. Although divine wrath/anger is always good, it does not follow that human wrath/anger is always wrong (see Jas 1:19; Eph 4:26).

carry the connotation of God's emotion in judgment (the affect), although they focus in this context upon God's action of judgment (the effect)."[89] The wrath of God, according to Romans 1:18–32, indicates *an abandonment of God's common grace (among other things) with respect to the objects of wrath*.[90] This divine rejection is reflected in Paul's repeated phrase "God gave them up/over" (Rom 1:24, 26, 28). The language assumes or at least intimates that prior to this "giving up" or "giving over" God is in some way presently restraining or withholding humankind's sinful tendencies as a matter of common grace.[91] The degree to which God unleashes his restraining power on or within the hearts of individuals depends to a greater or lesser extent on the level to which the suppression of the truth of/about God, or what Karl Barth called the "criminal arrogance of religion," reaches (Rom 1:18).[92] This rebellion is expressed not in a rejection of God's being per se but rather via a reinterpretation of God as God in some varied form of a-the-ism (and less likely atheism), or, as D. A. Carson refers to it as, "the degod-ding of God."[93] Stated more bluntly, Lesslie Newbigin argues, "We are not honest inquirers seeking the truth. We are alienated from truth and are

---

89. McFadden, *Judgment according to Works in Romans*, 47. See also 25–28.

90. Johnson calls it "the judicial infliction of the abandonment of men and women to the intensified cultivation of unnatural sexual enormities and other debasing and degrading devices" (S. Lewis Johnson, "Paul and the Knowledge of God," *BSac* 129 [1972]: 66).

91. For a defense and discussion of "common grace" see Anthony A. Hoekema, *Created in God's Image* (Grand Rapids: Eerdmans, 1986), 187–202. He defines common grace as "a grace that restrains sin in fallen humankind even though it does not take away man's sinfulness" (ibid., 189). Similarly, Grudem defines it as "the grace of God by which he gives people innumerable blessings that are not part of salvation" (Wayne Grudem, *Making Sense of Salvation: One of Seven Parts from Grudem's Systematic Theology* [Grand Rapids: Zondervan, 1994], 34). Common grace differs from saving grace "in its *results* (it does not bring about salvation), in its *recipients* (it is given to believers and unbelievers alike), and in its *source* (it does not directly flow from Christ's atoning work)" (ibid., 35). But it does flow *indirectly* from Christ's redeeming work, argues Grudem, because it functions to postpone immediate eschatological judgment until all the elect are saved (see 2 Pet 3:9). Finally, this view of *common* grace, although sharing some similarities with *prevenient* grace, differs from the Wesleyan view of *prevenient* grace in that *common* grace does not lead to salvation. See Thomas R. Schreiner, "Does Scripture Teach Prevenient Grace in the Wesleyan Sense?," in *Still Sovereign: Contemporary Perspectives on Election, Foreknowledge, and Grace*, ed. Thomas R. Schreiner and Bruce A. Ware (Grand Rapids: Baker, 2000), 369.

92. Karl Barth, *The Epistle to the Romans*, trans. Edwyn C. Hoskyns (Oxford: Oxford University Press, 1932), 37, 53; see also 50.

93. D. A. Carson, "The Vindication of Imputation: On Fields of Discourse and Semantic Fields," in *Justification: What's at Stake in the Current Debates*, ed. Mark Husbands and Daniel J. Treier (Downers Grove, IL: InterVarsity, 2004), 71. For an explanation of first-century views of a-theism (varied forms of nontheism) and atheism, see Donald E. Hartley, "Hebrews 11:6: A Reassessment of the Translation 'God Exists,'" *TJ* 27 (2006): 289–307.

enemies of it. We are by nature idolaters, constructing images of truth shaped by our own desires."[94] And these nontheistic (or in Newbigin's case, Cartesian) models and ideas have moral consequences. The root of the ethical breakdown appears to grow out of a religious rebellion or "from the perversion of faith."[95] And these perversions are the direct result of individuals being without excuse in terms of their suppressing-the-truth-of/about-God idolatry.[96]

How God hands individuals over to these sinful effects may be understood as a type of *addition* or even of *subtraction*. In other words, God may arguably *transform* the individual by (1) adding an element of unrighteousness, or (2) subtracting a moral ability as just retribution for godlessness. On the other hand, God may act in a *nontransformative* way such as by (3) passively letting a built-in moral cause-and-effect take its natural degenerative course(s), or by (4) unleashing the resident evil within the heart of humanity by actively withdrawing or ceasing to further provide his gracious restraining influence in an act of juridical irony.[97] Any one of these possible interpretive decisions results in the increase of sexual immorality (Rom 1:24–25), a degenerating of the original intent of sexuality to the point of homosexuality (Rom 1:26–27), and a justifying of all forms

---

94. Lesslie Newbigin, *Proper Confidence: Faith, Doubt, and Certainty in Christian Discipleship* (Grand Rapids: Eerdmans, 1995), 69.

95. Johnson, "Paul and the Knowledge of God," 62.

96. C. E. B. Cranfield, *The Epistle to the Romans*, ICC (Edinburgh: T&T Clark, 1975), 1:116 (consecutive); John Murray, *The Epistle to the Romans: The English Text with Introduction, Exposition and Notes*, NICNT (Grand Rapids: Eerdmans, 1968), 40 (result). Given the frequent blurring of purpose and result, the inexcusability of idolatry is most likely the *intended result*. See Leon Morris, *The Epistle to the Romans* (Grand Rapids: Eerdmans, 1988), 82.

97. These divine acts are parallel to both *hardening* and *fattening* in Exod 4–14 or Isa 6:9–10 (along with pars) respectively. The divine act in *fattening* and *hardening* involves *the withholding of special grace* or the new heart respecting either the mind (*fattening*) or the will (*hardening*), both involving the inseparably linked dual aspects of the heart. Here in Romans, the divine act entails *the withholding of common (not special) grace*. This latter act is never referred to as either *fattening* or *hardening*—although it (along with the other two) is certainly contingent on the congenital nature of the heart as being both *fat/hard*. Unlike *divine hardening* (Rom 9:18) but similar to what takes place here (Rom 1:18–32), *divine fattening* (Rom 11:7) involves the withholding of *salvific knowing*, while in Rom 1:18–32 it is the withdrawing of common grace *because* humanity suppresses what is *known* of/about God. However, whereas *fattening/hardening* are nonretributive, here (Rom 1:18–32) the divine withholding of common grace is clearly retributive. For a discussion of divine *hardening* and *fattening* see Donald E. Hartley, *The Wisdom Background and Parabolic Implications of Isaiah 6:9–10 in the Synoptics*, Studies in Biblical Literature 100 (New York: Lang, 2006); Hartley, "Destined to Disobey? Isaiah 6:10 in John 12:37–41," *CTJ* 44 (2009): 263–87.

of unrighteousness within a noetic framework of irrational animosity toward God (Rom 1:23–31).[98] The best explanation may be to describe this action (following option 4 above) as a *divine deprivation*, that is, *the withholding (rather than adding or subtracting something ontological in the heart, or passively permitting cause-and-effect to take place) of the gratuitous giving of common grace that in turn unleashes the congenital depravity bound up within the human heart.* It is a decisive, retributive, retaliatory, but apparently incremental divine abandonment. The subtraction of God's grace involves no actual transformation of humankind from what it is *by nature* but only what that innate nature is permitted to sinfully express *in function*. This divine activity instead allows humankind to be what it truly is in its sinful condition without God's grace perpetually restraining it. Therein lies the irony. Humanity suppresses who God actually is by nature through its idolatry, and God responds by permitting and punishing humanity to be what it actually is by nature in practice. Timothy Ward defines idolatry as identifying "something that humanity has created with God himself, and thus to give devotion to something that is not the living God."[99] Alain Gignac describes the divine response and activity to this idolatry as "an action-reaction revenge, in which God reestablishes his wounded honor with a kind of swap: since humanity *exchanged* God for idols, God will

---

98. The nature of this homosexuality, despite some recent *progressive* trends in scholarship, almost certainly includes both male and female. For samples of efforts to mitigate female homosexuality see James E. Miller, "The Practices of Romans 1:26: Homosexual or Heterosexual?," *NovT* 37 (1995): 1–11; Jamie A. Banister, "ὁμοίως and the Use of Parallelism in Romans 1:26–27," *JBL* 128 (2009): 569–90. For the link between Gnosticism and homosexuality see Jonathan Cahana, "Gnostically Queer: Gender Trouble in Gnosticism," *BTB* 41 (2011): 24–35. For both exegetical and theological treatments on homosexuality from a broadly *traditionalist* or *evangelical* perspective see Robert A. J. Gagnon, *The Bible and Homosexual Practice: Texts and Hermeneutics* (Nashville: Abingdon, 2001); Dan Otto Via and Robert A. J. Gagnon, *Homosexuality and the Bible: Two Views* (Minneapolis: Fortress, 2003); Preston M. Sprinkle, ed., *Two Views on Homosexuality: The Bible, and the Church*, Counterpoints: Bible & Theology (Grand Rapids: Zondervan, 2016); William R. G. Loader, *Making Sense of Sex: Attitudes towards Sexuality in Early Jewish and Christian Literature*, Attitudes to Sex in Early Jewish and Christian Literature (Grand Rapids: Eerdmans, 2013); (see also his five-volume series on sexuality in the ancient world); Michael L. Brown, *A Queer Thing Happened to America: And What a Long, Strange Trip It's Been* (Concord, NC: EqualTime Books, 2011); James R. White and Jeffrey D. Niell, *The Same Sex Controversy: Defending and Clarifying the Bible's Message about Homosexuality* (Minneapolis: Bethany House, 2002); Gorman, *Apostle of the Crucified Lord*, 413–14. For a more popular and pastoral treatment see James B. DeYoung, *Homosexuality: Contemporary Claims Examined in Light of the Bible and Other Ancient Literature and Law* (Grand Rapids: Kregel, 2000).

99. Timothy Ward, *Words of Life: Scripture As the Living and Active Word of God* (Downers Grove, IL: InterVarsity, 2009), 61.

deliver humanity to dishonor."[100] With God's restraining preservations partially if not entirely removed, the result is increased moral putrefaction. S. Lewis Johnson writes, "It is doubtful if there is a more perceptive analysis of human nature, its sin, guilt, and judgment than this Pauline one."[101] That this abandonment is reversible in the now time—not only in terms of common but special grace—ostensibly adds at least one element of discontinuity between the present and future wrath associated with the day of the Lord.

But in what way does this judgment in Romans 1:18-32 portend or foreshadow the consummate day of the Lord in its pinnacle if not in its permanence? Other factors may help in answering this question. Paul goes on in the second chapter of Romans to include Jews among these suppressors of the truth of/about God, but only less so in appearance than those individuals of Romans 1. The Jews' relative religiosity and morality, or in Paul's words, godliness and righteousness, even though grounded in God's special revelation and ethical injunctions, do not and will not safeguard them from "God's judgment," which is "in accordance with truth" (Rom 2:2, 3). On the contrary, their suppression of that truth is evidence that they are treasuring up for themselves "wrath . . . in the day of wrath, when God's righteous judgment will be revealed" (Rom 2:5). This future wrath that culminates in the day of the Lord does not automatically rule out that God's wrath is presently being revealed on or within these same unrepentant Jews, not unlike those individuals in Romans 1:18-32. Paul's point seems not so much to incidentally distinguish these groups but to link them together as part of the same humanity.[102] What appears different is that the present wrath with these Jews is less easily discernable or detectible as with those in Romans 1. Nevertheless, these Jews are no less subject to the final judgment. This present (Rom 1:18) and future (Rom 2:5) wrath of God, therefore, clearly implies an already/not-yet aspect to the day of the Lord. That this wrath connected to the day of the Lord is

---

100. Alain Gignac, "The Enunciative Device of Romans 1:18–4:25: A Succession of Discourses Attempting to Express the Multiple Dimensions of God's Justice," *CBQ* 77 (2015): 490.

101. Johnson, "Paul and the Knowledge of God," 62.

102. Gorman writes, "But he also has humanity more generally in mind, and he may in fact also have in view his Jewish readers, who would instantly recognize Gentiles in these verses but not—at least not before reading chapter 2—themselves" (Gorman, *Apostle of the Crucified Lord*, 412–13).

presently meted out in degrees, as a comparison of Romans 1–2 confirms, seems to suggest that the final day of judgment (and beyond) will likewise be summarily and incrementally executed.

Paul also appears to assume a parallel between what is known of God from the things that are made in Romans 1 to what is known of God from the law of God in Romans 2. While those in Romans 1 *suppress* the implicit truth of/about God in nature, the Jews of Romans 2 *transgress* the explicit commands of God in Scripture. In doing this, these unregenerate Jews, similarly to those individuals of Romans 1, suppress that which is known of/about God. Despite the privileges of having the Mosaic law, or special revelation, these serve only to *increase* the intensity of eschatological judgment. Evidences of God's "wealth of . . . kindness, and patience" (what is referred to above as common grace and expanded here to include special revelatory grace), instead of being incentives for salvific repentance, have become the bases of an arrogant usurpation of God's prosecutorial roles on the day of the Lord (2:4). Unlike the designated righteous Judge of the final judgment, these self-appointed judges "do the same things" as those earlier indicted—only to a putatively reduced degree (2:1–3).[103] If Paul's questions are more than rhetorical, then his unregenerate Jewish audience was guilty of hypocrisy, stealing, adultery, idolatry, and therefore dishonoring God and being the cause for gentiles blaspheming God (2:21–23). In this regard these Jews also "exchange the glory of the incorruptible for the image of the corruptible" and similarly elicit an already retaliatory wrath of God.[104] One may discern then an apparent but diminished "giving up" or "giving over" of God with respect to these Jews versus those in the previous context. And in a similar way, these Jews will also face eschatological judgment if not to a lesser (or greater?) degree. Determining whether condemnation or divine wrath will be greater or lesser—with respect to receiving only general revelation and rejecting it (in varying degrees) versus having both general and special revelation and rejecting them (in varying degrees)—is difficult to settle. Should those with greater sins but less revelation suffer more severity than those with greater revelation but less obvious sin? Is the incremental "giving up"

---

103. McFadden says Rom 2:1–29 "contains one of the clearest descriptions of the final judgment in Romans and the entire New Testament" (McFadden, *Judgment according to Works in Romans*, 62). He notes earlier that the Greek term used for "judge," κρίνω (krinō), "does not refer to the official judicial process of a court but to one person's finding fault with another" (ibid., 35).

104. Barth, *Romans*, 56.

of sinners in Romans 1 in some way quantitatively lesser to or greater than the "treasuring up" of wrath against ethnic but unregenerate Jews here in Romans 2 when it comes to the ultimate wrath on the final day of the Lord? No matter how one answers these questions, it is surely indisputable that Jewish judgment with respect to the final day of the Lord is increasing in severity, as noted by Paul's expression "treasuring up wrath."

Paul's view of God's *present* wrath as evidenced in varying degrees of unrighteousness (Rom 1:18–32) may not be used to make inconsequential the relative degree of righteousness (Rom 2:1–16) respecting the facing or not the *future* wrath of God in either the day of the Lord or thereafter. There remains a tension in Romans 2 concerning human merit versus righteous deeds as they relate to escaping or experiencing God's wrath. Paul seems to determine eschatological blessings or judgments on the basis of the general character of the persons under scrutiny (here unregenerate Jews versus regenerate gentiles). Suggestive is the evidence of a godly disposition and behavior or lack thereof as indications of regeneration, or what Paul would refer to in context as the writing of the law on the heart (2:15) and the circumcision of the heart (2:27–29).[105] While scholars may apply various interpretive schemes to Romans 2 in order to provide coherence and cohesion to Paul's rationale, the argument made here leans against positions of either advocating an outright *works/merit* salvation scenario or its opposite, a hypothetic *reductio ad absurdum* rejecting any notion of merit.[106] It seems unlikely that Paul argued that (1) *human merit* occupies

---

105. Some understand the phrase in Rom 2:15, "the work of the Law written in their hearts," as the Ten Commandments written in the hearts of all the children of Adam. For example, see Kim Riddlebarger, *A Case for Amillennialism: Understanding the End Times* (Grand Rapids: Baker, 2013), 62; Hoekema, *Created in God's Image*, 196–99 (refers to natural law derived from nature but uses Rom 2 for support). But the language here is new covenant and parallel with "circumcision of the heart" and therefore best understood as referring to regenerate gentiles in Rom 2 in contrast to unregenerate Jews. These gentiles certainly include those with only general revelation as well as those with both general and special revelation. See R. Todd Mangum, "Is There a Reformed Way to Get the Benefits of the Atonement to 'Those Who Have Never Heard?,'" *JETS* 47 (2004): 121–36. See McFadden, *Judgment according to Works in Romans*, 148–53, who understands 2:14–15 as "Gentiles in general who at times . . . do what the Mosaic law requires" (ibid., 48–49). However, he understands the gentiles of 2:26–29 as regenerate (ibid., 50–53).

106. While acknowledging that there are tensions within Pauline theology overall, one should certainly reject the notion that there are conflicting Pauline theologies generally or incoherencies in the Pauline text of Romans particularly. See Gignac, "Enunciative Device of Romans 1:18–4:25," 482–86. For a thorough discussion of the problems associated with works as an indicator of salvation and the impossibility of a human basis of merit for salvation see McFadden, *Judgment according to Works in Romans*, 139–53.

a determining role in one's eternal destiny but completely plausible that Paul would (2) only argue *hypothetically* that salvation could be obtained through a merit-based system. Given these alternative schemes, it nevertheless does not appear that Paul is either *directly* asserting a merit-based system or indirectly rejecting one by proposing a hypothetical scenario, ultimately setting it aside as unlikely and impossible. Instead, (3) this work proposes an *evidence-inference* paradigm for Romans 2 wherein one's works serve as concomitants of an eschatological orientation indicating a destiny of glory, honor, and peace (Rom 12:7, 10) or one meriting affliction and distress (Rom 2:8–9).[107] Based on these general assessments, one treasures up varying degrees of either just punishments or gratuitous rewards.[108] These eschatological degrees of punishments and rewards are then somewhat presently reflected in the judgments outlined in Romans 1–2. The point of Romans 2 is not to argue that the unregenerate ethnic Jews are absent of God's common as well as revelatory grace but rather to suggest that these same Jews are, no less certainly than their unregenerate gentile inferiors, presently without the special grace of the new heart and are therefore under the same, albeit less evident, wrath of God.[109]

One of the operational issues respecting the inbreaking of the wrath of God includes a *retributive* component. It is clear by the phrase διὸ παρέδωκεν αὐτοὺς ὁ θεὸς ἐν ταῖς ἐπιθυμίαις τῶν καρδιῶν αὐτῶν (*dio paredōken autous ho theos en tais epithymias tōn kardiōn autōn*), "therefore, God gave them over to the desires of their hearts," for example, that the sins and effects mentioned by Paul of the wrath of God originate from *within* the hearts of individuals rather than as something retributively *infused into* the hearts by God (Rom 1:24). David deSilva concurs, stating, "Being subject to the rule of the passions

---

107. Similarly see Rosscup, "Paul's Concept of Eternal Punishment," 173–76; McFadden, *Judgment according to Works in Romans*, 50, who describes these works in similar terms of "a holistic view" or "a holistic way" and a judgment based on "external actions and internal dispositions." He subsequently describes it as a "unitary view of human works" (ibid., 52).

108. Rosscup says the punishment comes in two pairs of terms. "The first pair of words spotlights God's anger in punishing (ὀργή [*orgē*] and θυμός [*thymos*]). The last pair deals with the offenders' anguish. They feel retribution that their own sin invited God to bring on them (θλῖψις [*thlipsis*] and στενοχώρια [*stenochōria*])" (Rosscup, "Paul's Concept of Eternal Punishment," 174).

109. McFadden is certainly correct when he says, "Interpreters must allow for the element of self-deception in the dialogue partner" (McFadden, *Judgment according to Works in Romans*, 61). With respect to the issue of self-deception of those in Rom 1, see Greg L. Bahnsen, "The Crucial Concept of Self-Deception in Presuppositional Apologetics," *WTJ* 57 (1995): 1–31.

of the heart is itself the penalty for the root problem, namely, not honoring God as Creator."[110] And although each one of the subsequent categories of sins are of themselves punishment for egregious forms of idolatry (Rom 1:18–23, 25b, 28a), nevertheless, these specific acts of sin also call for additional punishment of both immediate and eschatological death at the final day of the Lord (Rom 1:32).[111] In addition to sinning against general revelation, the unregenerate Jews of Romans 2 also reject the commands of the law in particular and thereby increase the wrath of a future reckoning as well (Rom 4:15). The divine response to their transgressions is parallel to that of the ungodliness of the gentiles in that both bring present as well as eschatological wrath. There is therefore not a sharp dichotomy between now (1:18–32) and later judgments (2:1–16; 3:1–20), although the distinction between the two elements is clearly evident. The nature of Jewish transgressions may be equated with gentile ungodliness in that both serve to bring further (and future) divine wrath. Commenting on Romans 4:15, Douglas Moo writes,

> For Paul does not use "transgression" as a synonym for "sin." "Transgression" denotes a specific kind of sin, the "passing beyond" the limits set by a definite, positive law or command. While every "transgression" is also a "sin," not every "sin" is a "transgression." Paul, then, is not indicating that there is no "sin" where there is no law, but, in almost a "truism," that there is no deliberate disobedience of positive commands where there is no positive command to disobey. . . . Paul's real point emerges in the application of this principle to the Mosaic law as an explanation of how it is that "the law works wrath." Before and outside of the Mosaic law wrath certainly exists, for all people, being sinners, stand under God's sentence of condemnation (1:18). But the Mosaic law "produces" even more wrath; rather than rescuing people from the sentence of condemnation, it confirms their condemnation.[112]

---

110. DeSilva, *Introduction to the New Testament*, 632.

111. The *causal* connectives are used repeatedly "because/for this reason" (διότι, διό, διὰ τοῦτο [*dioti, dio, dia touto*]) (vv. 19a, 21a, 24a, 26a) as well as *explanatory* conjunctions "for" in order to draw the connection between idolatry and just retribution (vv. 19b, 20a). "Paul argues not only that human sin follows idolatry but also that the proliferation of sin is itself the appropriate penalty of God's judgment against idolatry" (McFadden, *Judgment according to Works in Romans*, 30–31). See also Robert H. Gundry, "Grace, Works, and Staying Saved in Paul," *Biblia* 66 (1985): 22n56.

112. Douglas J. Moo, *The Epistle to the Romans*, NICNT (Grand Rapids: Eerdmans, 1996), 277.

And this Jewish disobedience to the law of God does not merely confirm their condemnation but also compounds it, says Moo. The results of divine abandonment in Romans 1:18–32 brought on by a measurable or *quantitative* spiritual atavism from theism to monism in a war against the Creator—or as Peter Jones would frame it, from two-ism to one-ism—involve a worsening or *qualitative* ethical insurrection against the creational order as the punishment.[113] The escalation of sinful activity solicits only additional wrath. This compounded unrighteousness becomes the fitting punishment of idolatry and the basis for future wrath (Rom 1:18; 2:5). This is not to suggest there is no relational, logical, or philosophical link with monism to deviant sexuality.[114] Peter Jones seems to suggest this very gravitation toward radical egalitarianism where no distinctives, including sexual, are maintained.[115] And though, according to Romans 1:18–32, these punishments are directed generally at all humankind, they are most notably and apparently aimed at the most egregious practitioners of idolatry. While Romans 1:18–2:14 focuses on men/man, Romans 2:14–19 focuses on Jew/gentile.[116] So although the day of the Lord will come catastrophically on all who do not call on the name of the Lord, Paul notes that there is presently an already/not-yet aspect of this coming wrath exercised discriminately and designedly on all humankind to a degree and most apparently if not more severely toward the most offensive offenders.[117] This present aspect of the day of the Lord with its portents elucidating the final par-excellent judgment in the day of the Lord together forms the backdrop to Paul's soteriological treatise beginning with justification.

In referring to this retributive action by God on all humankind generally and others more manifestly as *deprivation* (in Rom 1:18–32), it may be assumed that humankind therefore necessarily and congenitally possesses

---

113. See the perceptive treatment of Rom 1:18–32 in Peter Jones, *One or Two: Seeing a World of Difference: Romans 1 for the Twenty-First Century* (Escondido, CA: Main Entry Editions, 2010). "Unbroken naturalness is not pure" (Barth, *Romans*, 52).

114. See for example Wisdom of Solomon 11–19 and Gorman, *Apostle of the Crucified Lord*, 19, who says about idolatry "that immoralities of various kinds flow from that basis error."

115. See Jones, *One or Two*.

116. Horne, "Toward a Biblical Apologetic," 89. "This would establish the fact that up to 2:14 Paul has in mind a universal revelation that touches both Jew and Gentile" (ibid.).

117. Schmitt says in a footnote, "It is probably best to think of the wrath already being revealed in Romans 1 as the beginning of God's final, eschatological day of wrath anticipated in Romans 2:5–10. The two time periods are not fundamentally distinct" (Schmitt, "Peace and Wrath in Paul's Epistle to the Romans," 70n8).

all these unrighteous potentialities *ab initio* and that there is then a congenital *privation* with respect to the heart of humankind brought about by the fall—starkly depicted in the juridical indictment on the day of the Lord in Romans 3:9–20. It may be presupposed that Romans 1–4 maintains the prominence of the human condition in the *foreground* while the entirety of Romans has humanity's depravity in various proximities of *background*. The ungodliness and unrighteousness become the juridical penalties on all humankind in the sense that they are accompanying circumstances of the sin of Adam. But the specific activity in Romans 1:18–32 in particular involves both a further deprivation of God's goodness as well as an ironic (if not sardonic) retribution on those who grievously transform God's nature and character into something altogether foreign and false. Because of their opposition to God's goodness and in contrast to their utter perversion of God's holy character, God ceases his gracious restraining activities on the hearts of humanity and gives them over to their perverted selves.

To summarize, Paul, in the context of Romans 1:18–3:20, appears to be recreating for his readers the *Sitz im Leben* of the day of the Lord, namely, to those *existentially* carrying their guilt while *proleptically* facing it in utter silence before the throne of God's full and furious juridical wrath. This foretaste and foreboding dress rehearsal in turn becomes the forensic backdrop for his soteriological treatise, setting forth the only path of escape. This final judgment in the day of the Lord carries significant influence in Paul's correspondence to Rome and is reinforced by the bookends of the gospel (Rom 1:16–17; 3:21–5:21). What appears almost an interruption (Rom 1:18–3:20) in his exposition of the gospel (the bookends) turns out to be the most likely motivation behind it, thus hardly a mere digression or anacoluthon.[118] The wrath of God is therefore both future and present to some degree. Proof of its inauguration is evident in the divine deprivational acts of retribution (1:18–32) as well as the juridical indictment (2:1–16; 3:1–20), both aspects prefiguring as well as anticipating the final *performative* sentencing of unregenerate gentiles and Jews ("world" in 3:19) on the day of the Lord. With these issues in mind, the present wrath is not only *preemptive*

---

118. This is brought out syntactically when the γάρ (*gar*) clause in 1:18 is taken as an *explanation* of the gospel (or the phrase ἐκ πίστεως εἰς πίστιν [*ek pisteōs eis pistin*]) subordinate to either ἐπαισχύνομαι (*epaischynomai*, v. 16a) or ἀποκαλύπτεται (*apokalyptetai*, v. 17) and serving as a "cohesive device" (Porter, *Idioms of the Greek New Testament*, 305). See also McFadden, *Judgment according to Works in Romans*, 36–37.

but also *provisionary* and *prevenient*. The idea of God's inaugurated wrath may be understood to a large degree as a byproduct of Paul's encounter on the Damascus road, containing the husk of salvation within the trappings and tapestry of eschatological judgment, and consequently serving in a refractive manner on every aspect of his theology.

Having set the juridical context for the soteriological explanation of Christ's redemption, we may now revisit the question posed earlier. In what way does this divine retribution in Romans 1:18–32 portend or foreshadow the consummate day of the Lord in its fullness if not in its permanence? As shown above, the nature of the judgment is best understood as *a withdrawing of God's gracious restraining influence that in turn unleashes the congenital depravities of humanity*. This type of abandonment is surely included as part of the judgment in the day of the Lord. Instead of any restraints whatsoever or merely varying degrees of abandonment, the recipients of God's wrath on the final day of the Lord will be absolute, universal, and permanent. In Romans 1:18–32 in particular, God's wrath is merely giving humanity over to itself and its own corruptions to variable degrees. In the final day of the Lord, humankind will have added to this inward abandonment an external abandonment of benevolence and beneficence. Unsaved humankind will experience the double-edged sword of God's wrath in proportion to the evil deeds committed. If the above assessment is correct, then the present wrath serves as a true indicator of, or in Paul's words, a genuine *revealing* of the nature of the wrath to come.

ROMANS 3:21–5:21

Before briefly touching on other instances in Paul's epistle of God's wrath associated with the day of the Lord, it is important to understand how Paul may have construed his soteriological section on justification in light of his understanding of both the wrath of God and that day. Specifically, how does Paul see Romans 3:21–5:21 in light of the wrath of God and the day of the Lord regarding the saving act of Christ?

Having the final day of the Lord contextually in mind and specifically the emphasis resting on the wrath of God, we may then construe the crucifixion of Christ as an apocalyptic, proleptic, and vicarious day of vengeance for the sake of those represented in the person of Christ. *Redemption* brings to mind the exodus event or a type of the day of the

Lord in executing wrath on the Egyptians while rescuing the people of God (Rom 3:24).[119] Even in the exodus proper, redemption is intricately associated with the Passover event or the death of the firstborn as one (if not the primary) cause of escape from God's avenging death angel and Pharaoh's army.[120] In addition to this, its collocation with and reference to the *mercy seat* recalls the *propitiatory act* of the cult or the act of God's vengeance that is designed to turn away eschatological wrath by the satiation of divine justice (Rom 3:25).[121] "It is not simply the case that human beings stand under the condemnation of God's *Angriff*. Coordinate with this attack, God demands (and receives) the vicarious subjection of the incarnate one *to that very same attack*, the full force of which is concentrated in the

---

119. Richard H. Bell, "Sacrifice and Christology in Paul," *JTS* 53 (2002): 17. See Exod 6:6, where the exodus event is described as Yahweh's rescue and redemption of Israel.

120. Terms for redemption are associated with a host of issues (culled from biblical and extrabiblical sources), including: (1) *a price paid to secure an effect*—securing Jews from the diaspora, the blood of Christ, a once-for-all type of sacrifice, and with respect to the "many"; (2) *a regaining of something lost*—one's sanity, land or property, or people, freedom, purity of mind/freedom from worry, or justice; (3) *an escape from something bad*—judgment of Sodom, immoral situations, slavery, harm, or the curse of the law; or (4) *the addition of something good*—justification, forgiveness, or resurrection.

121. There is considerable debate whether the word translated as *propitiation* ἱλαστήριον (*hilistērion*) should be in reference to Christ as a *propitiatory sacrifice* or to the *place of propitiation* (*mercy seat*). There seems to be overwhelming evidence that the term refers to the "mercy seat" and therefore *place of propitiation* (see also Heb 9:5). "The ending-τήριον means 'place' so this is a 'place of propitiation' or 'mercy seat'" (A. T. Robertson, *A Grammar of the Greek New Testament in the Light of Historical Research* [Nashville: Broadman, 1934], 154). Some scholars have interpreted the *place of propitiation* as simply a cleansing element or the place where God is present but without vicarious or substitutionary atoning significance (Christian Eberhart and Don Schweitzer, "Did Paul See the Saving Significance of Jesus' Death as Resulting from Divine Violence? Dialogical Reflections on Romans 3:25," *Consensus [Online]* 34 [2012]: 1–20; Don Schweitzer, "Understanding Substitutionary Atonement in Spatial Terms," *Touchstone* 31 [2013]: 7–17). Schweitzer argues, "Christ's death is an expiation in that it overcomes human estrangement from God. However, its goal is not to satisfy God's wrath, for it is the love of God that bridges the distance between God and sinners, embracing the guilty despite their undeserving" (ibid., 12; see also 13–15, 17). But this explanation seems largely reductionistic, especially in light of additional appositional phrases further defining the *place* of propitiation as including a propitiatory sacrifice, namely, *through his faithfulness* (διὰ τῆς πίστεως [*dia tēs pisteōs*]) and *by his blood* (ἐν τῷ αὐτοῦ αἵματι [*en tō autou haimati*]). "It may sound paradoxical to say that God provides the propitiation, but it accounts for the facts" (Morris, *Romans*, 180n27; BDAG 474). For a discussion of incarnational-centered models of the atonement versus the forensic/vicarious views see Ross M. Wright, "Is There Life in Vicarious and Forensic Theories of the Atonement? An Assessment of J. K. Mozley's Interpretation of Propitiation," *Sewanee Theological Review* 57 (2014): 173–87. For an evangelical defense of (vicarious) substitutionary atonement in Paul see Simon J. Gathercole, *Defending Substitution: An Essay on Atonement in Paul*, Acadia Studies in Bible and Theology (Grand Rapids: Baker, 2015).

passion."[122] The picture Paul presents of God prior to this act is one of mercifully restraining his full fury while graciously dispensing his forgiveness in anticipation of this forensic, vindictive, vindicating, and apocalyptic action on the cross and on his Son. The soteriological collocation of terms (redemption and propitiation) used by Paul in 3:21–31 in particular suggests that the day of the Lord lies behind both the exodus event and the sacrificial motif of the Day of Atonement.[123] The latter's uniqueness (once a year) as well as the advent of God's presence in the Shekinah, bringing either forgiveness or condemnation, represents a type of the day of the Lord and an intermingling with the satisfying of God's wrath in the cult that prefigures the consummate atoning work of Christ.[124] In Christ's crucifixion, the day of the Lord intertwines with the exodus deliverance and the Day of Atonement in a par-excellent manner.[125] Propitiation, by turning away divine wrath through the satisfaction of justice at the place of the cross, offers the proleptic final escape from judgment for repentant sinners.[126] Christ has taken the full fury of God's

---

122. Paul Dafydd Jones, "The Rhetoric of War in Karl Barth's Epistle to the Romans: A Theological Analysis," *Zeitschrift für Neuere Theologiegeschichte* 17 (2010): 100. Of course Barth would apply this divine action in actual universalistic categories rather than limit it to the "many" and "all" represented by Christ—in distinction to the "all" and "many" represented by Adam (Rom 5:12–21). Equivocation of all/many seems necessary in light of the representative principle.

123. See Bell, "Sacrifice and Christology in Paul," 20–21; in Thomas Hieke and Tobias Nicklas, eds., *The Day of Atonement: Its Interpretations in Early Jewish and Christian Traditions*, Themes in Biblical Narrative: Jewish and Christian Traditions 15 (Leiden: Brill, 2012), see the essays written by Richard J. Bautch and Markus Tiwald.

124. "The Day of atonement . . . was sometimes called the day of reckoning, because that was the day when the books were audited, accounts reconciled, and debits were forgiven, cleared, or carried over into the next year" (George Wesley Buchanan, "The Day of Atonement and Paul's Doctrine of Redemption," *NovT* 32 [1990]: 238).

125. Although Paul directly states that Christ is the Passover lamb (1 Cor 5:7)—in agreement with the Synoptic Gospels (Matt 26:17–19; Mark 14:12–16; Luke 22:1–15) but in possible (but unlikely) discord with John (see John 1:29, 26; 12:1; 13:1; 18:28, 39; 19:14, 27)—there remain questions whether the Last Supper either actually took place on the Passover or was meant to be represented by the Passover meal. For a summary of issues see Drane, *Introducing the New Testament*, 142–46. Solutions may be found in the differing calendars (lunar versus solar) combined with the prevalent Jewish conflation of the Passover (proper) with the Feast of Unleavened Bread (Mark 14:12; Luke 22:1; Josephus, *Ant.* 14.21; 18.29; 20.106; *War* 2.10; 6.423).

126. Leon Morris, "The Use of ἱλάσκεσθαι etc. in Biblical Greek," *ExpTim* 62 (1950–51): 227–33; Morris, "The Meaning of ἱλαστήριον in Romans 3.25," *NTS* 2 (1955–56): 33–43. The violent nature of propitiation is the logical consequence to the wrath of God—depreciation of the extent of one seems to necessarily diminish that of the other. See Carson, "Vindication of Imputation," 46n2, 49.

wrath, paid it in full, and therefore offers forgiveness and escape from eschatological fury.[127]

Paul's final conclusion for the whole of Romans 3:21–4:25 reads, "Therefore, having been justified we have *peace* with God through our Lord Jesus Christ" (Rom 5:1). The exercise of God's wrath in the cross of Christ has secured peace for those who are justified. Thus, while wrath is both present (Rom 1:18) and future (Rom 2:5), so also is peace both present in justification (Rom 5:1) and future via vindication (Rom 2:10). This peace is a result of the divine war on sin having been won, divine wrath having been executed satisfactorily, and a divine reconstitution and restitution of what had been lost. It is not just a ceasefire or a surrender to God on humanity's part but rather a divine warrior's overcoming of innate human resistance to the revelation of God (both natural and special) through a revelatory and apocalyptic action in Christ as the divine foe subjugated to God's wrath on humankind's behalf.

Given the above scenario, the eschatological wrath and fury of God have been revealed in the present time and fully inflicted on Christ as the final place of divine judgment. While the "world" anticipates its ultimate day of reckoning (3:19–20), those designated as weak, ungodly, and sinners have already experienced both the final verdict and infliction of divine wrath via the vicarious actions of Christ on the cross—and moreover to the utter satisfaction of God's justice (5:6, 8). In a word, judgment day has already come and gone for "the many" in the person of Christ on the cross (5:12–21). It is this justification by the death of Christ that has bought and brought escape from both present and future wraths of God (Rom 5:9). For the saint, the wrath of God is therefore past, *fait accompli*, fully satisfied, and paid in full.

ROMANS 9–11

Romans 9–11 sets out to resolve the problem of the unbelief of most of ethnic Israel as it potentially threatens the faithfulness of God to his people. The key passage in this section contributing to the dominant theme of the

---

127. "Like God's holiness, then, his wrath is not something that sits awkwardly next to his love. Nor is it something unrelated to his love. God is angry at evil *because* he loves." And "in his pure love, God cannot tolerate evil" (Michael Reeves, *Delighting in the Trinity: An Introduction to the Christian Faith* [Downers Grove, IL: InterVarsity, 2012], 118).

future wrath of God in Romans and related to the day of the Lord is Romans 9:22–23.[128] Adding to the complexities of the passage is that it is one among several of Paul's notorious anacolutha in Romans.[129] It appears to be missing an apodosis.[130] John Piper reasons contextually that "Paul concludes his justification of God's unconditional election with the unfinished sentence of 9:23, and then with 9:24 returns to the level of 9:6–8 which had given rise to the issue of unconditional election."[131] A second issue is that 9:22–23 contain three adverbial clauses (if the καί [kai] is retained in v. 23), complicating the semantic relationship of the final ἵνα (hina) clause to the antecedent infinitives ἐνδείξασθαι and γνωρίσαι ([endeixasthai, gnōrisai] 22a–b). Piper suggests that the *purpose* infinitives are subordinate to the ἵνα (hina) clause and interprets the relationship as indicating that "the revealed character of God has integrity: it is not fragmented or contradictory. The acts of God come forth not in continuous reaction to autonomous external stimuli but

---

128. For a list of the difficulties of the passage in both translating and rightly construing the grammatical issues involved see Paul Ellingworth, "Translation and Exegesis: A Case Study (Rom 9:22ff)," *Bib* 59 (1978): 399–402.

129. Cranfield, *Epistle to the Romans*, 492–93; Morris, *Romans*, 366–67; BDF 242, §467. The anacoluthon is avoided if the καί [kai] in verse 23 is omitted, a situation that some manuscripts oblige (omitted in B, 326, pc, lat, Or, and 1739mg). See Bruce M. Metzger, *A Textual Commentary on the Greek New Testament: A Companion Volume to the United Bible Societies' Greek New Testament* (Stuttgart: Deutsche Bibelgesellschaft, 1994), 462. Piper notes that some argue for 9:23 being the *apodosis*, but, he says, "the arguments against this construction, however, are weighty" (John Piper, *The Justification of God: An Exegetical & Theological Study of Romans 9:1–23* [Grand Rapids: Baker, 1993], 205–7).

130. Contra Piper, Hoover argues that the *consequent* (*apodosis*) begins in v. 23 and therefore no anacoluthon. See Joseph Hoover, "The Wealth of God's Glory: A Response to John Piper's 'Four Problems in Romans 9:22–23,'" *Stone-Campbell Journal* 12 (2009): 48n7, 49–50. "The causal interpretation overlooks the counter-expectant nature of 9:22 and so holds wrath and power to be a direct purpose of God's patient endurance. Such an understanding of the relationship between God's wrath and God's enduring of sin is found nowhere else in the NT (Rom 2:4; 3:26; 2 Pet 3:9 on the contrary)" (ibid., 52). Hoover's limitation to the NT texts for ruling out the idea of God's forbearance of evil in order to build up wrath appears to be a case of special pleading (see Gen 15:16; 4 Ezra 7:72–74; 1 Macc 8:1–4; 2 Macc 6:12–14), besides having questionable interpretations of particular biblical passages such as 2 Pet 3:9 (ibid., 52–54). The *causal* interpretation does not limit one to Piper's understanding of the passage any more than taking the *counterexpectant* view confines one to Hoover's interpretation. See for example Wayne A. Brindle, "Prepared by Whom? Reprobation and Non-Calvinist Interpretations of Romans 9:22," *CTR* 12 (2015): 139.

131. Piper, *Justification of God*, 185. He adds, "Paul could have concluded his defense at this point. But since he does not, we see that he is not averse to reflecting more deeply on the problem of God's sovereignty in hardening some and having mercy on others. Romans 9:22, 23 is Paul's final insight into the whys and wherefores of unconditional election, and (together with 9:15–18) it is probably the closest that the Bible ever comes to offering us a justification of the mysterious ways of God with man" (ibid., 186–87).

from a unified, sovereign purpose."[132] Before commenting further with respect to the crux issue, Romans 9:22–23 reads as follows:

> But what if God, although desiring [or "because he desires"] to show his wrath and to make known his power, endured with much long-suffering vessels destined for wrath prepared for destruction? And in order that he might make known the riches of his glory to the vessels destined for mercy, namely, those whom he prepared before-hand for glory, ²⁴even us, whom he called, not only from out of the Jews but also out of the Gentiles—[Apodosis: then what will you say? Or will you then contest God's rights?]

Joseph Hoover argues that there is a parallel between Romans 9:22–23 and Romans 3:21–26, where in both texts "God's patient endurance serves God's desire to make known all his glorious attributes and not merely wrath and power."[133] Understood in this light, the affective element that Paul seems to be emphasizing or attempting to recreate in the reader is staked on the tolerance God exercises toward the vessels destined for wrath.[134] God is shown to exercise a great patience by withholding for the meantime his full fury until that day arrives, that is, until he gathers in all of his elect from among both Jews and gentiles. Underlying this assertion are arguably two rhetorical questions directed at the interlocutor: *Is not God therefore somewhat gracious for tolerating evil and evil folks for the sake of saving his elect? Do you, dear interlocutor, object to those undeniably more gracious aspects of God's sovereignty as well? Of course you don't! How consistent you are.*[135] Paul may be attempting to convey a frustration to the reader over the interlocutor's inconsistent moral outrage at the apostle's claims of God's absolute control over and noncontingent (in

---

132. Ibid., 188–89.

133. Hoover, "Wealth of God's Glory," 52.

134. Hoover refers to the participle θέλων (*thelōn*) as "the thesis of a contra-expectation clause the antithesis of which is the unmarked portion of 9:22" in contrast to a causal interpretation (ibid., 48, 50–51). He translates, "Desiring to show his wrath and to make known his power, [he] has *nevertheless* endured with much patience the vessels of wrath" (ibid., 48n4).

135. For an attempted outworking of this *pathos* toward the nonelect or unsaved Jew from a somewhat liberal perspective see James E. McNutt, "Vessels of Wrath, Prepared to Perish: Adolf Schlatter and the Spiritual Extermination of the Jews," *Theology Today* 63 (2006): 176–90. The author of this work is largely biased in his portrait of Adolf Schlatter's biblical positions toward Jews in pre-WWII Germany.

terms of human activities, actual or foreseen) bases of hardening versus mercying of individuals respecting salvation or damnation. Perhaps this exasperated tone of Paul, although admittedly speculative, may partially account (if most commentators are correct) for the anacoluthon here.[136] At any rate, a quantitative building up of eschatological wrath, which is not explicit here as elsewhere if the causative element is removed, is certainly not incompatible with the notion of showing patience to those very objects of wrath in the present. This divine patience toward the vessels of wrath has a goal, namely the gathering in of the elect of both Jews and gentiles for salvation.

An additional and perhaps more contested and contentious issue includes the nature of the *divine activity* with respect to the "vessels destined for wrath *prepared* for destruction" (9:22) versus "vessels destined for mercy, namely, those whom he *prepared beforehand* for glory" (9:23). The implications of double predestination are quite apparent and difficult to circumvent or mitigate.[137] Among all the contextual and grammatical issues involved in solving this complex and far-reaching text, the crux and perhaps key for unlocking the extent of divine involvement relates to how one reconciles the *active* voice of the finite verb in the relative clause, ἃ προητοίμασεν εἰς δόξαν (*ha proētoimasen eis doxan*), "those whom [referring to 'vessels destined for mercy'] *he prepared* beforehand for glory," versus the *passive* voice in the participle clause, σκεύη ὀργῆς κατητισμένα εἰς ἀπώλειαν (*skeuē orgēs katētismena eis apōleian*), "vessels destined for wrath *prepared* for destruction." How does one relate these ideas theologically or causatively to the *divine activity*? Daniel Wallace argues that the genitive in the Greek phrases σκεύη ἐλέους (*skeuē eleous*), "vessels of mercy," and σκεύη ὀργῆς (*skeuē orgēs*), "vessels of wrath," should be understood as *genitives of destination*, "vessels *destined* for mercy" and "vessels *destined*

136. Although the figure of *aposiopesis*, defined as "the breaking off of speech due to a strong emotion or to modesty," is unknown in the NT, according to one Greek grammar, this passage may be an exception. See BDF §482.

137. For an interesting study of the development of Luther's view of predestination as it was interpreted through Melanchthon, who rejected double predestination, versus Amsdorf, who endorsed it, see Robert Kolb, "Nikolaus von Amsdorf on Vessels of Wrath and Vessels of Mercy: A Lutheran's Doctrine of Double Predestination," *HTR* 69 (1976): 325–43; Monica Brands, "Vessels of Mercy: Aquinas and Barth on Election and Romans Chapters 9–11," *Journal of Theta Alpha Kappa* 37 (2013): 23–39. See also E. C. Blackman, "Divine Sovereignty and Missionary Strategy in Romans 9–11," *CJT* 11 (1965): 124–34; G. B. Caird, "Predestination—Romans 9–11," *ExpTim* 68 (1956–57): 324–27.

for wrath."[138] In addition to this, Wallace gives reasons for taking the middle/passive form of the perfect participle in the phrase κατηρτισμένα εἰς ἀπώλειαν (*katētismena eis apōleian*), "*having been prepared* for destruction," as *passive*, against the *direct middle*, "having *prepared themselves*."[139] He states the case as follows:

> The middle view has little to commend it. First, grammatically, the direct middle is quite rare and is used almost exclusively in certain idiomatic expressions, especially where the verb is used consistently with such a notion (as in the verbs for putting on clothes). This is decidedly not the case with καταρτίζω: nowhere else in the NT does it occur as a direct middle. Second, in the perfect tense, the middle-passive form is always to be taken as a passive in the NT (Luke 6:40; 1 Cor 1:10; Heb 11:3) — a fact that, in the least, argues against an idiomatic use of this verb as a direct middle. Third, the lexical nuance of καταρτίζω, coupled with the perfect tense, suggests something of a "done deal." Although some commentators suggest that the verb means that the vessels are *ready* for destruction, both the lexical nuance of complete preparation and the grammatical nuance of the perfect tense are against this. Fourth, the context argues strongly for a passive and completed notion. In v 20 the vessel is shaped by God's will, not its own ("Will that which is molded say to its maker, 'Why have you made me this way?'"). In v 21, Paul asks a question with οὐκ (thus expecting a positive answer): Is not the destiny of the vessels (one for honor, one for dishonor) entirely predetermined by their Creator? Verse 22 is the answer to that question. To argue, then, that κατητισμένα is a direct

---

138. Daniel B. Wallace, *Greek Grammar beyond the Basics: An Exegetical Syntax of the New Testament* (Grand Rapids: Zondervan, 1996), 101. Others classify the genitive as *attributive* (BDF §165; Max Zerwick, *Biblical Greek Illustrated by Examples*, trans. Joseph Smith, Scripta Pontificii 114 [Rome: Editrice Pontificio Istituto Biblico, 1963], §40; Nigel Turner, *A Grammar of New Testament Greek*, vol. 3, *Syntax*, ed. James Hope Moulton [Edinburgh: T&T Clark, 1963], 213). Robertson appears to take it as an *objective* genitive, interpreting it as vessels engaged in wrathful behaviors. See Robertson, *Grammar of the Greek New Testament*, 496. Morris prefers to translate "characterized by wrath," or a *descriptive* genitive (Morris, *Romans*, 368n104). Contrary to Brindle, there is no indication or hope that "vessels of wrath" may become "vessels of mercy" (Brindle, "Prepared by Whom?," 140; Cranfield, *Romans*, 495).

139. A fuller description of the participle would be as follows: *extensive* perfect, *simple* passive (without agency expressed), *adjectival* participle (fourth attendant position), modifying σκεύη (*skeuē*).

middle seems to fly in the face of grammar (the normal use of the voice and tense), lexeme, and context.[140]

The case against Wallace's observations and conclusions has not proved convincing.[141] One additional but incidental grammatical feature indirectly supporting Wallace is the use of the plural participle modifying a plural neuter noun for "vessels . . . prepared" (σκεύη . . . κατηρτισμένα [skeuē . . . katētismena]). This usage suggests a stress, similar to election, on *individual* rather than *group* reprobation.[142]

Supplemental to the grammatical arguments in favor of the *(divine) passive* for the perfect participle are two distinct views of double predestination. Each has arisen to further qualify either the similarity or dissimilarity of the divine actions. The first sees no distinction between God's actions toward vessels of wrath versus vessels of mercy and is labeled *symmetrical double predestination*.[143] This construal, according to R. C. Sproul, involves God positively working in the hearts of those prepared for glory to guarantee eternal life in the same way *(symmetrically)* he works positively in the hearts of the nonelect to guarantee their eternal perdition. Sproul rejects this view and associates it with hyper-Calvinism. In addition, this view

140. Wallace, *Greek Grammar beyond the Basics*, 418. Of course there are other possible agents or no agency at all, but God and the self are the two dominant views. See Piper, *Justification of God*, 208. Rosscup lists five possible arguments for the *direct* middle including (1) that God is mentioned in the active finite verb but not in the passive, suggesting God may not be involved in the latter; (2) God "endures" these vessels, hinting that it is they who are fitting themselves, not God; (3) frequent mention of "whoever" throughout Romans suggests a human response plays a part; (4) people are responsible and therefore able to positively respond; and (5) citing Jer 19, concerning vessels (Israelites), suggesting that by refusing to believe these Israelites fit themselves for destruction. See Rosscup, "Paul's Concept of Eternal Punishment," 177; Hoover, "Wealth of God's Glory," 54–56; Brindle, "Prepared by Whom?," 142–43. For a libertarian perspective see P. W. Gooch, "Sovereignty and Freedom: Some Pauline Compatibilisms," *SJT* 40 (1987): 531–42.

141. For the arguments based on extrabiblical examples of the perfect middle/passive participle understood as *direct* middles see Brindle, "Prepared by Whom?," 143–45.

142. See Friedrich Blass et al., *Grammatik des neutestamentlichen Griechisch: [Joachim Jeremias zum 75. Geburtstag]* (Göttingen: Vandenhoeck und Ruprecht, 1976), §133; Wallace, *Greek Grammar beyond the Basics*, 400; Robertson, *Grammar of the Greek New Testament*, 404; Thomas R. Schreiner, "Does Romans 9 Teach Individual Election unto Salvation? Some Evangelical and Theological Reflections," *JETS* 36 (1993): 25–40. Contrary to Brindle, the passage is not about "salvation history" (at least in the forefront) but about the glory of God in light of divine unconditional election and preterition. See Brindle, "Prepared by Whom?," 136.

143. See R. C. Sproul, *Chosen by God* (Wheaton, IL: Tyndale, 1986), 141–60. For a discussion of *single* predestination and *symmetrical* double predestination *(positive-positive)* as incompatible with the Reformed view of *asymmetrical* double predestination *(positive-negative)*, see R. C. Sproul, *"Double" Predestination*, available from www.ligonier.org/learn/articles/double-predestination/.

does not seem to adequately account for the divine activity respecting the *active* versus the *passive* verbal ideas noted above. A more plausible second view (which Sproul advocates) sees different divine activities and suggests that double predestination is *asymmetrical*. While God is the actor in both respects (the doctrine of *divine ultimacy*, as D. A. Carson refers to it), he acts *asymmetrically* with the objects of wrath versus objects of mercy. While God, on the basis of the atonement and through the instrumentality/agency of his Spirit, *positively* acts within the hearts of the elect to bring them to the saving knowledge of Christ (hence the active voice), he *negatively* works toward the nonelect (vessels of wrath) by *withholding* his saving activity and permitting these individuals to go their own way (hence the passive voice).[144] The divine activity toward one, *by means of the active voice*, is *transformative* (via regeneration), focusing directly on the *efficient* cause of salvation in the absence of a *material* cause, while the divine activity toward the other is *nontransformative* (via preterition). The latter is focused, *by means of the passive voice*, on the *material* cause of condemnation in the foreground while not negating the *efficient* cause lingering quite prominently in the background. In this way Paul seeks to link both the *material* cause of humanity's destruction to its responsibility as well as the *efficient* cause of its perdition to God's sovereignty.[145] So the differing voices in Greek are designed to differentiate the subject's respective actions toward the objects, not to distinguish acting agents. God is the sole actor either explicitly or elliptically (and inferentially) in *both* albeit *differing* respects.

While in Romans 1 the divine activity depicted in the phrase "God gave them over to the desires of their hearts" was earlier defined as *the withholding or withdrawing of common grace*, leading to increased moral putrefaction as juridical punishment for idolatry, the divine activity in Romans 9 includes the *withholding* of the special grace of *regeneration* or *effectual calling* and all its effects purely out of the divine will without consideration of evil deeds.[146] Contrary to Romans 1, where causative elements are given for

---

144. Similarly, see John Calvin, *Concerning the Eternal Predestination of God*, trans. John K. S. Reid (Louisville, KY: Westminster John Knox, 1997), 57–58.

145. Commenting on Rom 9:11, Pink writes, "God's acts both of election and preterition—choosing and passing by—were entirely irrespective of any foreseen 'good or evil.' Note, too, how this compound expression 'the purpose of God according to election' supports the contention of there being two parts to God's decree" (A. W. Pink, *The Doctrine of Election* [New York: Great Christian Books, 2013], 78). Pink takes a *supralapsarian* view (God determines the composition of the elect logically *prior* to determining the fall) and presents a convincing case for that position. See ibid., 73–88.

that divine action (which is never termed "hardening"), this negative divine activity of *hardening* in Romans 9 is *nonretributive*. There is no tit for tat, *quid pro quo*, or any notions of juridical reciprocities stated or implied in Romans 9 (or Rom 11). What takes place is simply the withholding of the gracious benefits of the atonement of Christ that are neither deserved nor earned by and for these individuals represented solely by Adam (Rom 5:12–21). This latter divine activity is usually given the theological name of *preterition*, that is, the divine passing over/by the nonelect for salvific benefits.[147]

From a biblical perspective, this negative divine activity in Romans is described as *hardening* (9:18) or *fattening* (11:7, 25) depending on whether the *volition* or the *cognition* of the heart is being emphasized. The *fattening* rubric in particular finds its genesis in Deuteronomy 29:3, where Moses records, "But to this very day the LORD *has not given* you an understanding mind, perceptive eyes, or discerning ears" (emphasis added). Isaiah transforms this divine passive activity (or *preterition*) in Deuteronomy with respect to the mind as God actively (but nontransformatively) *causes* the hearts to *remain* fat (unperceiving, unknowing, nonunderstanding) and thus guaranteeing a lack of repentance (volition), thereby ensuring disobedience to the law of Moses and bringing judgment for those violations, culminating in exile (Isa 6:9–10).[148] Paul picks up on the deprivational

---

146. For a typical example of conflating what happens in Rom 1 (juridical) with Rom 9 (nonjuridical) in terms of making election or preterition in some way a *quid pro quo*, see Brindle, "Prepared by Whom?," 137n8.

147. Likening theologians who hold to reprobation as turning God into the hypocritical priest and Levite in the story of the good Samaritan is to misunderstand both the parable of the good Samaritan and the basis of reprobation. The point of the story of the good Samaritan is to universalize the concept of neighbor (and love of neighbor) beyond Israel and to render the latter six of the Ten Commandments as mandatory toward all humankind (Rom 13:8–10). On that basis, reprobation is a fulfillment rather than a violation of the love-of-neighbor ethic precisely because it renders perfect justice toward God's enemies. See Walter Campbell Campbell-Jack, "Prolegomena for Reprobation," *EvQ* 61 (1989): 42; Brindle, "Prepared by Whom?," 146.

148. The fundamental issue behind the biblical concept of *fattening* or the *fat heart* is *noetic* and may be profitably studied through the psychology of *understanding* and best assessed as a *hermeneutic* construct or problem. See the helpful directives in Richard E. Palmer, *Hermeneutics: Interpretation Theory in Schleiermacher, Dilthey, Heidegger, and Gadamer*, Northwestern University Studies in Phenomenology & Existential Philosophy (Evanston, IL: Northwestern University Press, 1969), 7–11, 80, 105–6, 114–15, 130–39, 162–217, 227–53. Hermeneutics, according to Schleiermacher, is "the art of hearing" or "the art of understanding any utterance in language" (ibid., 86, 94). The task of interpreting any work of art involves three powers: *subtilitas intelligendi*, *subtilitas explicandi*, and *subtilitas applicandi*. According to Gadamer, each one of these powers is an essential component of *understanding* (ibid., 187–91). "Understanding always includes application to the present" (ibid., 191; see also 235–37). See also Hans-Georg Gadamer, *Truth and Method*, trans. Joel Weinsheimer and Donald G. Marshall (New York: Crossroad, 1989), 278–370.

nature of this negative divine activity by reusing Isaiah 6:9–10 via Isaiah 29:9–10 and Deuteronomy 29:3, phrasing it as "God gave them a spirit of stupor, eyes that they would not see and ears that they would not hear unto this very day" (Rom 11:8).[149] Thus an active sense in Isaiah of giving a spirit of stupor (parallel with "make fat" in Isa 6:10) is interpreted by Paul, who understood the divine activity in terms of the deprivational idea in Deuteronomy of "not giving" a heart that understands, perceives, and knows . . . salvifically. Only Deuteronomy specifically describes the divine activity—and it is clearly *deprivational* as well as nonretributional in nature. Thus all language of God *hardening* hearts (in the case of the will) or God *fattening* hearts (in the case of the mind) are to be viewed as emphasizing God's *efficient* causation and thus divine perpetuation of humankind's congenital state of hardheartedness and fat-heartedness (*material* causation), thereby guaranteeing its present foolishness and persistence in disobedience as well as its eventual eternal destruction and/or perdition. While Romans 1 depicts a present wrath in degrees as a deprivation of God's common grace due to idolatry by abandoning humanity to its heart's latent sinful desires, Romans 9 guarantees the destiny of wrath mentioned in Romans 2 by withholding the grace necessary to overcome those sinful desires and refusing to generate salvific wisdom, repentance, and faith that would in turn safeguard one into heaven's glory.[150]

Five additional comments may be made about the nature of the heart, as these aid in explaining the distinctive workings of the respective divine activities. First, the *cognitive* and *volitional* elements of the heart may be distinguished (as with fattening and hardening) but never separated from each other. Second, there is a priority of *cognition* to *volition* where the will is best described as the mind choosing, and choosing according to its best

---

149. For a detailed examination of the proposition that God has two contrary wills with respect to his salvation according to Calvin versus Amyraut, see Richard A. Muller, "A Tale of Two Wills? Calvin and Amyraut on Ezekiel 18:23," *CTJ* 44 (2009): 211–25.

150. Even highly informed Calvinists (here Edwards and Gerstner) sometimes blend *hardening* and *fattening* ideas together and indiscriminately join them to Rom 1:18–32 without making careful distinctions. For example, see John H. Gerstner, *Steps to Salvation: The Evangelistic Message of Jonathan Edwards* (Philadelphia: Westminster, 1960); Gerstner, "Edwardsean Preparation for Salvation," *WTJ* 42 (1979): 5–71. The confusion in the academic literature is not limited, therefore, to either non-Calvinists or incompatibilists. But see Hoover, "Wealth of God's Glory," 56, for an Arminian example of this confusion and conflation.

interests and strongest inclinations at the moment of choice.[151] Third, the divine *preparation* of these vessels of wrath and vessels of mercy finds its *formal* cause within the inscrutable or hidden will of God (9:8–21) in out-and-out contrast to punitive, *quid pro quo*, or retributive bases.[152] Fourth, because humankind is congenitally fat-hearted and hardhearted, for God to perpetuate those conditions requires neither transformative action nor a punitive basis but rather an executive decision to not transform a heart of stone into a heart of flesh. Fifth, although the *material* cause of this wrath lies within the vessels of wrath, the text nevertheless emphasizes the *formal, efficient,* and *final* cause of their deserved destruction as being *formally* and *efficiently* God and *finally* for his own glory (11:33–36). In concluding one element within this (*asymmetrical*) double-predestination perspective, Paul says, "Israel failed to obtain what it was diligently seeking, but the elect obtained it. The rest were *fattened*" (11:7). In other words, God refused to give salvific knowledge to the nonelect, thereby leaving them in their sinful condition, thereby guaranteeing their perdition; but he mercifully and graciously transforms the hearts of his elect so that they will and would salvifically understand, perceive, and know and as a result repent, believe, and be spared not strictly from exile out of the land (as the Deuteronomy and Isaiah texts typify) of Israel but actually and ultimately be rescued from both the wrath of God in that day as well as the consequential and consummate wrath of God in everlasting perdition.

---

151. This understanding of the will is heavily dependent on the work of Edwards on the subject. See Jonathan Edwards, *Freedom of the Will*, Works of Jonathan Edwards 1 (New Haven: Yale University Press, 1957).

152. The closest approximation to the explanation offered here is by A. W. Pink, *The Sovereignty of God* (Alachua, FL: Bridge-Logos, 2008), 94–98. He states, "The most common errant view is that this is speaking of nothing more than judicial hardening (i.e., a rejection by God of those who rejected Him first). . . . The Apostle is not speaking about those who had already turned their back on God's truth; instead he is dealing with God's sovereignty, as seen not only in showing mercy to whom He wills, but also in hardening whom He pleases. The exact words are that He hardens, 'Whom He will,' not 'all who have rejected His truth'" (ibid., 95). Although the literature on this subject is vast, a few recent works that promote the retribution view of divine hardening (from varying theological perspectives) are mentioned here. For example, see Edward P. Meadors, *Idolatry and the Hardening of the Heart: A Study in Biblical Theology* (New York: T&T Clark, 2006); G. K. Beale, *We Become What We Worship: A Biblical Theology of Idolatry* (Downers Grove, IL: InterVarsity, 2008); Aaron Sherwood, *The Word of God Has Not Failed: Paul's Use of the Old Testament in Romans 9*, Studies in Scripture and Biblical Theology 1 (Bellingham, WA: Lexham Press, 2015). These works, along with many previous others, simply assume a retributive or juridical basis for divine *hardening* and/or *fattening* without actually demonstrating it. For a sympathetic treatment but lacking the consistency of capturing the view enunciated here, see Gary V. Smith, "Spiritual Blindness, Deafness, and Fatness in Isaiah," *BSac* 170 (2013): 166–78.

How does the reality of double predestination, specifically, that associated with the dark side of wrath pertaining to preterition and perdition, relate to the day of the Lord? The first answer is that while the wrath of God is always associated with the day of the Lord proper, it extends far beyond that singular event. If previous occasions of God's wrath serve as types of the day of the Lord consummated at the second coming of Christ, then the everlasting state of perdition is a par-excellent fulfillment of this wrath. But taking into account Paul's soteriology, the day of the Lord's wrath has already been executed on the elect in Christ on the cross in full (Rom 3:21–31). Paul has left open, then, two ways of facing God's wrath: either by acknowledging that it has been inflicted on Christ in a fully satisfactory way or to accept that wrath on oneself both in an already limited degree and a later, more comprehensive level on the day of the Lord and thereafter.

The second answer is that the subject of divine hardening finds its origins in the life of Pharaoh in Exodus 4–14 during the exodus event, an event that typified the day of the Lord. Here divine hardening was the *cause*, not the *effect* of Pharaoh's sins. We earlier argued that redemption reaches back to the exodus event, composed of both divine rescue and divine judgment and uniquely united within the propitiation of the Passover. In Romans 9 there is a confluence of redemptive elements in the form of mercy and grace for God's people via unconditional election and a destined wrath for those who are not God's people via *preterition* (divine hardening). Just like the hardening of Pharaoh was not juridical, so the hardening of the non-elect in Romans 9 is not juridical either. Paul takes great pains to indicate that election is unconditional on humankind's part. Statements such as "before Jacob and Esau had done any good or evil as a basis of choosing," or "God has mercy on whom he will have mercy and hardens whom he will," or "the potter has power over the clay," and the all-encompassing statement "Therefore, it [God's mercy in individual election] is neither dependent on the one who wills nor on the one who runs but on God who shows mercy," all together suggest not only a nonjuridical basis of wrath but likewise a noncontingent basis of choosing within the objects of election (9:11, 15, 16, 18).[153] As Paul later states, "Therefore, in the same way, also at the present

---

153. John Calvin, *The Bondage and Liberation of the Will: A Defense of the Orthodox Doctrine of Human Choice against Pighius*, ed. Richard A. Muller, trans. Graham I. Davies, Texts and Studies in Reformation and Post-Reformation Thought 2 (Grand Rapids: Baker, 1996), 227;

time, there is a remnant according to electing grace. And if by grace, it is certainly then not of works, otherwise grace is certainly not grace" (11:3–4). Divine hardening, rather than being a judgment, instead points to sin's *material* cause, which provides the grounds from which wrong behaviors spring that in turn bring divine judgments culminating in the day of the Lord. Double predestination, or in Paul's terms, "the kindness and severity of God" (11:22), becomes the *formal* cause of both redemption and preterition, of both unconditional election and divine hardening, and of both elective love and nonelective hatred.

A third answer is that double predestination is exercised via the fattening motif taken up in Romans 11:7, 25 and is executed with respect to ethnic Israel until the eschatological day of the Lord. As stated earlier, this concept reaches back to Deuteronomy but is taken up by Isaiah in detail. And Isaiah focuses on the *cognitive* aspect of the heart due to polemic factors related to the conflicting wisdoms of the king's counselors versus God's prophets, necessitating the salvific wisdom of God to know the difference. The purpose of divine fattening in Isaiah's day was to guarantee the lack of repentance among most of Judah and therefore to generate violations of the law of Moses that would in turn culminate in exile and captivity. In other words, a day of the Lord would result in divine wrath being executed on ethnic Israel (Judah). But at the same time a promised restoration to the land would also be given to a remnant, but only after a period of disciplinary action by God. Paul indicates that part of the purpose of divine fattening is to gather in a great number of nonethnic Jews into the fold of salvation. Thus it is not a judgment per se on ethnic Israel. But it is followed by a salvific event for Israel. Paul indicates that it is the day of the Lord that will reverse the fattening condition of "all of Israel."[154] The result is that they will be saved. He writes,

---

Calvin, *Institutes of the Christian Religion: Calvin's Own "Essentials" Edition*, trans. Robert White (Edinburgh: Banner of Truth, 2014), 485.

154. For discussion of the conflicting interpretations of the phrase πᾶς Ἰσραήλ (*pas Israēl*), "all Israel," see Mark D. Nanos, "Romans 11 and Christian-Jewish Relations: Exegetical Options for Revisiting the Translation and Interpretation of This Central Text," *CTR* 9 (2012): 3–21; Jason A. Staples, "What Do the Gentiles Have to Do with 'All Israel'? A Fresh Look at Romans 11:25–27," *JBL* 130 (2011): 371–90; P. H. R. van Houwelingen, "The Redemptive-Historical Dynamics of the Salvation of 'All Israel' (Rom. 11:26a)," *CTJ* 46 (2011): 301–14; Cornelis P. Venema, "'In This Way All Israel Will Be Saved': A Study of Romans 11:26," *Mid-America Journal of Theology* 22 (2011): 19–40.

> For I do not want you to be ignorant, brethren, about this mystery, so that you are not wise to yourselves, that a fattening to part of Israel has come, until which [time] the fullness of the Gentiles should arrive. And in this way all Israel will be saved, just as it is written, "The Deliverer will come out of Israel, he will turn ungodliness from Jacob. And this is the covenant with them, when I will take away their sins." (Rom 11:25–27; citing Isa 59:20–21; 27:9)

So one of the experiences to be anticipated on the day of the Lord, for Paul, is the reversal of the partial *fattening* of the heart of ethnic Israel to include many if not most of ethnic and eschatological Israel—not simply because they are ethnic Israel but because they will be part of the elect. This reversal (chronological, not ontological) would be in fulfillment of the promises of both Ezekiel and Jeremiah to the extent that by all appearances a majority of ethnic Israel would then constitute a great number of the elect at that time.[155] Whether the phrase "all Israel" refers to the elect composed of both Jews and gentiles, or strictly only to the elect ethnic Jews, or somehow encompasses all of ethnic Israel, or merely includes the majority of ethnic Jews, remains a matter of continual scholarly debate. Given Paul's earlier statements in Romans 2 and Romans 9 in particular, however, where regenerate gentiles are labeled inwardly Jews while outwardly ethnic, but unregenerate Jews are rejected as inwardly Jews or the Israel (remnant) of Israel, it would appear that the most likely interpretive option is to view the pertinent phrase, "all Israel," as referring to all the elect among both Jews and gentiles but composed largely if not wholly of ethnic Jews. The pendulum of the composite nature of the elect having swung toward a majority of gentiles in Paul's day will swing back in the Jewish direction on the day of the Lord in fulfillment of the new covenant as part of the unfolding saga of *Heilsgeschichte*.

---

155. Hoekema reasons because οὕτως (outōs), "in this way," refers to *manner* and not *time* (as in τότε [tote] or ἔπειτα [epeita]) that therefore the salvation of the Jews is due to the means of jealousy over the divine reception of gentiles rather than simply a temporal indicator. See Hoekema, *Bible and the Future*, 144–45; BDAG 742. This particular manner of provoking Jews to jealousy is certainly true, but the overall context seems to suggest an additional temporal sequence to this event.

ROMANS 12–15

Romans 12:1-2 sets the stage for the remainder or paraenetic section of the epistle as well as initiates a conclusive response from the entirety of Paul's preceding argument(s).[156] These verses commence a section of the epistle (12:1-15:13) that seeks to implement the gospel's corollaries within the contexts of what Michael Gorman refers to as the "cruciform lives of holiness and hospitality."[157] Paul specifically desires to bring about a transformation among Christians that is in ethical and juridical conformity to the future age, set in contrast to a world system in which they still reside, and insistent on retaining them in a pattern of living other than that derived from having the mind of Christ. Paul's ethical injunctions rely on the realities associated specifically with the day of the Lord. The transformative process or the "already" in the "already/not yet" comprises a part of this apocalyptic activity that will be fully actualized in this new age ontologically, ethically, and judicially. Paul wanted his Roman readers to not only get a glimpse of the age that lies beyond the day of the Lord, but also to grasp, practice, and embody its ethical and judicial ambiance in the present. Paul's doctrine of present transformation, although not a concept entirely absent in the Old Testament, certainly receives more emphasis here—no doubt another corollary derived from his Damascus conversion/calling experience. That this transformation is only in degrees, as Paul suggests elsewhere (2 Cor 3:18), not only reflects the nature of the "already" as well as anticipates the "not yet" but also once again reveals the hermeneutical construct of Paul respecting practically every soteriological inbreaking, including those connected with the day of the Lord.

Romans 12:19-20 (13:4-5)

Romans 12:19-20 occurs in a section of Paul focusing on social ethics and utilizes two Old Testament texts, one in Deuteronomy (32:35) and the other in Proverbs (25:21-22) supporting a nonretaliatory attitude toward one's enemies in light of either impending or inevitable divine judgment associated with the day of the Lord.[158] The Deuteronomic text (mentioned in

---

156. See the excellent discussion of the basis for Christian transformation in J. Gerald Janzen, "A New Approach to 'logikān latreian' in Romans 12:1-2," *Enc* 69 (2008): 45-83. On the *inferential* nature of the particle (οὖν [oun]) to the preceding argument(s) see Wallace, *Greek Grammar beyond the Basics*, 673.

157. Gorman, *Apostle of the Crucified Lord*, 402.

158. On the use of the imperatival participles in this section see Philip Kanjuparambil, "Imperatival Participles in Rom 12:9-21," *JBL* 102 (1983): 285-88.

Rom 12:19) admonishes Christians not to take vengeance against those who have shown them injustice. Locating the reason for this reticence in Deuteronomy, Paul writes, "Do not avenge yourselves, dear friends, but give place to God's wrath, for it is written, 'vengeance is mine, I will repay,' says the Lord" (Rom 12:19). The Hebrew text Paul quotes occurs in a key location in Moses' song (Deut 31:1–43) depicting the retaliatory vengeance of God against Israel's enemies.[159] Having rejected the goodness of God while embracing idolatry, Israel had provoked God to jealousy and anger. God responded by determining to replicate his jealousy within them and recapitulate his wrath without as just (and ironic) retribution against Israel. He sparked jealousy by going after other nations in a salvific way and incited anger in Israel by bringing these very nations against them with fiery judgments including famines, plagues, diseases, wild-animal attacks, and wars (Deut 32:15–26).[160] But God subsequently redirected his vengeance toward Israel's enemies, promising to "get revenge" and "pay them back" for what they had done to Israel under God's providential control (Deut 32:31–35, 36–43). In an act of divine chastisement of his people, God had used Israel's enemies as disciplining tools only to afterward promise to punish these very instruments for their unjust treatment of Israel (see Isa 10:5–7, 12; Hab 1:12–13; 2:1–4, 16; Ps 73:2, 16–20).

It is the intervening time of chastisement, the period lying between God's anger with his people and the punishment via the instrumentality of their enemies, when God warns Israel to not take matters in their own hands and exact vengeance. God has promised to repay their enemies . . . and he does. Time indicators such as "at the time their foot slips" and that the "day of their disaster is near" and "impending judgment" heavily support a *near* interpretation for these judgments (vengeance) on Israel's enemies without necessarily excluding a more *remote* fulfillment.[161] If the Old Testament existential context is retained in Romans, then Paul wishes

---

159. Steyn has shown that Rom 12:19 and Heb 10:30 both reflect the Hebrew of the MT and "are even closer to Targum Onkelos and to the Peshitta" but differ more significantly from either the LXX or Odes of Solomon 2 (Gert Jacobus Steyn, "A Quest for the *Vorlage* of the 'Song of Moses' [Deut 32] Quotations in Hebrews," *Neot* 34 [2000]: 270).

160. Andrew Harper, *The Book of Deuteronomy*, Expositor's Bible Commentary (London: Hodder & Stoughton, 1903), 452–60.

161. If the Qumran text (1QS 10.17–20) is key to understanding Rom 12:19–20, then the attitude of nonretaliation on the part of Christians would be rectified in the "Day of Vengeance" by God. See Krister Stendahl, "Hate, Non-Retaliation, and Love," *HTR* 55 (1962): 343–55.

to convey to his readers that their antagonists, like Israel's enemies, are really no more than divine instruments of chastisement, not to be resisted in an unlawful manner. And as with Israel, divine judgment on one's enemies (who are also no doubt God's enemies) may come in the form of immediate and/or remote events of wrath without mitigating any idea of a still-future and ultimate par-excellent fulfillment of that wrath in the eschatological day of the Lord.

Paul's quotation of this Deuteronomic text omits the word "God" (δότε τόπον τῇ ὀργῇ [dote topon tē orgē]) and simply reads "give place to wrath" (Rom 12:19).[162] Some translators take this as referring to the wrath of an angry man, as in, "give place to *man's* wrath." Given this reading, believers are instructed to tolerate the wrath of an angry man on a personal level by either offering the other cheek or by fleeing to another city. Or it may mean that man's wrath is to be interpreted as the exercise on behalf of the righteous sufferer by a constituted or governmental means against these enemies. This second understanding would construe the admonition to permit government ("wrath of man") to fulfill its duty in executing wrath toward violators of justice (compare Rom 13).[163] There is no explicit mention by Paul, as there is with the Deuteronomic text, that God is ultimately behind these unjust (perceived or otherwise) events either from a wrathful man to be tolerated or by evil people deserving of governmental exercise of the sword. Furthermore, Paul leaves unstated whether or not God is merely operating from a position of rehabilitation or restitution with respect to his people by allowing these injustices to occur in the first place. Even under the wrath-of-an-angry-man interpretation, it remains God's role to take vengeance on *personal* enemies, whether or not they are proximate agents of God's disciplining activity on his people or, if possible, known not to be. Given the context of Romans 13, it would more likely be the case that these believers are being cautioned to forgo the taking of

---

162. The Hebrew text uses the pronoun "I" for the Lord and then Yahweh in Deut 32:36 explicitly. Given this explicit reference to Yahweh in Deut 32:36, one may infer that the "wrath" here is the "wrath of God" as opposed to the "wrath of man." John William Wevers, *LXX: Notes on the Greek Text of Deuteronomy*, Septuagint and Cognate Studies 39 (Atlanta: Scholars Press, 1995), 528.

163. And the exercise of wrath on those who violate justice is the main function of government. The "aim of the law is to prevent injustice from reigning," not to "cause justice to reign" (Frédéric Bastiat, *The Law*, trans. Dean Russell [Mountain View, CA: Creative Commons, 2013], 19).

the law into their own hands and instead being instructed to allow a constituted authority to deal with the perpetrator(s).[164] This interpretation
would also assume that the actions of their enemies are *prima facie* against
the laws of the state and therefore would justify if not require the state's
intervention. Most commentaries on Romans understand the reference
to wrath as divine and read it as "Give place to *God's* wrath," referring
either to near or more remote eschatological retribution and most likely
through mediate (or civil) if not immediate (God's direct involvement)
actions. This interpretation may then carry or imply a secondary sense
of "Get over your anger; calm yourself."[165] Arguing for the primary
sense of God's wrath, Edgar Smothers notes that "wrath" unqualified "is
a well established reading . . . for the wrath of God."[166] When this notion
is combined with the subject of the Deuteronomic text, context, and the
phrase "vengeance is mine, I will repay," it suggests God's ultimate role in
the activity of retribution both in the now and later eschatological day of
the Lord either by direct activity or via intermediary means and proximate
agents of that wrath. This being the general attitude, the "corresponding
specification of the appropriate Christian response to these specific forms
of opposition" would be likely to follow.[167]

The second text used by Paul is Proverbs 25:21–22 (Rom 12:20). Instead
of either taking personal vengeance out on an angry man or exercising
patience in the face of variegated wheels of juridical processes, a believer
is to respond by feeding and giving drink to his enemy, "for in doing this
you will be heaping burning coals on his head. Do not be overcome with
evil, but overcome evil with good" (Rom 12:20–21). There are generally
two interpretations of this passage, one that designates more and more
punishment to the one who resists kind deeds (going back to Origen and
Chrysostom) and one that suggests the burning refers to "burning pangs

---

164. Besides the contextual assumption, others have argued that the "sword" of 13:4 refers
to "the armed might of Rome on a war basis, not the administrative judicial machinery of
the empire" (Ray Barraclough, "Romans 13:1–7: Application in Context," *Colloq* 17 [1985]: 20).

165. The only other place in the NT that uses the phrase "give place" (δίδωμι + τόπος [*didōmi*
+ *topos*]) is Eph 4:27, "Do not give the Devil *an opportunity*."

166. Edgar R. Smothers, "Give Place to the Wrath (Rom. 12:19): An Essay in Verbal Exegesis,"
CBQ 6 (1944): 208.

167. John Piper, *"Love Your Enemies": Jesus' Love Command in the Synoptic Gospels and in the
Early Christian Paraenesis, a History of the Tradition and Interpretation of Its Uses*, SNTSMS 38
(Cambridge: Cambridge University Press, 1979), 17.

of shame" soliciting remorse and repentance from one's enemy (going back to Augustine and Jerome). The latter view, taking into consideration the "burning coals on his head" imagery, may be further nuanced and traced back to an Egyptian ritual of repentance recounted in the Tale of Khamuas, represented by a forked stick in the hand and a burning censer on the head. Others point to an even earlier source located in the Instruction of Amen-Em-Opet (chap. 2). But neither of these options has proved to be either a convincing background or a direct influence.[168] Krister Stendahl notes that the burning-coals symbolism suggests "an element of surprise" and carries a juridical motif contained in pagan (Babylonian Book of Proverbs), biblical (Ps 140:11; Prov 25:21–22), and extrabiblical Jewish texts (2 Esdras 16:52–53) — *all suggesting the notion of heightened punishment.*[169] John Day agrees, stating that this imagery "is invariably used in the Old Testament as a symbol of divine anger or judgment."[170] Based on the rabbinic understanding of Proverbs 25:21–22, Stendahl interprets Paul as follows: "If you act in non-retaliation your good deeds are stored up as a further accusation against your enemy for the day of Wrath to which you should defer all judgment."[171] Although absolute nonretaliation is sometimes derived from these verses, believers are generally to act in terms of a guiding principle or perhaps better react to injustices in an initially or attitudinally nonretaliatory manner while concealing hatred for one's enemies in what is referred to as a "spirit of concealment."[172]

---

168. See John N. Day, "'Coals of Fire' in Romans 12:19–20," *BSac* 160 (2003): 416–17. He notes the Egyptian Tale of Khamuas flounders on two points. First, there is no mention of a forked stick in Prov 25:22, and it mentions "coals," not "censer." Second, the date of the Egyptian Tale is approximated to 233–232 BC, much too late to influence the earlier Solomonic Proverbs. With respect to the Instruction of Amen-Em-Opet, although it is dated between the twelfth and sixth centuries BC, the borrowing or dependence is unclear either way, and the response in the Instruction is shame, not a "stick and censer" or "coals of fire."

169. Stendahl, "Hate, Non-Retaliation, and Love," 347.

170. Day, "'Coals of Fire' in Romans 12:19–20," 418. He adds, "For the apostle Paul to utilize this potent image in a manner foreign to its common usage—and without any clear contextual indicators to that effect—seems unlikely" (ibid.). In support of this interpretation are the parallel γάρ (*gar*) phrases, "Vengeance is mine, I will repay," and "for in doing this you will be heaping burning coals on his head," suggesting one and the same eschatological judgment (ibid., 419).

171. Stendahl, "Hate, Non-Retaliation, and Love," 348. One is reminded of the divine encouragement offered in Exod 23:32: "But if you diligently obey him [God's angel] and do all that I command, then I will be an enemy to your enemies, and I will be an adversary to your adversaries."

Romans 1 pictured the systematic abandonment of humanity's nature by God due to higher degrees of idolatry as a just retribution in the here and now. Romans 2 emphasized the notion of "treasuring up wrath" against those who had spurned special revelation if not general revelation. Here in Romans 12 the same idea of increased wrath is highlighted via the phrase "heaping burning coals on his head." Whether the overcoming of evil with good is intended to solicit remorse from one's enemy and eventual repentance or, more likely, suggests that God's punishment in the eschaton in light of the unrepentant enemies will be worse and worse remains a matter of continued dispute.[173] These interpretations are certainly not mutually exclusive ideas. Some may repent, while others may not. Given the previous indicators of Paul in Romans 1–2 and the use of Deuteronomy 32:35, there is likely a shadowy present as well as not-yet future aspect to this admonition as well as an intrinsic quantitative feature of punishment suggested by the heaping up of burning coals. The eschatological emphasis to this passage is most likely primary and the immediate application secondary. But given the context of human government as God's servant in Romans 13 to exercise "wrath on the wrongdoer" (Rom 13:4–5), the immediate understanding cannot be ruled out.[174] God's wrath is undeniably also mediated through human government primarily in mind. This God-ordained institution is to be the divine instrument in administering God's justice and retributive wrath in civil affairs while mirroring (albeit imperfectly) a jurisprudence in one accord with the just indictment and sentencing pronounced on the last day (3:19–20).[175]

---

172. Ibid., 349–50. There are of course Jewish examples of winning over someone by showing mercy and without the concealment of eternal hatred in the Testament of the Twelve Patriarchs (Testament of Benjamin 4–5; Testament of Gad 6–7; Testament of Joseph 18.2). But these are unrelated to the Proverbs passage and rabbinic understanding of it. Stendahl also cautions that the references for remorseful repentance may be in reference to fellow Jews, not outsiders (see the treatment of Joseph to his brothers in Testament of Benjamin 4–5). Here in Romans, it is enemies, a term never used of believers. For an example of an absolute nonretaliation perspective of these verses see Elizabeth Hershberger Bauman, *Ascuas de Fuego* (Scottdale, PA: Herald, 1982); Barbara Claassen Smucker, "Review of *Coals of Fire*. By Elizabeth Hershberger Bauman. Scottdale: Herald Press, 1954. Pp. 128, illustrated. $1.95.," *Mennonite Quarterly Review* 28 (1954): 228.

173. See Smothers, "Give Place to the Wrath (Rom. 12:19)," 206, 209.

174. Barraclough, "Romans 13:1–7," 17–18.

175. See C. E. B. Cranfield, "Christian's Political Responsibility according to the New Testament," *SJT* 15 (1962): 176–92.

Romans 13:8–14

On the tail end of Paul's discussion of the role of government and its exercise of divine wrath, he mentions the debt owed to government (in taxes) and transitions to the debt owed to one's fellow neighbor.[176] The fulfilling of these debts he labels love (13:8) and links them to the love-of-neighbor mandate. One cannot avoid the conclusion that in some way obedience to government as the civil hand of God in juridical affairs is somehow related to loving one's neighbor in the area of civil justice at the very least. Paul goes further and defines specifically what this love comprises by citing the latter half of the Ten Commandments (13:9).

1. Do not commit adultery (seventh commandment, Exod 20:14; Deut 5:18)

2. Do not murder (sixth commandment, Exod 20:13; Deut 5:17)

3. Do not steal (eighth commandment, Exod 20:15; Deut 5:19)

4. Do not covet (tenth commandment, Exod 20:17; Deut 5:21)

Paul gathers up any lingering commands that may be included in the love of neighbor by concluding, "and if there is any other command, it is summed up in this word, 'Love your neighbor as yourself.'" The two commands he leaves out from the second tablet of the Ten Commandments are the fifth, about honoring one's parents, and the ninth, about bearing false witness against one's neighbor (Exod 20:16; Deut 5:20). There is little doubt that Paul's omissions were only incidental and at any rate are to be inferred from the all-encompassing phrase and mandate. Elsewhere, in 1 Timothy 1:8–11, he includes all but one of the latter six commandments.[177] He continues by stating, "Love does no wrong to his neighbor, therefore love is

---

176. This transition is done by way of *Stichwort* for owe, ὀφειλή (*opheilē*) and owes, ὀφείλω (*opheilō*).

177. "Those who murder their fathers and mothers" (1 Tim 1:9a, fifth commandment), "murderers" (1 Tim 1:9b, sixth commandment), "the sexually immoral men who practice homosexuality" (1 Tim 1:10a, seventh commandment), "enslavers" (1 Tim 1:10b, eighth commandment), and "liars, perjurers" (1 Tim 1:10c, ninth commandment). He omits the prohibition on coveting or the tenth commandment, perhaps because government is primarily designed for the purpose of regulating certain *behaviors* rather than the *thoughts* of its citizens. See Joel McDurmon, *The Bounds of Love: An Introduction to God's Law of Liberty* (Braselton, GA: American Vision, 2016), 10–16.

the fulfillment of the law" (13:10). In this practical section of Romans, Paul appears mostly concerned about the just treatment of one's neighbor, both inside and outside the church.[178] And he reminds his Roman readers of their duty of love by fulfilling the moral law of God.[179]

The mention of moral duties in the Ten Commandments leads Paul to his primary eschatological concern. The *time* and the *hour* and the *day* that consummate their salvation are "nearer to us than when we believed" (13:11). What could Paul have in mind but most notably the time and hour and day that culminate in the day of the Lord and perhaps the judgment associated with it? He likens this heightened vigilance of moral sensitiv-ity in light of this proleptic occasion to being "awake from sleep." If citing the Ten Commandments was not moral direction enough in preparation for that day, Paul expands the metaphor of moral sleepiness in light of the eschatological daybreak of the new age to include all sorts of "works of darkness" that must be set aside (13:12). He even adds the metaphor that, like soldiers preparing for battle (of the day of the Lord?), they are to "put off the works of darkness" and instead "put on the armor of light" (13:12).[180] He states, "Let us walk honestly as in the day, not in excessive feasting and drunkenness, not in sexual immorality and sensuality, not in strife and jealousy. But put on the Lord Jesus Christ and do not make provisions for the flesh for the purpose of satisfying its desire" (13:13–14).

Thus this spiritual warring as soldiers is figurative for avoiding moral pitfalls and doing righteousness or reflecting and embodying virtues

---

178. On what the latter half of the Ten Commandments means for justice see William Ames, *The Marrow of Sacred Divinity, Drawn out of the Holy Scriptures, and the Interpreters thereof, and Brought into Method*, trans. John Dykstra Eusden (Boston: Pilgrim, 1968), §2.16–22. Chapters include "Justice and Charity toward Our Neighbor" (§2.16), "The Honor of Our Neighbor" (§2.17), "Humanity toward Our Neighbor" (§2.18), "Chastity" (§2.19), "Commutative Justice" (§2.20), "Telling the Truth" (§2.21), and "Contentment" (§2.22). "Justice is the virtue by which we are inclined to perform our duty to our neighbor" (ibid., §2.16.1). Justice here is "the mutual duty between those who are bound by the same law; in this sense it contains all the force of the second table" (ibid., §2.16.2). "Justice toward our neighbor affects him directly or as the result of some action" (ibid., §2.17.1).

179. This duty of loving one's neighbor is not restricted to believers but is a universal command that binds everyone to their Creator and fellow man. See Gundry, "Grace, Works, and Staying Saved in Paul," 7–8.

180. It reads ἐνδυσώμεθα δὲ τὰ ὅπλα τοῦ φωτός (*endusōmetha de ta hopla tou phōtos*), "but let us put on the armor of light." Some manuscripts (A, D) read for ὅπλα (*hopla*) ἔργα (*erga*), as in "*works* of light." For more on the day of the Lord/redemption and the armor of God, see the comments below on Ephesians.

commensurate with the work of Christ. It is evident as well that Paul is not against feasting per se but rather excessive feasting, not opposed to a godly intoxication but drunkenness, not prohibitive of every sort of sexual expression but only illicit sex and sensuality (namely, that conducted outside monogamous heterosexual marriage), not averse to contentions of every kind but strife (1 Cor 11:19), and not even averse to godly jealousy but rather sinful jealousy.[181] All of these works must be put aside and exchanged for godly behaviors, or what Paul figuratively refers to as putting on the armor of light and putting on the Lord Jesus Christ. Perspective of the day of the Lord calls for a biblical view of temperance, not a retroversion to asceticism but a thoroughgoing "creation-centered spirituality" leading toward an aesthetic enjoyment tempered within the confines of the moral law of God.[182]

Paul has taken the Old Testament concept of the day of the Lord and refracted it through his experience on the Damascus road, permitting him to regard an eschatological event as a present and future reality. Because Romans is not his first book—it is written approximately twenty years after his conversion—it therefore represents and reflects a conscientious maturity and highly developed understanding of the day of the Lord along

---

181. On the subject of feasting see Craig L. Blomberg, "Jesus, Sinners, and Table Fellowship," *BBR* 19 (2009): 35-62. And his earlier work, *Contagious Holiness: Jesus' Meals with Sinners*, NSBT 19 (Downers Grove, IL: InterVarsity, 2005). On "mild" and "gentle" intoxication see Gisela H. Kreglinger, *The Spirituality of Wine* (Grand Rapids: Eerdmans, 2016), 83-99. For the general position of alcohol taken in this work see Kenneth L. Gentry, *God Gave Wine: What the Bible Says about Alcohol* (Lincoln, CA: Oaklawn, 2001); Joel McDurmon, *What Would Jesus Drink? A Spirit-Filled Study* (White Hall, WV: Tolle Lege, 2011); Patrick E. McGovern, *Ancient Wine: The Search for the Origins of Viniculture* (Princeton: Princeton University Press, 2003); McGovern, *Uncorking the Past: The Quest for Wine, Beer, and Other Alcoholic Beverages* (Berkeley: University of California Press, 2009); Jim West, *Drinking with Calvin and Luther! A History of Alcohol in the Church* (Lincoln, CA: Oaklawn, 2003); Brad Whittington, *What Would Jesus Drink? What the Bible Really Says about Alcohol* (Austin, TX: Wunderfool, 2011). For a few representatives of a contrary view (mostly associated with "watering down the wine" in Jesus' day) advocating abstinence and/or prohibition, see Robert H. Stein, "Wine-Drinking in New Testament Times," *Christianity Today* 19 (1975): 9-11; Norman L. Geisler, "A Christian Perspective on Wine-Drinking," *BSac* 139 (1982): 46-56; Peter Lumpkins, *Alcohol Today: Abstinence in an Age of Indulgence* (Garland, TX: Hannibal Books, 2009); Robert P. Teachout, "The Use of 'Wine' in the Old Testament" (Ph.D. diss., Dallas Theological Seminary, 1979); Richard Teachout, *On the Fruit of the Vine: In Defense of Biblical Consistency* (Château-Richer, QC: EBPA-Etude Biblique pour Aujourd'hui [Bible Studies for Today], 2010); Richard Teachout, *Grape Juice: God's Blessing for His People!* (Château-Richer, QC: EBPA-Etude Biblique pour Aujourd'hui [Bible Studies for Today], 2011).

182. Drane, *Introducing the New Testament*, 438.

with the wrath it brings as well as serves to justify and affect other central tenets of his theology.

PHILIPPIANS

A good number of scholars affirm that Paul likely wrote the book of Philippians during his first Roman imprisonment (1:7, 13, 14, 17).[183] The apostle's overall intent in this brief letter is to encourage the persecuted Philippian church in their partnership for the advancement of the gospel (1:5). Both Paul and the Philippians were suffering for the sake of the gospel, and the apostle admonishes the congregation to remain united together as fellow soldiers marching forward into a hostile environment with the gospel. Paul encourages the church by reminding them that his own incarceration has turned out for the furtherance of the gospel (1:12–13). Even though Paul is imprisoned, that gospel is still advancing. Therefore, despite the fact that the Philippians are also suffering persecution they are exhorted to maintain their unity and continue living in a manner worthy of the gospel (1:27–28).

PHILIPPIANS 1:3–11

Paul's appeal to his Philippian partners to continue advancing the gospel as a united front was influenced by the day of the Lord motif. The apostle explicitly refers to the day of the Lord three times throughout the epistle (1:6, 10; 2:16). In his introductory prayer the apostle thanks God for the continual partnership of the Philippians in the gospel and prays that "the good work" he has accomplished among them he will bring to completion at the day of Christ Jesus. What exactly Paul means by the "good work" in verse 6 is debated.[184] However, it seems most plausible that the phrase is referring to the work of salvation that God accomplished in the Philippians when

---

183. There is extensive debate surrounding the location of his imprisonment at the time of writing the letter, but this is not relevant for the present inquiry. For helpful discussions of this issue see, for example, G. Walter Hansen, *The Letter to the Philippians*, PNTC (Grand Rapids: Eerdmans, 2009), 19–25; Bruce W. Longenecker and Todd D. Still, *Thinking through Paul: An Introduction to His Life, Letters, and Theology* (Grand Rapids: Zondervan, 2014), 198; Peter T. O'Brien, *The Epistle to the Philippians*, NIGTC (Grand Rapids: Eerdmans, 1991), 19–26; Jim Reiher, "Could Philippians Have Been Written from the *Second* Roman Imprisonment?," *EvQ* 84 (2012): 213–33; John Henry Paul Reumann, *Philippians: A New Translation with Introduction and Commentary*, AB 33B (New Haven: Yale University Press, 2008), 13–14.

184. See the discussion in Reumann, *Philippians*, 113–14, for the interpretive options.

they received the gospel. Paul offers thanks to God for the "good work" he
has inaugurated among the Philippians and that God is the one who will
bring his "good work" to consummation at the day of Christ Jesus (1:5–6).
But the apostle also thanks God because the genuineness of the Philippians'
salvation was validated by their being fellow partners with Paul in the
gospel (1:5–7). The Philippian congregation was living out the gospel in a
hostile environment (1:28; 3:2). But it was only the "good work" God had
begun that enabled the church to faithfully persevere as they anticipated
the day of the Lord.

That Paul is absolutely certain that God will bring to completion the
"good work" he began at the day of Jesus Christ emphasizes "the eschatological goal of present life in Christ."[185] The Philippians can presently live in a
manner worthy of the gospel, fully assured that God will continue his work
until the final day. The context seems to indicate a temporal progression of
the "good work," namely that God initiates the "good work," and he then
carries it forward, bringing it to completion, until the day of Jesus Christ.[186]
The context of the passage may also further suggest that the day of the Lord
motif in some way influences Paul's understanding of the "good work" that
God is doing among the Philippians until the eschatological day. As previously noted, Paul understands that the day of the Lord is both a present
and future reality. In verses 5–6 the apostle reminds the Philippians of the
fact that God began the "good work" among them. The implication of this is
that God has justified the Philippians, making them a new creation. Their
right relationship with God is validated in their current partnership with
Paul for the gospel and will also become evident to all (i.e., their persecutors) ultimately at the final assize. Heinz Giesen rightly comments: "The
completion of the divine redeeming work is here not [only] to be understood punctually, but as a process of inward sanctification which will be
brought to its end at the day of Christ Jesus. . . . That corresponds to the

---

185. Gordon D. Fee, *Paul's Letter to the Philippians*, NICNT (Grand Rapids: Eerdmans, 1995), 86.

186. The notion of progression seems evident from the combination of the passive participle ἐναρξάμενος (*enarxamenos*), "the one who began," which indicates a beginning point,
along with the future verb ἐπιτελέσει (*epitelesei*), "will complete," and the improper preposition ἄχρι (*achri*), "until," which denotes an endpoint. See Wallace, *Greek Grammar beyond the
Basics*, 568, who comments, "Wedged as it is between the past (ἐναρξάμενος) and an end-point
in the future (ἄχρι), the future tense seems to suggest a progressive idea. But the future in
itself says none of this."

engagement for the gospel from the very first day till now. . . . Their commitment to the gospel provides evidence of God being at work in them."[187]

In addition, the "good work" that God is accomplishing among them also has implications for their communal life. Because God will finish the "good work" he started at the coming day of the Lord, the Philippians can presently stand firm in one spirit as a unified front, striving together as faithful partners with Paul for the sake of the gospel (1:27). Despite their current hardships, the Philippians can be encouraged, knowing that God is the one at work in them and he has secured their future (2:12–13). The apostle can offer thanks to God for his Philippian partners, knowing that they all have the same mindset to advance the gospel as they press on to victory at the day of the Lord. Walter Hansen writes, "The hope of that future day of Christ gives strength to endure and persevere through all the trials, tensions, and disappointments of the present day."[188] Paul concludes this opening section by stating the goal of his prayer, namely that the Philippian believers would be pure and blameless *for the day of Christ* (1:10).[189] His point is to encourage the church to live in a manner that both is holy and does not bring offense to the gospel. Paul's appeal, rather, is "that Philippians should live accordingly in the face of the Day of Christ. Mission and ethical conduct are, consequently, founded and motivated eschatologically."[190]

PHILIPPIANS 2:12–18

In Philippians 2:1–18, Paul continues unpacking for the Philippian believers what it means to live in a manner worthy of the gospel (1:27–30). The church was encountering much hostility from their opponents because of their Christian faith, and the apostle provides instructions as to how they can maintain their unity in the midst of such opposition. As Paul remains

---

187. Heinz Giesen, "Eschatology in Philippians," in *Paul and His Theology*, vol. 3 of *Pauline Studies* (Leiden: Brill, 2006), 223.

188. Hansen, *Letter to the Philippians*, 51.

189. The preposition εἰς (*eis*) arguably has a telic force here. Fee, *Paul's Letter to the Philippians*, 102n23, contends that the idea in v. 10 is that Paul is praying that the Philippian church be pure and blameless "with the day of Christ in view as their ultimate goal." See Giesen, "Eschatology in Philippians," 228n76; Murray J. Harris, *Prepositions and Theology in the Greek New Testament: An Essential Reference Resource for Exegesis* (Grand Rapids: Zondervan, 2011), 88–90.

190. Giesen, "Eschatology in Philippians," 227–28.

incarcerated, it would complete his joy to know that his Philippian partners were continuing to advance the gospel with mutual love for one another, which is expressed through humility, by being concerned about the needs of others. Paul's appeal to the Philippians is grounded in Christ Jesus, who is the ultimate example of humility, selflessness, and obedience (vv. 6–11). In this christologically significant passage, Paul reminds the Philippians that the eternal Son of God did not seek self-aggrandizement but rather condescended himself to take on human nature and die on the cross for the sins of his people (vv. 6–8). Subsequently, the Father exalted him with the name that is above all names, and every tongue will confess that Jesus Christ is Lord (vv. 9–11). Paul exhorts the Philippians to have the self-sacrificial attitude of Christ as they continue marching forward with the gospel in hostile territory.[191]

In light of the tremendous significance of verses 6–11, it must be remembered that Paul's overall point in the context is *behavioral*. In other words, Christ is the model for how the Philippians should conduct themselves, particularly with respect to living in a manner worthy of the gospel. Verses 12–18 are also part of the apostle's entire paraenesis, which began back at 1:27 and provides specific applications for the Philippians.[192] Gerald Hawthorne contends that in verses 12–18 Paul "reaches back beyond the [Christ] hymn to link up with and add to the many other injunctions he had already given the church at Philippi for positive Christian living (1:27–2:5)."[193] Specifically, Paul urges the congregation to remain steadfast in their

---

191. The amount of literature written on Phil 2:6–11 is vast. In addition to the commentaries see, for example, Donald G. Dawe, *The Form of a Servant: A Historical Analysis of the Kenotic Motif* (Philadelphia: Westminster, 1963); C. Stephen Evans, ed., *Exploring Kenotic Christology: The Self-Emptying of God* (Oxford: Oxford University Press, 2006); Paul D. Feinberg, "The Kenosis and Christology: An Exegetical-Theological Analysis of Phil 2:6–11," *TJ* 1 (1980): 21–46; Michael J. Gorman, "'Although/Because He Was in the Form of God': The Theological Significance of Paul's Master Story (Phil 2:6–11)," *Journal of Theological Interpretation* 1 (2007): 147–69; Ralph P. Martin, *Carmen Christi: Philippians ii. 5–11 in Recent Interpretation and in the Setting of Early Christian Worship* (Grand Rapids: Eerdmans, 1983); Denny Burk, "Christ's Functional Subordination in Philippians 2:6: A Grammatical Note with Trinitarian Implications," *Journal of Biblical Manhood and Womanhood* 16 (2011): 25–37; Lawrence DiPaolo, *Hymn Fragments Embedded in the New Testament: Hellenistic Jewish and Greco-Roman Parallels* (Lewiston, NY: Mellen, 2008); Dennis W. Jowers, "The Meaning of MORFH in Philippians 2:6–7," *JETS* 49 (2006): 739–66.

192. The link is evident from the inferential conjunction ὥστε (*hōste*) in v. 12. See BDAG 1107; G. K. Beale, Daniel J. Brendsel, and William A. Ross, *An Interpretive Lexicon of New Testament Greek: Analysis of Prepositions, Adverbs, Particles, Relative Pronouns, and Conjunctions* (Grand Rapids: Zondervan, 2014), 96; L&N 784–85.

193. Gerald F. Hawthorne and Ralph P. Martin, *Philippians*, WBC 43 (Grand Rapids: Zondervan, 2015), 137.

obedience in advancing the gospel (vv. 12–13) and exhorts them to continual harmony as they live pure and blameless lives in which they shine as
lights amid a crooked and perverse world (vv. 14–18).[194]

Paul's appeal in verses 14–16 is of particular interest here, since he specifically mentions the day of Christ in verse 16. In verses 14–15 the apostle
urges the congregation to do everything without grumbling or arguing and
to live pure and blameless lives as children of God in shining as lights in
the world. The following participial clause in verse 16, λόγον ζωῆς ἐπέχοντες
(logon zōēs epechontes), "holding on to the word of life," is a matter of some
debate with respect to (1) the meaning of the verb ἐπέχω (epechō) and (2) the
syntactical function of the participial clause.

In the New Testament the verb ἐπέχω (epechō) occurs only five times
(Luke 14:7; Acts 3:5; 19:22; Phil 2:16; 1 Tim 4:16) and has three different
nuances: "hold fast" (i.e., to someone or something), "be mindful or obser-
vant," or "stop or stay at a place."[195] Traditionally the term has been translated in the standard English versions as either "hold forth/out" or "hold
fast." Scholars are divided over these distinct nuances and wrestle with
what meaning should be adopted. For instance, in an article examining the
lexical possibilities of ἐπέχω, Vern Poythress argues against the rendering
"hold forth" as a viable option due to insufficient evidence. He maintains,
"The meaning 'hold out' should not be considered unless we can first dis-
play unambiguous evidence that this is in fact a possible meaning for the
Greek word when accompanied by an accusative object."[196] He does consider "hold fast" to be an adequate translation but believes that rendering is
still somewhat corrigible and suggests the meaning of "having the word of

194. See Fee, *Paul's Letter to the Philippians*, 230–58; Mark J. Keown, *Congregational
Evangelism in Philippians: The Centrality of an Appeal for Gospel Proclamation to the Fabric of
Philippians*, PBM (Milton Keynes, UK: Paternoster, 2008), 128–35.

195. BDAG 262. See also the discussions in Keown, *Congregational Evangelism in Philippians*,
136–39; James P. Ware, *The Mission of the Church in Paul's Letter to the Philippians in the Context of
Ancient Judaism*, NovTSup 120 (Leiden: Brill, 2005), 257. Ware observes that even the standard
lexica are divided with respect to the meaning of ἐπέχω (epechō). For instance, LSJ 619 does
not list "hold fast" as an option, whereas BDAG 362 does list that as a possible meaning but
does not provide "holding forth" as an option. Interestingly, L&N provide both meanings and
mentions that either rendering is possible in Phil 2:16. J. H. Moulton and G. Milligan, *The
Vocabulary of the Greek Testament: Illustrated from the Papyri and Other Non-Literary Sources*
(London: Hodder & Stoughton, 1930), 232, also list both nuances for the term but attach
"holding fast" to Phil 2:16.

196. Vern S. Poythress, "Hold Fast Versus Hold Out in Philippians 2:16," *WTJ* 63 (2002): 52.

life" or "holding the word of life."[197] Poythress's analysis, however, is based
on a small sampling of ancient authors, and consequently he does not fully
explore the term's full semantic field of meaning.[198] Gordon Fee asserts
that the meaning of the verb is parallel to the phrase καὶ οἱ κατισχύοντες
τοὺς λόγος μου (kai oi katischyontes tous logos mou), "those who hold strong
my words," from Daniel 12:3 (LXX).[199] He contends that Paul had the apocalyptic vision of Daniel 12:1–4 in mind, which describes how the people of
God conduct themselves in a hostile environment, and relates that to the
Philippians' current situation. This leads Fee to surmise that the apostle
likely substituted ἐπέχοντες in place of the κατισχύοντες, because he wanted
to encourage the Philippian church to be steadfast in their evangelism
in the midst of such a crooked and perverse society. Thus Fee translates
ἐπέχοντες as "holding firm" because he believes that Paul's focus in the context was not that the Philippian congregation should "hold fast" to the
gospel so that the enemy does not take it away from them, but rather they
must hold firm to the gospel as they evangelize in a crooked and perverse
society.[200]

James Ware has arguably conducted the most exhaustive lexical analysis of ἐπέχοντες.[201] His examination encompasses a wide range of relevant
ancient literature and inscriptions, yielding the conclusion that the verb
ἐπέχω primarily has two major senses.[202] First, when used transitively, the
verb connotes "hostility" in the sense of the subject stopping an object.
When intransitive, it refers to the subject stopping itself. The second
major sense Ware discovered is that the term also connotes "extension."
Specifically, when the verb is transitive it refers to the subject "holding forth"
or "extending" an object, and when intransitive it denotes the "advance" or

---

197. Ibid. See also John P. Dickson, *Mission-Commitment in Ancient Judaism and in the Pauline Communities: The Shape, Extent and Background of Early Christian Mission*, WUNT 2/159 (Tübingen: Mohr Siebeck, 2003), 108–10; Hawthorne and Martin, *Philippians*, 146; Moisés Silva, *Philippians*, BECNT (Grand Rapids: Baker, 2005), 127, who support the translation "holding fast" or some variation of it.

198. This critique is offered by Ware, *Mission of the Church in Paul's Letter to the Philippians in the Context of Ancient Judaism*, 258.

199. Fee, *Paul's Letter to the Philippians*, 247n33. Fee is aware that the MT translates v. 3 as "and those bringing many to righteousness."

200. Ibid., 248.

201. Ware, *Mission of the Church in Paul's Letter to the Philippians in the Context of Ancient Judaism*, 256–70.

202. What follows is adopted from ibid., 269.

"extension" of the subject by itself. Furthermore, his analysis also concludes that the translation "holding fast" is not a viable rendering for Philippians 2:16. Ware comments, "It is telling that the sense 'hold' or 'hold fast' for the verb ἐπέχω, so popular among New Testament specialists, is virtually unknown to classical scholarship. It can be stated categorically that the verb ἐπέχω does not bear the sense 'hold' or 'hold fast' in any ancient passage."[203] Thus it seems that the most plausible rendering for the verb is "hold forth." In addition to the verb's semantic range as examined by Ware, the translation "holding forth" is substantiated from the context.[204] Paul's intent is to urge the Philippians to live in a manner worthy of the gospel. He exhorts the church to maintain their unity so that they can continue to focus on their evangelistic efforts. The Philippians are to shine as lights in the world, and the participial phrase λόγον ζωῆς ἐπέχοντες (logon zōēs epechontes) arguably expresses the manner by which they accomplish this, namely by "holding forth" (i.e., offering) the word of life to the residents of Philippi. The context seems to have a missional focus and the participial clause λόγον ζωῆς ἐπέχοντες functions "as an exhortation to spread the gospel."[205]

The purpose for Paul's exhortation that began back in verse 14 is now stated in the phrase εἰς καύχημα ἐμοὶ εἰς ἡμέραν Χριστοῦ (eis kauchēma emoi eis hēmeran Christou), "so that I can boast in the day of Christ."[206] The apostle's command, that the Philippians do all things without grumbling or complaining, that they live pure and blameless lives, shining as lights in the world, and that they "hold forth" the word of life, is so that he will be able to boast on the day of Christ. Paul only condones boasting if it is in the Lord (1 Cor 1:31; Phil 3:3), in the cross (Gal 6:14), or in sufferings (Rom 5:3).[207] In verse 16, Paul's boasting is focused on God and

---

203. Ibid., 268–69.

204. It is also worth noting that in a few instances the term is found in military contexts referring to an army advancing or overtaking an area. Paul may have been aware of this nuance especially when considering the other military terms used throughout the letter. See ibid., 265, who makes mention of this and provides a few references.

205. Ibid., 270. See also Fee, *Paul's Letter to the Philippians*, 247–48; Keown, *Congregational Evangelism in Philippians*, 145–47; Ben Witherington III, *Paul's Letter to the Philippians: A Socio-Rhetorical Commentary* (Grand Rapids: Eerdmans, 2011), 163.

206. εἰς καύχημα ἐμοὶ εἰς ἡμέραν Χριστοῦ (eis kauchēma emoi eis hēmeran Christou) seems to be functioning as a purpose clause of the entire sentence that began with the imperative in v. 14. So, Fee, *Paul's Letter to the Philippians*, 248; Hansen, *Letter to the Philippians*, 185n359; Keown, *Congregational Evangelism in Philippians*, 146–47; O'Brien, *Epistle to the Philippians*, 298.

207. See Hansen, *Letter to the Philippians*, 185.

the good work he had begun in the Philippians and was continuing to perfect until the day of Christ Jesus (1:6; 2:13). Boasting, then, in this context, "points to the ground of one's confidence and trust, Christ himself, in whom one therefore 'glories.'"[208] Thus for Paul the coming day of the Lord is a motivating factor for present ministry. The apostle understands that he himself will give an account of his ministry before the judgment seat of Christ. But he also urges the Philippians to continue faithfully advancing the gospel because on the day of the Lord they will give him a reason to boast in what God has accomplished among them. Paul recognizes that the church's mission and his own ministry are inextricably bound together, and when he stands before the Lord on that final day, the Philippians will serve as evidence that he did not labor in vain. In other words, the Philippian church will in essence provide testimony at the final assize that Paul faithfully carried out his new-covenant ministry. It seems reasonable, then, to surmise from verses 12–18 that the day of the Lord motif influenced Paul's view of ministry. The apostle exhorts the church to live in a manner worthy of the gospel in light of the coming eschatological day. The final day served as an incentive for both Paul and the Philippians to remain steadfast in carrying out their current mission of advancing the gospel, knowing that on that final day their work will be evaluated at God's court.

The book of Philippians demonstrates that the day of the Lord is directly related to Paul's theology of mission. The primary theme of the epistle is partnership for the advancement of the gospel. Paul appeals to the church to maintain their unity as they march forward with the gospel, knowing that they will be "pure and blameless for the day of Christ." Although Paul and the Philippians currently suffer at the hands of God's enemies, they can rejoice, knowing that their future is secure at the day of the Lord. The "good work" that God began and continues to accomplish among them enables Paul and the Philippians to faithfully carry out their current ministry, "holding forth" the gospel with a view toward the future day of the Lord, when they will ultimately stand before the judgment seat of Christ vindicated.

---

208. Fee, *Paul's Letter to the Philippians*, 249.

COLOSSIANS

The book of Colossians identifies the apostle Paul as its author (and writer; 1:1, 23; 4:18).[209] Although most scholars (approximately 60 percent, according to Raymond Brown) identify the work as pseudepigraphal, the evidence for this view has not proved compelling, and therefore this work remains committed to Pauline authorship.[210] Having adopted this perspective and because Paul mentions that he is writing the epistle from prison (Col 4:3, 10, 18), the most probable location and time of writing is his Roman imprisonment in AD 61–63 (according to Acts 28:11–31).[211] The location and date of the epistle (not to mention pseudonymity and pseudepigraphy) are key factors and relevant determinants when examining the epistle in light of the day of the Lord precisely because the further removed from Paul one gets chronologically, the

---

209. It is important to identify Paul as both *author* and *writer* because some scholars do not view these terms as synonymous. Raymond Brown, for example, holds to pseudonymity for Colossians but regards Paul as the *author* (the authority behind the writing), not the *writer* (referring to the actual writer either by himself or through an amanuensis). See Raymond Edward Brown, *An Introduction to the New Testament*, AYBRL (New York: Doubleday, 1997), 610n22. For the sake of brevity, this work will simply identify Paul as author with the sense of both author and writer.

210. See Craig A. Evans, "The Colossian Mystics," *Bib* 63 (1982): 188n1, who reaches similar conclusions. The standard scholarly tome arguing for pseudonymity in Colossians is Walter Bujard, *Stilanalytische Untersuchungen zum Kolosserbrief als Beitrag zur Methodik von Sprachvergleichen*, SUNT 11 (Göttingen: Vandenhoeck & Ruprecht, 1973). For other works dealing with NT pseudonymity see Kurt Aland, "The Problem of Anonymity and Pseudonymmity in Christian Literature of the First Two Centuries," *JTS* 12 (1961): 39–49; Johan Christiaan Beker, *Heirs of Paul: Paul's Legacy in the New Testament and in the Church Today* (Grand Rapids: Eerdmans, 1996); Raymond F. Collins, *Letters That Paul Did Not Write: The Epistle to the Hebrews and the Pauline Pseudepigrapha*, Good News Studies 28 (Wilmington, DE: Glazier, 1988); E. Earle Ellis, "Pseudonymity and Canonicity of New Testament Documents," in *Worship, Theology and Ministry in the Early Church: Essays in Honor of Ralph P. Martin*, ed. Michael J. Wilkins and Terence Paige (Sheffield, UK: JSOT, 1992), 212–24; Edgar J. Goodspeed, "Pseudonymity and Pseudepigraphy in Early Christian Literature," in *New Chapters in New Testament Study*, Ayer Lectures/Colgate-Rochester Divinity School (New York: Macmillan, 1937), 212–24; Mark Christopher Kiley, "Interplay with the Culture: What, Why, How," in *Colossians as Pseudepigraphy* (Sheffield, UK: JSOT, 1986), 15–35; Donald Guthrie, "The Development of the Idea of Canonical Pseudepigrapha in New Testament Criticism," *VE* 1 (1962): 43–59; A. P. Hayman, "Problem of Pseudonymity in the Ezra Apocalypse," *JSJ* 6 (1975): 47–56; Thomas D. Lea, "The Early Christian View of Pseudepigraphic Writings," *JETS* 27 (1984): 65–75; David G. Meade, *Pseudonymity and Canon: An Investigation into the Relationship of Authorship and Authority in Jewish and Earliest Christian Tradition*, WUNT 39 (Tübingen: Mohr, 1986), 194–218; Bruce M. Metzger, "Literary Forgeries and Canonical Pseudepigrapha," *JBL* 91 (1972): 3–24; Arthur G. Patzia, "The Deutero-Pauline Hypothesis: An Attempt at Clarification," *EvQ* 52 (1980): 27–42.

211. Ben Witherington III, "The Case of the Imprisonment That Did Not Happen: Paul at Ephesus," *JETS* 60 (2017): 525–32. Other proposals that assume Pauline authorship include Ephesus (AD 52–55 or 54–57, according to the Marcion prologue) and Caesarea (AD 56–58, according to Acts 24:27).

nearer one arrives at a full-blown Gnosticism of the second century. And as significant as the topic of Pauline authorship is to this epistle, it is intricately related to and rivaled by the equally difficult task, including the lack of unanimity, of determining the precise theological background of the epistle.[212]

Before examining the theology of the day of the Lord largely via a mirror reading of Paul's polemics, it is relevant to set forth the eschatology of the epistle in light of such an indeterminate background. Because of its almost exclusively realized eschatology and little by way of futuristic eschatology, scholars have sought to distance the writing from Paul. The idea behind this notion is that the further and further the church got from the historical Jesus, the more and more unlikely the imminent coming of Christ became. Recognizing this problem and to cover their embarrassment, later writers of the New Testament began to view the second coming of Christ in realized forms in order to save face. Any material that appears to stress a realized eschatology, so the theory goes, automatically falls under a later time period of the theological continuum. For example, according to Colossians, Christians are already in the kingdom of the Son (1:13; 4:11), raised with Christ (2:12; 3:1), and part of the heavenly assembly (3:1–4; see also Eph 2:6). The cataclysmic event of the day of the Lord associated with disarming all malevolent angelic powers, in addition, has already occurred (Col 2:15).[213]

---

212. On the issues of disputable Pauline authorship and Gnosticism, see the self-critical article on historical exegesis and modern scholarship by Michel R. Desjardins, "Rethinking the Study of Gnosticism," *R&T* 12 (2005): 370–84.

213. Moyo argues that the Colossian reference may be to so-called benevolent angelic figures whom Paul regards as threatening to the superiority of Christ. See Ambrose M. Moyo, "The Colossian Heresy in the Light of Some Gnostic Documents from Nag Hammadi," *Journal of Theology for Southern Africa* 48 (1984): 35. Bultmann (Rudolf Bultmann, "Die Bedeutung der neuerschlossenen mandäischen und manichäischen Quellen für das Verständnis des Johannesevangeliums," *ZNW* 24 [1925]: 100–46) compares this passage to the gnostic *descending-ascending redeemer myth* presented in the Apocalypse of Adam. The problem, as Combs notes, is that "it has not clearly been demonstrated that any of these tractates are free from Christian influences" and that "Yamauchi has demonstrated that The Apocalypse of Adam could not have been written before the second century" (William W. Combs, "Nag Hammadi, Gnosticism and New Testament Interpretation," *Grace Theological Journal* 8 [1987]: 209). Bultmann's views about a pre-Christian Gnosticism were not original to him but distilled from scholars such as Richard Reitzenstein, Wilhelm Bousset, and Mark Lidzbarski. See Edwin M. Yamauchi, "Pre-Christian Gnosticism in the Nag Hammadi Texts?," *Church History* 48 (1979): 129. Most gnostic scholars agree that "there are no Gnostic texts which date with certainty from the pre-Christian era" (Edwin M. Yamauchi, "Pre-Christian Gnosticism, the New Testament and Nag Hammadi in Recent Debate," *Them* 10 [1984]: 23). Nevertheless, other scholars insist on various trajectories of tradition stressing orthodoxy, liberalism, and Gnosticism, and that represented by Q and the Gospel of Thomas (ibid.). For an example of the activity of these hostile powers see Pheme Perkins, "John's Gospel and Gnostic Christologies: The Nag Hammadi Evidence," *Anglican Theological Review* 11 (1990): 71–73.

Ambrose Moyo writes, "He [Paul] argues that with the coming of Christ, the angelic powers have lost their right to influence the religious practices of man, and consequently the liturgical calendar need no longer be observed because the true substance (*sōma*), i.e., Jesus Christ, is now present. In other words the Christians live in the age of fulfillment."[214]

However, these realized (rather than overrealized) aspects of the day of the Lord are also present if not prominent in Paul's other undisputed epistles, such as Philippians (3:11–12, 20–21) and Romans (1:18, etc.) without denying future aspects. Paul had recognized early on in his ministry that even the par-excellent eschatological event of the day of the Lord could be overrealized to the extent that all futurity was quashed (2 Thess 2:2). Thus there appears to be an either-or mindset among some scholars lying at the heart of such objections to Pauline authorship if not taking into account adaptive eschatological perspectives on his part or simply recognizing the occasional nature and fluidity of his epistles. Rather than play into the hands of his theological opponents by merely stressing a competing realized eschatology in isolation from futuristic aspects, Paul added the latter as additional counterarguments as well as supplemental necessities comprising a total and complete salvation. Paul therefore pictures a future presentation of the church to Christ (1:22) as mature individuals (1:28), namely when Christ "appears" (φανερωθῇ [*phanerōthē*]) to save and reward his own (3:4, 24), judge the sons of disobedience with God's wrath (3:6, 25), and consummate the kingdom (4:11). Two points with reference to Paul's *realized* versus *futuristic* eschatology may be tentatively made.

First, the solution to Paul's emphasis on realized eschatology, then, seems to lie in the situation and circumstances surrounding the Colossian heresy that appears to postulate a salvation only in combination with or as supplemental to Christ's work, specifically challenging his work as mediator.[215] Paul may then have felt it necessary to emphasize the current eschatological realities of Christ's salvation in terms of status and state in order to counter a combination of Hellenistic, gnostic, and Judaistic elements

---

214. Moyo, "Colossian Heresy in the Light of Some Gnostic Documents from Nag Hammadi," 43. On the subject of astrological determinism in the so-called gnostic gospels see Pheme Perkins, "What Is a Gnostic Gospel?," *CBQ* 71 (2009): 121.

215. I assume, with most scholars, that there is indeed an "opponent paradigm" (or polemic) at work here and that, contrary to Asher's perspective—that universal language and the pseudepigraphal nature of the letter argue against such a notion—this polemic does not simply originate through the lens of the later church but rather within Paul himself. See Jeffrey R. Asher, "The Colossian Heresy: An Ecclesiastical Paradigm?," *Proceedings* 30 (2010): 113–14, 18–22.

seeking to detract and/or subtract by addition from Christ's sufficiency in redemption.[216] Because the illumined gnostic (or *biblical demiurgical traditions*, in Michael Williams's terms[217])—if what is known about later Gnosticism may be to some degree relevant here—routinely emphasized the present possession of salvation, Paul's response may be viewed then as a reformulation of gnostic ideas and thus a restoration of in-Christ theology to its proper place of all-sufficiency in light of such syncretism.[218] The stress placed on realized aspects of eschatology is, therefore, not simply a

---

216. See F. F. Bruce, "Colossian Problems Part 3: The Colossian Heresy," *BSac* 141 (1984): 195–208, where he discusses Platonic, Pythagorean, incipient Gnosticism, Essenism, and Merkabah mysticism (a form of Jewish Gnosticism). Bruce settles on the latter view; Yamauchi, "Pre-Christian Gnosticism, the New Testament and Nag Hammadi in Recent Debate," 25. For a summary of scholarly views (up to 1982) including incipient *Jewish Gnosticism* (Lightfoot), an established *priesthood of Gnostics* (Dibelius), a *Jewish Gnosticism of Persian origin* (Bornkamm), a form of *Jewish Qumranian mysticism and asceticism* (Lyonnet), a *tendency toward mysticism and asceticism broadly Hellenistic* (Francis), and a furthering of Francis's views by Bandastra, who sees this *mysticism and asceticism as particularly threatening to the role of Christ as mediator*, see Evans, "Colossian Mystics," 189–92. In 1973 Gunther had listed forty-four different perspectives on the identity of Paul's opponents (John J. Gunther, *St. Paul's Opponents and Their Background: A Study of Apocalyptic and Jewish Sectarian Teachings*, NovTSup 35 [Leiden: Brill, 1973], 3–4). For a more updated list see Asher, "Colossian Heresy," 108–9n4. See also the provocative study of Robert M. Royalty, "Dwelling on Visions: On the Nature of the So-Called 'Colossian Heresy,'" *Bib* 83 (2002): 329–30, 40, who argues that these opponents were other Christians or apocalyptic Christian prophets, specifically, those of the Johannine community who were unduly influenced by the book of Revelation; J. H. Roberts, "Jewish Mystical Experience in the Early Christian Era as Background to Understanding Colossians," *Neot* 32 (1998): 162–64. On the *history* of Gnosticism and gnostics, as well as gnostic theology, cosmology, and time (past, present, and future), see Edwin M. Yamauchi, "The Gnostics and History," *JETS* 14 (1971): 29–40. On the difficulty of *defining* Gnosticism see Jeffrey Kloha, "Jesus and the Gnostic Gospels," *Concordia Theological Quarterly* 71 (2007): 124–31.

217. See Desjardins, "Rethinking the Study of Gnosticism," 377. The work to which he refers is Michael A. Williams, *Rethinking "Gnosticism": An Argument for Dismantling a Dubious Category* (Princeton: Princeton University Press, 1996), 51. For a favorable assessment of Williams applied to the study of 1 Corinthians see Todd E. Klutz, "Re-Reading 1 Corinthians after Rethinking 'Gnosticism,'" *JSNT* 26 (2003): 193–216.

218. Yamauchi, "Gnostics and History," 34. For a fuller treatment of more advanced forms of docetism and Gnosticism in the second century onward see Yamauchi, "Pre-Christian Gnosticism in the Nag Hammadi Texts?," 129–41. Writing of the later-discovered Nag Hammadi documents, Combs writes, "Thus, though the Gnostic writings provide helpful insights into the heresies growing out of Christianity, it cannot be assumed that the NT grew out of Gnostic teachings" (Combs, "Nag Hammadi, Gnosticism and New Testament Interpretation," 195). He adds that "the roots of Gnosticism can be found in the Judaism, Christianity, and paganism of the first century, but classical Gnosticism has not yet been documented before the second century" (ibid., 212). There is no attempt here to be exhaustive on the subject of Gnosticism. Yamauchi wrote over thirty years ago (in 1984) that "nearly 3,000 books, articles and reviews on Gnosticism have been published in the last decade" (Yamauchi, "Pre-Christian Gnosticism, the New Testament and Nag Hammadi in Recent Debate," 22)! For how Irenaeus handled the gnostics in his time see Terrance L. Tiessen, "Gnosticism as Heresy: The Response of Irenaeus," *Didaskalia* 18 (2002): 31–48. For a popular summary of Gnosticism or what may be deemed the "new Gnosticism," see Mark A. Pierson, "Old Heresy, New Heretics: The Return of Gnosticism," *Modern Reformation* 17 (2008): 30–34.

"relaxation of the eschatological tension as Salvation came to be viewed as a possession in this present life," as Karl Kundsin has argued for the age in general; rather, it is an emphasis on present salvation's sufficiency to counter specious supplements to it.[219] Given these circumstances, the future aspects of the day of the Lord, at least thematically if not directly mentioned, may function together as an exclamation point in combating these ideas directly. Paul's references to the day of the Lord would then be specifically oriented at dismantling an overrealized and syncretistic soteriology that not only challenged the all-sufficiency of Christ's atonement by augmenting his work as mediator of that atonement but also minimizing the significance of that final day. Paul presents this final day of the Lord's appearing as the truly perfecting experience before the throne of God in contrast to the so-called perfecting mystical-ecstatic appearing before the throne promulgated by the errorists.

This leads to the second point. Because Gnosticism in general did not hold to a realistic (futuristic) eschatology, Paul's introduction of this future event in terms of perfecting the saints at the appearing of Christ seems to be directed at the supposed perfection putatively obtained (or at least viewed as obtainable) in this life apart from the final advent—precipitated by the resurrection (see also 2:10). Although the resurrection is not mentioned explicitly, it is difficult to imagine a perfection of the saint without it in Paul's eschatology, much less ecclesiology. At the crux of Gnosticism was what one scholar refers to as the embodiment of an "anti-cosmic religion."[220] Mehmet-Ali Ataç defines it as "the group of systems of cosmogony and anthropogony that establish a binary opposition between a transcendent god and matter, or creation, which could not be his work, but only of an inferior demiurge."[221] The resurrection being part of that cosmos would then be viewed as an equally untenable constituency of saintly perfection and therefore account for an exclusively realized eschatology of Paul's

219. Rudolf Bultmann and Karl Kundsin, *Form Criticism: Two Essays on New Testament Research: Study of the Synoptic Gospels, by Rudolf Bultmann, and Primitive Christianity in the Light of Gospel Research, by Karl Kundsin*, trans. Fredrick C. Grant (Chicago: Willett, Clark, 1934), 120.

220. Yamauchi, "Pre-Christian Gnosticism, the New Testament and Nag Hammadi in Recent Debate," 23, borrowing the phrase from K. W. Tröger but similar to Hans Jonas, who likewise identified the essential ingredient of Gnosticism as the anti-cosmic dualism.

221. Mehmet-Ali Ataç, "Manichaeism and Ancient Mesopotamian 'Gnosticism,'" *Journal of Ancient Near Eastern Religions* 5 (2005): 2.

errorists. On the one hand, there is no direct evidence that the errorists denied the *futurity* of the resurrection. But on the other hand, there is evidence that the *purpose* of the resurrection was likely minimized.

Closely associated with this future perfecting of the saints, the apostle mentions the repayment for wrongdoing that appears to refer to the final judgment on the day of the Lord (Col 3:25). Paul says, "for the one who does wrong will receive back that which he has done, and there is no favoritism" (ὁ γὰρ ἀδικῶν κομίσεται ὃ ἠδίκησεν, καὶ οὐκ ἔστιν προσωπολημψία [*ho gar adikōn komisetai ho ēdikēsen, kai ouk estin prosōpolēpsia*]).[222] Depending on how similar the incipient Gnosticism (or just pregnostic ideas of *gnōsis*) of Colossae was to the later gnostic theology, the introduction of an eschatological judgment would have come across as a particularly odious and unwelcome theme.[223] However, if the errorists were of the apocalyptic sort that is most likely, then a judgment theme would not be all that surprising. Taking a minimalist approach to the background or route of least resistance while operating within the milieu of first-century Judaism leads to favoring the views of Fred O. Francis as outlined by Craig Evans in his 1982 article. Francis understands the opposition Paul confronts to be a *tendency toward mysticism and asceticism that is broadly Hellenistic.* J. H. Roberts refers to the errorists as "a Jewish group of ascetic-mystics" who had interests in heavenly journeys such as those depicted in the Similitudes of Enoch.[224] He states, "They were Jews; they were ascetics; they were early Jewish mystics of the apocalyptic strain; they were a non-Christian group."[225] The

---

222. Some manuscripts add παρα τω θεω (*para tō theō*), "with God." See F, G, I, 629, it, vg^cl, Ambst, Pel, Cass. The meaning of "no partiality" *with God*, a term that occurs three other times in the NT (Rom 2:11; Eph 6:9; Jas 2:1) suggests (when it refers to God) that God has no meritorious incentives with respect to *status* (ethnic, social, or sexual) or *state* of sinners when exercising or dispensing either mercy or justice. Interestingly enough, the Similitudes contain a similar statement in 1 En. 63:8 pertaining to the hopelessness of salvation for wicked rulers because God shows no respect of persons. In using this phrase Paul reassures "his readers once more that not those opponents with their apocalyptic claims are the ones chosen by God for salvation, but those whose trust is in his Christ" (Roberts, "Jewish Mystical Experience in the Early Christian Era as Background to Understanding Colossians," 182).

223. William Richard Schoedel, "Parables in the Gospel of Thomas: Oral Tradition or Gnostic Exegesis?," *CTM* 43 (1972): 553–54, 559.

224. Roberts, "Jewish Mystical Experience in the Early Christian Era as Background to Understanding Colossians," 161. "We found the opponents against which the congregation at Colossae were warned to be a group of non-Christian Jewish mystics whose strict adherence to the law attained the proportions of an ascetic way of life and that their asceticism probably was a contributing factor towards the experience of heavenly journeys" (ibid., 185).

225. Ibid., 169, which he defends systematically.

Similitudes represent a revelation "on the throne chariot, and the throne room of God, with its accompanying phenomena such as fire and ice and thunder and crystal, angels and garments."[226] This experience would enable the initiate to worship God as the angels, aid in bringing about a moral perfection, and provide a competing source of authority.[227]

Added to this would be the feature provided by A. J. Bandstra that the central christological attack was aimed at Christ's role as mediator.[228] This is not to suggest that these errorists viewed angels in a competing role with Christ as mediator but rather that the mediatorial role of Christ with respect to issuing saving benefits was implicitly challenged by a self-made heavenly journey of sanctification and an earthly practice of asceticism.[229] Craig Evans suggests, in distinction to Bandstra, that the true problem is not christological but rather ecclesiological, namely, "by advocating that true worship and service are to be had only in heaven the errorists are neglecting and, indeed, perhaps despising, the functions of the body on earth."[230] Evans argues that the true substance of the shadow mentioned by

226. Ibid., 166. He also says that this entire undertaking and experiencing of the abode where God's throne is applies directly to Col 2:18, where the appeal of the errorists is what they have seen and heard while experiencing this place (ἅ ἑόρακεν ἐμβατεύων [ha heoraken embateuōn]). See 1 En. 14:5, 8–25; 17:2–18:16; 25:3–5.

227. Thus taking the genitive τῶν ἀγγέλων (tōn angelōn) in θρησκείᾳ τῶν ἀγγέλων (thrēskeia tōn angelōn) as subjective. "The author of Colossians can hardly deny the existence of angels or that angels worship God. He can only enjoin against a Christian prophet who makes a heavenly vision of the angels, rather than received tradition, the source of authority" (Royalty, "Dwelling on Visions," 351). For a detailed discussion on this matter see Clinton E. Arnold, *The Colossian Syncretism: The Interface between Christianity and Folk Belief at Colossae*, WUNT 77 (Tübingen: Mohr Siebeck, 1995), 90–102, though he quite strongly argues for the objective genitive. He argues that the angels were the objects of some kind of veneration, the purpose of which "was largely apotropaic" (ibid., 101).

228. Evans, "Colossian Mystics," 191–92. See also Fred O. Francis, "The Background of embateuein (Col 2:18) in Legal Papyri and Oracle Inscriptions," in *Conflict at Colossae: A Problem in the Interpretation of Early Christianity Illustrated by Selected Modern Studies*, ed. Fred O. Francis and Wayne A. Meeks (Missoula, MT: Scholars Press, 1975), 197–218; Francis, "Humility and Angelic Worship in Col 2:18," *ST* 16 (1962): 109–34; Francis, "Christological Argument of Colossians," in *God's Christ and His People: Studies in Honor of Nils Alstrup Dahl*, ed. Jacob Jervell and Wayne A. Meeks (Oslo: Universitetsforl, 1977), 192–208; Andrew J. Bandstra, "Did the Colossian Errorists Need a Mediator?," in *New Dimensions in New Testament Study*, ed. Richard N. Longenecker and Merrill C. Tenney (Grand Rapids: Zondervan, 1974), 329–43. See also Roy Yates, "'The Worship of Angels' (Col 2:18)," *ExpTim* 97 (1985): 12–15.

229. Arnold, taking a veneration-of-angels approach, indicates that "it appears that Christ is either neglected in favor of calling upon angels, or that he is regarded on the same level as the angels and is invoked in the same fashion as in the incantation texts" (Arnold, *Colossian Syncretism*, 102).

230. Evans, "Colossian Mystics," 199–200.

Paul is the church rather than Christ. This would suggest that the Colossian problem was not unlike that which occurred with the Corinthian church and less likely interpreted by Paul as a threat to Christ's role as mediator. These two areas of polemic, however, need not be mutually exclusive but instead *causally* if not *coordinately* related. In other words, the desire to worship God as the angels with some sanctifying benefits may have led directly to arrogance of a few as well as a dismissive attitude toward earthly congregational worship while only implicitly (if not unknowingly) posing a threat to the completed work of Christ.[231] This lack of explicit opposition to Christ's work may account for Paul's less-than-harsh response to these errorists as compared to how he handled his Galatian opponents. Or perhaps, as Roberts argues, these opponents were not part of the congregation at all but rather objects of the missionary activity of Colossae.[232] These heuristic assumptions are arguably the bare essentials gathered from a mirror reading of Colossians rather than one of approaching Colossians from a set of presupposed dogmas (late or otherwise) derived from either a speculative background or an assumed anachronistic line of continuity with later, full-blown Gnosticism. But how do the aspects connected with the day of the Lord in particular address these issues?

It is quite possible that references to the day of the Lord may be incidental or nonpolemical in nature. In other words, these delineated day of the Lord features may have nothing to do with opposing the aberrational, disruptive, and possibly heretical opinions affecting the Colossian believers directly (from within) or indirectly (in terms of evangelistic endeavors) over Christ's work as it affects their futurity. But this is an unlikely scenario. With the two prominent themes of the day of the Lord strategically included, namely the final perfection or salvation of the elect and the judgment of the ungodly (not to mention the future consummation of the kingdom), the particular emphasis appears to fall on the completion or perfection of the saints. Roberts refers to this as the *eschatological journey* in contrast to the hyped *mystical-ecstatic journey*, associating the former with a polemic directed at

---

231. This would certainly be in line with Gnosticism, "which had an overweening confidence in the ability of the self . . . to initiate and sustain a relationship with God" (Mark D. Tranvik, "Luther, Gerhard Forde, and the Gnostic Threat to the Gospel," *Lutheran Quarterly* 22 [2008]: 415).

232. Roberts, "Jewish Mystical Experience in the Early Christian Era as Background to Understanding Colossians," 171–75.

the implicit christological complements of the latter and including with it a sharp rebuke of the arrogant effects that this *mystical-ecstatic* experience brought (see 2 Cor 12:1–10). If anything, Paul combats the supposed sanctifying effects of this mystical journey with what Newman refers to as Paul's "Christoformic transformational mysticism."[233]

If this reconstruction is accurate, then the apocalyptic response would therefore not only address christological supplementations such as those associated with the "worship of angels"—most likely interpreted as a reference to being caught up to the divine counsel and therefore becoming participants of the worship angels perform (2:18)—but also offer criticisms of any remedial and/or auxiliary ascetic practices designed either to suppress the evil internal impulse or in some way serve as preparations for the heavenly journey.[234] These practices included advocating and observing particular festivals, new moons, and Sabbaths (2:16) and subjugating the body to extreme self-imposed regimented behaviors (2:23) including abstention from certain foods and drink (2:16, 21). Paul's use of the day of the Lord is therefore two-edged in the already/not-yet aspects of eschatology. The *already* in the already/not yet is wrought by Christ alone, whose sufficiency needs no heavenly journey or ascetic complementation. The *not yet* in the already/not yet is likewise supplied by Christ alone and alone promises ultimate perfection for the saint and certain wrath to the sinner. These factors, if Roberts's view of a missionary context is correct and contact with adversaries of the gospel is at stake, would certainly help the Colossians not only avoid being drawn into the false teachings themselves but also to properly evangelize those deeply inculcated within an ascetic-mystical piety of Jewish apocalypticism.

EPHESIANS

As with Colossians, a large segment (approximately 80 percent, according to Brown) of modern biblical scholarship rejects the Pauline authorship of Ephesians.[235] But this number is exaggerated. Contradicting this

---

233. Carey C. Newman, "Ephesians 1:3—A Primer to Paul's Grammar of God," *RevExp* 95 (1998): 89.

234. Roberts says similarly. See Roberts, "Jewish Mystical Experience in the Early Christian Era as Background to Understanding Colossians," 171.

235. Andrew T. Lincoln, *Ephesians*, WBC 42 (Dallas: Word Books, 1990), lx; Brown, *Introduction to the New Testament*, 620. For an introduction to pseudonymous works in the NT see Lee Martin McDonald, "Pseudonymous Writings and the New Testament," in *The World*

assessment, according to Harold Hoehner's careful tabulations, that portion of scholars disallowing Pauline authorship runs at about 39 percent from 1519–2001 and climbs to 50 percent when the years are limited to 1991–2001.[236] Thus the modern trend is certainly moving toward the rejection of Paul as the *actual* author and opting instead for his *implied* authorship. But the current crop of scholars has the numbers at about fifty-fifty. Early historical attestations to Paul's authorship are essentially unanimous beginning with Ignatius and continuing with Polycarp (referred to in the Muratorian canon), the Marcion canon (AD 140), Irenaeus, the Didache, Barnabas, Clement of Alexandria, Hermas, and even the Nag Hammadi documents. It has only been relatively recent scholarship that has questioned the epistle's authenticity, and largely on internal grounds, including language and style, theology, and the putative use of Colossians. Internal evidence supports Pauline authorship.[237] The epistle claims to be written by Paul (1:1; 3:1), who is currently a prisoner (3:1, 13; 4:1; 6:19–20). This claim alone puts the burden of proof on those who oppose the apostle's actual (not just implied) authorship (not withstanding the likely use of an amanuensis, of course) and those proposing some form of pseudonymity or even allonymity and allepigraphy.[238]

Chronological, geographical, and perhaps even background proximities of the cities of Ephesus and Colossae may explain similarities of the two epistles as well as help mitigate their distinctive features. In addition, that the letter is most likely circular may account for not only its impersonal tone with respect to the Ephesians in particular but also

of the New Testament: Cultural, Social, and Historical Contexts, ed. Joel B. Green and Lee Martin McDonald (Grand Rapids: Baker, 2013), 367–78. See also Metzger, "Literary Forgeries and Canonical Pseudepigrapha," 3–24; Bart D. Ehrman, *Lost Christianities: The Battles for Scripture and the Faiths We Never Knew* (Oxford: Oxford University Press, 2003), 67–89.

236. Harold W. Hoehner, *Ephesians: An Exegetical Commentary* (Grand Rapids: Baker, 2002), 18–20. Thus Hoehner demonstrated that the numbers provided by Brown were extremely prejudicial, a result of special pleading (at best), and uncritically influential to Ephesian studies.

237. For a thorough examination of the evidence for Pauline authorship and an examination of the arguments against it see ibid., 20–61.

238. McDonald, "Pseudonymous Writings and the New Testament," 374. If any weight may be given to one of the six subscriptions, namely that recorded in manuscript L, reading, "To the Ephesians written from Rome [an epistle of Paul from Rome] through Tychicus." For others see Metzger, *Textual Commentary on the Greek New Testament*, 543.

239. We "are not privy to the occasion of this epistle" is not to suggest that there really is no occasion. See David B. Capes, "Interpreting Ephesians 1–3: 'God's People in the Mystery of His Will,'" *SwJT* 39 (1996): 20.

its seemingly occasion-less (or least occasional) circumstance in writing altogether.[239] Rather than appear too dismissive of counterevidence, it may be stated that assuming or denying Pauline authorship is virtually inconsequential with respect to understanding the eschatology of the epistle in general or the allusions to the day of the Lord in particular. In the case of Ephesians (but less so with Colossians) this issue need not be entirely settled. But having stated this caveat, the position taken here is that Ephesians was written some time during Paul's imprisonment in Rome during the years AD 61–63 and most likely subsequent to the writing of Colossians.[240]

EPHESIANS 1–2

Although "the day of the Lord" is not an expression found in Ephesians, Paul does use the phrase "the day of redemption" as its eschatological near equivalent. Here Paul links the present possession of the Spirit as both the mark of ownership (believers are "sealed") and a guarantee (the Spirit functions as a "down payment") of all present and future items of inheritance connected with this redemption. In Ephesians 4:30 the believers are told not to grieve the Holy Spirit, "by whom you have been *sealed* unto the Day of redemption" (ἐν ᾧ ἐσφραγίσθητε εἰς ἡμέραν ἀπολυτρώσεως [*en hō esphragisthēte eis hēmeran apolytrōseōs*]). While Paul mentions that redemptive benefits are aspects the believer possesses in some respects *now* in Christ ("*in whom we have* redemption" [1:7]), these benefits are nevertheless incomplete and wait to be fully implemented in the future. The indwelling of the Spirit is earlier described as a down payment (ἀρραβών [*arrabōn*]) of these guarantees and therefore a pledge of all inheritances, including every aspect of this redemption promised and purchased for the elect (1:14). This future completion on the day of redemption, never mind its present installments, is referred to as the "*redemption* of the purchased possession" (εἰς ἀπολύτρωσιν τῆς περιποιήσεως [*eis apolytrōsin tēs peripoiēseōs*]), or when the finishing touches of redemption are applied to the entirety of the believer (and all believers), including the body (1:14). This future

---

240. Robert Hermans, "La christologie d'Ephésiens," *Bib* 92 (2011): 411–13. He sees the concepts of Christ as the head of all creation and believers' placement with Christ in heaven as two modifications of Colossians.

consummation of redemption is also referred to as a time or dispensation when all things will be gathered together in Christ (1:10) and most likely refers to an administration following the day of redemption or the new heavens and the new earth (to use Johannine language). And this futurity to the day of redemption is complemented by the symmetry or perhaps typology of present-day aspects of fulfillment.

Paul refers to the present and future *positive benefits* of the day of redemption. In perhaps the longest and highly subordinated sentence of the Greek New Testament, or as one scholar famously described it, *das monströseste Satzkonglomerat*, Paul lays out the spiritual blessings of the saints related to election, predestination unto adoption, and redemption that calls forth praises to the Father (1:3–14).[241] These blessings are partially realized now rather than later and grounded on an eternal unconditional election depicted as taking place prior to the creation of the world for the purposes of establishing a holy and blameless people in terms of their final perfection as everlasting participants of the Father's eternal love (1:3–4).[242] This is coordinate with predestination unto adoption as sons, secured through the work of redemption by the Son, and

---

241. The phrase describing this sentence as *das monströseste Satzkonglomerat* comes from Eduard Norden, *Agnostos Theos: Untersuchungen zur Formengeschichte religiöser Rede* (Leipzig: Teubner, 1923), 253n1.

242. It is utter nonsense to speak of this election as Capes does when he writes, "God chose Christ and then chose those who chose Christ" (Capes, "Interpreting Ephesians 1–3," 22; see also John Lewis, "Doing Theology through the Gates of Heaven: A Bible Study on Ephesians 1:3–14," ERT 28 [2004]: 365, who says, "But it is not election that is to be thought of in individualistic terms. God wills that all come to faith, but has also decreed that only those who do so will be counted among the elect"). Paul clearly rejects these types of claims, saying elsewhere about election: "Therefore, it [God's mercy in individual election] is neither dependent on *the one who wills* nor on the *one who runs* but on God who shows mercy" (Rom 9:16, emphasis added). For a straightforward refutation of corporate election see Leslie James Crawford, "Ephesians 1:3–4 and the Nature of Election," *MSJ* 11 (2000): 75–91. In similar fashion, it is equally without warrant to decry the nature of this election as eternal or nonhistorical as if by asserting such it "devalues or ignores a *real* incarnation, a *real* Gethsemane, a *real* cross, and a *real* resurrection" (Carey C. Newman, "Election and Predestination in Ephesians 1:4–6a: An Exegetical-Theological Study of the Historical, Christological Realization of God's Purpose," *RevExp* 93 [1996]: 239; Newman, "Ephesians 1:3," 94). Newman appears to confuse the historical effect for the eternal cause while jumping from the Hades of deism by diving into the Gehenna of Kantianism. In a later article Newman rightly emphasizes Eph 1:3 as a "one sentence summary of what is presented in the first three chapters of the letter" and "as the *leitmotif* for the entirety of the letter" ("Ephesians 1:3," 89).

unto the praise of the Father's will (1:5).[243] These divine activities are examples of the Father's abundant grace exercised through the Son's work, securing not only the forgiveness of sins but also spiritual and heavenly blessings (1:6–7). This effective redemption is generated by a pure graciousness within the eternal decree out of the Father's own interests and pleasure (1:8–9) and will eventually consummate in the gathering together of all things in Christ, both in heaven and on earth (1:10).[244] It applies especially to those who are the redemptive benefactors of this inheritance as sons who have been predestined as the eternal objects of this praise to the Father (1:11–12). Validation of the future blessings has already begun, and believers have been "sealed" by the Spirit of promise, who himself is a "guarantee" of all future inheritances of this redemption or unto the day of redemption (1:13–14). As Leslie Crawford has written, "It is God 'who has blessed' (verse 3), 'chosen' (verse 4), 'predestined,' 'freely bestowed' (verse 5), lavished redemption and forgiveness (verses 7–8), 'made known' and 'purposed' (verse 9), given an inheritance, working everything according to His will (verse 11), sealed (verse 13), and given the Holy Spirit (verse 14). Therefore it will be His glory that is praised (vv. 6, 12 and 14)."[245]

Other events associated with the day of the Lord are depicted as already at hand. For example, Paul prays that God gives them the Spirit of wisdom and revelation (1:17; see also 1:7). But the "giving" of the Spirit is linked

---

243. The relation of the aorist participle προορίσας (proorisas) with the main verb ἐξελέξατο (exelexato) may be modal and used to stress simultaneous action without any logical priority of either concept. "It is better to view God's act of election as being expressed in the predestination of the elect, so that the primacy of election remains without diminishing the importance of predestination" (Crawford, "Ephesians 1:3–4 and the Nature of Election," 81–82). However, one might point to the later aorist participles, "after having heard" (ἀκούσαντες [akousantes]) and "after having believed" (πιστεύσαντες [pisteusantes]) and their relationship to the aorist main verb, "you were sealed" (ἐσφραγίσθητε [esphragisthēte]) to indicate that the aorist participles occupy an antecedent (logical and temporal) relation with the main verb (1:13). That the former case (1:4–5) is addressing pretemporal divine aspects of the decree while the latter (1:13) is directed at the temporal application of those blessings may or may not be relevant. But even if the aorist participle referring to predestination is taken as temporally or (more likely) logically prior to election (1:4–5), then the primary point would be that election is a result of God's purpose to adopt sons. See Tucker S. Ferda, "'Sealed' with the Holy Spirit (Eph 1, 13–14) and Circumcision," Bib 93 (2012): 564–66.

244. Throughout this text (1:3–14), the phrase "in Christ" or its equivalents are repeated ten times. See ἐν Χριστῷ (v. 1), ἐν αὐτῷ (vv. 4, 9, 10), ἐν τῷ ἠγαπημένῳ (v. 6), ἐν ᾧ (vv. 7, 11, 13), and ἐν τῷ Χριστῷ (vv. 10, 12).

245. Crawford, "Ephesians 1:3–4 and the Nature of Election," 77.

with the day of the Lord, as Joel 2 testifies (and Acts 2 confirms).[246] Paul prays for the granting of this wisdom and revelation so that the saints might know more about what is awaiting them in terms of their inheritance and the hope of their calling and especially the power that has been exhibited toward them in this redemption (1:18–19). This powerful activity is likened to the might it took to raise Jesus from the dead and to position him in the heavenly realm, where he *presently* rules over both the enemies of the evil age and the church (1:20–23). This exaltation is derived from the enthronement psalm that sets Jesus on the throne of David exercising judgment, conducting battle, and subjugating his enemies (Ps 110).[247] The subsequent section in Ephesians (2:11–22) follows up with the ancient Near Eastern divine-warrior-victory pattern of "conflict, victory, kingship, house-building, celebration."[248] In Ephesians the pattern is specifically "Lordship (1.20–23), conflict-victory (2.1–16), victory shout (2.17), celebration (2.18), and house-building (2:20–22)."[249]

Along with this new reality of Christ's rule is the resurrection of the saints. Here their situation is shown in similar categories of Christ's resurrection, but rather than physical it is spiritual and linked to regeneration (see 1:20–21; 2:1–7). While dead in trespasses and sins, the elect (of 1:4) are, through the rich mercy and great love of the Father, resurrected or regenerated, made to ascend to the heavenly places, and ensconced with Christ on the throne next to God (2:1–10).[250] Thus the day of redemption

---

246. Paul also speaks in 1:13 of "the Holy Spirit of promise" or "the promised Spirit," no doubt referring to what was promised by Ezekiel, Jeremiah, and Joel. See Gordon D. Fee, *God's Empowering Presence: The Holy Spirit in the Letters of Paul* (Peabody, MA: Hendrickson, 1994), 670–71. For the view that Paul essentially uses the argument of Ezekiel as a unifying aspect of the letter to the Ephesians and that the believers were infused with an unwritten law, see Ira Jolivet, "The Ethical Instructions in Ephesians as the Unwritten Statutes and Ordinances of God's New Temple in Ezekiel," *ResQ* 48 (2006): 193–210.

247. Timothy G. Gombis, "Ephesians 2 as a Narrative of Divine Warfare," *JSNT* 26 (2004): 408–10. Psalm 110:3 states, "Your people willingly follow you when you go into battle." This suggests that the saints may play a part in the day of the Lord battle (see below).

248. Ibid., 405. The same pattern is noted in Exod 15 in the "Song of the Sea" and connected with redemption (ibid., 406). Thus the day of redemption follows the day of the Lord or constitutes the victory of that day.

249. Ibid., 408.

250. For an assessment of the human condition or "an incisive theological evaluation of the non-Christian world," see Peter T. O'Brien, "Divine Analysis and Comprehensive Solution: Some Priorities from Ephesians 2," *RTR* 53 (1994): 131, 130–42. This also sets up the basis for the *then–now* schema in Ephesians. See Daniel Darko, "What Does It Mean to Be Saved? An African Reading of Ephesians 2," *Journal of Pentecostal Theology* 24 (2015): 45.

has been inaugurated through the giving of the Spirit, the raising of the dead, and the ascension to the ruling throne along with the Son over the powers. And this post-day of the Lord reign has occurred precisely because the work of Christ on the cross (similar to Rom 1–3 and Col 2:15) is couched in terms of a victory over the enemies of the Lord associated with that final day. Timothy Gombis has argued that Ephesians 1:20–2:22 utilizes the "pattern of divine warfare" and expresses "the exaltation of Christ to cosmic lordship then delineates his triumphs over the powers that rule the present fallen age."[251] This portion of Ephesians, then, pictures Christ as the victorious conquering King who reigns and conducts war along with his warrior-like saints subsequent to the final day of the Lord victory, a battle Christ already won on the cross via his redemption.[252]

EPHESIANS 6:10–17

Despite the fulfillment of day of the Lord motifs that appear to place believers into the posteschaton or new age, Paul nevertheless avoids an overrealized eschatology. Instead he details the present and future *negative aspects* related to or in close proximity with the day of redemption. Aspects of the wrath of God are linked with the day of the Lord and directed at the disobedient. The inbreaking of this still-future wrath into the present age or "evil days/day" is every bit as certain as the benefits brought about by the day of the Lord victory of Christ described above (5:16; 6:13). While all those (including the elect) prior to experiencing the power of redemption fall under the description as those who are "by nature children of wrath" (ἤμεθα τέκνα φύσει ὀργῆς [*ēmetha tekna physei orgēs*], 2:3), Paul still anticipates a future day of wrath for those who remain without redemption or those regarded as the "sons of disobedience" (ἐπὶ υἱοὺς τῆς ἀπειθείας [*epi huious tēs apeitheias*], 5:6).[253] In contrast to the sons of disobedience (or

---

251. Gombis, "Ephesians 2 as a Narrative of Divine Warfare," 407, 18.

252. Kolb, in commenting on Luther's treatment of the armor of God and the devil, writes, "God is depicted as the victor over the devil's deception and murderous designs through Christ's death and resurrection" (Robert Kolb, "'The Armor of God and the Might of His Strength': Luther's Sermon on Ephesians 6 [1531/1533]," *Concordia Journal* 43 [2017]: 60).

253. For a discussion on the past life of believers and the behaviors left behind in order to embrace a new kind of existence, according to Ephesians, see Christoph W. Stenschke, "'Once You Were in Darkness': The Past of the Readers of Ephesians," *European Journal of Theology* 23 (2014): 123–39.

those characterized by disobedience), those characterized by the Spirit are instructed to "*redeem* the time," for the days are evil (5:16).[254] This sets up an inevitable showdown between what might be regarded as the sons of light (obedience) versus the sons of darkness (disobedience)—to borrow a Qumran motif (but cf. Eph 5:8–14).

While one might expect all aspects of this ethical dualism to be confined to the future day of redemption, where the Lord immediately deals with the disobedient and brings his full redemption to his elect, it is not quite the case. In one of the most descriptive passages in the epistle, located within the *peroratio* (6:10–20),[255] believers are portrayed as defending a city as fully armed warriors in active combat *now* with the forces of evil while in anticipation and preparation for the consummate "evil day" (ἐν τῇ ἡμέρᾳ τῇ πονηρᾷ [*en tē hēmera tē ponēra*] 6:13, 10–17).[256] Paul intentionally combines the activity of a wrestler (πάλη [*palē*], "wrestle") with that of a soldier in what amounts to a mixing of metaphors if not an example of the incompatibility of combining wrestling with the hardware of the panoply (6:12, 14–17).[257] Wrestlers in the ancient world grappled naked.[258] Although one need not make this metaphor walk on all fours, it should be stated that one neither goes to war naked (like a wrestler) nor wrestles

---

254. O'Brien, "Divine Analysis and Comprehensive Solution," 135.

255. The *peroratio* either summarizes both sections of Ephesians (indicative/imperative) or only covers the imperative section of the book. For a discussion of views see Donna R. Reinhard, "Ephesians 6:10–18: A Call to Personal Piety or Another Way of Describing Union," *JETS* 48 (2005): 522–23. Thus the *peroratio* may focus exclusively on the human response (covering only imperatival section) or covers the entirety of the book and therefore "invites us to consider some of the armor as divine attributes or gifts which God gives to believers and which have implications concerning how believers are to walk in accordance with these gifts" (ibid., 523).

256. "Only when we begin to identify the evils of our society in terms of Ephesians 6:10–13 will we be prepared to accept the guidance of Ephesians 6:14–17 as our appropriate strategy for defense" (Paul T. Eckel, "Ephesians 6:10–20," *Int* 45 [1991]: 290). On the flip side, each piece of armor "is fundamentally a mighty act of God's grace and only in a secondary and dependent way are they descriptions of virtuous behavior and Christian action" (ibid., 291–92). "Only the alert will stand in 'the evil day' (v. 13)—the final apocalyptic battle. . . . The initial skirmishes of the final all-out war with evil are being waged by the saints" (ibid., 292–93). For the picture of the battle as a defense of a city see Nils Neumann, "Die πανοπλία Gottes: Eph 6, 11–17 als Reflexion der Belagerung einer Stadt," *ZNW* 106 (2015): 40–64.

257. For a summarization of the notorious problem with the word for "struggle/wrestle" (παλή [*palē*]) as it relates to the armor, see Michael E. Gudorf, "The Use of *Palē* in Ephesians 6:12," *JBL* 117 (1998): 331n1.

258. Ibid., 332. Thus 6:13 is a bit ironic. Rather than "Therefore take off your clothes," Paul says, "Take up (or put on) the full armor of God." Gudorf suggests μάχη (*machē*), "battle," might have been a more consistent term here, all things being equal.

while wearing the armor (like a soldier). Obviously Paul has something altogether different in mind for the Christian.

Rather than view this description as a mixing of mutually exclusive metaphors, Paul provides a well-known combination of wrestling and warfare drawn from ancient sources that directly applies to how the church conducts its day of the Lord–like warfare in the present time.[259] Michael Gudorf locates the source of Paul's metaphor in Plutarch. He writes,

> In Plutarch's *Moralia*, there occurs an interesting word that combines the concept of a heavily armored soldier (ὁπλίτης) with that of wrestling (πάλη). The resulting compound, ὁπλιτοπάλας, is a term used to describe a heavily armored soldier who also happens to be an accomplished wrestler. As one might easily imagine, such an individual would be particularly formidable in the arena of close-quarter military combat, where only one is left standing.[260]

The first thing to note is that Paul's combination of wrestling and soldiering is not accidental or even original but rather by design. The second thing to note is the importance attributed to the wrestler himself, who, according to Plutarch and in distinction to the boxer or runner, has within his arsenal a well-developed set of skills that enable him to both stay on his feet and to execute the practiced proficiencies of cunning as well as deception against his opponent.[261] By way of analogy, the Christian is presented as a sure-footed, skillful, and cunning wrestler-in-armor engaged in hand-to-hand combat with a formidable opponent (even though the technical term in Plutarch, ὁπλιτοπάλης [oplitopalēs], is not used by Paul).[262] Likewise the Christian is to exercise cunning, skill, and even forms of deception against

---

259. The par-excellent source of the warrior image of strength and open battle in ancient Greece is Homer's Achilles. On this topic see the bibliography provided in Jeffrey R. Asher, "An Unworthy Foe: Heroic ἔθη, Trickery, and an Insult in Ephesians 6:11," *JBL* 130 (2011): 733n11. Odysseus, on the other hand, "served as the paradigm of the heroic virtues of trickery and cunning" (ibid., 737–38). These two images are diametrically opposed in Eph 6:10–20, where the former refers primarily to believers and the latter to the devil. This is not to suggest that the images are mutually exclusive, for, as indicated above, the wrestler-warrior image applied to believers includes the use of deception and cunning.

260. Gudorf, "Use of *Palē* in Ephesians 6:12," 332.

261. Ibid., 332–33. For an extended list of ancient authors and the use of wrestling in association with deception and warfare (including Lucian, Philostratus, and Aristophanes) see Asher, "Unworthy Foe," 738–40.

262. ὁπλιτοπάλης is defined as "heavy-armed warrior" (LSJ 1240).

a predominantly cunning and deceptive opponent using his own methods of combat in opposition to the gospel (μεθοδεία [methodeia], 6:11).

By mixing these metaphors it is most likely that Paul intended to borrow Plutarch's (and other ancient writers') wrestler-warrior archetype to remind the saint that he is a formidable wrestler-in-armor trained to conduct militant close-quarter combat tactical warfare with the Lord's enemies as a preview of the eschatological consummation of that war pending the day of the Lord. The reference to "standing" as opposed to, say, "attacking" should not be understood as merely defensive actions, nor should the wrestler-warrior image be limited to close-quarter combat.[263] Paul includes the reality of missile warfare as undertaken by the enemy. In this way the enemy is portrayed in terms of the trickster or within the cast of the "Odysseus ethos." The believer's shield of faith is therefore designed to "extinguish all the fiery arrows of the wicked one" (6:16). Stripping back the metaphors, these enemies of the church are likely represented in terms of unjust political, economic, and intellectual organizations as well as unseen angelic forces aligned against the gospel (see also 2 Cor 10:3–6).[264] Given the usage of the panoply, Jeffrey Asher has correctly framed the entirety of Ephesians in terms of institutional identity and argues that "Eph 6:10–20 functions not as moral paraenesis but, more specifically, as paraenesis aimed at defining the community in sharp, even harsh contrast with the world that lay outside its boundaries."[265] Asher concludes that Ephesians is therefore much more introversional (borrowing from MacDonald) than Colossians.

---

263. Asher, "Unworthy Foe," 736–37. Luther presented both offensive and defensive strategies, represented by the expression, "One power protects the city; the other goes to battle and wins the victory" (Kolb, "'Armor of God and the Might of His Strength,'" 64).

264. Similar to Eph 6:10–17, Paul says in 2 Cor 10:3–5 that (1) the war is not according to human standards, (2) the weapons of warfare, τὰ ὅπλα τῆς στρατείας ἡμων οὐ σαρκικὰ (ta hopla tēs strateias hēmōn ou sarkika), are not "fleshly" or "human," (3) but they are powerful for tearing down strongholds (arguments and every obstacle opposed to the knowledge of God). This indicates that the warfare is primarily intellectual, philosophical, or discursive and intended to be included within ethics and the practice of virtue. See Richard Jungkuntz, "Weapons of Their Warfare: A Study in Early Christian Polemic," CTM 38 (1967): 436–57, for the four methods of argumentation largely misused (according to the author) by the church fathers in opposing Epicureanism. But this does not rule out direct intrusions of the spirit world such as demon possession, spiritism, witchcraft, sorcery, the occult, etc. For a much-needed corrective on this issue, see J. Ayodeji Adewuya, "The Spiritual Powers of Ephesians 6:10–18 in the Light of African Pentecostal Spirituality," BBR 22 (2012): 251–58.

265. Asher, "Unworthy Foe," 746.

Far from the church being cast in a role of a docile victim or even a pacifistic-oriented organization, while taking into account the metaphorical nature of this description, of course, its members are portrayed in militaristic tones as well as physically and tactically intimidating characters. The entire panoply may be serving, then, as an elaborate piece of "counterideology," not against warfare or armory in general but rather in behalf of the deconstruction of the variegated intellectual counterpoints to the gospel from the spheres of power.[266] It is important to note, in addition to this, that the wrestler-warrior image need not be regarded as that of an intellectual (or otherwise) bully but rather of a defender. Paul calls on these combatants to "stand" (πρὸς τὸ δύνασθαι ὑμᾶς στῆναι, pros to dynasthai hymas stēnai) or "stand firm" (στῆτε [stēte] 6:11, 14).[267] The battle associated with the day of the Lord (and day of redemption) should therefore encompass both activities, namely, the divine immediacy of that future advent as well as the mediate activity of God's people in the here and now. In the words of Carey Newman, "In Christ, God's future rule, his eschatological acts of judgment and salvation, have *already* broken-in upon the world."[268] And these acts have no less broken in *at the present time* through the sanctifying actions of his saints and their wrestler-warrior activities wrought by the power of God and aimed at the authorities of this present evil age.

According to Donna Reinhard, the individual pieces of armor most likely follow a pattern of *divine provisions* (truth, righteousness, peace, faith, salvation, word/Spirit) followed by *human responsibilities* respecting those provisions.[269] This pattern roughly corresponds with the indicative (1:3–3:21)

---

266. The term "counterideology" comes from Gregory Wong, "A Farewell to Arms: Goliath's Death as Rhetoric against Faith in Arms," *BBR* 23 (2013): 45, who in turn gets it from Fokkelman. Wong uses counterideology to stand for the mitigation of the faith in armament altogether. But here it is the "armor of God" (as opposed to the armor of Goliath or Saul). See also Ariella Deem, "Short Notes: '. . . And the Stone Sank into His Forehead.' A Note on 1 Samuel 17.49," *VT* 28 (1978): 349–51.

267. Asher notes that "three specific motifs are associated with believers: strength, armoring, and standing. These three motifs not only describe the believers but are also essential to understanding the structure of this paraenetic section" (Asher, "Unworthy Foe," 732). He later states with respect to the soldier's "standing" that "it was used as a description of one of the two types of warfare described in the *Iliad* (the σταδίη μαχή [the 'standing fight'] versus missile warfare) and was the standard term for describing the warrior engaged in open, close-order battle" (ibid., 735).

268. Newman, "Ephesians 1:3," 96.

269. So Reinhard, "Ephesians 6:10–18," 524.

and imperative divisions of the book (4:1–6:20)—the latter half with the armor in the *peroratio* (6:10–20). While correspondence of the *divine provisions* is accomplished and applied through mercy and grace, the *human responses* arise out of a grateful heart; both divine and human aspects are then conceptually united in the particulars of the armor. The complementation is made evident by uniting earlier statements in Ephesians with those linked to the armor. This includes the *truth* in the belt of truth (1:13; 4:25), *righteousness* in the breastplate of righteousness (4:22–24), *peace* in the feet shod with the preparation of the gospel of peace (1:2; 2:14; 4:3), *faith* in the shield of faith (2:8–9; 4:11–14), *salvation* in the helmet of salvation (2:5, 8–9; 5:23), and the *word of God* or the *Spirit* in the sword of the Spirit (1:13; 5:18–19). Reinhard writes, "With the exception of the term 'righteousness,' every other attribute of the armor is mentioned in both indicative and imperative sections of the letter and then repeated in the 'whole armor of God' pericope."[270] In addition to this, the armor section brings together various themes including divine strengthening (3:16–19; 6:10) and reliance on God to conquer the dark forces (2:1–5; 6:11–12). Reinhard concludes that the armor of God is parallel with Ephesians 3 (Christ dwelling in their hearts by faith) and therefore equivalent to being in union with or putting on Christ.[271] Thus the armor of God is represented as the virtuous acts of believers that have their efficiency due to the mercy of the Father and the objective work of Christ.

Paul not only sets forth the basis of divine accomplishments and human responsibilities but by doing so identifies the *ideological* components of the battle(s) and areas of opposition. The *strategies* appear to be summarized by the phrase "machinations of the Devil" (πρὸς τὰς μεθοδείας τοῦ διαβόλου [*pros*

---

270. Ibid., 526.

271. Ibid., 529–31. The concepts of Christ living in the heart (indwelling) and being "in Christ" are unlikely to be interchangeable or identical. But the thesis up to this point appears to be quite valid. On the argument concerning whether "righteousness" in "the breastplate of righteousness" refers to imputation (and forensic declarations) or virtues see David H. Wenkel, "The 'Breastplate of Righteousness' in Ephesians 6:14: Imputation or Virtue?," *TynBul* 58 (2007): 275–87. Wenkel argues for the latter, stating, "The armor of God appears to be a rigid metaphor while the individual pieces appear to have a small degree of flexibility" (ibid., 280). Later he states, "if the whole 'armour of God' is referencing both imputation and virtue, it loses all meaning as a metaphor" (ibid., 284). Choosing one or the other is not simply a matter of being consistent, but according to Wenkel, a necessity in maintaining the single framework of a metaphor.

tas methodias tou diabolou]).[272] The *opponents* include those in the governing structures, such as "powers" (πρὸς τὰς ἀρχάς [*pros tas archas*]), "authorities" (πρὸς τὰς ἐξουσίας [*pros tas exousias*]), and "world rulers of this darkness" (πρὸς τούς κοσμοκράτορας τοῦ σκότους τούτου [*pros tous kosmokratoras tou skotous toutou*]) as well as more supernaturally oriented adversaries noted by the phrase "spiritual wickedness in heavenly places" (τὰ πνευματικὰ τῆς πονηρίας ἐν τοῖς ἐπουρανίοις [*ta pneumatika tēs ponērias en tois epouraniois*]) (6:11–12).[273] Because Paul prefaces this list by saying that the struggle is not "against flesh and blood" (ὅτι οὐκ ἔστιν ἡμῖν πρὸς αἷμα καὶ σάρκα [*hoti ouk estin hēmin pros haima kai sarka*]), one should not assume that therefore "flesh and blood" has no part in the struggle or is not involved at all in carrying out this *spiritual* warfare.[274] Who else are these *powers, authorities,* and *world rulers* utilizing the strategies and ideologies of the devil against the gospel under the influence of spiritual wickedness in heavenly places but those comprised of flesh and blood? The enemy, as depicted here with its multifaceted front, is that to whom the believer was once in allegiance (Eph 2:2–3). This adversary is behind the "age" that Paul depicted in Ephesians 2:2–3 as that which directs the "unhealthy and ungodly social, cultural, economic, and political environment in which we live."[275] These are the fronts on which the Christian as wrestler-warrior is to be engaged and conquering as part of the proleptic day of the Lord conflict. And as Jeffrey Niehaus has rightly stated, "the purpose of warfare is to bring unsubmissive territory under the effectual rule of the god."[276]

---

272. The term for "machinations" is μεθοδεία (*methodeia*). It occurs only twice in the NT (Eph 4:14; 6:11) and is always used negatively. It may be translated "scheming, craftiness" (BDAG 625; L&N §88.158). For the history of its usage see *TLNT* 2:462; Asher, "Unworthy Foe," 737. See also Everett L. Wheeler, *Stratagem and the Vocabulary of Military Trickery*, Mnemosyne, Bibliotheca Classica Batava Supplementum 108 (Leiden: Brill, 1988).

273. Other texts using the armor of God or that are regarded as parallel to Eph 6:10–20 include Isa 11:5; 52:7; 59:17–20; Wis 5:15–23; Rom 13:12; 2 Cor 6:7; 1 Thess 5:8; T. Levi 8:2. See Asher, "Unworthy Foe," 729n1.

274. Arnold takes all these terms as designating malevolent spiritual powers derived from the magical or astrological tradition. See Clinton E. Arnold, *Ephesians, Power and Magic: The Concept of Power in Ephesians in Light of Its Historical Setting*, SNTSMS 63 (Cambridge; New York: Cambridge University Press, 1989), 64–68. Later he asserts, "No human opposition is mentioned in this context" (ibid., 118). See also his *Powers of Darkness: Principalities & Powers in Paul's Letters* (Downers Grove, IL: InterVarsity, 1992), 148–60. He may not be excluding humanity entirely out of the equation, but they are mere pawns. See Stenschke, "'Once You Were in Darkness,'" 127.

275. Darko, "What Does It Mean to Be Saved?," 47.

276. Jeffrey Jay Niehaus, "Joshua and Ancient Near Eastern Warfare," *JETS* 31 (1988): 49.

The point of Paul is not to exclude evil humanity as occupiers of the strategic places of assault within this warfare but to point beyond it to the spiritual source(s) motivating, manipulating, and moving within the larger cosmic battle associated with the day of the Lord. Likewise, one should not assume that because the battle is described as a spiritual one that therefore it *necessarily* eliminates all possibility of physical warfare whatsoever as part of that spiritual battle.[277] "No sword of steel or iron is appropriate or allowed in this conflict" appears to be an unwarranted conclusion derived from an unnecessary reductionism.[278] What Paul is likely warning about here is the danger of focusing exclusively on sinful humanity's role in the battles to the exclusion of recognizing the perennially malevolent spiritual forces orchestrating them. The solution to exclusively (or largely) focusing on humanity is certainly not to bypass or eliminate all sinful human involvement whatsoever from the spiritual battle against the church. By construing the environment of the participants in entirely supernatural categories, one comes dangerously close to projecting docetic-like metaphysics into the nature of spiritual warfare.

Further insight into the imagery of the wrestler-in-armor is to ask whether this metaphor is restricted to the Roman (or Greek) wrestler-warrior or is also (or even primarily) derived from the Old Testament as well. Scholars have pointed to Isaiah 59:17–18 as the most extended reference of the armor metaphor (see also Isa 11:5). Here it is clearly the Lord in the role of Divine Warrior who wears the armor: "And he put on righteousness like a breastplate and placed a helmet of salvation on his head, and he clothed himself with a garment of vengeance and with his cloak, as one about to render retribution, reproach to his adversaries" (Isa 59:17–18 NETS LXX).

Unfortunately for Israel, this vengeance is directed against them. In contrast to the character and moral condition of Israel, David Wenkel

---

277. Contra Hollie M. Holt-Woehl, "Putting on the Whole Armor of God: Preaching Ephesians 6:10–20 in a Multicultural Congregation," *WW* 29 (2009): 298. Thus these caveats should not be taken as prescriptions for following the modus operandi of Thomas Müntzer in establishing God's rule on earth. On the other hand, for a powerful examination of three historical abuses of government intervention on religious settlements (including the Branch Davidians), leading to a final conflagration, see Brent D. Shaw, "State Intervention and Holy Violence: Timgad/Paleostrovsk/Waco," *Journal of the American Academy of Religion* 77 (2009): 853–94.

278. Kolb, "'Armor of God and the Might of His Strength,'" 71. For similar sentiments against the use of "holy war" by human governments today see McDurmon, *Bounds of Love*, 58–59.

notes that here the "armour metaphor as a whole refers to YHWH's attributes in opposition to Israel's moral corruption."[279] While Isaiah's use of the armor metaphor includes justice as both a belt (11:5) and as a breastplate (59:17), Paul uses the belt for truth (Eph 6:14a) and the breastplate for justice/righteousness (Eph 6:14b). Aside from the fluid use of the armor metaphor by both Isaiah and Paul, the essential idea is that the armor in Isaiah represents the righteous character and actions of God in contrast to the people of Israel. This suggests when Paul exhorts Christians to "put on the whole armor *of God*" (ἐνδύσασθε τὴν πανοπλίαν τοῦ θεοῦ [*endysasthe tēn panoplian tou theou*]) or to "take up the whole armor *of God*" (διὰ τοῦτο ἀναλάβετε τὴν πανοπλίαν τοῦ θεοῦ [*dia touto analabete tēn panoplian tou theou*]) that he primarily intends and expects there to be a virtuous, functional, or ethical righteousness in mind rather than (but not necessarily excluding) a forensic feature. The armor of God in Isaiah and Ephesians would then represent a carrying out of the righteousness of God. By extension, the various pieces of armor likely signify various truths and aspects of the gospel, but without necessarily implying a hierarchy of doctrine, perhaps much more akin to spokes on a wheel.[280] It is also liable that the "breastplate of righteousness" is equivalent to the pregnant expression "the righteousness of God."[281] In distinction to Paul, however, the Isaianic reference represents a day of the Lord in a fashion that is in opposition to the people of God instead of her enemies. Paul then uses the metaphor for carrying out the day of the Lord battles in the interim

---

279. Wenkel, "'Breastplate of Righteousness' in Ephesians 6:14," 282.

280. Ibid., 286.

281. The phrase "righteousness of God" is highly disputed and discussed within a vast amount of scholarly literature. It is without dispute that the phrase is essentially elastic without a strict technical meaning. Thus it is subject to an array of specific and diverse nuances depending on the context, collocations, and literary refractions (as in Rom 1:17). For a sampling of literature see Michael F. Bird, *The Saving Righteousness of God: Studies on Paul, Justification and the New Perspective*, PBM (Milton Keynes, UK: Paternoster, 2007); Hays, *Conversion of the Imagination*; Yung Suk Kim, *A Theological Introduction to Paul's Letters: Exploring a Threefold Theology of Paul* (Eugene, OR: Cascade Books, 2011); J. R. Daniel Kirk, *Unlocking Romans: Resurrection and the Justification of God* (Grand Rapids: Eerdmans, 2008); Dane Calvin Ortlund and Matthew S. Harmon, eds., *Studies in the Pauline Epistles: Essays in Honor of Douglas J. Moo* (Grand Rapids: Zondervan, 2014); Stanley E. Porter and Craig A. Evans, eds., *The Pauline Writings* (London: T&T Clark, 2004); Cornelis P. Venema, *The Gospel of Free Acceptance in Christ: An Assessment of the Reformation and New Perspectives on Paul* (Edinburgh: Banner of Truth Trust, 2006); N. T. Wright, "On Becoming the Righteousness of God: 2 Corinthians 5:21," in *Pauline Theology*, ed. David M. Hay (Minneapolis: Augsburg, 1993), 200–208.

between the victory of God in Christ on the cross and the final consummation on the day of redemption.

Paul has used the day of redemption as both a past and future reality designed by the Father, contingent on an effective salvific work of Christ and applied as well as guaranteed by the application and possession of the Spirit. While Ephesians presents aspects of the day of the Lord as accomplished and followed to some extent by stations associated with the day of redemption, nevertheless, phases of both days persist in the present age. For example, believers enjoy the future eschatological benefits of reigning with Christ in heaven as if the day of the Lord has taken place and the day of redemption has already arrived. Nevertheless, believers are presently engaged in day of the Lord activities such as spiritual warfare, awaiting the final execution of the day of the Lord and day of redemption for all of creation. Paul has communicated to the Ephesians that there are already/not-yet aspects of each of these grand day-of schemes intersecting, intruding, foreshadowing, and integrating within the warp and woof of Pauline eschatology in such a way that gives purpose and meaning to the church's mission. And until the final perfection of the bride of Christ, these days await their ultimate par-excellent fulfillment, when the eschaton climaxes in the redemptive matrix of universal cosmic salvation.

THE PASTORAL EPISTLES

The letters of 1 and 2 Timothy and Titus[282] are often referred to as the "Pastoral Epistles."[283] This nomenclature is helpful in that it broadly summarizes Paul's purpose for writing these epistles. However, the occasion for

---

282. It is beyond the sphere of this work to discuss the issues surrounding the authorship of these letters. Pauline authorship, however, has historically been the consensus view of the ancient church up until the nineteenth century. From the nineteenth century into the modern era, the debate has continued, and a sizable portion of scholarship has concluded that Paul did not author the Pastoral Epistles. However, when examining both the internal and external evidence of the letters, it seems that the preponderance of proof arguably favors Pauline authorship, and thus the authenticity of all three epistles is assumed here. For helpful discussions regarding the issue of authorship see, for example, George William Knight, *The Pastoral Epistles: A Commentary on the Greek Text*, NIGTC (Grand Rapids: Eerdmans, 1992), 4–52; Terry L. Wilder, "Pseudonymity, the New Testament, and the Pastoral Epistles," in *Entrusted with the Gospel: Paul's Theology in the Pastoral Epistles*, ed. Andreas J. Köstenberger and Terry L. Wilder (Nashville: Broadman & Holman, 2010), 28–51; William D. Mounce, *Pastoral Epistles*, WBC 46 (Nashville: Nelson, 2000), cxviii–cxxix.

283. For discussion on the origin of this nomenclature see Knight, *Pastoral Epistles*, 3; Luke Timothy Johnson, *The First and Second Letters to Timothy: A New Translation with Introduction and Commentary*, AB 35A (New Haven: Yale University Press, 2008), 13n3.

each letter is unique, as the apostle provides both instruction and exhortation to his fellow workers regarding specific issues that had arisen in the churches they served.

In 1 Timothy Paul is seemingly focused on the importance of Timothy demonstrating what it means to be a faithful steward who manages the household of God well.[284] Certain opponents had infiltrated the church and were teaching contrary to the gospel. Apparently these false teachers had accumulated much influence (2:11-15; 5:15, 17-25), and thus Paul writes to Timothy with instructions on how to deal with those who were wreaking havoc within the house of God (1:3-4, 18-20). Moreover, Alan Tomlinson observes that the removal of the false teachers was only a part of the broader purpose for which Paul writes:

> Timothy's de facto mission involves much more than just the initial charge to correct false teachers. Timothy is more than a troubleshooter; he is going to be the model and example of appropriate devotion for leaders with the household. With this expanded mission for Timothy in view, Paul then turned to more personal instructions, charging the "steward-delegate" to expose false teachers and thus prove to be a "good servant" (4:1-7a), to be an example to the household of God with devotion to the Savior God (4:9-16), and to relate properly to the church in good order (5:2-6:2).[285]

In Titus, Paul instructs his son in the faith to remain in Crete with a twofold purpose: (1) he is to set things in order in the churches, and (2) he is to appoint elders in every city (1:5). The "setting things in order" likely refers to silencing those whom Paul refers to as idle talkers and deceivers who were teaching contrary to the gospel for dishonest gain (1:10-11). To combat these opponents, Paul instructs Titus to establish elders within the churches who would faithfully teach the gospel and live in a manner worthy of it. In addition, the apostle provides a "household code" delineating directives for how those within the congregations should behave. The purpose for this is that "the visibly good and attractive lives of God's

---

284. This language is adopted from F. Alan Tomlinson, "The Purpose and Stewardship Theme within the Pastoral Epistles," in Köstenberger and Wilder, *Entrusted with the Gospel*, 52-60.

285. Ibid., 60.

household are a revelation to all people of the blessing that the crucified Savior has in store for those who put their faith in him (2:11–14)."[286]

In 2 Timothy, Paul realizes that he does not have long to live (4:6–7) and thus requests Timothy to visit him as soon as possible (4:9, 21). But the epistle is more than just Paul urging his coworker to come visit; it is also a "final will and testament" as the apostle writes to encourage Timothy "to follow the pattern established by Paul as a 'loyal man of God' who did indeed guard the deposit [i.e. the gospel] and did entrust it to faithful men like Timothy. Timothy is to do the same (2:1–2; 4:1–2)."[287] The imminency of death compels Paul to admonish his son in the faith to follow his example and continue to faithfully proclaim the gospel.[288]

In a general sense these epistles do contain specific "pastoral" instructions that Paul expects both Timothy and Titus to implement among their respective congregations. Interpreting these epistles through this "pastoral" framework has led commentators to focus on certain themes throughout the letters such as church structure, soteriology, combating false teachers, and the importance of sound doctrine.[289] While such themes are certainly prevalent throughout these epistles, what is often missing from the discussion is reference to the eschatology of the letters.[290] Nevertheless, a careful reading of the Pastoral Epistles demonstrates that Paul's theology

---

286. Jerome D. Quinn, *The Letter to Titus: A New Translation with Notes and Commentary and an Introduction to Titus, I and II Timothy, the Pastoral Epistles*, AB 35 (New Haven: Yale University Press, 2005), 50. See also Tomlinson, "Purpose and Stewardship Theme within the Pastoral Epistles," 60–62.

287. Tomlinson, "Purpose and Stewardship Theme within the Pastoral Epistles," 63.

288. Ibid.

289. See, for example, Knight, *Pastoral Epistles*, 10, 24–32; I. Howard Marshall and Philip H. Towner, *A Critical and Exegetical Commentary on the Pastoral Epistles*, ICC (London: T&T Clark, 2004), 42–57; Mounce, *Pastoral Epistles*, cxxx–cxxxv.

290. See, for example, Brown, *Introduction to the New Testament*, 638–80; deSilva, *Introduction to the New Testament*, 733–75; Drane, *Introducing the New Testament*, 344–48; Donald A. Hagner, *The New Testament: A Historical and Theological Introduction* (Grand Rapids: Baker, 2012), 626–34; Köstenberger and Wilder, *Entrusted with the Gospel*, in which none of the essays in the volume address the eschatology of the Pastoral Epistles; Longenecker and Still, *Thinking through Paul*, 261–91; I. Howard Marshall, "Theological Interpretation of the New Testament," in *Theological Interpretation of the New Testament: A Book-by-Book Survey*, ed. Kevin J. Vanhoozer, Daniel J. Treier, and N. T. Wright (Grand Rapids: Baker, 2008), 161–81. Notable exceptions to this are Beale, *New Testament Biblical Theology*, 140–41; Matthew Y. Emerson, "Paul's Eschatological Outlook in the Pastoral Epistles," *CTR* 12 (2015): 83–98; Philip H. Towner, "The Present Age in the Eschatology of the Pastoral Epistles," *NTS* 32 (1986): 427–48; Frances M. Young, *The Theology of the Pastoral Letters*, New Testament Theology (Cambridge: Cambridge University Press, 1994), 70–73.

of the day of the Lord motif influences how he addresses the ecclesiological issues of each letter. Throughout the Pastoral Epistles the apostle seemingly understands the day of the Lord to be both a present and future reality. For Paul, the day of the Lord is not a footnote that the church occasionally considers, but rather the day has tremendous influence on the apostle's ecclesiology. In other words, the coming eschatological day should affect how the household of God, and all the various ministries associated with it, operates in the present. A cumulative survey of the epistles will help substantiate this claim.

It is evident in the Pastoral Epistles that Paul understands the church is presently living in the last days, which were inaugurated at Christ's first advent and will be consummated at his second advent (1 Tim 4:1; 2 Tim 3:1).[291] The apostle is not concerned about *when* the Day will arrive but rather that it *will* arrive. Even though the eschatological day is still future, Paul reminds Timothy and Titus that the difficult circumstances their congregations are facing demonstrate that the final day is *proleptic* and thus should affect how the church presently functions. It seems, then, that the day of the Lord shaped Paul's instructions to both Timothy and Titus, urging them to faithfully steward the household of God in light of the coming final day. For Paul, the future has an enormous influence on the present.

That the day of the Lord is a fundamental concept influencing Paul's instructions and exhortations in the Pastorals is likely derived from certain features that, when viewed *collectively*, verify this claim. For instance, the presence of false teachers in the church attempting to lead congregants astray from sound doctrine is a portent that the day of the Lord is approaching (1 Tim 1:3–4; 4:7; 6:20–21; 2 Tim 2:16–19).[292] The apostle likely derived this understanding from the teaching of Jesus, who warned that the onslaught of false teachers served as evidence that the "last days" have been inaugurated and that the day of the Lord is closer than ever before (Matt 24:11; see also 2 Pet 2:1–3). Likewise, Paul understands that the

---

291. See Emerson, "Paul's Eschatological Outlook in the Pastoral Epistles," 93–94; Towner, "Present Age in the Eschatology of the Pastoral Epistles," 431–33.

292. This theme is observed by G. K. Beale, "The Eschatology of Paul," in Harmon and Smith, *Studies in the Pauline Epistles*, 202; Bernhard Mutschler, "Eschatology in the Pastoral Epistles," in Watt, *Eschatology in the New Testament and Some Related Documents*, 379; Emerson, "Paul's Eschatological Outlook in the Pastoral Epistles," 10–11.

presence of false teachers and opponents to the gospel is one indication that the church is living in the last days and that the consummate day is drawing near. Consequently, he exhorts Timothy and Titus to protect their congregations against the false teachers, who, unless they repent, will face severe consequences at the final assize. G. K. Beale notes, "The presence of tribulation in the form of false, deceptive teaching [in the church] is also one of the signs that the long-awaited latter days had finally come. That this idea in 1 and 2 Timothy is not a reference to only a distant, future time is evident from recognizing that the [church] is already experiencing the latter-day tribulation of deceptive teaching and apostasy."[293] Paul urges his fellow coworkers to act swiftly by removing the false teachers in their midst, some of whom he has already "handed over to Satan" (1 Tim 1:20). The aim in removing these false teachers or "handing them over to Satan" is certainly to protect the church from doctrinal error, but it is also intended to be remedial for the false teachers (Matt 18:15–20; 1 Cor 5:1–5). In other words, the action taken against the false teachers is carried out in hope that they will be restored. Since the church is living in the last days, it is all the more urgent that these false teachers repent because of the impending day of the Lord. If they fail to repent and persist in undermining the faith, they will ultimately suffer divine retribution on that final day. Conversely, the apostle encourages Timothy and Titus to remain diligent in their teaching of sound doctrine, knowing they will receive a reward at the coming of the Lord Jesus. As Timothy, Titus, and all believers are faithful to the deposit (i.e., the gospel) that has been entrusted to them, they can look forward to the day of the Lord with great anticipation.

Another feature demonstrating the influence of the day of the Lord motif in the Pastorals is evident in the terms and idioms Paul uses throughout the letters. One particular term is the noun ἐπιφάνεια (epiphaneia), "appearance."[294] This word is not entirely synonymous with the term παρουσία (parousia), which is always used by Paul in reference to the future coming

---

293. Beale, "Eschatology of Paul," 202. See also Emerson, "Paul's Eschatological Outlook in the Pastoral Epistles," 93.

294. See BDAG 385; NIDNTTE 4:585–91. The noun is found six times in the NT, all in the Pauline corpus (2 Thess 2:8; 1 Tim 6:14; 2 Tim 1:10; 4:1, 8; Titus 2:13). With the exception of 2 Tim 1:10, the term always refers to the day of the Lord. The verb ἐπιφαίνω (epiphainō) occurs four times in the NT (Luke 1:79; Acts 27:20; Titus 2:11; 3:4), none of which are in reference to the second coming.

of the Lord, whereas *epiphaneia* can refer to a past event such as Christ's redemptive act (2 Tim 1:10; Titus 2:11; 3:4). But even these contexts demonstrate that what Christ accomplished in the past for his people must also be understood in light of his future coming. In other words, "The ἐπιφάνεια of Christ must be considered as a comprehensive salvation-historical event in which God's redemptive acts in the past stand in immediate relation to the present as well as to the future."[295] The term *epiphaneia* is also used in the Pastoral Epistles in eschatological contexts referring to the second coming or final appearing of the Lord (1 Tim 6:14; 2 Tim 4:1, 8; Titus 2:13).[296] In all four occurrences, the apostle exhorts Timothy and Titus to keep away from evil, to live virtuously and remain steadfast in the faith until the appearing of the Lord Jesus. From Paul's perspective, the future day of the Lord is a motivating factor for how Timothy and Titus carry out their present ministries. In light of the consummate day, the apostle exhorts his coworkers to manage the household of God well, knowing that on that day they will receive the crown of righteousness (2 Tim 4:8). Moreover, Paul's instructions also have implications for the congregations Timothy and Titus serve, for he expects that the church will diligently fulfill its ministry, living an ethical and moral life in the present with a future orientation. As these congregations faithfully carry out their new-covenant ministry, they can do so with joyful anticipation as they await the day of the Lord. The apostle's use of ἐπιφάνεια (*epiphaneia*) in the context of the Pastoral Epistles serves to remind his coworkers and the congregations they serve that the imminent appearance of the Lord should influence how they function as the household of God.

In addition to the term *epiphaneia*, Paul also uses other locutions in reference to the day of the Lord. In 2 Timothy the apostle employs his typical idiom "on that day" or "in that day," reminding Timothy that those who have served faithfully will be rewarded on the final day (2 Tim 1:12, 18; 4:8).[297] Furthermore, the phrases "in later times" and "in last days" (1 Tim 4:1; 2 Tim 3:1) may also connote an eschatological nuance. Although these

---

295. Andrew Y. Lau, *Manifest in Flesh: The Epiphany Christology of the Pastoral Epistles*, WUNT 2/86 (Tübingen: Mohr, 1996), 235.

296. For a helpful discussion on the similarities and distinct nuances between *epiphaneia* and *parousia* see Collins, "Παρουσία to Ἐπιφάνεια," 294–99.

297. See, for example, Mutschler, "Eschatology in the Pastoral Epistles," 382–84.

terms primarily focus on the *present* age, which has been inaugurated by Christ's first advent, these idioms are not devoid of a future understanding.[298] In other words, that the "last days" have arrived indicates that the future consummation of history is more imminent than ever. These last days are currently filled with those who pervert the gospel and abandon the faith. Thus Paul reminds Timothy to be a faithful steward of the gospel and endure hardship, knowing that the final day will come. Additional terms throughout the Pastorals such as "save" (1 Tim 4:16; 2 Tim 4:18), "eternal life" (1 Tim 1:16; Titus 1:2; 3:7), and "hope" also have eschatological nuances, as Paul understands that these are ultimately consummated at the day of the Lord.[299] The language Paul uses in the Pastorals once again demonstrates his already/not-yet mindset as he continues to remind his coworkers that while many "days" of the Lord have come, evidenced in the reality that they are living in the last days, the ultimate day is imminent. Thus the apostle urges Timothy and Titus to be diligent stewards of the gospel that they have been entrusted with and teach others to do likewise in light of the second coming (1 Tim 6:17–19).

The final feature evident in the Pastorals demonstrating that the day of the Lord is a significant motif in Paul's instructions to Timothy and Titus is his statements about the final judgment. In conjunction with the terms and idioms mentioned above, the apostle incorporates judicial language as a reminder to his coworkers and their congregations that the final day of the Lord is a forensic day (1 Tim 3:6; 5:12, 24–25; 2 Tim 4:1; Titus 3:12). For instance, in 1 Timothy 5:22 Paul warns Timothy not to lay hands on someone too hastily. The grounds for this are stated in verse 24, namely that there are some whose sins are obvious going before them into judgment, but for others their sins are revealed later. The point is that Timothy must carefully discern those who are fit for leadership within the church. But Paul's statement "going before them into judgment" may also have an eschatological nuance. As Philip Towner observes, "God's eschatological

---

298. On the meaning of these phrases see, for example, ibid., 378–82; Emerson, "Paul's Eschatological Outlook in the Pastoral Epistles," 92; Towner, "Present Age in the Eschatology of the Pastoral Epistles," 431–33.

299. This observation is taken from Mutschler, "Eschatology in the Pastoral Epistles," 366–69, 373–76. He also lists several additional terms and phrases throughout the Pastorals that have eschatological nuances, such as conformity with Christ, the eschatological wreath, the coming kingdom, and others.

decision is thus the framework within which Timothy's own act of discernment takes place. The blatant sin of obvious sinners forges the path to the
ineluctable eschatological judgment, and one in a role such as Timothy's
becomes a participant in the judicial process."[300] It is obvious that those
who commit blatant sin are not fit for leadership. But the statement "there
are those whose sin will be made evident later" does not mean that Timothy
should wait a long period of time before appointing leaders. Rather, the
phrase likely means that "it is not an adequate period of waiting that brings
sins to light, but the final judgment."[301] The point is that Timothy must use
great discernment when appointing leaders, for they will ultimately give
an account before the Lord's tribunal. The forensic nature of the day of
the Lord is also evident in 2 Timothy 4:1–2, where Paul charges Timothy
by appealing to the divine witness of the Father and the Son to preach the
word. Moreover, the importance of the charge to preach the word is to be
understood in light of the day of the Lord. Paul urges Timothy to remain
steadfast in preaching the word because Christ Jesus is the one who is about
to judge the living and the dead.[302] As Paul prepares for death, he exhorts
Timothy to follow his example and finish the race well, knowing that the
reward will come at the final assize, where he and all those who set their
affections on the Lord's return will receive the crown of righteousness
(4:7–8). Thus Paul reminds Timothy that preaching is to be eschatologically
motivated. And as Timothy faithfully preaches the word in the midst of a
hostile culture, he must do so with a future orientation knowing that on
that final court day when the true Judge arrives he will receive ultimate
vindication.

As in his earlier letters, so also here in his final letters Paul demonstrates that the day of the Lord is a prominent motif in his overall theological framework. When viewed collectively, the aforementioned features
of the Pastoral Epistles reveal that the apostle understands that the day of
the Lord is the final assize where Jesus returns as the true and righteous
Judge, meting out either retribution or reward. Consequently, the reality

---

300. Philip H. Towner, *The Letters to Timothy and Titus*, NICNT (Grand Rapids: Eerdmans,
2006), 377. Contra Knight, *Pastoral Epistles*, 241, who argues this is strictly human judgment.

301. Knight, *Pastoral Epistles*, 378n94. See also Marshall and Towner, *Critical and Exegetical
Commentary on the Pastoral Epistles*, 625–26.

302. μέλλοντος κρίνειν is a periphrastic future construction emphasizing the imminence
of the day of the Lord. See Mounce, *Pastoral Epistles*, 572.

of the coming final day must influence every aspect of the church's present ministry. More specifically, "The eschatological statements of the Pastoral Epistles form the framework for self-understanding and behavior— personally and ecclesiastically—from the present up to the parousia."[303] Therefore, Paul exhorts his coworkers to manage the household of God well, knowing that they and their congregations will one day stand before the judgment bench of the Lord Jesus, who serves as the Father's judicial agent and has absolute authority to pronounce the final verdict.

---

303. Mutschler, "Eschatology in the Pastoral Epistles," 400.

Conclusion

The purpose of this work was to examine how the day of the Lord should be understood as a major motif that influenced all of Paul's theological paradigm. More specifically, the argument presented here was that the day of the Lord was so significant for Paul that every aspect of his theology is in some way affected by this concept. Even in contexts where he does not explicitly mention the day of the Lord, we argued that the reality of this consummate day is in some way shaping the totality of his theology. The argument here is not that the day of the Lord should be considered the "center" of Paul's theology but rather that the day of the Lord is a fundamental component influencing all of Pauline theology. In other words, the day of the Lord is not an afterthought. Therefore, this study has *thematically* examined the day of the Lord motif throughout Paul's writings and concluded that his understanding of this theological concept had a much greater influence on the totality of his theological framework than scholarship previously suggested.

Chapter 1 examined several of the major treatments pertaining to the day of the Lord in modern scholarship. It was noted that much of the current literature on this subject focuses on the *origin* of the concept of the day of the Lord. The survey demonstrated that scholarly consensus regarding the origin of the day of the Lord is elusive. The various theories put forth by modern scholarship indicate that the concept is fluid and has been approached from a variety of different angles. And while there is little agreement regarding the origin of the day, the majority of scholars surveyed appreciate the diverse features used throughout the Old Testament to portray the concept of the day of the Lord. Despite the diversity among scholarly opinion, the survey helped elucidate a more precise understanding of the importance of the day of the Lord throughout the Old Testament and how this ultimately impacted Paul's theological framework.

The intention of chapter 2 was to examine how the day of the Lord is *thematically* evident throughout the entire Old Testament. We argued that the concept, while certainly embryonic, is evident beginning in the Torah, where several passages depict Yahweh either coming or that he will come to visit his people with blessings or curses depending on their faithfulness to the covenant stipulations he prescribed. The day of Yahweh's visitation may be a day that his people should fear, or it may be a day they can joyfully anticipate. This phenomenon of the Lord coming to visit his people likely served as the foundation for the origin of the day of the Lord phrase that was later annotated by the Prophets.

Building on the foundation established in the Torah, the Prophets interpreted the day of the Lord as a *terminus technicus* for the final day of judgment. But the Prophets also revealed that they understood there to be "days" of the Lord.[1] The circumstances that affected God's people (famine, sickness, war, exile, etc.) seemingly were understood as typological patterns pointing to the consummate day of the Lord. The hardships that the covenant people faced were to be interpreted as warnings to repent of their sins and return to Yahweh before the ultimate day arrived and all the nations would appear before him at the final assize. For the Prophets, the day of the Lord sometimes describes imminent judgment, while in other passages the locution clearly refers to the final eschatological judgment when God will ultimately make all things right.[2]

A brief exposition of the Writings demonstrated that the people understood the consequence of exile as a day of the Lord in which they were currently living. Specific examples from Lamentations and Daniel provide evidence that these authors interpreted life in exile as an actual day of the Lord but were encouraged by God that the final day had not arrived and that Yahweh would restore his people and share his kingdom with them. This survey not only offered a firmer understanding of the day of the Lord as a central theme depicted throughout the entire Old Testament but also set the stage for properly understanding Paul's theology of the day of the Lord, which he interprets as finding fulfillment at the second coming of Jesus.

Chapter 3 offered an examination of extracanonical literature and its teaching concerning the day of the Lord. The chapter established that not only was the extracanonical literature familiar with the day of the Lord, but, in keeping with the Old Testament's teaching concerning this motif,

---

1. William J. Dumbrell, *The Search for Order: Biblical Eschatology in Focus* (Grand Rapids: Baker, 1994), 109.

2. See George Eldon Ladd, *A Theology of the New Testament* (Grand Rapids: Eerdmans, 1993), 198–99.

these ancient texts are replete with numerous idioms that depict the final day when God will render perfect justice. The authors of these writings understood that God had decreed that the consummate day will come at the appointed time. Until then, the readers are encouraged to remain steadfast in their obedience to God and his commands as they suffer persecution at the hands of his enemies. Those who are loyal to Yahweh can have a firm hope, knowing that on this final day God will come to put all things right. These extracanonical texts echo the Old Testament's teaching that the day of the Lord is a day of judgment and salvation, a day to be feared or celebrated, a day of doom or rejoicing, and that whatever the outcome may be, it is clear that this is the consummate day toward which all history is heading.

The purpose of chapter 4 was to establish that Paul's encounter with the risen Christ on the Damascus road was in essence a *proleptic* day of the Lord. The final Judge appeared to Paul on that day and instead of administering retribution granted him mercy. The apostle was not only transformed into a Christ follower but was also divinely appointed to a new vocation that was parallel with the Old Testament prophetic tradition in many respects. Paul was made aware of the true identity of Jesus, who was the culmination of all the Old Testament promises and the one who inaugurated the end of the age. This "day" on the Damascus road verified for the apostle that the final day was closer than ever. Consequently, the numerous references and allusions to the eschatological day throughout Paul's writings demonstrate that the day of the Lord was one of the primary components of his theological matrix. For Paul the day of the Lord was exceedingly more than just an afterthought in his theology. Rather, the day of the Lord, and the many implications associated with it, are notably pervasive throughout his letters. Paul repeatedly mentions or alludes to the fact that Jesus' coming again on that last day to bring final judgment and salvation veritably impacts every facet of his theology. In other words, the conclusion of this chapter is that there is no part of Paul's theological schema that was not in some way influenced by the day of the Lord.

Chapter 5 provided a survey of the various terminology and idioms that Paul uses through his corpus when referring to the day of the Lord.

In order to substantiate the claims made from this study, chapter 6 analyzed how Paul perceived the day of the Lord, evident throughout his writings. This was accomplished by (1) offering a brief overview of the various terms and idioms found throughout Paul's epistles that are synonymous with the day of the Lord motif and (2) by exploring several texts throughout Paul's writings relevant to the day of the Lord. The intention in this chapter was not to provide a detailed exegesis of either the various terms or passages, but rather to offer a *thematic* analysis of how Paul understood the day of the Lord throughout his epistles.

This study shows that the day of the Lord was a major lens through which Paul operated. The intent here was to offer a *thematic* survey of this doctrine, which has yielded the conclusion that the day of the Lord saturates the apostle's entire corpus and is a paramount motif significantly affecting his entire theological purview. Further in-depth investigation into how the day of the Lord impacts the other areas of Pauline theology is needed and would seemingly provide insight into how the day of the Lord affects Paul's understanding in such areas as election, justification, adoption, and sanctification. For now, this work surmises that Paul understood the day of the Lord as a past, present, and future reality that ultimately finds fulfillment at the second coming of Christ, who, as the Father's judicial agent, will ultimately judge the living and the dead at the final assize. This day will be a day of retribution for those who do not know God and a day of vindication for those who do.

Bibliography

Abegg, Martin. "War Scroll (1QM) and Related Texts." In *Dictionary of New Testament Background,* edited by Craig A. Evans and Stanley E. Porter, 1260–63. Downers Grove, IL: IVP Academic, 2000.

Achtemeier, Paul J. "Finding the Way to Paul's Theology: A Response to J. Christiaan Beker and J. Paul Sampley." In *Pauline Theology,* edited by Jouette M. Bassler, 25–31. SBLSS 21. Minneapolis: Fortress, 2002.

Adewuya, J. Ayodeji. "The Spiritual Powers of Ephesians 6:10–18 in the Light of African Pentecostal Spirituality." *BBR* 22 (2012): 251–58.

Aernie, Jeffrey W. *Is Paul Also among the Prophets? An Examination of the Relationship between Paul and the Old Testament Prophetic Tradition in 2 Corinthians.* LNTS 467. London: T&T Clark, 2012.

Aernie, Matthew D. *Forensic Language and the Day of the Lord Motif in 2 Thessalonians 1 and the Effects on the Meaning of the Text.* West Theological Monographs Series. Eugene, OR: Wipf & Stock, 2011.

Aland, Kurt. "The Problem of Anonymity and Pseudonymmity in Christian Literature of the First Two Centuries." *JTS* 12 (1961): 39–49.

Albani, Matthias. "'The One Like a Son of Man' and the Royal Ideology." In *Enoch and Qumran Origins: New Light on a Forgotten Connection,* edited by Gabriele Boccaccini, 47–53.

Alexander, T. Desmond. *From Paradise to the Promised Land: An Introduction to the Pentateuch.* 3rd ed. Grand Rapids: Baker, 2012.

Allen, Leslie C., and R. K. Harrison. *The Books of Joel, Obadiah, Jonah, and Micah.* NICOT. Grand Rapids: Eerdmans, 1976.

Ames, William. *The Marrow of Sacred Divinity, Drawn out of the Holy Scriptures, and the Interpreters thereof, and Brought into Method.* Translated by John Dykstra Eusden. Boston: Pilgrim, 1968. Reprint, Grand Rapids: Baker, 1997.

Andiñach, Pablo R. "The Locusts in the Message of Joel." *VT* 42 (1992): 433–41.

Arnold, Clinton E. *The Colossian Syncretism: The Interface between Christianity and Folk Belief at Colossae.* 2 vols. WUNT 77. Tübingen: Mohr Siebeck, 1995.

———. *Ephesians, Power and Magic: The Concept of Power in Ephesians in Light of Its Historical Setting.* SNTSMS 63. Cambridge: Cambridge University Press, 1989.

———. *Powers of Darkness: Principalities & Powers in Paul's Letters.* Downers Grove, IL: InterVarsity, 1992.

Ascough, Richard S. "A Question of Death: Paul's Community-Building Language in 1 Thessalonians 4:13–18." *JBL* 123 (2004): 509–30.

Asher, Jeffrey R. "The Colossian Heresy: An Ecclesiastical Paradigm?" *Proceedings* 30 (2010): 107–22.

———. "An Unworthy Foe: Heroic ἔθη, Trickery, and an Insult in Ephesians 6:11." *JBL* 130 (2011): 729–48.

Ataç, Mehmet-Ali. "Manichaeism and Ancient Mesopotamian 'Gnosticism.'" *Journal of Ancient Near Eastern Religions* 5 (2005): 1–39.

Atkinson, Kenneth. "Theodicy in the Psalms of Solomon." In *Theodicy in the World of the Bible,* edited by Antti Laato and Johannes C. de Moor, 546–75. Leiden: Brill, 2003.

Aune, David E., T. J. Geddert, and Craig A. Evans. "Apocalypticism." In *Dictionary of New Testament Background,* edited by Craig A. Evans and Stanley E. Porter, 45–58. Downers Grove, IL: IVP Academic, 2000.

Bahnsen, Greg L. "The Crucial Concept of Self-Deception in Presuppositional Apologetics." *WTJ* 57 (1995): 1–31.

Bakon, Shimon. "The Day of the Lord." *JBQ* 38 (2010): 149–56.

Ball, Ivan Jay. "A Rhetorical Study of Zephaniah." Ph.D. diss., Graduate Theological Union, 1972.

Balla, Peter. "2 Corinthians 6:2." In *Commentary on the New Testament Use of the Old Testament,* edited by G. K. Beale and D. A. Carson, 766–68. Grand Rapids: Baker, 2007.

Bandstra, Andrew J. "Did the Colossian Errorists Need a Mediator?" In *New Dimensions in New Testament Study,* edited by Richard N. Longenecker and Merrill C. Tenney, 329–43. Grand Rapids: Zondervan, 1974.

Banister, Jamie A. "ὁμοίως and the Use of Parallelism in Romans 1:26–27." *JBL* 128 (2009): 569–90.

Barclay, John M. G. "Conflict at Thessalonica." *CBQ* 55 (1993): 512–30.

Barker, J. D. "Day of the Lord." In *Dictionary of the Old Testament Prophets,* edited by Mark J. Boda and J. G. McConville, 132–43. Downers Grove, IL: InterVarsity, 2012.

Barker, Kenneth L., and D. Waylon Bailey. *Micah, Nahum, Habakkuk, Zephaniah.* NAC 20. Nashville: Broadman & Holman, 1999.

Barnett, Paul. *The Second Epistle to the Corinthians.* NICNT. Grand Rapids: Eerdmans, 1997.

Barraclough, Ray. "Romans 13:1–7: Application in Context." *Colloq* 17 (1985): 16–21.

Barth, Karl. *The Epistle to the Romans.* Translated by Edwyn C. Hoskyns. Oxford: Oxford University Press, 1932.

Bastiat, Frédéric. *The Law.* Translated by Dean Russell. Annotated ed. Mountain View, CA: Creative Commons, 2013.

Bauckham, Richard J. *Jude, 2 Peter.* WBC 50. Waco, TX: Word, 1983.

Bauman, Elizabeth Hershberger. *Ascuas de Fuego.* Scottdale, PA: Herald, 1982.

Beale, G. K. "The Eschatology of Paul." In *Studies in the Pauline Epistles: Essays in Honor of Douglas J. Moo,* edited by Matthew S. Harmon and Jay E. Smith, 198–213. Grand Rapids: Zondervan, 2014.

———. *Handbook on the New Testament Use of the Old Testament: Exegesis and Interpretation.* Grand Rapids: Baker, 2012.

———. *A New Testament Biblical Theology: The Unfolding of the Old Testament in the New.* Grand Rapids: Baker, 2011.

———. "The Old Testament Background of Reconciliation in 2 Corinthians 5–7 and Its Bearing on the Literary Problem of 2 Corinthians 6:14–7:1." In *The Right Doctrine from the Wrong Texts? Essays on the Use of the Old Testament in the New,* edited by G. K. Beale, 217–47. Grand Rapids: Baker, 1994.

———. *We Become What We Worship: A Biblical Theology of Idolatry.* Downers Grove, IL: InterVarsity, 2008.

Beale, G. K., Daniel J. Brendsel, and William A. Ross. *An Interpretive Lexicon of New Testament Greek: Analysis of Prepositions, Adverbs, Particles, Relative Pronouns, and Conjunctions.* Grand Rapids: Zondervan, 2014.

Beasley-Murray, G. R. "Resurrection and Parousia of the Son of Man." *TynBul* 42 (1991): 296–309.

Beecher, Willis. "The Day of the Lord before Joel's Time." *Homiletical Review* 18 (1889): 449–51.

Beker, Johan Christiaan. *Heirs of Paul: Paul's Legacy in the New Testament and in the Church Today.* Grand Rapids: Eerdmans, 1996.

———. *Paul's Apocalyptic Gospel: The Coming Triumph of God.* Philadelphia: Fortress, 1982.

———. *The Triumph of God: The Essence of Paul's Thought.* Translated by Loren T. Stuckenbruck. Minneapolis: Fortress, 1990.

Bell, Richard H. "Sacrifice and Christology in Paul." *JTS* 53 (2002): 1–27.

Belleville, Linda L. "Tradition or Creation? Paul's Use of the Exodus 34 Tradition in 2 Corinthians 3.7–18." In *Paul and the Scriptures of Israel,* edited by Craig A. Evans and James A. Sanders, 169–86. JSOTSup 83. Sheffield: JSOT, 1993.

Ben Zvi, Ehud. *A Historical-Critical Study of the Book of Zephaniah.* BZAW 198. Berlin: de Gruyter, 1991.

Berlin, Adele. *Lamentations: A Commentary.* OTL. Louisville, KY: Westminster John Knox, 2002.

———. *Zephaniah.* AB 25a. New York: Doubleday, 1994.

Bernstein, Moshe J. "Pesher Habakkuk." In *Encyclopedia of the Dead Sea Scrolls,* edited by Lawrence H. Schiffman and James C. VanderKam, 647–50. New York: Oxford Univesity Press, 2000.

Beyerle, Stefan. "'One Like a Son of Man': Innuendoes of a Heavenly Individual." In *Enoch and Qumran Origins: New Light on a Forgotten Connection,* edited by Gabriele Boccaccini, 54–58. Grand Rapids: Eerdmans, 2005.

Bird, Michael F. *Introducing Paul: The Man, His Mission and His Message.* Downers Grove, IL: InterVarsity, 2008.

———. *The Saving Righteousness of God: Studies on Paul, Justification and the New Perspective.* PBM. Milton Keynes, UK: Paternoster, 2007.

Blackman, E. C. "Divine Sovereignty and Missionary Strategy in Romans 9–11." *Canadian Journal of Theology* 11 (1965): 124–34.

Blass, Friedrich, Albert Debrunner, and Friedrich Rehkopf. *Grammatik des neutestamentlichen Griechisch: [Joachim Jeremias zum 75. Geburtstag].* 17., völlig neubearb. u. erw. Aufl. ed. Göttingen: Vandenhoeck & Ruprecht, 1976.

Blomberg, Craig L. *Contagious Holiness: Jesus' Meals with Sinners.* NSBT 19. Downers Grove, IL: InterVarsity, 2005.

———. "Jesus, Sinners, and Table Fellowship." *BBR* 19 (2009): 35–62.

Boase, Elizabeth. *The Fulfilment of Doom? The Dialogic Interaction between the Book of Lamentations and the Pre-Exilic/Early Exilic Prophetic Literature.* Library of Hebrew Bible/Old Testament Studies 437. New York: T&T Clark, 2006.

Boccaccini, Gabriele, ed. *Enoch and the Messiah Son of Man: Revisiting the Book of Parables.* Grand Rapids: Eerdmans, 2007.

Bock, Darrell L. "Son of Man." In *Dictionary of Jesus and the Gospels,* edited by Joel B. Green, Jeannine K. Brown, and Nicholas Perrin, 894–900. Downers Grove, IL: InterVarsity, 2013.

Boer, Martinus C. de. *The Defeat of Death: Apocalyptic Eschatology in 1 Corinthians 15 and Romans 5.* JSNTSup 22. Sheffield, UK: JSOT, 1988.

———. *Galatians: A Commentary.* NTL. Louisville, KY: Westminster John Knox, 2011.

Bosman, Jan P. "The Paradoxical Presence of Exodus 34:6–7 in the Book of the Twelve." *Scriptura* 87 (2004): 233–43.

Brands, Monica. "Vessels of Mercy: Aquinas and Barth on Election and Romans Chapters 9–11." *Journal of Theta Alpha Kappa* 37 (2013): 23–39.

Branick, Vincent P. "Apocalyptic Paul?" *CBQ* 47 (1985): 664–75.

Brichto, Herbert Chanan. "The Worship of the Golden Calf: A Literary Analysis of a Fable on Idolatry." *HUCA* 54 (1983): 1–44.

Brindle, Wayne A. "Prepared by Whom? Reprobation and Non-Calvinist Interpretations of Romans 9:22." *CTR* 12 (2015): 135–46.

Brown, Michael L. *A Queer Thing Happened to America: And What a Long, Strange Trip It's Been.* Concord, NC: EqualTime Books, 2011.

Brown, Raymond Edward. *An Introduction to the New Testament.* AYBRL. New York: Doubleday, 1997.

Bruce, F. F. *1 & 2 Thessalonians.* WBC 45. Waco, TX: Word Books, 1982.

———. *The Acts of the Apostles: The Greek Text with Introduction and Commentary.* 3rd rev. and enl. ed. Grand Rapids: Eerdmans, 1990.

———. "Colossian Problems Part 3: The Colossian Heresy." *BSac* 141 (1984): 195–208.

Buchanan, George Wesley. "The Day of Atonement and Paul's Doctrine of Redemption." *NovT* 32 (1990): 236–49.

Bujard, Walter. *Stilanalytische Untersuchungen zum Kolosserbrief als Beitrag zur Methodik von Sprachvergleichen.* SUNT 11. Göttingen: Vandenhoeck & Ruprecht, 1973.

Bultmann, Rudolf. "Die Bedeutung der neuerschlossenen mandäischen und manichäischen Quellen für das Verständnis des Johannesevangeliums." *ZNW* 24 (1925): 100–146.

Bultmann, Rudolf, and Karl Kundsin. *Form Criticism: Two Essays on New Testament Research: Study of the Synoptic Gospels, by Rudolf Bultmann, and Primitive Christianity in the Light of Gospel Research, by Karl Kundsin.* Translated by Frederick C. Grant. Chicago: Willett, Clark, 1934.

Burk, Denny. "Christ's Functional Subordination in Philippians 2:6: A Grammatical Note with Trinitarian Implications." *Journal of Biblical Manhood and Womanhood* 16 (2011): 25–37.

Cahana, Jonathan. "Gnostically Queer: Gender Trouble in Gnosticism." *BTB* 41 (2011): 24–35.

Caird, G. B. "Predestination—Romans 9–11." *ExpTim* 68 (1956–57): 324–27.

Calvin, John. *The Bondage and Liberation of the Will: A Defense of the Orthodox Doctrine of Human Choice against Pighius.* Edited by Richard A. Muller. Translated by Graham I. Davies. Texts and Studies in Reformation and Post-Reformation Thought 2. Grand Rapids: Baker, 1996.

———. *Concerning the Eternal Predestination of God.* Translated by John K. S. Reid. Louisville, KY: Westminster John Knox, 1997.

———. *Institutes of the Christian Religion: Calvin's Own "Essentials" Edition.* Translated by Robert White. Edinburgh, UK: Banner of Truth, 2014.

Campbell, Barth Lynn. "Flesh and Spirit in 1 Cor 5:5: An Exercise in Rhetorical Criticism of the NT." *JETS* 36 (1993): 331–42.

Campbell, Constantine R. *Verbal Aspect, the Indicative Mood, and Narrative: Soundings in the Greek of the New Testament.* Edited by D. A. Carson. Studies in Biblical Greek Series 13. New York: Lang, 2012.

Campbell-Jack, Walter Campbell. "Prolegomena for Reprobation." *EvQ* 61 (1989): 39–50.

Capes, David B. "Interpreting Ephesians 1–3: 'God's People in the Mystery of His Will.'" *SwJT* 39 (1996): 20–31.

Capes, David B., Rodney Reeves, and E. Randolph Richards. *Rediscovering Paul: An Introduction to His World, Letters, and Theology.* Downers Grove, IL: InterVarsity, 2007.

Caragounis, Chrys C. *The Son of Man: Vision and Interpretation.* WUNT 38. Tübingen: Mohr Siebeck, 1986.

Carson, D. A. "The Vindication of Imputation: On Fields of Discourse and Semantic Fields." In *Justification: What's at Stake in the Current Debates,* edited by Mark Husbands and Daniel J. Treier, 46–78. Downers Grove, IL: InterVarsity, 2004.

Carson, D. A., and Douglas J. Moo. *An Introduction to the New Testament.* 2nd ed. Grand Rapids: Zondervan, 2005.

Casey, Maurice. *The Solution to the "Son of Man" Problem.* LNTS. London: T&T Clark, 2009.

Cassuto, Umberto. *A Commentary on the Book of Genesis.* Translated by Israel Abrahams. 2 vols. Publications of the Perry Foundation for Biblical Research in the Hebrew University of Jerusalem. Jerusalem: Magnes, 1961.

Cathcart, K. J. "Day of Yahweh." In *Anchor Bible Dictionary,* edited by David Noel Freedman, 84–85. New York: Doubleday, 1992.

Černý, Ladislav. *The Day of Yahweh and Some Relevant Problems.* Práce z Vědeckých Ústavù 53. Praze: Nákl. Filosofické Fakulty University Karlovy, 1948.

Chae, Young S. *Jesus as the Eschatological Davidic Shepherd: Studies in the Old Testament, Second Temple Judaism, and in the Gospel of Matthew.* 2 vols. WUNT 216. Tübingen: Mohr Siebeck, 2006.

Charles, R. H. *A Critical History of the Doctrine of a Future Life in Israel.* 2nd ed. London: Adam & Charles Black, 1913.

Charlesworth, James H. "Community Organization in the Rule of the Community." In *Encyclopedia of the Dead Sea Scrolls,* edited by Lawrence H. Schiffman and James C. VanderKam, 133–36. New York: Oxford University Press, 2000.

———, ed. *The Old Testament Pseudepigrapha.* Vol. 2, *Expansions of the "Old Testament" and Legends, Wisdom and Philosophical Literature, Prayers, Psalms, and Odes, Fragments of Lost Judeo-Hellenistic Works.* AYBRL. New York: Doubleday, 1985.

———. "Pseudepigrapha, OT." In *Anchor Bible Dictionary,* edited by David Noel Freedman, 537–40. Vol. 5. New York: Doubleday, 1992.

Childs, Brevard S. *The Book of Exodus: A Critical, Theological Commentary.* OTL 2. Philadelphia: Westminster, 1974.

———. *Isaiah.* OTL. Louisville, KY: Westminster John Knox, 2001.

Christensen, Duane L. *Deuteronomy 21:10–34:12.* WBC 6B. Nashville: Thomas Nelson, 2002.

Ciampa, Roy E., and Brian S. Rosner. *The First Letter to the Corinthians.* PNTC. Grand Rapids: Eerdmans, 2010.

Clines, David J. A. *The Esther Scroll: The Story of the Story.* JSOTSup 30. Sheffield, UK: JSOT, 1984.

Coggins, R. J., and Michael A. Knibb. *The First and Second Books of Esdras.* CBC. Cambridge: Cambridge University Press, 1979.

Collins, Adela Yarbro. "The Function of 'Excommunication' in Paul." *HTR* 73 (1980): 251–63.

Collins, C. John. *Genesis 1–4: A Linguistic, Literary, and Theological Commentary.* Phillipsburg, NJ: Presbyterian & Reformed, 2006.

Collins, John J. "Apocalyptic Literature." In *Dictionary of New Testament Background,* edited by Craig A. Evans and Stanley E. Porter, 40–45. Downers Grove, IL: IVP Academic, 2000.

———. "The Expectation of the End in the Dead Sea Scrolls." In *Eschatology, Messianism, and the Dead Sea Scrolls,* edited by Martin Abegg Jr. and Peter W. Flint, 74–90. Grand Rapids: Eerdmans, 1997.

Collins, Raymond F. *Letters That Paul Did Not Write: The Epistle to the Hebrews and the Pauline Pseudepigrapha.* Good News Studies 28. Wilmington, DE: Glazier, 1988.

———. "Παρουσὶα to ᾿Επιφάνεια: The Transformation of a Pauline Motif." *In Unity and Diversity in the Gospels and Paul: Essays in Honor of Frank J. Matera,* edited by Christopher W. Skinner and Kelly R. Iverson, 273–99. Atlanta: Society of Biblical Literature, 2012.

Combs, William W. "Nag Hammadi, Gnosticism and New Testament Interpretation." *Grace Theological Journal* 8 (1987): 195–212.

Coppins, Wayne. "Doing Justice to the Two Perspectives of 1 Corinthians 15:1–11." *Neot* 44 (2010): 282–91.

Corley, Bruce. "Interpreting Paul's Conversion—Then and Now." In *The Road from Damascus: The Impact of Paul's Conversion on His Life, Thought, and Ministry,* 1–17. McMaster New Testament Studies. Grand Rapids: Eerdmans, 1997.

Costa, Tony. "Is Saul of Tarsus Also among the Prophets? Paul's Calling as Prophetic Divine Commissioning." In *Christian Origins and Hellenistic Judaism: Social and*

Literary Contexts for the New Testament, edited by Stanley E. Porter and Andrew W. Pitts, 203–35. TENTS 10. Leiden: Brill, 2013.

Craghan, John F. *Esther, Judith, Tobit, Jonah, Ruth.* Old Testament Message 16. Wilmington, DE: Glazier, 1982.

Cranfield, C. E. B. "The Christian's Political Responsibility according to the New Testament." *SJT* 15 (1962): 176–92.

———. *The Epistle to the Romans.* Vol. 1. ICC. Edinburgh: T&T Clark, 1975.

———. *The Epistle to the Romans.* Vol. 2. ICC. Edinburgh: T&T Clark, 1979.

Craven, Toni. *Artistry and Faith in the Book of Judith.* SBLDS 70. Chico, CA: Scholars Press, 1983.

Crawford, Leslie James. "Ephesians 1:3–4 and the Nature of Election." *MSJ* 11 (2000): 75–91.

Crawford, Sidnie White. "The Additions to Esther: Introduction, Commentary, and Reflections." In *New Interpreter's Bible,* edited by C. L. Seow, Leslie C. Allen, Ralph W. Klein, Irene Nowell, Sidnie Crawford White, and Lawrence M. Wills, 945–72. Nashville: Abingdon, 1999.

Cross, Frank M. "The Divine Warrior in Israel's Early Cult." In *Biblical Motifs: Origins and Transformations,* edited by Alexander Altmann, 11–30. Cambridge, MA: Harvard University Press, 1966.

Darko, Daniel. "What Does It Mean to Be Saved? An African Reading of Ephesians 2." *Journal of Pentecostal Theology* 24 (2015): 44–56.

Davies, W. D. *Paul and Rabbinic Judaism: Some Rabbinic Elements in Pauline Theology.* 4th ed. Philadelphia: Fortress, 1980.

Davila, James R. "Pseudepigrapha, Old Testament." In *Eerdmans Dictionary of Early Judaism,* edited by John J. Collins and Daniel C. Harlow, 1110–14. Grand Rapids: Eerdmans, 2010.

Dawe, Donald G. *The Form of a Servant: A Historical Analysis of the Kenotic Motif.* Philadelphia: Westminster, 1963.

Day, John N. "'Coals of Fire' in Romans 12:19–20." *BSac* 160 (2003): 414–20.

De Roche, Michael. "Zephaniah 1:2–3: The 'Sweeping' of Creation." *VT* 30 (1980): 104–9.

De Vos, Craig Steve. "Stepmothers, Concubines, and the Case of Πορνεία in 1 Corinthians 5." *NTS* 44 (1998): 104–14.

Deem, Ariella. "Short Notes: '. . . And the Stone Sank into His Forehead.' A Note on 1 Samuel 17.49." *VT* 28 (1978): 349–51.

Deissmann, Adolf. *Light from the Ancient East: The New Testament Illustrated by Recently Discovered Texts of the Graeco-Roman World.* Translated by Lionel R. M. Strachan. 4th ed. New York: Dorian, 1927. Reprint, Peabody, MA: Hendrickson, 1995.

Dequeker, Luc. "'The Saints of the Most High' in Qumran and Daniel." In *Syntax and Meaning: Studies in Hebrew Syntax and Biblical Exegesis,* edited by C. J. Labuschagne, 108–87. OtSt 18. Leiden: Brill, 1973.

DeSilva, David Arthur. *Introducing the Apocrypha: Message, Context, and Significance.* Grand Rapids: Baker, 2002.

———. *An Introduction to the New Testament: Contexts, Methods, and Ministry Formation.* Downers Grove, IL: InterVarsity, 2004.

———. *The Jewish Teachers of Jesus, James, and Jude: What the First Family of Christianity Learned from the Apocrypha and Pseudepigrapha*. New York: Oxford University Press, 2012.

Desjardins, Michel R. "Rethinking the Study of Gnosticism." *R&T* 12 (2005): 370–84.

DeYoung, James B. *Homosexuality: Contemporary Claims Examined in Light of the Bible and Other Ancient Literature and Law*. Grand Rapids: Kregel, 2000.

Dickson, John P. *Mission-Commitment in Ancient Judaism and in the Pauline Communities: The Shape, Extent and Background of Early Christian Mission*. WUNT 2/159. Tübingen: Mohr Siebeck, 2003.

DiPaolo, Lawrence. *Hymn Fragments Embedded in the New Testament: Hellenistic Jewish and Greco-Roman Parallels*. Lewiston, NY: Mellen, 2008.

Donfried, Karl P. "Justification and Last Judgment in Paul." *Int* 39 (1976): 140–52.

Drane, John William. *Introducing the New Testament*. 3rd ed. Minneapolis: Fortress, 2011.

Dumbrell, William J. *The Search for Order: Biblical Eshatology in Focus*. Grand Rapids: Baker, 1994.

Dunn, James D. G. "Paul and Justification by Faith." In *The Road to Damascus: The Impact of Paul's Conversion on His Life, Thought, and Ministry*, edited by Richard N. Longenecker, 85–101. Grand Rapids: Eerdmans, 1997.

———. "Paul's Conversion—A Light to Twentieth Century Disputes." In *Evangelium, Schriftauslegung, Kirche: Festschrift für Peter Stuhlmacher zum 65. Geburtstag*, edited by Jostein Ådna, Scott J. Hafemann, and Otfried Hofius, 77–93. Göttingen: Vandenhoeck & Ruprecht, 1997.

———. *The Theology of Paul the Apostle*. Grand Rapids: Eerdmans, 1998.

Dupont, Jacques. *ΣΥΝ ΧΡΙΣΤΩΙ: L'union avec le Christ Suivant Saint Paul*. Leuven: Desclée de Brouwer, 1952.

Durham, John I. *Exodus*. WBC 3. Waco, TX: Word Books, 1987.

Eberhart, Christian, and Don Schweitzer. "Did Paul See the Saving Significance of Jesus' Death as Resulting from Divine Violence? Dialogical Reflections on Romans 3:25." *Consensus (Online)* 34 (2012): 1–20.

Eckel, Paul T. "Ephesians 6:10–20." *Int* 45 (1991): 288–93.

Eckstein, Hans-Joachim. "'Denn Gottes Zorn wird vom Himmel her offenbar werden': Exegetische Erwägungen zu Röm 1:18." *ZNW* 78 (1987): 74–89.

Edwards, Jonathan. *Freedom of the Will*. Edited by Perry Miller. Works of Jonathan Edwards 1. New Haven: Yale University Press, 1957.

Ehrman, Bart D. *Lost Christianities: The Battles for Scripture and the Faiths We Never Knew*. Oxford: Oxford University Press, 2003.

Ellingworth, Paul. "Translation and Exegesis: A Case Study (Rom 9:22ff)." *Bib* 59 (1978): 396–402.

Ellis, E. Earle. "Pseudonymity and Canonicity of New Testament Documents." In *Worship, Theology and Ministry in the Early Church: Essays in Honor of Ralph P. Martin*, edited by Michael J. Wilkins and Terence Paige, 212–24. Sheffield, UK: JSOT, 1992.

Emerson, Matthew Y. "Paul's Eschatological Outlook in the Pastoral Epistles." *CTR* 12 (2015): 83–98.

Estes, Joel D. "Calling on the Name of the Lord: The Meaning and Significance of ἐπικαλέω in Romans 10:13." *Them* 41 (2016): 20–36.

Evans, C. Stephen, ed. *Exploring Kenotic Christology: The Self-Emptying of God.* Oxford: Oxford University Press, 2006.

Evans, Craig A. "The Colossian Mystics." *Bib* 63 (1982): 188–205.

———. "Prophet, Paul as." In *Dictionary of Paul and His Letters,* edited by Gerald F. Hawthorne, Ralph P. Martin, and Daniel G. Reid, 762–65. Downers Grove, IL: InterVarsity, 1993.

———. *Ancient Texts for New Testament Studies: A Guide to the Background Literature.* Peabody, MA: Hendrickson, 2005.

Everson, A. Joseph. "Days of Yahweh." *JBL* 93 (1974): 329–37.

Everts, J. M. "Conversion and Call of Paul." In *Dictionary of Paul and His Letters,* edited by Gerald F. Hawthorne, Ralph P. Martin, and Daniel G. Reid, 156–63. Downers Grove, IL: InterVarsity, 1993.

Fanning, Buist M. *Verbal Aspect in New Testament Greek.* Edited by J. Barton, R. C. Morgan, B. R. White, J. MacQuarrie, K. Ware, and R. D. Williams. Oxford Theological Monographs. Oxford: Clarendon, 1990.

Fass, David E. "The Molten Calf: Judgment, Motive, and Meaning." *Judaism* 39 (1990): 171–83.

Fee, Gordon D. *The First and Second Letters to the Thessalonians.* NICNT. Grand Rapids: Eerdmans, 2009.

———. *The First Epistle to the Corinthians.* Rev. ed. NICNT. Grand Rapids: Eerdmans, 2014.

———. *God's Empowering Presence: The Holy Spirit in the Letters of Paul.* Peabody, MA: Hendrickson, 1994.

———. *Paul's Letter to the Philippians.* NICNT. Grand Rapids: Eerdmans, 1995.

———. "Toward a Theology of 1 Corinthians." In *Pauline Theology,* edited by David M. Hay, 37–58. Minneapolis: Fortress, 2002.

Feinberg, Paul D. "The Kenosis and Christology: An Exegetical-Theological Analysis of Phil 2:6–11." *TJ* 1 (1980): 21–46.

Fensham, Frank C. "A Possible Origin of the Concept of the Day of the Lord." In *Proceedings of the Ninth meeting of Die Ou-Testamentiese Werkgemeenskap in Suid-Afrika held at the University of Stellenbosch 26th–29th July 1966, and Proceedings of the Second Meeting of Die Nuwe-Testamentiese Werkgemeenskap van Suid-Afrika Held at the University of Stellenbosch 22nd–25th July 1966,* 90–97. Potchefstroom: Bepeck, 1966.

Ferda, Tucker S. "'Sealed' with the Holy Spirit (Eph 1, 13–14) and Circumcision." *Bib* 93 (2012): 557–79.

Fitzmyer, Joseph A. *The Impact of the Dead Sea Scrolls.* New York: Paulist, 2009.

Fleer, David. "Exegesis of Joel 2:1–11." *ResQ* 26 (1983): 149–60.

Flint, Peter W. "Habakkuk Commentary (1QpHab)." In *Dictionary of New Testament Background,* edited by Craig A. Evans and Stanley E. Porter, 437–38. Downers Grove, IL: IVP Academic, 2000.

Foster, Paul. "Who Wrote 2 Thessalonians? A Fresh Look at an Old Problem." *JSNT* 35 (2012): 150–75.

Fox, Michael V. *Characters and Ideology in the Book of Esther*. Columbia: Univesity of South Carolina Press, 1991.

Francis, Fred O. "The Background of *embateuein* (Col 2:18) in Legal Papyri and Oracle Inscriptions." In *Conflict at Colossae: A Problem in the Interpretation of Early Christianity Illustrated by Selected Modern Studies*, edited by Fred O. Francis and Wayne A. Meeks, 197–218. Vol. 4 of *Sources for Biblical Study*. Missoula, MT: Scholars Press, 1975.

———. "Christological Argument of Colossians." In *God's Christ and His People: Studies in Honor of Nils Alstrup Dahl*, edited by Jacob Jervell and Wayne A. Meeks, 192–208. Oslo: Universitetsforl, 1977.

———. "Humility and Angelic Worship in Col 2:18." *Studia theologica* 16 (1962): 109–34.

Fuerst, W. J. "The Rest of the Chapters of the Book of Esther." In *The Shorter Books of the Apocrypha: Tobit, Judith, Rest of Esther, Baruch, Letter of Jeremiah, Additions to Daniel and Prayer of Manasseh*, 132–38. Cambridge: Cambridge University Press, 1972.

Furnish, Victor Paul. *II Corinthians*. AB 32A. Garden City, NY: Doubleday, 1984.

Gadamer, Hans-Georg. *Truth and Method*. Translated by Joel Weinsheimer and Donald G. Marshall. 2nd ed. New York: Crossroad, 1989.

Gagnon, Robert A. J. *The Bible and Homosexual Practice: Texts and Hermeneutics*. Nashville: Abingdon, 2001.

Garland, David E. *1 Corinthians*. BECNT. Grand Rapids: Baker, 2003.

Garrett, Duane A. *Hosea, Joel*. NAC 19A. Nashville: Broadman & Holman, 1997.

———. "Joel, Book of." In *Dictionary of the Old Testament Prophets*, edited by Mark J. Boda and J. G. McConville, 452–54. Downers Grove, IL: InterVarsity, 2012.

Garrett, Duane A., and Paul R. House. *Song of Songs/Lamentations*. WBC 23B. Nashville: Thomas Nelson, 2004.

Gathercole, Simon J. *Defending Substitution: An Essay on Atonement in Paul*. Acadia Studies in Bible and Theology. Grand Rapids: Baker, 2015.

Geisler, Norman L. "A Christian Perspective on Wine-Drinking." *BSac* 139 (1982): 46–56.

Gentry, Kenneth L. *God Gave Wine: What the Bible Says about Alcohol*. Lincoln, CA: Oaklawn, 2001.

Gerstner, John H. "Edwardsean Preparation for Salvation." *WTJ* 42 (1979): 5–71.

———. *Steps to Salvation: The Evangelistic Message of Jonathan Edwards*. Philadelphia: Westminster, 1960.

Giesen, Heinz. "Eschatology in Philippians." In *Paul and His Theology*. Vol. 3 of *Pauline Studies*. Edited by Stanley E. Porter, 217–82. Leiden: Brill, 2006.

Gignac, Alain. "The Enunciative Device of Romans 1:18–4:25: A Succession of Discourses Attempting to Express the Multiple Dimensions of God's Justice." *CBQ* 77 (2015): 481–502.

Gignilliat, Mark S. "2 Corinthians 6:2: Paul's Eschatological 'Now' and Hermeneutical Invitation." *WTJ* 67 (2005): 147–61.

Goldingay, John. *The Theology of the Book of Isaiah*. Downers Grove, IL: InterVarsity, 2014.

Gombis, Timothy G. "Ephesians 2 As a Narrative of Divine Warfare." *JSNT* 26 (2004): 403–18.

Gooch, P. W. "Sovereignty and Freedom: Some Pauline Compatibilisms." *SJT* 40 (1987): 531–42.

Goodspeed, Edgar J. "Pseudonymity and Pseudepigraphy in Early Christian Literature." In *New Chapters in New Testament Study,* 212–24. Ayer Lectures/Colgate-Rochester Divinity School. New York: Macmillan, 1937.

Gorman, Michael J. "'Although/Because He Was in the Form of God': The Theological Significance of Paul's Master Story (Phil 2:6–11)." *Journal of Theological Interpretation* 1 (2007): 147–69.

————. *Apostle of the Crucified Lord: A Theological Introduction to Paul & His Letters.* 2nd ed. Grand Rapids: Eerdmans, 2017.

Gottwald, Norman K. *Studies in the Book of Lamentations.* SBT 14. Eugene, OR: Wipf & Stock, 2009.

Gray, John A. "The Day of Yahweh in Cultic Experience and Eschatological Prospect." *Svensk exegetisk årsbok* 39 (1974): 5–37.

Green, Gene L. *Jude and 2 Peter.* BECNT. Grand Rapids: Baker, 2008.

————. *The Letters to the Thessalonians.* PNTC. Grand Rapids: Eerdmans, 2002.

Gressmann, Hugo. *Der Ursprung der israelitisch-jüdischen Eschatologie.* Forschungen zur Religion und Literatur des Alten und Neuen Testaments 6. Göttingen: Vandenhoeck & Ruprecht, 1905.

Grieb, A. Katherine. "Last Things First: Karl Barth's Theological Exegesis of 1 Corinthians in the Resurrection of the Dead." *SJT* 56 (2003): 49–64.

Grindheim, Sigurd. *God's Equal: What Can We Know about Jesus' Self-Understanding?* LNTS 446. London: T&T Clark, 2011.

Grudem, Wayne. *Making Sense of Salvation: One of Seven Parts from Grudem's Systematic Theology.* Grand Rapids: Zondervan, 1994.

Grundmann, Walter. "ἀνέγκλητος." Page 357 in *TDNT.*

Gudorf, Michael E. "The Use of *Palē* in Ephesians 6:12." *JBL* 117 (1998): 331–35.

Gundry, Robert H. "Grace, Works, and Staying Saved in Paul." *Biblia* 66 (1985): 1–38.

Gunther, John J. *St. Paul's Opponents and Their Background. A Study of Apocalyptic and Jewish Sectarian Teachings.* NovTSup 35. Leiden: Brill, 1973.

Guthrie, Donald. "The Development of the Idea of Canonical Pseudepigrapha in New Testament Criticism." *VE* 1 (1962): 43–59.

Guthrie, George H. *2 Corinthians.* BECNT. Grand Rapids: Baker, 2015.

Hafemann, Scott J. "The Glory and Veil of Moses in 2 Cor 3:7–14: An Example of Paul's Contextual Exegesis of the OT—A Proposal." *Horizons in Biblical Theology* 14 (1992): 31–49.

————. *Paul, Moses, and the History of Israel: The Letter/Spirit Contrast and the Argument from Scripture in 2 Corinthians 3.* WUNT 81. Tübingen: Mohr Siebeck, 1995.

Hagner, Donald A. *The New Testament: A Historical and Theological Introduction.* Grand Rapids: Baker, 2012.

Hamilton, James M. *With the Clouds of Heaven: The Book of Daniel in Biblical Theology.* NSBT 32. Downers Grove, IL: InterVarsity, 2014.

Hamilton, Victor P. *Exodus: An Exegetical Commentary.* Grand Rapids: Baker, 2011.

Hansen, G. Walter. *The Letter to the Philippians.* PNTC. Grand Rapids: Eerdmans, 2009.

Harper, Andrew. *The Book of Deuteronomy*. Expositor's Bible Commentary. London: Hodder & Stoughton, 1903.

Harrington, Daniel J. *Invitation to the Apocrypha: Message, Context, and Significance.* Grand Rapids: Eerdmans, 1999.

Harris, Murray J. *Prepositions and Theology in the Greek New Testament: An Essential Reference Resource for Exegesis.* Grand Rapids: Zondervan, 2011.

———. *The Second Epistle to the Corinthians: A Commentary on the Greek Text.* NIGTC. Grand Rapids: Eerdmans, 2004.

Hartley, Donald E. "Destined to Disobey? Isaiah 6:10 in John 12:37–41." *CTJ* 44 (2009): 263–87.

———. "Hebrews 11:6: A Reassessment of the Translation 'God Exists.'" *TJ* 27 (2006): 289–307.

———. *The Wisdom Background and Parabolic Implications of Isaiah 6:9–10 in the Synoptics.* Edited by Hemchand Gossai. Studies in Biblical Literature 100. New York: Lang, 2006.

Hartman, Lars. *Prophecy Interpreted: The Formation of Some Jewish Apocalyptic Texts and of the Eschatological Discourse Mark 13 Par.* ConBNT 1. Lund: Gleerup, 1966.

———. *Asking for a Meaning: A Study of 1 Enoch 1–5.* ConBNT 12. Lund: LiberLaromedel/Gleerup, 1979.

Hartman, Louis Francis, and Alexander A. Di Lella. *The Book of Daniel.* AB 23. Garden City, NY: Doubleday, 1978.

Harvey, A. E. "Opposition to Paul." In *The Galatians Debate: Contemporary Issues in Rhetorical and Historical Interpretation,* edited by Mark D. Nanos, 321–33. Peabody, MA: Hendrickson, 2002.

Hawthorne, Gerald F., and Ralph P. Martin. *Philippians.* Rev. ed. WBC 43. Grand Rapids: Zondervan, 2015.

Hayman, A. P. "Problem of Pseudonymity in the Ezra Apocalypse." *JSJ* 6 (1975): 47–56.

Hays, Richard B. *The Conversion of the Imagination: Paul as Interpreter of Israel's Scripture.* Grand Rapids: Eerdmans, 2005.

———. *Echoes of Scripture in the Letters of Paul.* New Haven: Yale University Press, 1989.

Head, Peter M. "The Curse of the Covenant Reversal: Deuteronomy 28:58–68 and Israel's Exile." *Churchman* 111 (1997): 218–26.

Hedrick, Charles W. "Paul's Conversion/Call: A Comparative Analysis of the Three Reports in Acts." *JBL* 100 (1981): 415–32.

Helyer, Larry R. *Exploring Jewish Literature of the Second Temple Period: A Guide for New Testament Students.* Downers Grove, IL: InterVarsity, 2002.

———. *The Witness of Jesus, Paul, and John: An Exploration in Biblical Theology.* Downers Grove, IL: InterVarsity, 2008.

Hermans, Robert. "La christologie d'Ephésiens." *Bib* 92 (2011): 411–26.

Hieke, Thomas, and Tobias Nicklas, eds. *The Day of Atonement: Its Interpretations in Early Jewish and Christian Traditions.* Themes in Biblical Narrative: Jewish and Christian Traditions 15. Leiden: Brill, 2012.

Hiers, Richard H. "Day of the Lord." In *Anchor Bible Dictionary,* edited by David Noel Freedman, 82–83. Vol. 2. New York: Doubleday, 1992.

Hoehner, Harold W. *Ephesians: An Exegetical Commentary.* Grand Rapids: Baker, 2002.

Hoekema, Anthony A. *The Bible and the Future.* Grand Rapids: Eerdmans, 1979.

―――. *Created in God's Image.* Grand Rapids: Eerdmans, 1986.

Hoffmann, Yair. "The Day of the Lord as a Concept and a Term in the Prophetic Literature." *ZAW* 93 (1981): 37–50.

Holladay, William Lee, and Ludwig Köhler. *A Concise Hebrew and Aramaic Lexicon of the Old Testament: Based upon the Lexical Work of Ludwig Köhler and Walter Baumgartner.* Grand Rapids: Eerdmans, 1971.

Holland, Glenn Stanfield. "The Tradition That You Received from Us: 2 Thessalonians in the Pauline Tradition." PhD diss., University of Chicago Divinity School, 1988.

Holland, Tom. *Contours of Pauline Theology: A Radical New Survey of the Influences on Paul's Biblical Writings.* Fearn, UK: Mentor, 2004.

Holleman, Joost. *Resurrection and Parousia: A Traditio-Historical Study of Paul's Eschatology in I Corinthians 15.* NovTSup 84. Leiden: Brill, 1996.

Holt-Woehl, Hollie M. "Putting on the Whole Armor of God: Preaching Ephesians 6:10–20 in a Multicultural Congregation." *WW* 29 (2009): 292–99.

Hoover, Joseph. "The Wealth of God's Glory: A Response to John Piper's 'Four Problems in Romans 9:22–23.'" *Stone-Campbell Journal* 12 (2009): 47–58.

Horne, Charles M. "Toward a Biblical Apologetic." *Bulletin of the Evangelical Theological Society* 4 (1961): 89–92.

Horsley, G. H. R., and S. R. Llewelyn. *New Documents Illustrating Early Christianity: Greek and Other Inscriptions and Papyri Published 1988–1992.* 10 vols. Grand Rapids: Eerdmans, 1981–2012.

Horsley, Richard A. *Revolt of the Scribes: Resistance and Apocalyptic Origins.* Minneapolis: Fortress, 2010.

House, Paul R. "The Day of the Lord." In *Central Themes in Biblical Theology: Mapping Unity in Diversity,* edited by Scott J. Hafemann and Paul R. House, 179–224. Grand Rapids: Baker, 2007.

―――. "Endings and New Beginnings: Returning to the Lord, the Day of the Lord, and Renewal in the Book of the Twelve." In *Thematic Threads in the Book of the Twelve,* edited by Paul L. Redditt and Aaron Schart, 313–39. BZAW 325. Berlin: de Gruyter, 2003.

Houwelingen, P. H. R. van. "The Redemptive-Historical Dynamics of the Salvation of 'All Israel' (Rom. 11:26a)." *CTJ* 46 (2011): 301–14.

Howard, James K. "Christ Our Passover: A Study of the Passover-Exodus Theme in 1 Corinthians." *EvQ* 41 (1969): 97–108.

Howell, Don N. "The Center of Pauline Theology." *BSac* 151 (1998): 50–70.

Ishai-Rosenboim, Daniella. "Is יום ה (Day of the Lord) a Term in Biblical Language?" *Bib* 87 (2006): 395–401.

Jacobson, Rolf A. "Moses, the Golden Calf, and the False Images of the True God." *WW* 33 (2013): 130–39.

Janzen, J. Gerald. "A New Approach to '*logikēn latreian*' in Romans 12:1–2." *Encounter* 69 (2008): 45–83.

Jensen, Peter. *The Revelation of God.* Contours of Christian Theology. Downers Grove, IL: InterVarsity, 2002.

Johnson, Luke Timothy. *The First and Second Letters to Timothy: A New Translation with Introduction and Commentary.* AB 35A. New Haven: Yale University Press, 2008.

———. *The Writings of the New Testament: An Interpretation.* 3rd ed. Minneapolis: Fortress, 2010.

Johnson, S. Lewis. "Paul and the Knowledge of God." *BSac* 129 (1972): 61–74.

Jolivet, Ira. "The Ethical Instructions in Ephesians as the Unwritten Statutes and Ordinances of God's New Temple in Ezekiel." *ResQ* 48 (2006): 193–210.

Jones, Paul Dafydd. "The Rhetoric of War in Karl Barth's Epistle to the Romans: A Theological Analysis." *Zeitschrift für neuere Theologiegeschichte* 17 (2010): 90–111.

Jones, Peter. *One or Two: Seeing a World of Difference: Romans 1 for the Twenty-First Century.* Escondido, CA: Main Entry Editions, 2010.

Joubert, Stephan. "Paul's Apocalyptic Eschatology in 2 Corinthians." In *Eschatology of the New Testament and Some Related Documents,* edited by Jan G. van der Watt, 225–38. WUNT. Tübingen: Mohr Siebeck, 2011.

Jowers, Dennis W. "The Meaning of MORFH in Philippians 2:6–7." *JETS* 49 (2006): 739–66.

Judge, Edwin A. "The Decrees of Caesar at Thessalonica." *RTR* 30 (1971): 1–7.

Jungkuntz, Richard. "Weapons of Their Warfare: A Study in Early Christian Polemic." *CTM* 38 (1967): 436–57.

Kaiser, Walter C. *Exodus.* Expositor's Bible Commentary 2. Grand Rapids: Zondervan, 1990.

———. *The Messiah in the Old Testament.* SOTBT. Grand Rapids: Zondervan, 1995.

Kanjuparambil, Philip. "Imperative Participles in Rom 12:9–21." *JBL* 102 (1983): 285–88.

Kaye, B. N. "Eschatology and Ethics in 1 and 2 Thessalonians." *NovT* 17 (1975): 47–57.

Keener, Craig S. *Acts: An Exegetical Commentary.* Vol. 1, *Introduction and 1:1–2:47.* Grand Rapids: Baker, 2012.

———. *Acts: An Exegetical Commentary.* Vol. 3, *Acts 15:1–23:35.* Grand Rapids: Baker, 2014.

Keown, Mark J. *Congregational Evangelism in Philippians: The Centrality of an Appeal for Gospel Proclamation to the Fabric of Philippians.* PBM. Milton Keynes, UK: Paternoster, 2008.

Kidner, Derek. *Psalms 1–72: An Introduction and Commentary.* TOTC 15. Downers Grove, IL: InterVarsity, 2008.

Kiley, Mark Christopher. "Interplay with the Culture: What, Why, How." In *Colossians as Pseudepigraphy,* 15–35. Sheffield, UK: JSOT, 1986.

Kim, Seyoon. "The Jesus Tradition in 1 Thess 4:13–5:11." *NTS* 48 (2002): 225–42.

———. *The Origin of Paul's Gospel.* Tübingen: Mohr Siebeck, 1981. Reprint, Eugene, OR: Wipf & Stock, 2007.

———. *Paul and the New Perspective: Second Thoughts on the Origin of Paul's Gospel.* WUNT 140. Tübingen: Mohr Siebeck, 2002.

Kim, Yung Suk. *A Theological Introduction to Paul's Letters: Exploring a Threefold Theology of Paul.* Eugene, OR: Cascade Books, 2011.

King, Greg A. "The Day of the Lord in Zephaniah." *BSac* 152 (1995): 16–32.

Kirk, J. R. Daniel. *Unlocking Romans: Resurrection and the Justification of God.* Grand Rapids: Eerdmans, 2008.

Klein, Ralph W. "Day of the Lord." *CTM* 39 (1968): 517–25.

Kline, Meredith G. *Images of the Spirit.* BBMS. Grand Rapids: Baker, 1980.

———. "Primal Parousia." *WTJ* 40 (1978): 245–80.

Kloha, Jeffrey. "Jesus and the Gnostic Gospels." *Concordia Theological Quarterly* 71 (2007): 121–44.

Klutz, Todd E. "Re-Reading 1 Corinthians after Rethinking 'Gnosticism.'" *JSNT* 26 (2003): 193–216.

Knibb, Michael A. "Enoch, Similitudes of (1 Enoch 37–71)." In *Eerdmans Dictionary of Early Judaism,* edited by John J. Collins and Daniel C. Harlow, 584–87. Grand Rapids: Eerdmans, 2010.

Knight, George William. *The Pastoral Epistles: A Commentary on the Greek Text.* NIGTC. Grand Rapids: Eerdmans, 1992.

Kolb, Robert. "'The Armor of God and the Might of His Strength': Luther's Sermon on Ephesians 6 (1531/1533)." *Concordia Journal* 43 (2017): 59–73.

———. "Nikolaus von Amsdorf on Vessels of Wrath and Vessels of Mercy: A Lutheran's Doctrine of Double Predestination." *HTR* 69 (1976): 325–43.

Köstenberger, Andreas J., and Terry L. Wilder, eds. *Entrusted with the Gospel: Paul's Theology in the Pastoral Epistles.* Nashville: Broadman & Holman, 2010.

Kreglinger, Gisela H. *The Spirituality of Wine.* Grand Rapids: Eerdmans, 2016.

Kreitzer, L. Joseph. *Jesus and God in Paul's Eschatology.* JSNTSup 19. Sheffield, UK: JSOT, 1987.

Ladd, George Eldon. *A Theology of the New Testament.* Rev. ed. Grand Rapids: Eerdmans, 1993.

Lambrecht, Jan. "The Favorable Time: A Study of 2 Cor 6,2a in Its Context." In *Vom Urchristentum zu Jesus: für Joachim Gnilka,* edited by Hubert Frankemölle and Karl Kertelge, 377–91. Freiburg: Herder, 1989.

———. "The Paul Who Wants to Die: A Close Reading of 2 Cor 4:16–5:10." In *Theologizing in the Corinthian Conflict: Studies in the Exegesis and Theology of 2 Corinthians,* edited by R. Bieringer, Ma Marilou, S. Ibita, Dominika Kurek-Chomycz, and Thomas A. Vollmer, 158–59. Biblical Tools and Studies 16. Leuven: Peeters, 2013.

Lanier, David Emory. "The Day of the Lord in the New Testament: A Historical and Exegetical Analysis of Its Background and Usage." PhD diss., Southwestern Baptist Theological Seminary, 1988.

Lattke, Michael. "Psalms of Solomon." In *Dictionary of New Testament Background,* edited by Craig A. Evans and Stanley E. Porter, 853–57. Downers Grove, IL: IVP Academic, 2000.

Lau, Andrew Y. *Manifest in Flesh: The Epiphany Christology of the Pastoral Epistles.* WUNT 2/86. Tübingen: Mohr, 1996.

Lea, Thomas D. "The Early Christian View of Pseudepigraphic Writings." *JETS* 27 (1984): 65–75.

Lewis, John. "Doing Theology through the Gates of Heaven: A Bible Study on Ephesians 1:3–14." *ERT* 28 (2004): 363–68.

Lewis, Scott M. *What Are They Saying about New Testament Apocalyptic?* New York: Paulist, 2004.

Licona, Michael. *The Resurrection of Jesus: A New Historiographical Approach.* Downers Grove, IL: InterVarsity, 2010.

Lincoln, Andrew T. *Ephesians*. WBC 42. Dallas: Word Books, 1990.

Lindgård, Fredrik. *Paul's Line of Thought in 2 Corinthians 4:16–5:10*. WUNT 189. Tübingen: Mohr Siebeck, 2005.

Loader, William R. G. *Making Sense of Sex: Attitudes towards Sexuality in Early Jewish and Christian Literature*. Attitudes to Sex in Early Jewish and Christian Literature. Grand Rapids: Eerdmans, 2013.

Long, Fredrick J. *2 Corinthians: A Handbook on the Greek Text*. Baylor Handbook on the Greek New Testament. Waco, TX: Baylor University Press, 2015.

Longenecker, Bruce W., and Todd D. Still. *Thinking through Paul: An Introduction to His Life, Letters, and Theology*. Grand Rapids: Zondervan, 2014.

Longenecker, Richard N. *Galatians*. WBC 41. Dallas: Word Books, 1990.

Luckensmeyer, David. *The Eschatology of First Thessalonians*. Novum Testamentum et Orbis Antiquus, Studien zur Umwelt des Neuen Testaments 71. Göttingen: Vandenhoeck & Ruprecht, 2009.

Lumpkins, Peter. *Alcohol Today: Abstinence in An Age of Indulgence*. Garland, TX: Hannibal Books, 2009.

Luz, Ulrich. *Das Geschichtsverständnis des Paulus*. München: Kaiser, 1968.

Malherbe, Abraham J. *The Letters to the Thessalonians: A New Translation with Introduction and Commentary*. AB 32B. New York: Doubleday, 2000.

Mangum, R. Todd. "Is There a Reformed Way to Get the Benefits of the Atonement to 'Those Who Have Never Heard'?" *JETS* 47 (2004): 121–36.

Mare, W. Harold. "A Study of the New Testament Concept of the Parousia." In *Current Issues in Biblical and Patristic Interpretation: Studies in Honor of Merrill C. Tenney Presented by His Former Students,* edited by Gerald F. Hawthorne, 336–45. Grand Rapids: Eerdmans, 1975.

Marshall, I. Howard. *The Acts of the Apostles*. New Testament Guides. Sheffield: Sheffield Academic Press, 1997.

———. "Theological Interpretation of the New Testament." In *Theological Interpretation of the New Testament: A Book-by-Book Survey,* edited by Kevin J. Vanhoozer, Daniel J. Treier, and N. T. Wright, 162–81. Grand Rapids: Baker, 2008.

Marshall, I. Howard, and Philip H. Towner. *A Critical and Exegetical Commentary on the Pastoral Epistles*. ICC. London: T&T Clark, 2004.

Martin, Ralph P. *2 Corinthians*. WBC. Waco, TX: Word, 1986.

———. *Carmen Christi: Philippians ii. 5–11 in Recent Interpretation and in the Setting of Early Christian Worship*. Rev. ed. Grand Rapids: Eerdmans, 1983.

Martínez, Florentino García. "Apocalypticism in the Dead Sea Scrolls." In *The Continuum History of Apocalypticism,* edited by Bernard McGinn, John J. Collins, and Stephen J. Stein, 100–101. New York: Continuum, 2003.

Matera, Frank J. *New Testament Theology: Exploring Diversity and Unity*. Louisville, KY: Westminster John Knox, 2007.

Matthews, Victor Harold. *The Hebrew Prophets and Their Social World: An Introduction*. 2nd ed. Grand Rapids: Baker, 2012.

McCarthy, Michael C. "Divine Wrath and Human Anger: Embarrassment Ancient and New." *TS* 70 (2009): 845–74.

McConville, J. G. *Deuteronomy*. Apollos Old Testament Commentary 5. Downers Grove, IL: InterVarsity, 2002.

McDonald, Lee Martin. "Pseudonymous Writings and the New Testament." In *The World of the New Testament: Cultural, Social, and Historical Contexts*, edited by Joel B. Green and Lee Martin McDonald, 367–78. Grand Rapids: Baker, 2013.

McDurmon, Joel. *The Bounds of Love: An Introduction to God's Law of Liberty*. Braselton, GA: American Vision, 2016.

———. *What Would Jesus Drink? A Spirit-Filled Study*. White Hall, WV: Tolle Lege, 2011.

McFadden, Kevin W. *Judgment according to Works in Romans: The Meaning and Function of Divine Judgment in Paul's Most Important Letter*. Minneapolis: Fortress, 2013.

McGovern, Patrick E. *Ancient Wine: The Search for the Origins of Viniculture*. Princeton: Princeton University Press, 2003.

———. *Uncorking the Past: The Quest for Wine, Beer, and Other Alcoholic Beverages*. Berkeley: University of California Press, 2009.

McKnight, Scot. *Jesus and His Death: Historiography, the Historical Jesus, and Atonement Theory*. Waco, TX: Baylor University Press, 2005.

McNutt, James E. "Vessels of Wrath, Prepared to Perish: Adolf Schlatter and the Spiritual Extermination of the Jews." *Theology Today* 63 (2006): 176–90.

Meade, David G. *Pseudonymity and Canon: An Investigation into the Relationship of Authorship and Authority in Jewish and Earliest Christian Tradition*. WUNT 39. Tübingen: Mohr, 1986.

Meadors, Edward P. *Idolatry and the Hardening of the Heart: A Study in Biblical Theology*. New York: T&T Clark, 2006.

Menken, Maarten J. J. *2 Thessalonians*. New Testament Readings. London: Routledge, 1994.

Metso, Sarianna. "Rule of the Community/Manual of Discipline (1QS)." In *Dictionary of New Testament Background*, edited by Craig A. Evans and Stanley E. Porter, 1018–24. Downers Grove, IL: IVP Academic, 2000.

Metzger, Bruce M. *An Introduction to the Apocrypha*. New York: Oxford University Press, 1957.

———. "Literary Forgeries and Canonical Pseudepigrapha." *JBL* 91 (1972): 3–24.

———. *A Textual Commentary on the Greek New Testament: A Companion Volume to the United Bible Societies' Greek New Testament*. 2nd ed. Stuttgart: Deutsche Biblegesellschaft, 1994.

Michaelis, Wilhelm. "εἴσοδος, ἔξοδος, διέξοδος." In *Theological Dictionary of the New Testament*, edited by Gerhard Kittel and Gerhard Friedrich, 103–9. Grand Rapids: Eerdmans, 1964–76.

Miller, James E. "The Practices of Romans 1:26: Homosexual or Heterosexual?" *NovT* 37 (1995): 1–11.

Mitton, Charles L. "New Wine in Old Wine Skins: IV." *ExpTim* 84 (1973): 339–43.

Moltmann, Jürgen. *Theology of Hope: On the Ground and the Implications of a Christian Eschatology*. New York: Harper & Row, 1967.

Moo, Douglas J. *The Epistle to the Romans*. NICNT. Grand Rapids: Eerdmans, 1996.

———. *Galatians*. BECNT. Grand Rapids: Baker, 2013.

Moore, Carey A. *Daniel, Esther, and Jeremiah: The Additions.* AB 44. Garden City, NY: Doubleday, 1977.

———. *Judith: A New Translation with Introduction and Commentary.* AB 40. Garden City, NY: Doubleday, 1985.

———. "The Origins of the LXX Additions to the Book of Esther." *JBL* 92 (1973): 382–93.

Morris, Leon. *The Epistle to the Romans.* Grand Rapids: Eerdmans, 1988.

———. "The Meaning of ἱλαστήριον in Romans 3.25." *NTS* 2 (1955–56): 33–43.

———. "The Use of ἱλάσκεσθαι etc. in Biblical Greek." *ExpTim* 62 (1950–51): 227–33.

Motyer, J. Alec. *The Prophecy of Isaiah: An Introduction and Commentary.* Downers Grove, IL: InterVarsity, 1993.

Moule, C. F. D. *An Idiom Book of New Testament Greek.* 2nd ed. Cambridge: Cambridge University Press, 1959.

Moulton, J. H., and G. Milligan. *The Vocabulary of the Greek Testament: Illustrated from the Papyri and Other Non-Literary Sources.* London: Hodder & Stoughton, 1930.

Mounce, William D. *Pastoral Epistles.* WBC 46. Nashville: Thomas Nelson, 2000.

Mowinckel, Sigmund. *He That Cometh: The Messiah Concept in the Old Testament and Later Judaism.* Translated by G. W. Anderson. BRS. Grand Rapids: Eerdmans, 2005.

———. *The Psalms in Israel's Worship.* Translated by D. R. Ap-Thomas. 2 vols. BRS. Grand Rapids: Eerdmans, 2004.

Moyo, Ambrose M. "The Colossian Heresy in the Light of Some Gnostic Documents from Nag Hammadi." *Journal of Theology for Southern Africa* 48 (1984): 30–44.

Muller, Richard A. "A Tale of Two Wills? Calvin and Amyraut on Ezekiel 18:23." *CTJ* 44 (2009): 211–25.

Murray, John. *The Epistle to the Romans: The English Text with Introduction, Exposition and Notes.* 2 vols. NICNT. Grand Rapids: Eerdmans, 1968.

Mutschler, Bernhard. "Eschatology in the Pastoral Epistles." In *Eschatology in the New Testament and Some Related Documents,* edited by Jan G. van der Watt, 362–401. Tübingen: Mohr Siebeck, 2011.

Myers, Jacob Martin. *I and II Esdras: Introduction, Translation and Commentary.* AB 42. Garden City, NY: Doubleday, 1974.

Nanos, Mark D. "Romans 11 and Christian-Jewish Relations: Exegetical Options for Revisiting the Translation and Interpretation of This Central Text." *CTR* 9 (2012): 3–21.

Neumann, Nils. "Die πανοπλία Gottes: Eph 6, 11–17 als Reflexion der Belagerung einer Stadt." *ZNW* 106 (2015): 40–64.

Newbigin, Lesslie. *Proper Confidence: Faith, Doubt, and Certainty in Christian Discipleship.* Grand Rapids: Eerdmans, 1995.

Newman, Carey C. "Christophany as a Sign of 'The End.'" In *Israel's God and Rebecca's Children: Christology and Community in Early Judaism and Christianity: Essays in Honor of Larry W. Hurtado and Alan F. Segal,* edited by David B. Capes, 155–67. Waco, TX: Baylor University Press, 2007.

———. "Election and Predestination in Ephesians 1:4–6a: An Exegetical-Theological Study of the Historical, Christological Realization of God's Purpose." *RevExp* 93 (1996): 237–47.

———. "Ephesians 1:3—A Primer to Paul's Grammar of God." *RevExp* 95 (1998): 89–101.

Nicholl, Colin R. *From Hope to Despair in Thessalonica: Situating 1 and 2 Thessalonians.* SNTSMS 126. Cambridge: Cambridge University Press, 2004.

Nickelsburg, George W. E. *1 Enoch 1: A Commentary on the Book of 1 Enoch Chapters 1–36.* Hermeneia. Minneapolis: Fortress, 2001.

———. "The Bible Rewritten and Expanded." In *Jewish Writings of the Second Temple Period: Apocrypha, Pseudepigrapha, Qumran Sectarian Writings, Philo, Joseph,* edited by Michael E. Stone, 135–38. Literature of the Jewish People in the Period of the Second Temple and the Talmud 2. Philadelphia: Fortress, 1984.

———. "Deliverance, Judgment, and Vindication." In *Faith and Piety in Early Judaism: Texts and Documents,* edited by George W. E. Nickelsburg and Michael E. Stone, 122–26. Philadelphia: Fortress, 1983.

———. "Enoch, First Book of." In *Anchor Bible Dictionary,* edited by David Noel Freedman, 508–16. Vol. 2. New York: Doubleday, 1992.

———. *Jewish Literature between the Bible and the Mishnah: A Historical and Literary Introduction.* 2nd ed. Minneapolis: Fortress, 2005.

———. *Resurrection, Immortality, and Eternal Life in Intertestamental Judaism and Early Christianity.* Expanded ed. HTS 56. Cambridge, MA: Harvard University Press, 2006.

———. "Son of Man." In *Anchor Bible Dictionary,* edited by David Noel Freedman, 137–50. New York: Doubleday, 1992.

Niehaus, Jeffrey Jay. *God at Sinai: Covenant and Theophany in the Bible and Ancient Near East.* SOTBT. Grand Rapids: Zondervan, 1995.

———. "Joshua and Ancient Near Eastern Warfare." *JETS* 31 (1988): 37–50.

Nir, Rivkah. *The Destruction of Jerusalem and the Idea of Redemption in the Syriac Apocalypse of Baruch.* Early Judaism and Its Literature 20. Atlanta: Society of Biblical Literature, 2003.

Nogalski, James D. "The Day(s) of YHWH in the Book of the Twelve." In *Thematic Threads in the Book of the Twelve,* edited by Paul L. Redditt and Aaron Schart, 192–213. BZAW 325. Berlin: de Gruyter, 2003.

Norden, Eduard. *Agnostos Theos: Untersuchungen zur Formengeschichte religiöser Rede.* Leipzig: Teubner, 1923.

Noth, Martin. *Exodus: A Commentary.* Translated by J. S. Bowden. OTL. Philadelphia: Westminster, 1962.

———. *The Laws in the Pentateuch, and Other Studies.* Translated by D. R. Ap-Thomas. Philadelphia: Fortress, 1967.

O'Brien, Peter T. "Divine Analysis and Comprehensive Solution: Some Priorities from Ephesians 2." *RTR* 53 (1994): 130–42.

———. *The Epistle to the Philippians.* NIGTC. Grand Rapids: Eerdmans, 1991.

———. "Was Paul Converted?" In *Justification and Variegated Nomism: A Fresh Appraisal of Paul and Second Temple Judaism,* edited by D. A. Carson and Peter T. O'Brien, 361–91. Grand Rapids: Baker, 2004.

O'Neill, J. C. *The Theology of Acts in Its Historical Setting.* 2nd ed. London: Society for Promoting Christian Knowledge, 1970.

Oepke, Albrecht. "παρουσία, πάρειμι." In *The Theological Dictionary of the New Testament,* edited and translated by Geoffrey W. Bromiley, 858–71. Vol. 5. Grand Rapids: Eerdmans, 1964–76.

Oesterley, W. O. E. *An Introduction to the Books of the Apocrypha.* London: Society for Promoting Christian Knowledge, 1958.

Ortlund, Dane Calvin, and Matthew S. Harmon, eds. *Studies in the Pauline Epistles: Essays in Honor of Douglas J. Moo.* Grand Rapids: Zondervan, 2014.

Osborne, Grant R. *Matthew.* ZECNT 1. Grand Rapids: Zondervan, 2009.

———. *Romans.* IVP New Testament Commentary Series. Downers Grove, IL: InterVarsity, 2004.

Oster, Richard. *1 Corinthians.* College Press NIV Commentary. Joplin, MO: College Press, 1995.

Oswalt, John N. "The Golden Calves and the Egyptian Concept of Deity." *Evangelical Quarterly* 45 (1973): 13–20.

Otzen, Benedikt. *Tobit and Judith.* Guides to Apocrypha and Pseudepigrapha. London: Sheffield Academic, 2002.

Palmer, Richard E. *Hermeneutics: Interpretation Theory in Schleiermacher, Dilthey, Heidegger, and Gadamer.* Edited by John Wild, James M. Edie, Herbert Spiegelberg, William Earle, George A. Schrader, Maurice Natanson, Paul Ricoeur, Aron Gurwitsch, and Calvin O. Schrag. Northwestern University Studies in Phenomenology & Existential Philosophy. Evanston, IL: Northwestern University Press, 1969.

Patterson, Richard Duane. *Nahum, Habakkuk, Zephaniah.* Wycliffe Exegetical Commentary. Chicago: Moody, 1991.

Patzia, Arthur G. "The Deutero-Pauline Hypothesis: An Attempt at Clarification." *EvQ* 52 (1980): 27–42.

Paul, Shalom M. *Amos.* Hermeneia. Minneapolis: Fortress, 1991.

Perkins, Pheme. "John's Gospel and Gnostic Christologies: The Nag Hammadi Evidence." *Anglican Theological Review* 11 (1990): 68–76.

———. "What Is a Gnostic Gospel?" *CBQ* 71 (2009): 104–29.

Phillip, Mario. "Delivery into the Hands of Satan—A Church in Apostasy and Not Knowing It: An Exegetical Analysis of 1 Corinthians 5:5." *ERT* 39 (2015): 45–60.

Pierson, Mark A. "Old Heresy, New Heretics: The Return of Gnosticism." *Modern Reformation* 17 (2008): 30–34.

Pink, A. W. *The Doctrine of Election.* New York: Great Christian Books, 2013.

———. *The Sovereignty of God.* 3rd ed. Alachua, FL: Bridge-Logos, 2008.

Piper, John. *The Justification of God: An Exegetical & Theological Study of Romans 9:1–23.* 2nd ed. Grand Rapids: Baker, 1993.

———. *"Love Your Enemies": Jesus' Love Command in the Synoptic Gospels and in the Early Christian Paraenesis, a History of the Tradition and Interpretation of Its Uses.* SNTSMS 38. Cambridge: Cambridge University Press, 1979.

Plevnik, Joseph. "The Center of Pauline Theology." *CBQ* 51 (1989): 461–78.

———. *Paul and the Parousia: An Exegetical and Theological Investigation.* Peabody, MA: Hendrickson, 1997.

Polaski, Donald C. *Authorizing an End: The Isaiah Apocalypse and Intertextuality.* BibInt 50. Leiden: Brill, 2001.

Polhill, John B. *Paul and His Letters.* Nashville: Broadman & Holman, 1999.

Porter, Stanley E. *The Apostle Paul: His Life, Thought, and Letters.* Grand Rapids: Eerdmans, 2016.

——. *Idioms of the Greek New Testament.* 2nd ed. Biblical Languages 2. Sheffield: Sheffield Academic, 1994.

——. "Is There a Center to Paul's Theology? An Introduction to the Study of Paul and his Theology." In *Paul and His Theology,* edited by Stanley E. Porter, 1–19. Vol. 3 of *Pauline Studies.* Leiden: Brill, 2006.

——. *Verbal Aspect in the Greek of the New Testament, with Reference to Tense and Mood.* Edited by D. A. Carson. Studies in Biblical Greek 1. New York: Lang, 1989.

Porter, Stanley E., and Craig A. Evans, eds. *The Pauline Writings.* London: T&T Clark, 2004.

Poythress, Vern S. "Hold Fast Versus Hold Out in Philippians 2:16." *WTJ* 63 (2002): 45–53.

——. "Holy Ones of the Most High in Daniel 7." *VT* 26 (1976): 208–13.

Quinn, Jerome D. *The Letter to Titus: A New Translation with Notes and Commentary and an Introduction to Titus, I and II Timothy, the Pastoral Epistles.* AB 35. New Haven: Yale University Press, 2005.

Rad, Gerhard von. *Old Testament Theology: The Theology of Israel's Prophetic Traditions.* Translated by D. M. G. Stalker. 2 vols. New York: Harper, 1962.

——. "Origin of the Concept of the Day of Yahweh." *Journal of Semitic Studies* 4 (1959): 97–108.

Ralston, Timothy J. "The Theological Significance of Paul's Conversion." *BSac* 147 (1990): 198–215.

Reed, Stephen A. *The Dead Sea Scrolls Catalogue: Documents, Photographs, and Museum Inventory Numbers.* Resources for Biblical Study 32. Atlanta: Scholars Press, 1994.

Reeves, Michael. *Delighting in the Trinity: An Introduction to the Christian Faith.* Downers Grove, IL: InterVarsity, 2012.

Reiher, Jim. "Could Philippians Have Been Written from the *Second* Roman Imprisonment?" *EvQ* 84 (2012): 213–33.

Reinhard, Donna R. "Ephesians 6:10–18: A Call to Personal Piety or Another Way of Describing Union." *JETS* 48 (2005): 521–32.

Rendtorff, Rolf. "How to Read the Book of the Twelve as a Theological Unity." In *Reading and Hearing the Book of the Twelve,* edited by James Nogalski and Marvin A. Sweeney, 75–87. SBLSS 15. Atlanta: Society of Biblical Literature, 2000.

Reumann, John Henry Paul. *Philippians: A New Translation with Introduction and Commentary.* AB 33B. New Haven: Yale University Press, 2008.

Richard, Earl. *First and Second Thessalonians.* Sacra Pagina 11. Collegeville, MN: Liturgical, 1995.

Ridderbos, Herman. *Paul: An Outline of His Theology.* Translated by John Richard De Witt. Grand Rapids: Eerdmans, 1975.

Riddlebarger, Kim. *A Case for Amillennialism: Understanding the End Times.* Expanded ed. Grand Rapids: Baker, 2013.

Roberts, J. H. "Jewish Mystical Experience in the Early Christian Era as Background to Understanding Colossians." *Neot* 32 (1998): 161–89.

Robertson, A. T. *A Grammar of the Greek New Testament in the Light of Historical Research.* 4th ed. Nashville: Broadman, 1934.

Roetzel, Calvin J. *Paul, a Jew on the Margins.* Louisville, KY: Westminster John Knox, 2003.

Rosner, Brian S. *Paul, Scripture and Ethics: A Study of 1 Corinthians 5–7.* Biblical Studies Library 22. Grand Rapids: Baker, 1999.

Rosscup, James E. "Paul's Concept of Eternal Punishment." *MSJ* 9 (1998): 169–89.

Rost, Leonhard, and Robert Morris Johnston. *Judaism outside the Hebrew Canon: An Introduction to the Documents [Review].* Translated by David E. Green. Andrews University Seminary Studies 18. Berrien Springs, MI: Andrews University Press, 1980.

Royalty, Robert M. "Dwelling on Visions: On the Nature of the So-Called 'Colossian Heresy.'" *Bib* 83 (2002): 329–57.

Russell, Ronald. "The Idle in 2 Thess 3:6–12: An Eschatological or a Social Problem?" *NTS* 34 (1988): 105–11.

Rydelnik, Michael. *The Messianic Hope: Is the Hebrew Bible Really Messianic?* NAC Studies in Bible & Theology 9. Nashville: Broadman & Holman, 2010.

Sæbø, M. "אוֹר." In *Theological Lexicon of the Old Testament,* edited by Jenni, Ernst, and Claus Westermann, 63–66. Vol. 1. Peabody, MA: Hendrickson, 1997.

Sailhamer, John. "Genesis." In *Expositor's Bible Commentary*, edited by Frank E. Gaebelein. Grand Rapids: Zondervan, 1990.

———. *The Pentateuch as Narrative: A Biblical-Theological Commentary.* Library of Biblical Interpretation. Grand Rapids: Zondervan, 1992.

Salters, Robert B. *A Critical and Exegetical Commentary on Lamentations.* ICC. London: T&T Clark, 2010.

Sandnes, Karl Olav. *Paul, One of the Prophets? A Contribution to the Apostle's Self-Understanding.* WUNT 43. Tübingen: Mohr Siebeck, 1991.

Savage, Timothy B. *Power through Weakness: Paul's Understanding of the Christian Ministry in 2 Corinthians.* Edited by Margaret E. Thrall. SNTSMS 86. Cambridge: Cambridge University Press, 1996.

Sayler, Gwendolyn B. *Have the Promises Failed? A Literary Analysis of 2 Baruch.* SBLDS 72. Chico, CA: Scholars Press, 1984.

Schmid, Hans Heinrich. "גורל." Page 311 in *TLOT.*

Schmitt, Mary. "Peace and Wrath in Paul's Epistle to the Romans." *Conrad Grebel Review* 32 (2014): 67–79.

Schnabel, Eckhard J. *Acts.* ZECNT 5. Grand Rapids: Zondervan, 2012.

Schnelle, Udo. *Apostle Paul: His Life and Theology.* Translated by M. Eugene Boring. Grand Rapids: Baker, 2005.

Schoedel, William Richard. "Parables in the Gospel of Thomas: Oral Tradition or Gnostic Exegesis?" *CTM* 43 (1972): 548–60.

Schottroff, W. "פקד." In *Theological Lexicon of the Old Testament,* edited by Jenni, Ernst, and Claus Westermann, 1018–31. Vol. 2. Peabody, MA: Hendrickson, 1997.

Schreiner, Thomas R. "Does Romans 9 Teach Individual Election unto Salvation? Some Evangelical and Theological Reflections." *JETS* 36 (1993): 25–40.

———. "Does Scripture Teach Prevenient Grace in the Wesleyan Sense?" In *Still Sovereign: Contemporary Perspectives on Election, Foreknowledge, and Grace,* edited by Thomas R. Schreiner and Bruce A. Ware, 365–82. Grand Rapids: Baker, 2000.

———. *Galatians.* Exegetical Commentary on the New Testament. Grand Rapids: Zondervan, 2010.

———. *The King in His Beauty: A Biblical Theology of the Old and New Testaments.* Grand Rapids: Baker, 2013.

———. *Paul, Apostle of God's Glory in Christ: A Pauline Theology.* Downers Grove, IL: InterVarsity, 2001.

———. *Romans.* Edited by Moisés Silva. BECNT. Grand Rapids: Baker, 1998.

Schultz, Richard L. "The King in the Book of Isaiah." In *The Lord's Anointed: Interpretation of Old Testament Messianic Texts*, edited by P. E. Satterthwaite, Richard S. Hess, and Gordon J. Wenham, 141–65. Tyndale House Studies. Grand Rapids: Baker, 1995.

Schweitzer, Don. "Understanding Substitutionary Atonement in Spatial Terms." *Touchstone* 31 (2013): 7–17.

Scott, J. Julius. "Paul and Late-Jewish Eschatology: A Case Study of 1 Thess 4:13–18 and 2 Thess 2:1–12." *JETS* 15 (1972): 133–43.

Seifrid, Mark A. *The Second Letter to the Corinthians.* PNTC. Grand Rapids: Eerdmans, 2014.

Shaw, Brent D. "State Intervention and Holy Violence: Timgad/Paleostrovsk/Waco." *Journal of the American Academy of Religion* 77 (2009): 853–94.

Sherwood, Aaron. *The Word of God Has Not Failed: Paul's Use of the Old Testament in Romans 9.* Studies in Scripture and Biblical Theology 1. Bellingham, WA: Lexham Press, 2015.

Shogren, Gary Steven. *1 and 2 Thessalonians.* ZECNT. Grand Rapids: Zondervan, 2012.

Silva, Moisés. "ἐπιφάνεια." In *New International Dictionary of New Testament Theology and Exegesis*, edited by Moisés Silva, 585–90. 2nd ed. Vol. 4. Grand Rapids: Zondervan, 2014.

———. "παρουσία." In *New International Dictionary of New Testament Theology and Exegesis*, edited by Moisés Silva, 858–71. 2nd ed. Vol. 3. Grand Rapids: Zondervan, 2014.

———. *Philippians.* 2nd ed. BECNT. Grand Rapids: Baker, 2005.

Skeen, Judy. "Not as Enemies, but Kin: Discipline in the Family of God; 2 Thessalonians 3:6–12." *RevExp* 96 (1999): 287–94.

Skinner, John. *A Critical and Exegetical Commentary on Genesis.* 2nd ed. ICC 1. Edinburgh: T&T Clark, 1969.

Smith, Gary V. "Spiritual Blindness, Deafness, and Fatness in Isaiah." *BSac* 170 (2013): 166–78.

Smith, Jay E., and Matthew S. Harmon, eds. *Studies in the Pauline Epistles: Essays in Honor of Douglas J. Moo.* Grand Rapids: Zondervan, 2014.

Smith, John M. P. "The Day of Yahweh." *Ashland Theological Journal* 5 (1901): 505–33.

Smith, Murray J. "The Thessalonian Correspondence." In *All Things to All Cultures: Paul among Jews, Greeks, and Romans*, edited by Mark Harding and Alanna Nobbs, 269–301. Grand Rapids: Eerdmans, 2013.

Smith, Ralph L. *Micah-Malachi.* WBC 32. Waco, TX: Word Books, 1984.

Smothers, Edgar R. "Give Place to the Wrath (Rom. 12:19): An Essay in Verbal Exegesis." *CBQ* 6 (1944): 205–15.

Smucker, Barbara Claassen. "Review of *Coals of Fire*. By Elizabeth Hershberger Bauman. Scottdale: Herald Press, 1954. Pp. 128, illustrated. $1.95." *Mennonite Quarterly Review* 28 (1954): 228.

Spicq, Ceslas. *Theological Lexicon of the New Testament*. Edited and translated by James D. Ernst. 3 vols. Peabody, MA: Hendrickson, 1994.

Sprinkle, Preston M., ed. *Two Views on Homosexuality, the Bible, and the Church*. Counterpoints: Bible & Theology. Grand Rapids: Zondervan, 2016.

Sproul, R. C. *Chosen by God*. Wheaton, IL: Tyndale, 1986.

———. *"Double" Predestination*. Available from www.ligonier.org/learn/articles/double-predestination/.

Stanley, David M. "Paul's Conversion in Acts: Why the Three Reports?" *CBQ* 15 (1953): 315–38.

Staples, Jason A. "What Do the Gentiles Have to Do with 'All Israel'? A Fresh Look at Romans 11:25–27." *JBL* 130 (2011): 371–90.

Stein, Robert H. "Wine-Drinking in New Testament Times." *Christianity Today* 19 (1975): 9–11.

Stendahl, Krister. "Hate, Non-Retaliation, and Love." *HTR* 55 (1962): 343–55.

———. *Paul among Jews and Gentiles, and Other Essays*. Philadelphia: Fortress, 1976.

Stenschke, Christoph W. "'Once You Were in Darkness': The Past of the Readers of Ephesians." *European Journal of Theology* 23 (2014): 123–39.

Steudel, Annette. "'CHRYT HYMYM in the Texts from Qumran." *Revue de Qumran* 16 (1993): 225–46.

Steyn, Gert Jacobus. "A Quest for the *Vorlage* of the 'Song of Moses' (Deut 32) Quotations in Hebrews." *Neot* 34 (2000): 263–72.

Still, Todd D. *Conflict at Thessalonica: A Pauline Church and Its Neighbours*. JSNTSup 183. Sheffield: Sheffield Academic Press, 1999.

———. "Eschatology in the Thessalonian Letters." *RevExp* 96 (1999): 195–210.

Stockhausen, Carol Kern. *Moses' Veil and the Glory of the New Covenant: The Exegetical Substructure of II Cor. 3,1–4,6*. AnBib 116. Rome: Editrice Pontificio Istituto Biblico, 1989.

Stone, Michael E. "Apocalyptic Literature." In *Jewish Writings of the Second Temple Period: Apocrypha, Pseudepigrapha, Qumran Sectarian Writings, Philo, Josephus*, edited by Michael E. Stone, 383–441. Compendia Rerum Iudaicarum ad Novum Testamentum 2. Philadelphia: Fortress, 1984.

———. "Greek Apocalypse of Ezra." In *The Old Testament Pseudepigrapha*, edited by James H. Charlesworth, 561–70. Vol. 1. AYBRL. New York: Doubleday, 1983.

———. *Features of the Eschatology of IV Ezra*. Harvard Semitic Studies 35. Atlanta: Scholars Press, 1989.

Strazicich, John. *Joel's Use of Scripture and Scripture's Use of Joel: Appropriation and Resignification in Second Temple Judaism and Early Christianity*. BibInt 82. Leiden: Brill, 2007.

Stuart, Douglas K. *Exodus*. NAC 2. Nashville: Broadman & Holman, 2006.

———. *Hosea-Jonah*. WBC 31. Waco, TX: Word Books, 1987.

———. "The Sovererign's Day of Conquest." *Bulletin of the American Schools of Oriental Research* 221 (1976): 159–64.

Stuckenbruck, Loren T. "Apocrypha and Pseudepigrapha." In *Early Judaism: A Comprehensive Overview*, edited by John J. Collins and Daniel C. Harlow, 179–203. Grand Rapids: Eerdmans, 2012.

Sweeney, Marvin A. *Form and Intertextuality in Prophetic and Apocalyptic Literature.* FAT 45. Tübingen: Mohr Siebeck, 2005.

———. *Isaiah 1–39: With an Introduction to Prophetic Literature.* FOTL 16. Grand Rapids: Eerdmans, 1996.

———. *The Twelve Prophets.* 2 vols. Berit Olam. Collegeville, MN: Liturgical, 2000.

———. *Zephaniah: A Commentary.* Hermeneia. Philadelphia: Fortress, 2003.

Teachout, Richard. *Grape Juice: God's Blessing for His People!* Château-Richer, QC: EBPA–Etude Biblique pour Aujourd'hui (Bible Studies for Today), 2011.

———. *On the Fruit of the Vine: In Defense of Biblical Consistency.* Château-Richer, QC: EBPA–Etude Biblique pour Aujourd'hui (Bible Studies for Today), 2010.

Teachout, Robert P. "The Use of 'Wine' in the Old Testament." PhD diss., Dallas Theological Seminary, 1979.

Theissen, Gerd. *The Social Setting of Pauline Christianity: Essays on Corinth.* Philadelphia: Fortress, 1982.

Thielman, Frank. *Theology of the New Testament: A Canonical and Synthetic Approach.* Grand Rapids: Zondervan, 2005.

Thiselton, Anthony C. *The First Epistle to the Corinthians: A Commentary on the Greek Text.* NIGTC. Grand Rapids: Eerdmans, 2000.

Tiessen, Terrance L. "Gnosticism as Heresy: The Response of Irenaeus." *Didaskalia* 18 (2002): 31–48.

Tigchelaar, Eibert. "The Dead Sea Scrolls." In *Eerdmans Dictionary of Early Judaism,* edited by John J. Collins and Daniel C. Harlow, 163–80. Grand Rapids: Eerdmans, 2010.

Timmer, Daniel C. "Variegated Nomism Indeed: Multiphase Eschatology and Soteriology in the Qumranite Community Rule (1QS) and the New Perspective on Paul." *JETS* 52 (2009): 341–56.

Tomlinson, F. Alan. "The Purpose and Stewardship Theme within the Pastoral Epistles." In *Entrusted with the Gospel: Paul's Theology in the Pastoral Epistles,* edited by Andreas J. Köstenberger and Terry L. Wilder, 52–60. Nashville: Broadman & Holman, 2010.

Towner, Philip H. *The Letters to Timothy and Titus.* NICNT. Grand Rapids: Eerdmans, 2006.

———. "The Present Age in the Eschatology of the Pastoral Epistles." *NTS* 32 (1986): 427–48.

Tranvik, Mark D. "Luther, Gerhard Forde, and the Gnostic Threat to the Gospel." *Lutheran Quarterly* 22 (2008): 415–26.

Tromp, Johannes. "The Sinners and the Lawless in Psalm of Solomon 17." *NovT* 35 (1993): 344–61.

Turner, Nigel. *A Grammar of New Testament Greek.* Vol. 3, *Syntax.* Edited by James Hope Moulton. Edinburgh: T&T Clark, 1963.

Tzoref, Shani Berrin. "Pesher on Habakkuk." Page 1054 in *EDEJ.*

Vander Hart, Mark D. "The Transition of the Old Testament Day of the Lord into the New Testament Day of the Lord Jesus Christ." *Mid-America Journal of Theology* 9 (1993): 3–25.

VanderKam, James C. *From Revelation to Canon: Studies in the Hebrew Bible and Second Temple Literature.* Supplements to the Journal for the Study of Judaism 62. Leiden: Brill, 2000.

———. "Studies in the Apocalypse of Weeks (1 Enoch 93:1–10, 91:11–17)." *CBQ* 46 (1984): 511–23.

———. "Theophany of Enoch 1:3b–7, 9." *VT* 23 (1973): 130–50.

VanGemeren, Willem. *Interpreting the Prophetic Word: An Introduction to the Prophetic Literature of the Old Testament*. Grand Rapids: Zondervan, 1996.

Vaux, Roland de. *Ancient Israel: Its Life and Institutions*. Translated by John McHugh. BRS. Grand Rapids: Eerdmans, 1997.

Vena, Osvaldo D. *The Parousia and Its Rereadings: The Development of the Eschatological Consciousness in the Writings of the New Testament*. Studies in Biblical Literature 27. New York: Lang, 2001.

Venema, Cornelis P. *The Gospel of Free Acceptance in Christ: An Assessment of the Reformation and New Perspectives on Paul*. Edinburgh: Banner of Truth Trust, 2006.

———. "'In This Way All Israel Will Be Saved': A Study of Romans 11:26." *Mid-America Journal of Theology* 22 (2011): 19–40.

Via, Dan Otto, and Robert A. J. Gagnon. *Homosexuality and the Bible: Two Views*. Minneapolis: Fortress, 2003.

Vlaardingerbroek, Johannes. *Zephaniah*. Historical Commentary on the Old Testament. Leuven: Peeters, 1999.

Waldman, Nahum M. "The Breaking of the Tablets." *Judaism* 27 (1978): 442–47.

Wallace, Daniel B. *Greek Grammar beyond the Basics: An Exegetical Syntax of the New Testament*. Grand Rapids: Zondervan, 1996.

Wanamaker, Charles A. *The Epistles to the Thessalonians: A Commentary on the Greek Text*. NIGTC. Grand Rapids: Eerdmans, 1990.

Ward, Timothy. *Words of Life: Scripture as the Living and Active Word of God*. Downers Grove, IL: InterVarsity, 2009.

Ware, James P. *The Mission of the Church in Paul's Letter to the Philippians in the Context of Ancient Judaism*. NovTSup 120. Leiden: Brill, 2005.

Waterman, C. Henry. "The Sources of Paul's Teaching on the 2nd Coming of Christ in 1 and 2 Thessalonians." *JETS* 18 (1975): 105–13.

Waters, Guy. "Curse Redux? 1 Corinthians 5:13, Deuteronomy, and Identity in Corinth." *WTJ* 77 (2015): 237–50.

Webb, Barry G. *Five Festal Garments: Christian Reflections on the Song of Songs, Ruth, Lamentations, Ecclesiastes, Esther*. NSBT 10. Downers Grove, IL: InterVarsity, 2000.

Weima, Jeffrey A. D. *1–2 Thessalonians*. BECNT. Grand Rapids: Baker, 2014.

Weiss, Meir. "The Origin of the 'Day of the Lord' Reconsidered." *HUCA* 37 (1966): 29–71.

Wenham, Gordon J. *Genesis 1–15*. WBC 1. Waco, TX: Word, 1987.

Wenkel, David H. "The 'Breastplate of Righteousness' in Ephesians 6:14: Imputation or Virtue?" *TynBul* 58 (2007): 275–87.

West, Jim. *Drinking with Calvin and Luther! A History of Alcohol in the Church*. Lincoln, CA: Oaklawn, 2003.

Westermann, Claus. *Genesis 1–11: A Commentary*. Translated by John J. Scullion. London: Society for Promoting Christian Knowledge, 1984.

———. *Lamentations: Issues and Interpretation*. Translated by Charles Muenchow. Minneapolis: Fortress, 1994.

Wevers, John William. *LXX: Notes on the Greek Text of Deuteronomy.* Edited by Bernard A. Taylor. Septuagint and Cognate Studies Series 39. Atlanta: Scholars Press, 1995.

Wheeler, Everett L. *Stratagem and the Vocabulary of Military Trickery.* Mnemosyne, Bibliotheca Classica Batava Supplementum 108. Leiden: Brill, 1988.

White, James R., and Jeffrey D. Niell. *The Same Sex Controversy: Defending and Clarifying the Bible's Message about Homosexuality.* Minneapolis: Bethany House, 2002.

Whittington, Brad. *What Would Jesus Drink? What the Bible Really Says about Alcohol.* Austin, TX: Wunderfool, 2011.

Wilder, Terry L. "Pseudonymity, the New Testament, and the Pastoral Epistles." In *Entrusted with the Gospel: Paul's Theology in the Pastoral Epistles,* edited by Andreas J. Köstenberger and Terry L. Wilder, 28–51. Nashville: Broadman & Holman, 2010.

Willett, Tom W. *Eschatology in the Theodicies of 2 Baruch and 4 Ezra.* Journal for the Study of the Pseudepigrapha Supplement Series 4. Sheffield, UK: JSOT, 1989.

Williams, Michael A. *Rethinking "Gnosticism": An Argument for Dismantling a Dubious Category.* Princeton: Princeton University Press, 1996.

Winninge, Mikael. *Sinners and the Righteous: A Comparative Study of the Psalms of Solomon and Paul's Letters.* Coniectanea Biblica: New Testament Series 26. Stockholm: Almqvist & Wiksell International, 1995.

Winter, Bruce W. *After Paul Left Corinth: The Influence of Secular Ethics and Social Change.* Grand Rapids: Eerdmans, 2001.

———. "'If a Man Does Not Wish to Work . . .' A Cultural and Historical Setting for 2 Thessalonians 3:6–16." *TynBul* 40 (1989): 303–15.

———. "'The Seasons' of this Life and Eschatology in 1 Corinthians 7:29–31." In *"The Reader Must Understand": Studies in Eschatology in Bible and Theology,* edited by K. E. Brower and M. Elliot, 323–34. Leicester, UK: Apollos, 1997.

Wise, Michael O. "The Dead Sea Scrolls: General Introduction." In *Dictionary of New Testament Background,* edited by Craig A. Evans and Stanley E. Porter, 252–66. Downers Grove, IL: IVP Academic, 2000.

Wise, Michael O., Martin Abegg Jr., and Edwin Cook, eds. *The Dead Sea Scrolls: A New Translation.* San Francisco: HarperSanFrancisco, 1996.

Witherington, Ben, III. "The Case of the Imprisonment That Did Not Happen: Paul at Ephesus." *JETS* 60 (2017): 525–32.

———. *Jesus, Paul, and the End of the World: A Comparative Study in New Testament Eschatology.* Downers Grove, IL: InterVarsity, 1992.

———. *Paul's Letter to the Philippians: A Socio-Rhetorical Commentary.* Grand Rapids: Eerdmans, 2011.

———. "Transcending Imminence: The Gordian Knot of Pauline Eschatology." In *Eschatology in Bible & Theology: Evangelical Essays at the Dawn of a New Millennium,* edited by K. E. Brower and M. W. Elliott, 171–86. Downers Grove, IL: InterVarsity, 1997.

Witherup, Ronald D. "Functional Redundancy in the Acts of the Apostles: A Case Study." *JSNT* 48 (1992): 67–86.

Wolf, Herbert M. *Interpreting Isaiah: The Suffering and Glory of the Messiah.* Grand Rapids: Academie Books, 1985.

Wolff, Hans Walter. *Joel and Amos.* Translated by Waldemar Janzen, S. Dean McBride Jr., and Charles A. Muenchow. Hermeneia 14. Minneapolis: Fortress, 1977.

Wong, Gregory. "A Farewell to Arms: Goliath's Death as Rhetoric against Faith in Arms." *BBR* 23 (2013): 43–55.

Wright, Christopher J. H. *Knowing Jesus through the Old Testament.* Downers Grove, IL: InterVarsity, 1995.

Wright, N. T. *The Climax of the Covenant: Christ and the Law in Pauline Theology.* Minneapolis: Fortress, 1992.

———. *The New Testament and the People of God.* COQG 1. Minneapolis: Fortress, 1992.

———. "On Becoming the Righteousness of God: 2 Corinthians 5:21." In *Pauline Theology*, edited by David M. Hay, 200–208. Minneapolis: Augsburg, 1993.

———. *Paul and the Faithfulness of God.* 2 vols. COQG 4. Minneapolis: Fortress, 2013.

———. *The Resurrection of the Son of God.* COQG 3. Minneapolis: Fortress, 2003.

———. *What Saint Paul Really Said: Was Paul of Tarsus the Real Founder of Christianity?* Grand Rapids: Eerdmans, 1997.

Wright, Ross M. "Is There Life in Vicarious and Forensic Theories of the Atonement? An Assessment of J. K. Mozley's Interpretation of Propitiation." *Sewanee Theological Review* 57 (2014): 173–87.

Yamauchi, Edwin M. "The Gnostics and History." *JETS* 14 (1971): 29–40.

———. "Pre-Christian Gnosticism in the Nag Hammadi Texts?" *Church History* 48 (1979): 129–41.

———. "Pre-Christian Gnosticism, the New Testament and Nag Hammadi in Recent Debate." *Them* 10 (1984): 22–27.

Yates, Roy. "'The Worship of Angels' (Col 2:18)." *ExpTim* 97 (1985): 12–15.

Young, Frances M. *The Theology of the Pastoral Letters.* New Testament Theology. Cambridge: Cambridge University Press, 1994.

Young, R. Garland. "The Times and the Seasons: 1 Thessalonians 4:13–5:11." *RevExp* 96 (1999): 265–76.

Zacharias, H. Daniel. "The Son of David in *Psalms of Solomon* 17." In *"Non-Canonical" Religious Texts in Early Judaism and Early Christianity*, edited by Lee Martin McDonald and James H. Charlesworth, 73–87. Jewish and Christian Texts in Contexts and Related Studies Series. London: T&T Clark, 2012.

Zerwick, Max. *Biblical Greek Illustrated by Examples.* Translated by Joseph Smith. Scripta Pontificii 114. Rome: Editrice Pontificio Istituto Biblico, 1963.

Scripture Index

239

Other Ancient Witnesses

Subject Index